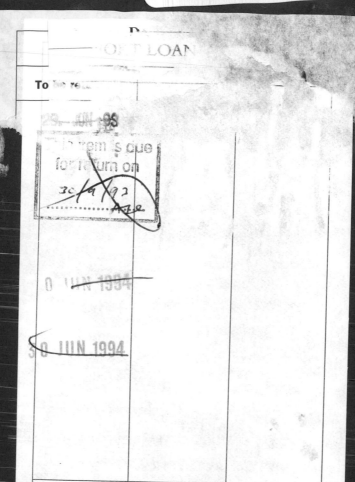

OF T LOAN

To be re...

This item is due
for return on

This book may be recalled
before the above date

Red Data Birds
in Britain

Red Data Birds in Britain

ACTION FOR RARE, THREATENED
AND IMPORTANT SPECIES

EDITED BY

L. A. Batten, C. J. Bibby, P. Clement
G. D. Elliott and R. F. Porter

ILLUSTRATED BY

Ian Willis

Published for
THE NATURE CONSERVANCY COUNCIL
and
THE ROYAL SOCIETY FOR THE PROTECTION OF BIRDS

T & A D POYSER

LONDON

First published in 1990 by T & A D Poyser Ltd
24–28 Oval Road, London NW1 7DX

United States Edition published by
ACADEMIC PRESS INC.
San Diego, CA 92101

Text set in Linotronic Baskerville
Typeset by Paston Press, Loddon, Norfolk
and printed in Great Britain by Mackays of Chatham PLC, *Chatham, Kent.*

British Library Cataloguing in Publication Data
Red data birds in Britain.
  1. Great Britain. Birds. Conservation
  I. Batten, L. A.
  639.9780941

ISBN 0-85661-056-9

Contents

List of photographs of bird habitats

1. Montane
2. Upland heath
3. Peat bog
4. Hanging oak wood
5. Native pine wood
6. Lowland heath
7. Reed bed
8. Wet lowland grassland
9. Marine
10. Sea cliff
11. Intertidal mudflat
12. Salt marsh
13. Shingle beach
14. Machair
15. Coastal lagoon
16. Scottish loch
17. Lowland lake
18. Upland stream
19. Reservoir
20. Conifer plantation
21. Arable farmland
22. Downland
23. Improved pasture
24. Built-up area

Acknowledgements

This book has been possible only because many people have given their time and expertise to help the editors in many ways.

Particular thanks must go to I. J. Ferguson-Lees for initially helping with the selection of species and for providing draft texts for many of the species accounts while under contract to the NCC. These texts were later updated by the late P. J. Grant and formed the basis of the book as it was first envisaged. M. J. Nugent and H. B. Ginn also helped with editing and commenting on the texts at this time. Later, in 1986, when the unpublished manuscript was reviewed with the RSPB, it was decided to expand the species account sections dealing with threats and conservation actions, to update the other sections (particularly that on populations) and to add general chapters on threats and bird conservation in Britain.

The editors are extremely grateful to S. D. Housden for writing the chapter on conservation and for commenting on virtually all the texts; to Dr G. J. Thomas for assisting with species selection and the threats analysis; to A. J. Prater for preparing drafts of many of the wader texts and for providing the material for the threats related to the estuarine environment; to Dr M. W. Pienkowski, who contributed a section on bird conservation in the wider countryside, and who commented on sections of the book; to Dr C. A. Galbraith who helped with the threats chapter; to Dr N. Davidson for his comments on material related to estuaries; to P. H. Oswald for his help with organizational aspects of the work and to the NCC and RSPB typists, especially Maureen Symons.

The following are thanked for their comments on various species texts: G. Allport, Dr M. I. Avery, Dr I. P. Bainbridge, Dr E. M. Bignal, C. G. R. Bowden, Dr A. F. Brown, Y. M. Brown, Dr N. D. Burgess, J. J. Buxton, N. Buxton, Dr P. Byle, Dr C. J. Cadbury, Dr L. H. Campbell, C. Carson, Dr J. T. Cayford, S. J. da Prato, P. Davis, M. Davies, S. Davies, I. K. Dawson, J. C. U. Day, R. H. Dennis, T. D. Dick, Dr A. Douse, P. J. Ellis, Dr A. D. Fox, Dr R. J. Fuller, Dr R. W. Furness, Dr H. Galbraith, D. E. Glue, Dr J. D. Goss-Custard, Dr R. E. Green, Dr J. J. D. Greenwood, Dr M. P. Harris, Dr D. A. Hill, Dr G. Hirons, Dr A. V. Hudson, Dr P. J. Hudson, D. Ireland, Dr M. J. Kelsey, J. A. Love, J. A. Marchant, Dr M. Marquiss, Dr P. Monaghan, Dr M. E. Moser, Dr R. Moss, Dr G. P. Mudge, Dr I. Newton, M. J. Nugent, Dr M. Owen, Dr I. J. Patterson, S. J. Petty, Dr N. Picozzi, Dr G. R. Potts, D. E. Pritchard, Dr D. A. Ratcliffe, S. Redpath, Dr M. J. Richardson, D. G. Salmon, R. E. Scott, H. P. Sitters, R. Spencer, A. K. M. St Joseph, Dr T. J. Stowe, D. A. Stroud, Dr R. W. Summers, G. Sweet, M. L. Tasker, Dr D. B. A. Thompson, P. Thompson, Dr D. J. Townshend, J. Waldon, Dr S. Wanless, Dr A. D. Watson, D. Watson, Dr J. Watson, A. Webb and H. Young.

The following members of NCC's Advisory Committee on Birds are also thanked for their general comments on certain sections of the book: R. H. Dennis, Professor P. R. Evans, Dr J. J. D. Greenwood, Dr C. J. O. Harrison, Professor G. V. T. Matthews, Dr M. Owen, I. Prestt, Dr G. R. Potts, J. Swift and V. Thorn.

We would like to thank the following photographers who supplied the photographs used in the Habitats chapter, M. I. Avery, E. A. Clack, C. H. Gomersall, S. C. Porter, P. Wakely and G. Williams.

Key abbreviations used in this book

AOB   Area of outstanding natural beauty
BTO   British Trust for Ornithology
CITES   Convention on International Trade in Endangered Species
EC   European Communities
EEC   European Economic Community
ESA   Environmentally sensitive area
ITE   Institute of Terrestrial Ecology
ICBP   International Council for Bird Preservation
IUCN   International Union for Conservation of Nature and Natural Resources
IWRB   International Waterfowl and Wetlands Research Bureau
LNR   Local nature reserve
NC   Nature conservancy
NCC   Nature Conservancy Council
NNR   National nature reserve
RBBP   Rare Birds Breeding Panel
RSNC   Royal Society for Nature Conservation
RSPB   Royal Society for the Protection of Birds
SPA   Special protection area
SSSI   Site of special scientific interest
WCA   Wildlife and Countryside Act 1981
WWI   Wetland of international importance
WWT   Wildfowl and Wetlands Trust

Introduction

International Red Data Books have been published by the International Union for Conservation of Nature and Natural Resources (IUCN). For birds, these have been compiled by the International Council for Bird Preservation (ICBP). These works cover species which, on a world scale, are *endangered* to the extent of being likely to become extinct if the causal factors are not altered, or are *vulnerable* if they could move into the endangered category without intervention. An additional category of *rare* recognizes the potential vulnerability of many species with very small numbers or world ranges, often those on single islands or in rain forest fragments.

Compared with the swelling crisis of worldwide extinctions of birds and other wildlife, Europe is privileged and Britain still more so. One or two European birds could fall to worldwide extinction in our lifetimes but it is most unlikely that a British species will. Three British species (Red Kite, White-tailed Eagle and Corncrake) probably qualify for inclusion in the next international Red Data Book (Collar & Andrew, 1988). This relatively happy circumstance might owe something to a long history of concern and action for nature conservation. On the other hand, large land masses such as Europe, and ones subject to recent (on an evolutionary time-scale) glaciation, do not have many of the most vulnerable kinds of birds. Most such species have rather small populations or occur in restricted areas not subject, before man's arrival, to major upheaval. The 1979 EC Birds Directive formally charges the British government with the preparation of a list of threatened species, and this book aims to meet this requirement. Having set out the challenge in these terms, it is desirable to take continuing stock of progress and to alter future actions in the light of further knowledge. We hope that the book will be subject to ongoing revision and that another edition in five or ten years time will be better informed. The editors welcome any comment or factual contribution towards improving the next edition.

In an era of consciousness about habitats and ecosystems, a species-based approach may seem unfashionable. Birds, however, have a special popularity which makes them a visible symbol of conservation aspirations. With a large public following, they can bring support to the more esoteric notions of habitat or community conservation. Birds are mobile and wide-ranging and cannot be supported in small reserves alone. For this reason they epitomize the struggle to

1

achieve a better standard of nature conservation within the commercial country-side.

Mobility adds an international responsibility for species which may spend only part of their year with us but which no less belong elsewhere as well. By the same token it can sharpen appreciation of threats faced by 'our' birds while they are in other countries. Birds face some special problems over and above those directly for habitat, most obviously their predation or persecution by humans and the indirect effects of pesticides or pollution, for which they can be powerful indicators. For these reasons we feel that a species-based bird conservation book is important. Similar Red Data books have been prepared for plants and insects in Britain (Perring & Farrell, 1983; Shirt, 1987).

The prime thrust of habitat conservation in Britain is still directed towards key sites whose preservation is the very minimum needed to maintain the range and diversity of the best of Britain's wild places. The rationale and details of this approach are set out in *A Nature Conservation Review* (Ratcliffe, 1977). The very best sites should ideally be managed as national nature reserves (NNRs) or similarly strongly protected. A series of sites of special scientific interest (SSSIs) are protected by the provisions of the Wildlife and Countryside Act (1981) while usually remaining in private use and ownership. The wider countryside presents a major opportunity for new conservation initiatives especially as agriculture strives to come to terms with surplus production. Bird conservation spans the range of concerns from special habitats and sites to those in the wider countryside while adding its own distinctive contribution. Conservation action for birds is hence often likely to be beneficial to a wide range of wildlife.

AREA OF COVERAGE

This book covers the birds of Great Britain. The Channel Islands are not included because their location puts them into the biogeographic context of the continental mainland. They are included in some, but not all, major studies of British birds, so their uniform treatment would be difficult. Because they are small, and thus rather poor in species, their inclusion would not have made an appreciable difference to most species texts or to the number of species included.

The whole of Ireland is excluded partly for scientific but more for administrative reasons. Many fairly common British breeding birds are naturally very scarce—or even locally endangered—in Ireland, mostly because of Ireland's position as an outlying European island. More importantly, the legal and administrative frameworks of nature conservation differ between Britain, the Irish Republic and Northern Ireland. The Irish Wildlife Service is drafting a similar publication for Ireland, and we trust that our enthusiasm for such a project will satisfy any regional sensibilities which we may have offended.

THE BRITISH AVIFAUNA

Over 520 bird species have been recorded in Britain during this century and, of these, 210 nest every year and 27 more have nested at least once. Apart from the regular breeders, 54 species are common passage migrants or winter visitors. The rest are rare passage migrants or vagrants, many of which have been recorded only on a small number of occasions.

Viewed on a European scale, Britain has a rather restricted breeding land-bird fauna which is commensurate with its being an island at one corner of the Palearctic faunal region. Many of our breeding land birds have a wide continental distribution and thus occur in substantially greater numbers elsewhere. Two particular features of Britain's breeding birds stand out as special. First is the wealth of the north-west Atlantic seabirds which breed from Iceland to Britain, Ireland and the coasts of Scandinavia and the Russian arctic. Second is the assemblage of upland birds whose closest affinities are with the tundra regions but which show some important differences from Scandinavian bird communities.

In the winter, our mild oceanic climate attracts many wildfowl and waders which breed to the north, both east and west. Many of these species migrate no further than they have to from their breeding grounds, and Britain provides an attractive wintering area. Our long coastline provides abundant habitat, especially estuaries, suitable for northern breeding waders to pass the winter. High proportions of some wader and wildfowl populations winter or make migration stages in Britain.

On the whole, the record of effectiveness of bird conservation in Britain in the last fifty years has been good. Britain has lost one previously regular breeding species (Kentish Plover) and is about to lose another two (Red-backed Shrike and Wryneck). Several species have recolonized after human impact partly led to earlier extinction (eg, Osprey, Avocet, Black-tailed Godwit and, hopefully, White-tailed Eagle if its re-introduction is successful). There have also been new colonists of both southern (eg, Collared Dove and Cetti's Warbler) and northern (eg, Wood Sandpiper and Redwing) origins. A crisis of pesticide contamination was averted, possibly just in time, and there are now thriving populations of Golden Eagles and Peregrines.

There is however a more worrying aspect. Birds with exacting habitat requirements can be held from the brink of national extinction on a small number of reserves (for instance Avocet, Bittern and Red-necked Phalarope). On the other hand, there are, as elaborated in this book, many species which are vulnerable to the impact of man and which have shown a reduction in their range and numbers. This is of concern for two reasons. If man can reduce a species' range and numbers, there is no reason why, without curative action, the process should not continue to national extinction. Secondly, the support for nature conservation comes from people. If species dwindle and become rare, so that people can no longer see them, it is a small consolation to know that they just hang on in a few remote reserves. The final and national loss of species in Britain has so far been limited. The same cannot be said regionally. The maintenance of a natural geographical range of individual birds is of critical importance to the people who support nature conservation. The species described in this book as suffering range reduction at the hand of man testify both to a risk of national extinctions and international censure but more immediately to a reduction in the quality of life for people who care about their own natural environment.

THE CRITERIA FOR SELECTION OF RED DATA SPECIES

Species have been selected for inclusion here on the basis of the five criteria given below. The first three are objective and measurable, though the thresholds set are arbitrary. In practice, the data on species abundance or trends vary in quality, both from species to species and regionally over a single species' range. Future research should improve our information, but for the present we must often rely on subjective or estimated quantification of the data available. Furthermore, the different criteria vary in their objectivity and cannot be compared directly to each other. Judging the case for each species independently for each category should ensure that the species included are valid candidates, even though their claims for inclusion vary in strength.

Rightly or wrongly, we decided against including species introduced beyond their natural ranges. Some, such as Canada Goose, would be included by virtue of a high proportion of the European breeding population being in Britain. A notable candidate would have been the Mandarin Duck which is a Red Data Book species in its native range which gives the feral British population an unusual claim to importance. Categories 1, 4 and 5 apply to both breeding and non-breeding birds, while categories 2 and 3 refer to breeding species only.

1. INTERNATIONAL SIGNIFICANCE OF BRITISH POPULATIONS

There should be no doubt that conservation is an international concern. We have special responsibility to maintain species for which Britain supports numbers of international importance. For a few species, this can be judged on a world scale which would be the ideal yardstick. For most this is not yet realistic because of the lack of adequate census data, especially outside Britain and western Europe.

The definition of the area for which the British population is important presents difficulties. If we cannot compare our populations to the world populations, where shall we draw our larger boundary? 'Europe' in some sense seems appropriate, but should we consider the whole continent, just the EEC, or some other part. Here we take a biogeographical view. A north-west European flyway clearly exists for geese and waders, with little interchange across central Europe between this western and other, eastern populations. We shall take a similar view for songbirds and seabirds, setting a national grouping of the western European countries from Scandinavia to Iberia, including Iceland, as shown in the map opposite.

A threshold British population of 20% of this north-west European wintering or breeding population has been set for a species inclusion. Judgement has had to be made on the inclusion or otherwise of a small number of marginal species and where census data are poor.

2. SCARCITY AS BRITISH BREEDERS

Scarcity is important because of the extent to which it indicates the susceptibility of a population to loss of range or numbers. In some cases, it also indicates an association with scarce and thus otherwise valuable habitats. All species with recent breeding records in Britain but numbers below 300 pairs have been included. This number is arbitrary, and some of the species that would be included by raising it are rare enough to be vulnerable. However, this is the cut-off point usually used by the Rare Breeding Birds Panel (Spencer *et al.*, 1988) and we have chosen to follow it. Species with very variable populations (eg, Dartford Warbler) have been included if low counts in the last 20 years have been below this threshold.

The ranges of breeding birds are in constant flux, so that it is no surprise that oddities arrive and breed sporadically and that some species on the edges of their range are very scarce. Amongst these, it is difficult to judge the importance of conservation. Potential new colonists and species with smaller ranges or numbers

Areas of western Europe used to compare the international significance of British bird populations. Breeding numbers are compared with those in the stippled zone. Wintering numbers are compared with those north of the broken line (the 'north-west European population') and follows the convention used by the International Waterfowl and Wetlands Research Bureau (IWRB).

than could naturally be expected to occur (eg, Purple Sandpiper or Little Gull) deserve support in the vulnerable phase of scarcity. By comparison, accidentals are of little more than curiosity value. Since there is no reliable way of making a separation within this range of scarce breeding birds, we have had to include them all, except Spotted Sandpiper in 1975, an event which is most unlikely to recur. In spite of their numbers, we hope that this book will dispel the notion that these are the species of highest importance in current thinking about nature conservation.

3.   DECLINING BREEDING NUMBERS

Populations fluctuate or change systematically for natural reasons. Long-term downward trends may—but do not necessarily—indicate the adverse impact of man and are potentially reversible. The case of the Grey Partridge is a good example of a declining species for which the causes are well understood and have wide ramifications. The condition for inclusion in this category has arbitrarily been set as a persistent decline of more than 50% in the last 25 years. Sudden crashes due to cold winters or similar natural causes have been excluded. Thus Whitethroats declined in numbers by about 75% between 1968 and 1969 and have not since recovered. However, they are not included as this sharp change is believed to have been due to drought in the Sahel. It has proved very difficult to assign this category because of lack of adequate data for several species which might be eligible. These species deserve better monitoring so as to be given better attention if needed.

4.   RESTRICTED DISTRIBUTION IN VULNERABLE SITES OR HABITATS

Populations of some species are believed to be especially vulnerable by virtue of confinement to rather few sites or particularly vulnerable habitats. We have taken species where more than 50% of the population is confined to 10 or fewer sites as qualifying. In some cases, these species live in rare and vulnerable habitats: for Dartford Warbler or Bearded Tit further loss of heaths or reed-beds would be disastrous. Others, especially several seabirds, breed in colonies or, in the case of wildfowl and waders, winter in concentrations at rather few sites. Any adverse impact on such sites could have a quite disproportionate impact on bird numbers. This condition differs from the others in that its interpretation is relatively arbitrary when it comes to defining site boundaries. However, it admits only six species which do not also qualify on other criteria. A further 20 species included for other reasons also qualify by this criterion.

5.   SPECIES OF SPECIAL CONCERN

In eight cases, texts were prepared for species which were expected to qualify for inclusion, but which did not in fact do so. In one case (Dotterel) this was because of a sudden increase in numbers during the writing of this book. Until it is known whether this increase is real or merely the result of improved survey data we thought it better to keep Dotterel in under this special heading. The other special cases (Black Grouse, Merlin, Greenshank, Whimbrel, Barn Owl and Nightjar) may well have qualified on the grounds of declining range and numbers if only there were adequate data to show it. In all cases we believe that the species are potentially at risk and merit future attention both to assess whether they are actually entitled to a place in this listing and to avert any threats identified. We follow Collar and Stuart (1985) in admitting a special, discretionary category.

THE SPECIES SELECTED AND FUTURE CANDIDATES

The birds selected are listed on pp. 339–344. As discussed above, it is by no means easy to assess whether a particular species meets any one criterion because information, especially on changes of range or numbers, is often not good enough. Now that attention has been focused on this deficiency, we can seek to increase the monitoring effort on some of the most critical species.

We have addressed the question of species which may be close to deserving inclusion in another way. A complete list of British birds was assessed and species noted where we could be reasonably confident that their numbers and ranges would be maintained during the next 25 years in the absence of unexpected events. This might be seen as a green list; the species are in no way endangered. It is from among the remaining species that future candidates for the Red Data Book might arise. At the moment, many do not meet its criteria, but we cannot be confident that they will maintain their range or numbers. The 30 extra species are listed on page 345. Their future status ought to be watched carefully.

THE CONTENTS OF THE SPECIES TEXTS

The texts follow a standard format to cover the following points.

INTRODUCTION

This indicates the reasons for which the species is included, and summarizes the salient points from the text.

LEGAL STATUS

Status is shown for the species under the Wildlife and Countryside Act (WCA) 1981, the EC Birds Directive and the Berne Convention. Further detail on the significance of these legal safeguards is given on pages 321–322.

ECOLOGY

Sufficient information is given to set the context for the following discussion of threats and conservation. References are given to specific sources on the species if any exist beyond the general works.

DISTRIBUTION

Sufficient information is given to indicate the distribution of the species on a world scale and within Britain. This section does not aim to be exhaustive. Further detail can be found in the standard faunal works, the most recent and comprehensive being *The Birds of the Western Palearctic*. For species not yet covered in this work, Vaurie's *Birds of the Palaearctic Fauna* is a good source. For Britain, greater details are given in the two atlases of breeding and wintering birds produced by the British Trust for Ornithology.

POPULATION

Numbers and trends are outlined for Britain and elsewhere if relevant information exists.

THREATS

The extent to which species are threatened can in part be inferred from previous range and population changes, though it will be clear that for many species these have by no means always been adequately documented. In some cases, threats are inferred from general trends, such as the rate of demand for development land and other losses of natural habitat. Only in rare cases is it clear from explicit research just what the key threats to particular birds are.

CONSERVATION

A good deal of conservation work has already been done, and this is outlined before going on to discuss the further requirements. The areas in need of attention and the major challenges are described. It will be possible to review future progress both by future measurement of range or numbers and by the extent to which the factors outlined here have received effective attention.

REFERENCES

Texts include reference to major papers on the species concerned but do not give a full bibliography for each. Three major references contribute to most texts but are not cited repeatedly:

CRAMP, S. *et al.* (eds) 1977, 1980, 1983, 1985, 1988. The Birds of the Western Palearctic,Vols 1–5. Oxford: Oxford University Press.
LACK, P. (compiler) 1986. The Atlas of Wintering Birds in Britain and Ireland. Calton: Poyser.
SHARROCK, J.T.R. (ed.) (1976). The Atlas of Breeding Birds in Britain and Ireland. Berkhamsted: Poyser.

REFERENCES

COLLAR, N.J. & ANDREW. P. 1988. Birds to Watch: the ICBP World Check-list of Threatened Birds. Cambridge: ICBP.
COLLAR, N.J. & STUART, S.N. 1985. Threatened Birds of Africa and Related Islands. Cambridge: ICBP & IUCN.
PERRING, F.H. & FARRELL, L. 1983. Red Data Books. 1: Vascular Plants, 2nd edition. Nettleham: RSNC.
RATCLIFFE, D. A. (ed.) 1977. A Nature Conservation Review. Cambridge: Cambridge University Press.
SHIRT, D.B. 1987. British Red Data Books. 2: Insects. Peterborough: NCC.
SPENCER and The Rare Breeding Birds Panel. 1988. Rare breeding birds in the United Kingdom in 1986. Brit. Birds 81: 417–444.

Red-throated Diver

Gavia stellata

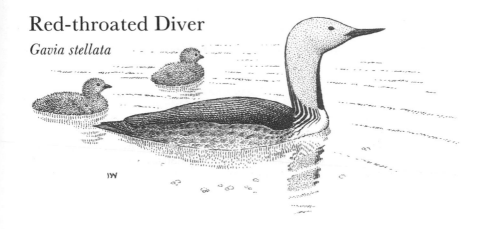

The breeding and wintering populations of this bird in Britain are of international importance. Breeding is confined to Scotland, particularly the northern Isles and the northern part of the mainland. After a decline in the 19th century there has been a good recovery and a slight extension of range in the 20th century: over 1,200 breeding pairs, with over 10,000 wintering.

Greater controls over oil pollution and the safeguarding of breeding areas through SSSI and SPA designations and water quality of the breeding lochs are the most important conservation objectives.

LEGAL STATUS

Protected under Schedule 1 of WCA 1981; Annex 1 of EC Birds Directive; Appendix II of the Berne Convention.

ECOLOGY

Open moorland is the most typical breeding habitat, but nesting may also occur in more forested areas. Most pools and lochs hold only a single pair, but in areas where pools are abundant there may be several pairs within a few hundred metres of each other, and densities over large areas may be high (eg about one pair per square kilometre in a 2,800-ha area of moorland in Shetland). Nest: usually an open scrape, variably lined with rotting vegetation, which is situated on an islet, or on the shore of pools or of small or occasionally large lochs. The nest may also consist of a heap of rotting vegetation in water. Eggs: laid from mid-May to the end of July, but mainly from the end of May to mid-July. Clutch: 2 (1–3); single-brooded, but early clutch losses may often be replaced. The young fledge by mid-September. In Shetland, breeding success averages 0·45 young fledged per pair and does not appear to have changed much this century (Gomersall, 1987).

In coastal areas, where the bulk of the population is found, feeding is carried out in inshore waters, fish being brought to the young. Pairs breeding further inland feed on large lochs close to the nesting site. The nesting pool or loch is not usually used for feeding.

9

DISTRIBUTION AND POPULATION

North Holarctic. Breeds in west and north Scotland, north-west Ireland, Iceland, Fenno-Scandia and northern Russia; it winters along the coasts of south-west Iceland, north-west and west Europe, the northern Mediterranean, the Black and Caspian seas, eastern Asia and North America.

The main breeding strongholds are in Shetland, Orkney, the Western Isles and the north of mainland Scotland. Breeding extends southwards to the north of Perth (Tayside), to south Argyll and Arran (Strathclyde), and sporadically to south-west Scotland and also parts of Morayshire (Grampian).

Since the 19th century, when persecution appeared to have caused a decline, there has been a steady recovery, with expansion into areas such as Kintyre, Islay, Jura, Perth and south-west Scotland. The breeding population in Shetland has been estimated to be about 700 pairs (Gomersall *et al.*, 1984) and in Orkney 90–95 pairs (Booth *et al.*, 1984) and in Argyll 55 pairs (Broad *et al.*, 1986). No comprehensive surveys have been carried out elsewhere, but pairs are widespread and relatively numerous over much of the north of Scotland, and the total population is probably between 1,200 and 1,500 pairs. Elsewhere in western Europe substantial populations exist only in Finland (2,000 pairs), Iceland (1,000 pairs), Norway (1,000 pairs) and Sweden (where an accurate estimate is not available).

Moulting concentrations (of up to 1,500) are found regularly in the Moray Firth and off Aberdeen. In winter, inshore waters of the Moray Firth and southwards to Northumberland are particularly important, although in smaller numbers birds may be found around the rest of the southern coasts and the west as far north as Skye. Larger numbers are noted off the East Anglian coast and in the Thames estuary. Parrack (1986) suggested that the total population in Britain and Ireland in October might be as high as 20,000, but, in the light of estimates made by Tasker *et al.* (1987) of 3,100–4,200 on the east coast of Britain, a figure of 10,000 for the whole British wintering population seems more likely.

THREATS TO SURVIVAL

Threats (actual or potential) include human disturbance, the taking of eggs, predation by foxes, gulls and (particularly in Shetland and Orkney) skuas, varying water levels, marine pollution (especially oil), and the use of monofilament and static fishing nets. Marine pollution is the main year-round threat.

Although individual pairs may suffer from the effects of disturbance, predation and water level fluctuations, there is no evidence that these factors are, at present levels, having any general effect on the population as a whole. The majority of the population breeds on relatively isolated small pools where pressure from angling and other activities is light. On Foula, where densities of skuas are high but disturbance rates are low, breeding success is as good or better than elsewhere (Furness, 1983).

In common with all diver species, the Red-throated Diver is at high risk from pollution, particularly oil spillage, both in the breeding season and in winter. During the eight winters 1971/72–1978/79, 418 divers were found ashore during surveys carried out by the RSPB Beached Bird Survey (Stowe, 1982). Of these, 247 were oiled, and 201 of those oiled were Red-throated. In addition to these data from routine surveys, divers are regularly recorded amongst the list of species killed in specific oil incidents such as the 'Amoco Cadiz' in the English Channel and the 'Esso Bernicia' in Shetland. In the latter incident, oil was spilled in January, 1979, the diver mainly affected being the Great Northern Diver. A similar spill in summer would have killed many Red-throated Divers, as 12% of the British population breeds within the immediate vicinity of the oil terminal and its associated shipping lanes.

Problems may occur where there is persistent or deliberate disturbance by birdwatchers or photographers (Booth, 1982), and in a detailed two-year study in Shetland, Gomersall (1987) found that water level fluctuations were a minor problem, 4·5% of eggs being lost to flooding. Although detailed ringing data are not yet available, the present fledging rate would appear to be sufficient to maintain a stable population.

Breeding Red-throated Divers have also been found drowned in fixed nets in coastal waters off the Outer Hebrides (Buxton, 1983), in Shetland, and in the Moray Firth. Although these have been apparently small and localized incidents, extension of such fishing activities to waters used by large numbers of divers could have more serious implications. A more generalized threat is posed by possible changes in fish populations in waters around Shetland and Orkney which are already having an impact on inshore feeding species such as Arctic Terns.

Divers are threatened by continuing afforestation of moorland in the north of Scotland, and by future extensive peat extraction; the population as a whole may be affected if these operations were carried out on an extremely large scale.

CONSERVATION

The current overall status is, as far as is currently known, stable but remains potentially at risk, and the designation of SSSIs and creation of SPAs for the most important breeding areas must be actively pursued. Local protection measures should be considered in areas where new breeding occurs (eg, south-west Scotland) and visitors to major breeding areas should be asked to avoid disturbing nesting divers. There should be a presumption against large scale conifer afforestation in the catchment areas of the breeding lochs supporting Red-throated Divers.

The main threat throughout the year, marine pollution, can be controlled and limited only by the continued effective implementation of legislative controls on pollution, and up-to-date oil-spill contingency plans and monitoring.

The impact on the Red-throated Diver, and other sea birds, of entanglement with fixed or monofilament nets requires urgent investigation.

Breeding success and population levels should continue to be monitored, and further work is needed to identify areas used by wintering and moulting flocks. Ringing studies to obtain data on population parameters and movements, which are already underway in Shetland, should be continued.

REFERENCES

BOOTH, C.J. 1982. Fledging success of some Red-throated Divers in Orkney. Scot. Birds 12: 33–38.
BOOTH, C.J., CUTHBERT, M. & REYNOLDS, P. 1984. The birds of Orkney. The Orkney Press.
BROAD, R.A., SEDDON, A.J.E. & STROUD, D.A. 1986. The waterfowl of freshwater lochs in Argyll. The third Argyll Bird Report pp. 77–84.

Buxton, N.E. 1983. Unnatural mortality of Red-throated Divers. Scot. Birds 12: 227–228.

Furness, R.W. 1983. Foula, Shetland: the birds of Foula. The Brathay Hall Trust.

Gomersall, C.H. 1987. Breeding performance of the Red-throated Diver *Gavia stellata* in Shetland. Holarctic Ecol. 9: 227–284.

Gomersall, C.H., Morton, J.S. & Wynde, R.M. 1984. Status of breeding Red-throated Divers in Shetland 1983. Bird Study 31: 223–229.

Párrack, J.D. 1986. Red-throated Diver *Gavia stellata*. *In* Lack, P. (ed.), The atlas of wintering birds in Britain and Ireland: pp. 34–35. Calton: Poyser.

Stowe, T.J. 1982. Beached Bird Surveys. Sandy (RSPB).

Tasker, M.L., Webb, A., Hall, A.J., Pienkowski, M.W. & Langslow, D.R. 1987. Seabirds in the North Sea. Peterborough: NCC.

Consultant: L.H. Campbell

Black-throated Diver

Gavia arctica

The Black-throated Diver is a rare breeding bird in Britain. Breeding is confined to Scotland. Trends in the population are unclear, but numbers are about 150 territorial pairs in recent years. Moulting and wintering populations are relatively small. In addition to the designation of SSSIs and SPAs, conservation measures include the use of floating nesting rafts to reduce losses of eggs from flooding and ground predators. Maintenance of water quality is important throughout the catchment area of the breeding lochs.

LEGAL STATUS

Protected under Schedule 1 of WCA 1981; Annex 1 of EC Birds Directive; Appendix II of the Berne Convention.

ECOLOGY

Breeding occurs on lochs amongst mountains, on open moorland, or in lightly forested areas. Nest: usually an open scrape close to the water's edge, variably lined with rotting vegetation, or a heap of waterplants and moss. Islets in large freshwater lochs are preferred (76% of nests in a study area in north-western Scotland were on islands), but the main shoreline may be used. Eggs: laid in late April, mainly in May and June, but also in July. Clutch: 2 (1–3); single-brooded, but up to two replacement clutches may be laid. Most young fledge by the end of August, but some fledge as late as the third week in September. Hatching success in Scotland is usually rather low (<50%) and overall chick productivity is poor; 0·2–0·3 fledged chicks per territorial pair.

Feeding during the breeding season is carried out on the nesting loch and other adjacent freshwater lochs, where fish are the main food.

DISTRIBUTION AND POPULATION

Northern Holarctic. Breeds in Scotland, Fenno-Scandia, the Baltic States and northern Russia, but not in Iceland; it winters mainly along coasts of north and west Europe, the Balkans, the Black and Caspian Seas, eastern Asia and western North America. In Britain it nests in western and northern Scotland (but not Orkney and Shetland), the main areas being Sutherland, Wester Ross and the Outer Hebrides; it is increasingly scarce southwards into Perthshire and Argyll. The Black-throated Diver was first recorded breeding in Ayrshire in 1956, and in Dumfries and Galloway in 1974.

Trends in the population are difficult to assess owing to the lack of systematic information. The population is believed to have declined in the 19th century as a result of persecution, and this decline may have continued during this century. A full survey in 1985 (Campbell & Talbot, 1987) estimated that the breeding population was 150 territorial pairs. There are indications that there has been a contraction from eastern and south-western areas in Scotland (Mudge et al., in prep.).

Post-breeding and moulting flocks occur regularly in various sea lochs in the west and north-west of Scotland.

This is the least common of the three main wintering divers; it occurs in small numbers along most of the east and southern coasts of Britain and also in western Scotland. Tasker et al. (1987) estimated that there were only about 100 of these birds wintering along the east coast of Britain, and Parrack (1986) estimated about 1,300 for the total wintering population in Britain and Ireland; this seems reasonable, the bulk of the wintering population occurring off southern and western coasts.

THREATS TO SURVIVAL

Threats include human disturbance, the taking of eggs, predation, varying water levels, afforestation, acidification, and marine pollution.

Losses of eggs and chicks are usually high. Recent research (RSPB, unpublished) has shown that flooding and predation are the main primary causes of egg loss, disturbance and the taking of eggs being of secondary importance. The rate of chick-loss after hatching is also high, but it is uncertain whether this is due to poor feeding conditions or to other factors such as weather.

Flooding is a problem on both natural lochs and those affected by hydro-electric schemes.

Whilst predation by birds is known to occur in both disturbed and undisturbed conditions, nocturnal predation appears to be widespread—with otters, foxes and pine martens being the likely predators. Human theft of eggs is also known to occur during almost every breeding season.

Afforestation and other changes in land use may adversely affect breeding by changing water quality, affecting food stocks, changing water regimes and altering habitats around lochs and nest sites. Poor chick survival may possibly reflect shortages of suitably sized fish.

Outside the breeding season, and in common with other divers, Black-throated Divers are at risk from marine pollution, particularly oil pollution. More details are included under Red-throated Diver, but 58 Black-throated Divers were killed in the 'Amoco Cadiz' incident in the English Channel in March, 1978.

CONSERVATION

Several practical conservation measures could be taken to improve hatching success. Nesting rafts have been used with success for Great Northern Divers in North America and could be used to reduce egg losses from both flooding and predation, their use with this species is working and should be developed further. Wardening, the use of signposts, and the circulation of leaflets to landowners and visitors may help to reduce losses arising from disturbance at some sites, and visits to nests by birdwatchers and photographers should continue to be restricted.

There should be a presumption against the large-scale conifer afforestation of water catchments of lochs supporting Black-throated Divers, and steps should be taken to protect the water quality of breeding lochs and their feeder streams. The designation of Special Protection Areas, based on appropriate SSSIs, should be given early consideration. About 30% of breeding pairs are located in proposed SPAs or other SSSIs.

Oil pollution, notably during the moulting and wintering periods, can be controlled and limited only by the continued effective operation of legislative controls and up-to-date oil-spill contingency plans.

Breeding success and population levels should continue to be monitored, and further research is needed to identify the relative importance of different predators and the causes of chick mortality.

REFERENCES

CAMPBELL, L.H. & TALBOT, T.R. 1987. Breeding status of Black-throated Divers in Scotland. Brit. Birds 80: 1–8.
MUDGE, G.P., DENNIS, R.H., TALBOT, T.R. & BROAD, R.A. In prep. Changes in the breeding status of Black-throated Divers in Scotland.
PARRACK, J.D. 1986. Black-throated Diver *Gavia arctica. In* Lack, P. (ed.), The atlas of wintering birds in Britain and Ireland: 36–37. Calton: Poyser.
TASKER, M.L., WEBB, A., HALL, A.J., PIENKOWSKI, M.W. & LANGSLOW, D.R. 1987. Seabirds in the North Sea. Peterborough: NCC.

Consultant: L.H. Campbell

Great Northern Diver
Gavia immer

The wintering population of this bird in Britain is of international importance, and it probably includes most of the western Palearctic breeding population. It is known that breeding has occurred once in Scotland. Oil pollution is the main threat, and conservation depends mainly on minimizing the occurrence and impact of oil spillage.

LEGAL STATUS

Protected under Schedule 1 of WCA 1981; Annex 1 of EC Birds Directive; Appendix II of the Berne Convention.

ECOLOGY

The Great Northern Diver breeds on open and fairly deep freshwater lochs in treeless or forested country. In winter, most are found in coastal waters, feeding up to 10 km offshore. Nest: an open scrape or mound of grass and rushes, close to the water's edge on an islet or promontory on large lakes. Eggs: laid (in Iceland) from late May to mid-July, mainly in June. Clutch: 2 (1–3); single-brooded, but early losses are often replaced. The young fledge by late September.

Food in the breeding season is mainly fish but may also include crustaceans, insects, molluscs, worms and frogs.

DISTRIBUTION AND POPULATION

This is mainly a northern Nearctic breeding species, with a small Palearctic population (100–300 pairs) breeding in Iceland. Although summering adult pairs or singles are not infrequent in northern and western Scotland, breeding has been confirmed only once in Scotland (Hunter, 1970). A mixed Great Northern and Black-throated Diver pair has nested quite regularly on one loch in recent years (Hunter & Dennis, 1972; RSPB, unpublished). The bird is a regular passage migrant and winter visitor along the coasts of northern and western Scotland, western England and Wales, and less commonly off eastern England. Tasker et al. (1987) estimated that 1,000 wintered on the North Sea coasts of Britain, and Parrack (1986) suggested that the total wintering population in Britain and Ireland was between 3,500 and 4,500. This is well in excess of the likely total Icelandic population, and it is assumed that birds from Greenland, and perhaps eastern Canada, must winter in British waters.

THREATS TO SURVIVAL

Threats to unpredictable future breeding attempts may include a range of factors such as disturbance, egg collecting, and water level fluctuations, but marine oil pollution is the main threat to the wintering population and Nearctic visitors, for which British waters are particularly important. By way of example, the 'Torrey Canyon' incident in April, 1967, destroyed about 40 of these birds, which were believed to constitute most of the Cornish wintering population. In March, 1978, the 'Amoco Cadiz' incident resulted in 66 oiled birds in north-west France and the Channel Islands (Jones et al., 1978), and the 'Esso Bernicia' spill at Sullom Voe, Shetland, in January, 1979, killed 146 (Heubeck & Richardson, 1980). The Icelandic population may be particularly at risk if it traditionally winters within the same small area.

CONSERVATION

Although there may be a need for active protection measures if future breeding attempts occur in Scotland, successful conservation of the Palearctic breeding and wintering populations will depend mostly on measures taken to prevent and minimize the impact of oil spillage at sea. Further research is needed into the size of the Icelandic breeding population and the size and distribution of the wintering population off British coasts.

REFERENCES

HEUBECK, M. & RICHARDSON, M.G. 1980. Bird mortality following the Esso Bernicia oil spill, Shetland, December 1978. Scot. Birds 11: 97–107.
HUNTER, E.N. 1970. Great Northern Diver breeding in Scotland. Scot. Birds 6: 195.
HUNTER, E.N. & DENNIS, R.H. 1972. Hybrid Great Northern Diver × Black-throated Diver in Wester Ross. Scot. Birds 7: 89–91.
JONES, P.H., MONNAT, J.-Y., CADBURY, C.J. & STOWE,T.J. 1978. Birds oiled during the Amoco Cadiz incident—an interim report. Marine Pollution Bull. 9: 307–310.
PARRACK, J.D. 1986. Great Northern Diver *Gavia immer*. *In* Lack, P. (ed.), The atlas of wintering birds in Britain and Ireland: 38–39. Calton: Poyser.
TASKER, M.L., WEBB, A., HALL, A.J., PIENKOWSKI, M.W. & LANGSLOW, D.R. 1987. Seabirds in the North Sea. Peterborough: Nature Conservancy Council.

Consultant: L.H. Campbell

Red-necked Grebe
Podiceps grisegena

The Red-necked Grebe is only an occasional breeder in Britain, having attempted to breed on at least two occasions since 1980. Otherwise a winter visitor in small numbers. The increasing instances of summering birds indicate that this may be a potential colonist. There is little conservation action required other than safe-guarding potential breeding pairs and sites from disturbance.

LEGAL STATUS

Protected under WCA 1981; EC Birds Directive; Appendix II of the Berne Convention.

ECOLOGY

During the breeding season Red-necked Grebes occur mainly on shallow lowland lakes with a high ratio of dense, tall, emergent vegetation—typically *Phragmites*—often associated with breeding colonies of *Larus* gulls or other water-birds. Breeding has also been recorded on the backwaters of large rivers or estuaries and on pools cut off from the sea (Cramp et al., 1977). In Britain, breeding has been attempted or suspected on freshwater reservoirs and flooded gravel pits. Nest: usually floating amongst dense vegetation or, occasionally, in more open situations; built from aquatic vegetation, usually solitary. Eggs: laid between April and June. Clutch: 4–5; normally one brood. Outside the breeding season these birds move to estuaries or coastal waters. In Britain, Red-necked Grebes regularly winter along the east and south coasts from the Firth of Forth to Poole Harbour (Lack, 1986).

Food consists mainly of invertebrates—especially aquatic and terrestrial insects and their larvae— and, to a lesser extent, fish (Cramp et al., 1977).

DISTRIBUTION AND POPULATION

Holarctic. Breeds from Denmark, Sweden, Finland and northern Russia south to Germany, the Balkans and the Ukraine, east to the Kirgiz Steppes; from east Siberia south to Manchuria, and in Alaska, Canada and the northern USA. It winters south to the Mediterranean, south-east China and the southern USA (British Ornithologists Union, 1971; Cramp et al., 1977). The bird has bred in the Netherlands (Cramp et al., 1977), and summering birds have been recorded there in recent years (Ovweneel, 1985). The north-west European population appears to fluctuate: Denmark 350–400 pairs, Finland about 2,000 pairs, West Germany about 120 pairs (Cramp et al., 1977) and Sweden 600 pairs (Grenmyr, 1984).

In Britain, attempts at breeding have been suspected at a site in Scotland on up to five occasions since 1980, and eggs were laid but failed to hatch; a similar failure occurred at a site in England in 1988. Single birds and pairs have summered on a number of other occasions in recent years.

The European population apparently winters mainly in coastal areas of the Baltic and North Sea.

THREATS TO SURVIVAL

Threats include disturbance by man and his activities.

There would appear to be suitable habitat available in Britain should this species show continuing signs of colonization.

The main threat to breeding birds would appear to be disturbance caused by human activities, such as water sports and angling. Disturbance by birdwatchers would have been a problem at a site in England in 1988 if it had not been wardened.

CONSERVATION

In the event of breeding becoming regular, then site safeguard measures should be examined and implemented as appropriate; otherwise, birds showing indications of breeding should be protected from disturbance by site wardening.

REFERENCES

BRITISH ORNITHOLOGISTS UNION 1971. The Status of birds in Britain and Ireland. British Ornithologists Union.
GRENMYR, V. 1984. The occurrence of red-necked grebe *Podiceps grisegena* in Northern Sweden, Vär Fagelvärld 43: 27–34.
OVWENEEL, G.L. 1985. Overzomerende Roodhalsfuten *Podiceps grisegena* op de Gvevelingen. Limosa 58: 74–75.

Slavonian Grebe

Podiceps auritus

The Slavonian Grebe is a rare breeding species which is confined to Scotland; it is mainly a regular (principally coastal) winter visitor to the British Isles. Slavonian Grebes first bred in the Scottish Highlands in 1908, slowly increasing in numbers until a peak of about 80 pairs occurred in the late 1970s; the population had decreased to about 60 pairs by the mid-1980s. It has bred in seven Scottish counties, but Inverness-shire has always been the headquarters. Threats include human disturbance, a decrease in invertebrate populations due to overstocking of fish, and a change in the nutrient status of lochs as a result of adjacent operations; all of these factors require addressing. The creation of SSSIs on the most important sites is the first priority.

LEGAL STATUS

Protected under Schedule 1 of WCA 1981; Annex 1 of EC Birds Directive; Appendix II of the Berne Convention.

ECOLOGY

Slavonian Grebes breed on large and small freshwater lakes and pools, often those which are poorly vegetated and less productive in nature. In Scotland, nests tend to be on mesotrophic lochs which have relatively little emergent vegetation. Nesting waters can range in size from 2 km in length to pools of 100 m in width. In winter the birds favour sheltered estuaries and coastal bays. Nest: built in emergent vegetation in shallow water [nearly always bottle sedge (*Carex rostrata*) but occasionally horsetail (*Equisetum* spp.)] and in the branches of overhanging trees which are in water. Sometimes the birds nest in loose colonies. Eggs: laid mid-May to early August, mainly in mid-May to June; eggs are frequently laid again after failure. Clutch: 4–5 (3–6); a double brood is rarely produced. Young fledge by late August to early September.

Food, gained by diving, consists mainly of aquatic insects and larvae in breeding season, but molluscs, crustaceans, small fish and worms are also taken.

The young are cared for by both parents.

DISTRIBUTION AND POPULATION

Holarctic and Circumpolar. Breeds in Scotland, Iceland, Fenno-Scandia eastwards through the USSR, and in North America; wintering on coastal and freshwater sites south of the breeding range (Fjeldsa, 1973). The population in north-west Europe is estimated to be: 500–750 pairs in Iceland, 60–80 pairs in Scotland, 500 pairs in Norway, 1,000 pairs in Sweden and 3,000 pairs in Finland.

Breeding in Inverness-shire (Highland Region) was first recorded in 1908, and most are still in that county. Slavonian Grebes bred in Sutherland (1–4 pairs) from 1929 to the early 1960s; in Caithness from 1929 to 1975, reaching a peak of 10 pairs in 1971; and in Morayshire in the 1950s, and regularly since, with a peak of seven pairs in 1971. Single pairs nested in Aberdeenshire in 1960–62 and again in 1974. More recently, this species colonized the Spey Valley in 1971 and now occurs there regularly, with a maximum of 10 pairs being recorded in 1984; it colonized Perthshire in 1973, with a maximum of three pairs in 1982, but bred there last in 1983.

The total population is monitored by the RSPB; the results are published in the Scottish Bird Report and the annual report of the Rare Breeding Birds Panel. The population in Scotland was estimated at 50 pairs in 1966; 52 pairs were counted in 1971, and 63 pairs in 1972. A peak of 80 pairs was recorded in 1978–80, and 81 pairs were seen in 1984; since then, numbers have dropped to 74–76 pairs in 1985, 66 pairs in 1986, and 61–62 pairs in 1987 (Thom, 1986).

Breeding success is generally poor, with 0.4 chicks reared per pair in poor years and 0.8 chicks per breeding pair in good years (Crooke, 1987).

The wintering population in Britain has been reported to be about 400 birds (Lack, 1986).

THREATS TO SURVIVAL

Threats include human disturbance by fishermen, birdwatchers, photographers and tourists; egg-collecting is common. Fluctuating water levels cause problems, and there has been evidence of predation of eggs, young and even adults by mammals, birds and pike. Coots have taken over nest platforms and harried adults. At least one loch has been damaged by afforestation, and has become unsuitable for breeding, while another loch has been subjected to run-off from forestry operations. Conifer afforestation adjacent to breeding sites may result in changes in hydrology, nutrient status and acidity—reducing levels of invertebrates to the detriment of the grebes. The stocking of lochs with rainbow trout has resulted in a decrease in the number of these birds on some lochs owing to competition for aquatic insect food. One small breeding site containing one pair has been lost following the building of a waterside house. On tidal waters in winter, and on passage, the birds are at risk from oil pollution; 8–16% of the Shetland wintering population were killed by an oil tanker spill in the winter of 1978–79.

CONSERVATION

One of the most important sites, Loch Ruthven, has been designated an SSSI for the species; recently, part of this site has also been purchased by the RSPB as a reserve. The remainder of the more important nesting sites have been recommended for SSSI designation.

All regular breeding sites should be safeguarded from damaging land-use changes, and the creation of Special Protection Areas requires consideration.

Increasing commercialization of trout fisheries on these lochs is a cause for concern, and efforts should be made to prevent overstocking of fish with the resulting damage to the aquatic food supplies of these birds.

Proposals for conifer afforestation beside the grebe lochs should be carefully examined and rejected where inappropriate. Proposals for broadleaf woodlands in watersheds would sometimes be more acceptable.

Detailed research is required to study the species' ecological requirements and also the reasons for the low breeding success. Management techniques for enhancing breeding success need to be continued and increased. Viewing facilities are needed for birdwatchers to watch nesting grebes without causing disturbance, and the RSPB have now provided an observation hide at Loch Ruthven.

REFERENCES

CROOKE, C.H. *et al.* 1987. Breeding Slavonian Grebes in Great Britain. RSPB Highland Office Report.
FJELDSA, J. 1973. Distribution and geographical variation of the Horned Grebe *Podiceps auritus* (Linn. 1758). Orn. Scand. 4: 55–86.
THOM, V.M. 1986. Birds in Scotland. Calton: Poyser.

Consultant: R.H. Dennis

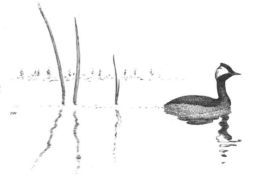

Black-necked Grebe
Podiceps nigricollis

The Black-necked Grebe is a rare breeding bird in Britain, and a scarce winter visitor and passage migrant. Breeding was first recorded in the British Isles, in Wales, in 1904, subsequently in England, in 1918, and then in Scotland in 1930. Now breeds regularly in England and Scotland, with a population of 25–30 pairs. There is a need to ensure that main colony sites are adequately safeguarded, and for research work to determine the requirements of breeding birds and the effects of disturbance and predation.

LEGAL STATUS

Protected under Schedule 1 of WCA 1981; EC Birds Directive; Appendix II of the Berne Convention.

ECOLOGY

The breeding population in Britain has been little studied, but it shows an apparent preference for lowland eutrophic meres, ponds, lochs and reservoirs with extensive emergent vegetation, and often areas of amphibious bistort (*Polygonum amphibium*). Nest: in shallow water, consisting of a heap of water plants and dead leaves usually well hidden in dense reeds or sedges. At suitable sites, colonies of up to 10–12 pairs may develop. Eggs: usually laid during late April to July. Clutch: 3–5 (2–8); there are occasionally two broods. Most young fledge by early August.

Food in the breeding season consists mainly of insects and larvae caught by diving (Madon, 1931; Dementiev & Gladkov, 1967). In the winter an increased number of small fish are taken.

DISTRIBUTION AND POPULATION

Holarctic and Afro-tropical. Breeds in Britain, in central, eastern and southern Europe north to Denmark (up to 200 pairs), and in southern Sweden. The European breeding population fluctuates from year to year, but has shown a tendency to increase on the western and northern edges of its range in the last 10 years.

The original colonization of Britain in 1904, and the main periods of spread since then, have reflected wider colonizations of Europe (eg, Poland, Czechoslovakia and Denmark in the late 19th century; Ireland in 1915; the Netherlands in 1918; Sweden in 1927; Belgium in 1931, and Finland in 1932); these colonizations have often been attributed to population shifts following the desiccation of the Caspian steppe lakes (Kalela, 1949).

First recorded nesting in Wales 1904, England 1918 and Scotland 1930 and subsequently sporadically in many counties. In recent years, in Britain, breeding records have come from four or five main colonies with occasional pairs elsewhere. At least two of the recently occupied colonies within Scotland have declined and may no longer be regularly occupied. The species can be very mobile during the pre-breeding period, and in areas with suitable water sites pairs can be difficult to locate.

There is no evidence that the British population ever numbered more than 10 pairs before 1970; since then the population has fluctuated, but it has sustained a slow but steady increase: up to 1987 there were between 26 and 37 breeding pairs (Spencer, 1988) and in 1988 up to 33 pairs (Spencer, *in litt*).

At one time there was a large colony in County Roscommon, Ireland (about 250 pairs in 1930, perhaps 300 in 1932), but in 1934 drainage reduced these to a handful, the last of which nested in 1957 (Ruttledge, 1966).

Outside the breeding season birds can be seen on passage in small numbers at many inland sites during July to October, and more rarely in March to May. Pairs in breeding plumage often linger at suitable sites during the spring before moving on. In winter, small concentrations occur on the London area reservoirs and in several south coast estuaries and harbours.

The wintering population of Britain and Ireland is about 120 birds (Lack, 1986).

The population and breeding success of known colonies are monitored annually by the RSPB and the Rare Breeding Birds Panel.

THREATS TO SURVIVAL

Threats include human disturbance, predation and habitat loss; these appear to be the main problems facing the small British population. Sites may be occupied for a number of years before being deserted for no obvious reason, although the effects of human disturbance and of predation, particularly by pike, may be important. Most of the important colonies that have developed have been on quiet undisturbed lakes or lochs. In southern England pairs have apparently attempted to breed on a number of suitable waters but have left after disturbance caused by recreational activities.

The effects of predation are relatively unknown, but pike have often been implicated at sites where breeding success is low. In 1987, a pair of birds on an RSPB reserve lost two broods to pike.

The events in Ireland in the 1930s show the danger of lowered water tables and drainage. Birds may transfer to suitable habitats nearby, but, without the core site, adverse factors may cause the species to disappear.

It is not known where the British population winters, but Black-necked Grebes have been killed by oil spills which could pose a serious threat to such a small population.

CONSERVATION

In recent years all important colonies, except one, have been within areas protected by SSSI status. It is important that all sites which regularly support breeding Black-necked Grebes should have adequate safeguards either as nature reserves or SSSIs, or through the creation of Special Protection Areas. Further research to determine the specific requirements of breeding Black-necked Grebes is required, but, in any case, human disturbance should be kept to a minimum. The composition of fish stocks within occupied waters should be maintained to prevent predation by pike or competition from insectivorous species of fish.

REFERENCES

DEMENTIEV, G.P. & GLADKOV, N.A. 1967. Birds of the Soviet Union, vol. IV. Israel Program for Scientific Translations Ltd., Jerusalem.

KALELA, O. 1949. Changes in geographic ranges in the avifauna of northern and central Europe in relation to recent changes in climate. Bird Banding 20: 77–103.

MADON, P. 1931. Le secret du grèbe. Alauda 3: 264–310.

RUTTLEDGE, R.F. 1966. Ireland's Birds. London: Witherby.

SPENCER, R. 1988. Rare breeding birds in the United Kingdom in 1986. British Birds 81: 417–444.

Manx Shearwater

Puffinus puffinus

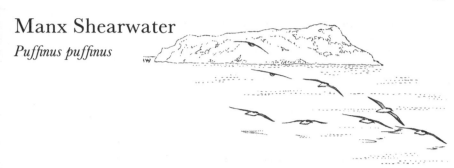

The Manx Shearwater is a localized breeding bird which is found in internationally important numbers in Britain. It has been estimated that over 235,000 pairs nest in Britain in about 30 present or past colonies. Some 225,000 or more of these birds (90–95%) breed on the islands of Rhum, Skomer and Skokholm. The British total is likely to represent 65–80% of the north European population of the race *P. p. puffinus*, considered by some authorities to be a separate species. Cats and rats are threats that need to be removed or prevented from colonizing those islands containing breeding colonies.

LEGAL STATUS

Protected under WCA 1981; EC Birds Directive; Appendix II of the Berne Convention.

ECOLOGY

A summer visitor which breeds on grassy islands and headlands to which it returns in early February–March, spending winters at sea. Nest: a chamber at the end of an excavated burrow or adapted rabbit hole, usually 90–180 cm long (occasionally as little as 45 cm), in a turf or sometimes scree slope; nests are found up to 800 m above sea level, and some 3 km inland on insular hilltops (Rhum) (Wormell, 1976). The birds are highly colonial. Eggs: laid from the end of April to late July, mainly mid-May to mid-July. Clutch: 1; one brood. Most of the young are fledged by the end of September, but a few are not fledged until mid-October.

Food consists of small fish, cephalopods, small crustaceans and floating offal (Cramp & Simmons, 1977).

DISTRIBUTION AND POPULATION

Holarctic and Australasian. In Europe the North Atlantic race (*P. p. puffinus*) is confined to Iceland (one colony), Faeroes, Ireland, Britain and north-west France. The Balearic race (*P. p. mauretanicus*) and the east Mediterranean race (*P. p. yelkouan*) breed on Mediterranean islands. The North Atlantic race winters mostly off eastern South America, apparently also reaching South Africa.

When breeding occurs locally, the birds can be numerous in various parts of north and west Scotland, the Isle of Man, Wales and south-west England, from Shetland to the Isles of Scilly; there were some decreases in the 19th and early 20th centuries due to human persecution and to the introduction of rats, especially at unprotected smaller colonies. Birds can be seen at or near colonies from late February to October, and at other times are at sea, particularly off the north and west coasts. In late summer they occur in smaller numbers off the east coast south to Norfolk; they are scarce off south-east England, and rare everywhere off coastal Britain in winter.

About 22 colonies were present in 1985–87 and there are several other sites where breeding, or possible breeding, has been recorded in the past. The combined population in Britain and Ireland is considered to be between 250,000–300,000 pairs (Lloyd *et al.*, in press). Skokholm (Dyfed) is estimated to support 30,000–40,000 pairs, while Skomer and Middlesholm (Dyfed) have been shown subsequently to hold over 100,000 pairs, and Rhum (Highland) over 100,000 pairs. Although the remaining colonies are much smaller, mostly less than 1,000 pairs and all but a few under 100 pairs, their total must be at least 10,000, so that the British total alone apparently exceeds 235,000 pairs at the most conservative figure. Only one of the Irish colonies is known to hold over 10,000 pairs (perhaps 20,000), and on the published figures the total in the whole of Ireland seems unlikely to be more than 35,000.

Elsewhere, the only European colonies of this race are in Iceland (Vestmann Islands), Faeroes (estimated 10,000–15,000 pairs) and north-west France (formerly numerous, but greatly decreased to around 50 pairs by the 1980s).

It seems improbable that the European population of the North Atlantic race exceeds 350,000 pairs (Cramp *et al.*, 1977)—on which basis the British total may represent nearly 70%.

Outside Europe, *P. p. puffinus* nests only on Madeira, the Azores and more recently, in Massachusetts.

THREATS TO SURVIVAL

Threats include rats and cats, perhaps large gulls, and marine pollution (Corkhill, 1973). The taking of young for human consumption may have caused reductions in numbers at some places in the past.

The accidental introduction of brown rats resulted in the desertion of several island colonies in the 19th century. More recently, rats are considered to be the underlying cause of the decline since 1930 on Eigg, Highland (Inverness-shire) where up to 10 km of the cliffs were once occupied and where now there are probably less than 50 pairs.

Although Great Black-backed Gulls (*Larus marinus*) prey on Shearwaters and have increased considerably in the last 100 years, as have many other gull species, there is no evidence that they have ever seriously affected the numbers at any British colony, presumably because Shearwaters come to land, and change over at the nest burrow, only at night.

The results of marine pollution are hardly known because this species features little among beached corpses; however, some must become oiled as they frequently settle on the water to swim and dive for food. Problems may also be caused by the ingestion of discarded plastic articles.

CONSERVATION

The main needs are to continue monitoring the population level, to control the rat population, and to prevent rats and other land-based predators getting onto rat-free islands which have breeding colonies of Shearwaters. The three main colonies—on Rhum, Skomer and Skokholm—have SSSI status.

REFERENCES

CORKHILL, P. 1973. Manx Shearwaters on Skomer: population and mortality due to gull predation. Brit. Birds 66: 136–143.
CRAMP, S., BOURNE, W.R.P. & SAUNDERS, D. 1974. The seabirds of Britain and Ireland. London: Collins.
LLOYD, C.S., TASKER, M.L. & PARTRIDGE, K.E. In press. The status of seabirds in Britain and Ireland. London, Poyser.
WORMELL, P. 1976. The Manx Shearwaters of Rhum. Scot. Birds 9: 103–113.

Storm Petrel

Hydrobates pelagicus

The Storm Petrel is a localized breeding bird found in internationally important numbers in Britain. This colonial species is difficult to census, but it is estimated that there are at least 20,000 pairs in Britain, representing over 30% of the European (and world) population. The main threats are cats and rats (and other land-based predators), and it is essential to prevent the introduction of these animals to the breeding islands.

LEGAL STATUS

Protected under WCA 1981; Annex 1 of EC Birds Directive; Appendix II of the Berne Convention.

ECOLOGY

The Storm Petrel is a maritime species which breeds on islands and coastal headlands from late April to October, spending winter in the Atlantic. Nest: in a rock crevice, under a boulder, among loose stones, in an old wall or ruin, on a storm beach or in a rabbit or Shearwater hole, occasionally at the end of its own excavated burrow on a turf-topped rocky island. The birds are colonial, though often rather loosely. Eggs: laid from the end of May to August, but mainly mid-June to early August. Clutch: 1; one brood. Most of the young fledge by early October, but a few do not do so until November.

Food consists of small crustaceans, cephalopods, fish, medusae, oily and fatty materials (Davis, 1957).

DISTRIBUTION AND POPULATION

West Palearctic. Confined to Iceland (one colony), the Faeroes, Ireland, Britain, the Channel Islands, north-west and south-west France, north and east

Spain, and various west Mediterranean islands, though they may nest in Norway and have recently been found in the Canaries; they winter at sea, mostly off western and southern Africa.

Over 50 breeding colonies are known along the north and west coasts of Britain, from Shetland to the Isles of Scilly, but these birds are extremely difficult to census, and it is difficult even to know whether or not some sites are still occupied (local declines have been noted in Scotland and in south-west England over the past 100 years). Birds are seen at the colonies from April to November, but are otherwise at sea. The largest colonies occur in St Kilda, the Summer Isles, Shetland, Orkney, Dyfed and the Isles of Scilly, but many are small, and probably most hold well under 100 pairs—none, apparently exceeding 10,000. It is likely that there are at least 20,000 pairs in Britain, and perhaps four or five times that number. Some 24 colonies are known in Ireland, and two of those are known to have over 10,000 pairs (one over 20,000). With generally very local and apparently small numbers in Iceland, France, Spain and the Mediterranean (though probably rather more in the Faeroes), it seems likely that the British population may represent at least 30% of the European and world totals (Cramp *et al.*, 1974).

Very few quantitative data are available to show population trends.

THREATS TO SURVIVAL

Threats include predation by rats, cats, large gulls and skuas, and possibly contamination by marine pollution.

The accidental introduction of rats is the main problem and few, if any, Storm Petrels breed on islands where rats are present. Cats have also had an impact on some islands where lighthouse keepers have introduced them in the past. There is a tendency for Storm Petrels to desert nests if disturbed (Furness & Baillie, 1981).

The effects of marine pollution are not understood, since this pelagic species features little among beached corpses.

CONSERVATION

Some of the islands with the largest colonies, such as Skokholm (Dyfed) are already reserves. It is essential however, because of Britain's international responsibility for this species, that at least all nesting sites with over 200 pairs be designated SSSIs and in some instances SPAs.

The control of rats on any breeding island is essential; it is also essential to prevent the introduction of rats and cats (and any other small carnivore) to islands where they are not already present.

Research is also needed on the impact of trampling by herbivores, introduced by man, on turf structure, and the effect this has on the petrels' ability to make burrows.

Despite the difficulties, urgent steps should be taken to introduce a population-monitoring programme, without which it would be very easy for numbers to decline dramatically without anyone being aware.

REFERENCES

CRAMP, S., BOURNE, W.R.P. & SAUNDERS, D. 1974. The seabirds of Britain and Ireland. London: Collins.

Davis, P.E. 1957. The breeding of the Storm Petrel. Brit. Birds 50: 85–101, 371–384.
Furness, R.W. & Baillie, S.R. 1981. Factors affecting capture rate and biometrics of Storm Petrels on St Kilda. Ringing Migr. 3: 137–148.

Leach's Petrel

Oceanodroma leucorhoa

Leach's Petrel is a localized breeding bird which is found in internationally important numbers in Britain. There are several thousand pairs which may represent well over half of the eastern Atlantic total. Nests on a small number of remote Scottish island groups; the introduction of mammalian predators to the islands must be prevented as they are the main known threats to breeding birds.

LEGAL STATUS

Protected under Schedule 1 of WCA 1981; Annex 1 of EC Birds Directive; Appendix II of the Berne Convention.

ECOLOGY

A maritime species, the Leach's Petrel breeds on undisturbed offshore islands from May to October, spending the non-breeding season in the sub-arctic, sub-tropical and tropical Atlantic. Nest: a variably lined chamber at the end of an excavated burrow, 0·5–1 m long, in open turf, sometimes under a boulder or in a crevice in rocks or in a ruined building, on thickly turfed, rocky, oceanic islands. The birds are loosely colonial, but all activity ashore is nocturnal. Eggs: laid from the end of May to mid-August. Clutch: 1; one brood. The young fledge by mid-October.

Food consists of planktonic crustaceans, molluscs, tiny fish, oily and fatty substances (eg, fish offal thrown overboard from fishing boats, whale faeces, etc.) (Cramp et al., 1977). This species is subject to periodic large-scale wrecks, fortunately these are rare and usually occur during persistent severe westerly gales in late September–November. As a result of these gales, birds (occasionally numbering several hundred) become emaciated, because of difficulties with feeding, and are then blown inshore through weakness.

DISTRIBUTION AND POPULATION

Holarctic. Breeds very locally on small islands off northern Scotland, the Faeroes, south Iceland, north-west Norway, and western Ireland; wintering in tropical areas of the Atlantic south to latitudes of southern Africa.

The British population may represent well over half the eastern Atlantic total, though only a minute proportion of the world figure, Newfoundland colonies alone being estimated in millions.

The British population is largely restricted to a few long-established breeding areas on remote islands or groups off northern Scotland. Breeds mainly on St Kilda, Flannans, Sula Sgeir and North Rona, but also on Foula and Ramna Stacks (Shetland), and possibly on Sule Skerry (Orkney) and Bearasay (off Lewis, Outer Hebrides) as well as elsewhere in the Northern and Western Isles.

At sea, birds are normally found over or beyond the edge of the continental shelf, a region which may be associated with increased food—both from trawling activities and from natural sources. On southward migration, in October and November, the birds may appear close inshore in western Britain, especially during or after prolonged westerly gales.

Nocturnal behaviour and the remoteness of colonies make population estimates almost impossible, but there are certainly several thousand pairs on St Kilda, several hundred to a few thousand pairs on North Rona, a few hundred pairs on the Flannans and Sula Sgeir, and 50–100 pairs on Foula; the British total is probably under 10,000 pairs (Cramp *et al.*, 1974).

THREATS TO SURVIVAL

Threats include potential predation and marine pollution. As the bird has a very local distribution, the accidental introduction of mammalian predators is an ever-present threat which could have a major impact on numbers.

Marine pollution is always a threat.

CONSERVATION

Three of the four main Scottish breeding sites are scheduled National Nature Reserves, and all other sites and probable sites are SSSIs. Furthermore, all sites are, at least in part, candidate SPAs. Continued monitoring of populations is essential, combined with checks for the presence of rats in the colonies. It is absolutely essential that mammalian predators, particularly rats, be kept off the breeding islands.

REFERENCE

CRAMP, S., BOURNE, W.R.P. & SAUNDERS, D. 1974. The seabirds of Britain and Ireland. London: Collins.

Gannet
Sula bassana

The Gannet is a localized breeding bird found in internationally important numbers in Britain. Gannets have increased from about 30,000 pairs in seven

British colonies in the first decade of the 20th century to about 159,000 pairs in 14 colonies by 1984–85, representing 72% of the European population and 61% of the world population. Disturbance to the most accessible breeding colonies needs to be regulated, and the population—and potential threats—should be monitored closely.

LEGAL STATUS

Protected under WCA 1981; EC Birds Directive; Appendix III of the Berne Convention.

ECOLOGY

Gannets breed on cliff ledges or cliff-top slopes, stacks and headlands, and on precipitous islands; they are highly colonial. A few breed in their fourth year but most do not do so until their sixth year (Nelson, 1978). Around Shetland, the majority of breeding adults are found within 37 km of the colony, virtually all being found within 120 km (Tasker *et al.*, 1985). Nest: consists of a substantial pile of seaweed, other vegetation and flotsam. Eggs: laid in March to June, mainly late April to mid-May. Clutch: 1; one brood. Fledging occurs mainly between late August and early September, but a few do not fledge until November. About 75% of the eggs laid result in fledged young (Nelson, 1978).

Food consists largely of pelagic shoaling fish, up to 30 cm long, which are caught following a plunge-dive from heights of up to 40 m, and submerging usually no deeper than 15 m into the water. Offal is also eaten.

Adult mortality averages 6·1% on the Bass Rock, but mortality in the first year of life may be over 70%.

DISTRIBUTION AND POPULATION

Holarctic, but present only in the Atlantic and adjoining seas. In Europe, Gannets breed in Iceland, the Faeroes, Ireland, Britain, the Channel Islands, north-west France and Norway; they winter in the North Sea and the Atlantic south to west Africa, and also increasingly in the western Mediterranean. Passage and feeding movements occur along all coasts in most months. Most first-year birds disperse south in September–October together with birds from Iceland, the Faeroes and Norway, while many adults and older immatures remain in British waters throughout the year (Nelson, 1978).

There were 14 well-established British colonies in 1988; birds have 'prospected' the Shiant Isles since 1975, but breeding has not been proved. The largest colony is on St Kilda (50,100 pairs in 1985, 22·4% of the European population) (Wanless, 1987). Other colonies (in decreasing order of size) are: Grassholm, Ailsa Craig, Bass Rock, Hermaness, Sula Sgeir, Noss, Sule Stack, Bempton (colonized in the 1920s), Scar Rocks (recolonized about 1939), Flannan Isles (discovered 1969), Fair Isle (prospecting 1972–3, first bred in 1975), Troup Head (first bred in 1988), and Foula (prospecting 1970, first bred in 1980); all of these colonies are in Scotland, except Grassholm (Wales) and Bempton (England). Numbers declined during the 19th century due to persecution and harvesting for food (Fisher & Vevers, 1943–44).

The total of around 30,000 pairs in seven colonies (Lundy was deserted in 1906 or 1909) in the first decade of the 20th century increased steadily to nearly 44,500 by 1939 (Fisher & Vevers, 1943–44), about 107,000 by 1968–70 (assuming a total of 45,000 for St Kilda: Cramp *et al.*, 1974), and 161,000 by 1984–85, the rate of increase being 2·6% per annum in the period 1969–85 (Wanless, 1987). The increase has been most rapid in recently established colonies. In 1985–87 there were also about 25,000 pairs in Ireland, about 24,700 pairs in Iceland, and smaller numbers in the Faeroes (about 2,000), the Channel Islands (4,370), north-west France (6,000) and Norway (2,300) (the last three areas were all colonized since 1939); there were also some 40,000 pairs on the west side of the Atlantic in 1984 (three colonies in Newfoundland and three in the Gulf of St Lawrence). The British figure of 161,000 pairs in 1984–85 was 72% of the European total and 61% of the world population of 263,200 pairs (Wanless, 1987).

THREATS TO SURVIVAL

Threats include human exploitation, oil pollution near colonies, and (potentially) chemical pollution and over-fishing by man. Human exploitation had a serious effect last century, and it is thought to have reduced the world population by nearly 70% from perhaps 170,000 pairs to around 53,000 pairs (Fisher and Vevers, 1943–44). Although most colonies are now protected, some young are still legally taken on Sula Sgeir NNR, the Faeroes and Iceland.

Oil pollution is generally not a serious problem for Gannets as they probably do not see fish beneath oil and so do not dive into it and are unlikely to swim far enough to come up in an oil slick.

Oil slicks near colonies may pose a hazard, as birds may sit on the water in thousands near their colony (Nelson, 1978).

Although entanglement in discarded nets and plastic rings etc., either at sea or when incorporated in nesting material, affects some birds it is unlikely to be important in population terms.

Chemical pollution is potentially serious, particularly that due to PCBs, DDE, dieldrin, mercury, copper and zinc. All of these substances were found in Gannet eggs collected at Ailsa Craig, Scar Rocks and the Bass Rock in 1974. Furthermore, evidence of eggshell thinning was also found (Parslow & Jefferies, 1977).

Changes in abundance of surface shoaling fish (due, perhaps, to climatic variations or to increased industrial fishing) is a potential threat, but so far colonies have increased despite the collapse of the herring fishery in the Clyde, the North Sea and Norway (Wanless, 1987).

The major food of the Gannet is herring, but it will, however, take almost any fish. Nevertheless, continuing over-exploitation of fish by man could have major effects on Gannet populations in the future.

CONSERVATION

There is a unique series of counts which document the change in numbers of the world population this century. A full census should continue to be repeated every 10 years, and, where possible, individual colonies should be counted more frequently.

The taking of young for human food, and the disturbance caused on Sula Sgeir during the 'Guga' hunt, needs monitoring in view of the fact that the colony there is not increasing as are other colonies in Scotland.

Chemical pollutants in Gannets and their eggs need to be monitored on a continuing basis.

The main feeding areas of major colonies during the breeding season need to be identified.

Breeding colonies need protection, and disturbance to the most accessible ones should be controlled in order to avoid a reduction in breeding success.

Research is required into the possible effects of human exploitation of fish stocks.

REFERENCES

CRAMP, S., BOURNE, W.R.P. & SAUNDERS, D. 1974. The seabirds of Britain and Ireland. London: Collins.

FISHER, J. & VEVERS, H.G. 1943–44. The breeding distribution, history and population of the North Atlantic Gannet (*Sula bassana*). J. Anim. Ecol. 12: 173–213; 13: 49–62.

NELSON, B. 1978. The Gannet. Berkhamsted: Poyser.

PARSLOW, J.L.F. & JEFFERIES, D.J. 1977. Gannets and toxic chemicals. Brit. Birds 70: 366–372.

TASKER, M.L., JONES, P.H., BLAKE, B.F. & DIXON, T.J. 1985. The marine distribution of the gannet *Sula bassana* in the North Sea. Bird Study 32: 82–90.

WANLESS, S. 1987. A survey of the numbers and breeding distribution of the North Atlantic Gannet *Sula bassana* and an assessment of the changes which have occurred since Operation Seafarer 1969–70. Nature Conservancy Council. Research and survey in Nature Conservation Series No. 4. Peterborough.

Consultants: S. Wanless and M.L. Tasker

Bittern

Botaurus stellaris

The Bittern is a rare and declining resident in Britain which is confined almost entirely to lowland marshes dominated by *Phragmites australis*. In winter the population is supplemented by birds from elsewhere in Europe. The Bittern ceased to breed in Britain by about 1886, due to persecution; recolonization took place in Norfolk in the early 1900s, and this was followed by a slow increase and spread up to the mid-1950s. After this there began a decline which is still continuing. By 1987, there were probably no more than 22–25 pairs. Protection and management of reed beds and further research into the bird's ecology are required.

LEGAL STATUS

Protected under Schedule 1 of WCA 1981; Annex 1 of EC Birds Directive; Appendix II of the Berne Convention.

ECOLOGY

In Britain, breeding Bitterns are confined to large reed beds, although in central Europe they also breed in *Typha* swamps. Males advertise their presence by booming; this feature provides the only possible way of obtaining a census of their numbers, though this may not be reliable as males move around and can have several booming sites. Research is being carried out into booming, and there is evidence that males can be recognized individually by their booms. It is hoped that this may lead to a technique for monitoring male survival. Males may also be polygamous—each having up to five females (Gauckler & Kraus, 1965). Nest: built primarily of reed stems forming a small platform about 30 cm in diameter. Nests are built in the standing reeds of the previous year. Eggs: laid in late March and April. Clutch: 4–5 (3–7). Parental care is thought to be exercised by female alone. Chicks leave the nest and disperse into the reeds about 12 days after hatching. No reliable data are available on the fledged brood size or on chick survival. The chicks fledge between June and early August (Cramp & Simmons, 1977).

Food consists mainly of fish (including eels), amphibians (both adult and larval), insects, molluscs, crustaceans, small mammals, and birds (Gentz, 1965; Vasvári, 1927–28; Witherby *et al.*, 1940). Little is known about the diet of chicks or of post-fledging dispersal.

DISTRIBUTION AND POPULATION

Palearctic. The bird breeds throughout Europe, north Africa and central and eastern Asia. Northern populations migrate further south to central Europe in winter. In Britain, Bitterns are now confined to three main sites in East Anglia and Lancashire. A few pairs breed regularly at several smaller sites. The British population is thought to be sedentary although local movements by individuals have been recorded between nearby sites (eg, Leighton Moss and Haweswater Moss, Lancashire).

Following extinction in Britain in the late 18th century, Bitterns were found breeding again on the Norfolk Broads in 1911. The population slowly increased to about 25 'boomers' in two counties by 1930. By 1954 the population had increased and spread, with Bitterns breeding regularly in seven counties and having bred in an eighth. At this time there were an estimated 78–83 'boomers', 60 of which were in Norfolk, mainly on the Broads. A decline probably began in the 1950s, so that by 1976 the population was estimated at 45–47 'boomers' falling to 26–29 in 1986 and 20 in 1990 including just four on the Norfolk Broads (Day & Wilson, 1978; Day, pers. comm. and G. Tyler, pers. comm.). It should be noted that these figures do not accord with those given in the annual reports of the Rare Breeding Birds Panel (Spencer *et al.*, 1989). This is because RSPB research has shown that previous survey methods have not enabled an accurate estimate to be made. In winter, between 30 and 190 are recorded away from the breeding areas, the number depending on the severity of the winter. Recorded sightings of these birds are scattered throughout England and Wales—but mainly south of a line from Pembroke to the Humber (Lack, 1986). About 12% of such records are of birds found dead or dying (Bibby, 1981).

The population of Bitterns in Britain is monitored by counting the booming of the males on the main sites, and periodically at all sites.

The European population of Bitterns, excluding those in the USSR, was estimated as 2,500–2,700 'boomers' in 1976, although a decline of 30–50% probably occurred following the 1978/79 winter (Day, 1981). The decline appears to be continuing in the Continental populations, with both the French and Dutch populations decreasing (Duhautois, 1984; Osieck, pers. comm.).

THREATS TO SURVIVAL

Threats include the actual or potential effects of pesticides and heavy metals, the eutrophication and turbidity of waters, the die-back of reeds, and the encroachment of scrub onto breeding sites.

The drop in numbers from the late 1950s may have been caused by pesticides. Work presently being carried out into the effects of pesticides and heavy metals suggests that environmental contaminants such as PCBs and mercury may be a problem.

Since the 1950s the further fall in numbers on the Norfolk Broads may have been caused by a combination of factors; these include water eutrophication and turbidity — together with reed die-back — and also scrub encroachment and lack of ditch management due to a decline in reed cutting. Elsewhere, apparently suitable habitat is still available but is not being used.

Climatic factors, such as harsh winters and dry summers, may be a major factor. Studies into these and other ecological factors are currently underway.

CONSERVATION

About 85% of the British Bittern population breed on protected reserves, 65% of the population breeding at three sites: Walberswick and Minsmere in Suffolk, and Leighton Moss in Lancashire. These three sites are SSSIs and the latter is a designated and the former two are proposed SPAs. All the other remaining sites are SSSIs.

Research on breeding biology, feeding ecology and population dynamics in Britain has only just started, and there is an urgent need to learn more about these aspects of this shy and secretive bird.

Some management is undertaken on nature reserves, particularly ditch clearance, reed cutting and control of scrub. However, more needs to be known about the effectiveness of such management schemes. At some sites artificial feeding is undertaken in severe winters. Protection and proper management of extensive reed beds is essential for the survival of this species, and the need to buy potential breeding sites and create new reed beds should be given urgent consideration

REFERENCES

BIBBY, C.J. 1981. Wintering bitterns in Britain. Brit. Birds 74: 1–10.
DAY, J.C.U. 1981. Status of Bitterns in Europe since 1976. Brit. Birds 74: 10–16.
DAY, J.C.U. & WILSON, J. 1978. Breeding Bitterns in Britain. Brit. Birds 71: 285–300.
DUHAUTOIS, L. 1984. Inventaire des colonies de Herons Pourpres en France: Evaluation des effectifs reproducteurs du Butor Etoile et du Blongios Nain en France: saison de Nidification 1983. Société Nationale de Protection de la Nature.
GAUCKLER, V.A. & KRAUS, M. 1965. Zut Brutbiologie der Großen Rohrdommel (Botaurus stellaris). Die Vogelwelt. 86: 129–145.
GENTZ, K. 1965. Die Grosse Dommel. Lutherstadt: Wittenberg.

SPENCER, R. and the RARE BREEDING BIRDS PANEL, 1989. Rare breeding birds in the United Kingdom in 1987. Brit. Birds 82: 477–504.

VASVÁRI, M. (1927–28). Adalékok a bölömbika és pocgém táplálko-zási oekologiájá-hoz. Aquila 34–35: 342–361.

WITHERBY, H.F., JOURDAIN, F.C.R., TICEHURST, N.F. & TUCKER, B.W. 1940. The Handbook of British Birds, Vol. III (Hawks to Ducks): 156–160.

Consultants: J.C.U. Day and P.A.F. Byle

Little Bittern

Ixobrychus minutus

The Little Bittern is a rare but annual visitor to the British Isles, with small influxes in some years, mainly during the spring. Breeding has been suspected on a number of occasions and has been proven once, in 1984. No special conservation measures are required.

LEGAL STATUS

Protected under Schedule 1 of WCA 1981; Annex 1 of EC Birds Directive; Appendix II of the Berne Convention.

ECOLOGY

The Little Bittern is a summer visitor to Europe, occupying a wide range of freshwater swamps, riverine zones, fringes of lakes or pools, and areas of tall dense stands of reeds (*Phragmites*) or similar emergent plants. It is also found in more artificial habitats such as fish ponds, canals, ditches and ornamental waters. Unlike the Bittern (*Botaurus stellaris*) the Little Bittern does not require large unbroken tracts of suitable habitat (Cramp *et al.*, 1977). The only confirmed British breeding record was from an area of *Phragmites* surrounding a shallow eutrophic lake. Nest: dead reed stems and leaves, usually situated over water amongst reeds, willows and other emergent vegetation. Clutch: 5–6; one brood. Incubation: 17–19 days. Fledging occurs in 25–30 days.

Food consists primarily of fish, amphibians and insects (Cramp *et al.*, 1977).

DISTRIBUTION AND POPULATION

Palearctic, Afro-tropical and Australasian. Breeds from Iberia, France, the Netherlands and the Baltic States across Europe into western Asia, south to the Mediterranean basin, Iran and north-western India, and also in tropical and southern Africa, Madagascar and Australia. The Palearctic population winters mainly in tropical east Africa from Sudan and Ethiopia west to the Congo and south to Transvaal and eastern Cape Province.

The population in western Europe is known to have declined in recent years; Belgium had 100–200 pairs before 1960, and it now has about 60 pairs, the decline being due mainly to pollution and drainage (Lippens & Wille, 1972). The Netherlands had up to 225 pairs in good years, but some local decreases occurred due to loss of habitat (Braaksma, 1968). In France the population has declined by 64% from 1,260 pairs in 1970 to 453 pairs in 1983 (Duhautois, 1984).

In Britain, there has been only one confirmed breeding record from Yorkshire, in 1984, when a pair raised four young. Birds were seen at the same site in 1985, although breeding was not proven. Breeding was suspected in East Anglia in the 19th century, and also in England in 1947, while apparent pairs summered in Britain in 1956, 1958 and 1960 (British Ornithologists Union, 1971).

THREATS TO SURVIVAL

While the population in adjacent parts of Europe continues to decline it is considered unlikely that the Little Bittern will colonize Britain. Should breeding take place again, then human and predatory disturbance at nest sites could be the main problems.

CONSERVATION

As instances of breeding in Britain are likely to remain casual events, there are few if any conservation measures that can be usefully taken. Pairs should be safeguarded from human disturbance, and the location of any sites should not be disclosed unless appropriate protective measures have been taken.

REFERENCES

BRAAKSMA, S. 1968. De verspreiding van het Wadaapje (*Ixobrychus minutus*) als broedsvogel. Limosa 31: 41–61.
BRITISH ORNITHOLOGISTS UNION. 1971. The status of birds in Britain and Ireland.
DUHAUTOIS, L. 1984. Heron pourpre, butors: le declin. Le Courrier de la Nature 92: 24–26.
LIPPENS, L. & WILLE, H. 1972. Atlas des Oiseaux de Belgique et d'Europe occidentale.

Bewick's Swan
Cygnus columbianus bewickii

The Bewick's Swan winters in Britain in internationally important numbers. The bird breeds in northern Russia and winters in western Europe, about 30% of the birds wintering in Britain (mainly in three localities). The population is increasing in Britain, and to secure the future presence of large numbers, habitat safeguard and protection from disturbance are needed for all the wintering areas. Bewick's Swan is one of two subspecies of the circumpolar 'Tundra Swan', *C. columbianus*; the other, the Whistling Swan (*C. c. columbianus*), breeds and winters in North America.

LEGAL STATUS

Protected under Schedule 1 of WCA 1981; Annex 1 of EC Birds Directive; Appendix II of the Berne Convention.

ECOLOGY

In winter Bewick's Swans frequent flat lowland areas below 100 m, including lakes, reservoirs, pools and rivers, usually with nearby extensive open ground— especially damp or flooded grassland or arable farmland free from disturbance (Scott, 1980).

In winter, food consists mainly of grasses and aquatic plants. Since the early 1970s these swans have increasingly taken to foraging also on waste root crops, grain stubbles and winter cereals (Owen & Cadbury, 1975). The average breeding success is about 16% of young surviving annually, ranging between 7% and 23% in recent years, and the calculated annual survival of adults is at least 87%.

DISTRIBUTION AND POPULATION

Palearctic. Breeds across the whole of northern Russia eastwards from the White Sea above 65°N. Some 16,000 to 16,500 birds regularly winter in north-west Europe where they are strongly attached to traditional sites. Over 6,000 now winter in Britain, from mid-October until early April, with peak numbers usually in January. The three main wintering areas are the Ouse Washes (Cambridgeshire/Norfolk), Slimbridge (Gloucestershire), and Martin Mere (Lancashire), together with their surrounding areas.

In the 19th and early 20th centuries, the main British wintering areas were in Scotland, but wintering birds have become scarce there since the 1930s, and increasing numbers are found in England following influxes in 1938–39 and 1955–56. At Slimbridge and Ouse Washes, numbers have increased; recent peak counts are given in the following table.

Bewick's Swan: numbers at Slimbridge and Ouse Washes since 1979

Slimbridge

1979/80	1980/81	1981/82	1982/83	1983/84	1984/85	1985/86	1986/87	1987/88	1988/89
390	412	576	285	281	421	475	414	240	245

Ouse Washes

1979/80	1980/81	1981/82	1982/83	1983/84	1984/85	1985/86	1986/87	1987/88	1988/89
2,120	2,995	2,842	2,792	3,364	5,227	4,743	6,160	3,787	3,834

Other important sites are the Ribble estuary (Lancashire), where the flock, which interchanges with Martin Mere, now averages 320; Romney Marsh (Kent), where up to about 180 have been recorded in recent winters; and Nene Washes (Cambridgeshire) with an average of 473 during 1981–86.

Annual variations at particular sites, and fluctuations in the total population, are caused by varying breeding success and influxes from the continent in periods of severe weather. Many of the records outside the main population centres shown in the winter Atlas distribution map result from such influxes and from birds moving to and from these centres.

THREATS TO SURVIVAL

Threats include disturbance to the main wintering areas and illegal shooting on the continent and possibly in Britain: of 53 first-winter birds X-rayed, 12% carried lead shot (Evans et al., 1973).

Drainage of agricultural land, where flocks occur outside the main wintering areas (eg, Idle Washlands in north Nottinghamshire/south Yorkshire), and reduction in winter flooding at localities such as the Somerset Levels and Amberley Wild Brooks (Sussex), continue to reduce the winter spread of the population.

CONSERVATION

At the Ouse Washes and Slimbridge, artificial feeding with grain has been carried out as well as the creation and management of a suitable grazing habitat. This, together with freedom from human disturbance, has been highly successful in ensuring site fidelity and increasing numbers at these sites. Observation hides have also been provided so that the public can watch the swans at close range without causing disturbance.

The future presence of large numbers at the Ouse Washes, Slimbridge and Martin Mere seems assured, but firm protection is needed for the other wintering areas frequented by significant numbers. Establishment of further reserves, such as those at Slimbridge and Welney, with provision of grain for food—especially in periods of severe weather—would be ideal. In addition, there is a continuing need to protect wetland areas used by this species through notification as SSSI. It is essential in all cases that proper management of the water regime is undertaken to ensure the right conditions on these 'refuge' areas. Furthermore, agricultural surpluses provide the opportunity to consider the constructive set-aside of land in low-lying areas for this and other waterfowl species.

REFERENCES

EVANS, M.E., WOOD, N.A. & KEAR, J. 1973. Lead shot in Bewick's Swans. Wildfowl 24: 56–60.
OWEN, M. & CADBURY, C.J. 1975. The ecology and mortality of swans at the Ouse Washes, England. Wildfowl 26: 31–42.
SCOTT, D.K. 1980. The behaviour of Bewick's Swans at the Welney Wildfowl Refuge, Norfolk and on the surrounding fens: a comparison. Wildfowl 31: 5–18.

Whooper Swan

Cygnus cygnus

The Whooper Swan is a rare breeding bird which also winters in numbers of international importance. The Whooper Swan became extinct as a breeding bird in Great Britain in Orkney, in the 18th century, since when only sporadic nesting has been recorded in Scotland—involving one or two pairs some of which are thought to be feral. Over 5,000 of the birds winter in Britain; these come mainly from Iceland and represent about 20% of the north-west European population. Control of disturbance on breeding and wintering sites in Britain, and reduction of lead shot on certain wintering sites, are necessary conservation measures.

LEGAL STATUS

Protected under Schedule 1 of WCA 1981; Annex 1 of EC Birds Directive; Appendix II of the Berne Convention.

ECOLOGY

Breeds on banks or islets of lochs, or on hummocks in northern marshes; it is solitary. Nest: a large heap of reeds (*Phragmites*), sedges (*Carex*) and moss. Eggs: laid mid-May in Scotland. Clutch: 3–5 (3–8), incubated by the female for 31–40 days; one brood (Campbell & Ferguson-Lees, 1972). Fledging occurs in about 12 weeks.

Food in the breeding season includes roots and shoots of aquatic plants and aquatic invertebrates. In winter the birds eat a variety of emergent and submerged water plants as well as grass, spilled grain and winter cereals. In some areas Whooper Swans also feed on waste potatoes and turnips (Thom, 1986; Black & Rees, 1984).

DISTRIBUTION AND POPULATION

Palearctic. The bird breeds in Iceland, Fenno-Scandia and across northern Russia; it winters west to Britain and Ireland, and south to Biscay, the Adriatic, Aegean, Black Sea and Caspian coasts and eastern Asia. It is a regular winter visitor to Britain during October–April. Since becoming extinct in Orkney in the 18th century, the Whooper Swan has only sporadically been recorded nesting in Britain; however, odd birds or pairs (sometimes sick or injured) summer in Scotland in most years. Probably only about ten instances of eggs or young have been recorded in the 20th century until the 1980s, the most recent being in the Western Isles in 1947, Highland (Inverness) in 1963, 'Scotland' in 1978 (the pair hatched three young), two pairs in 1979 (a wild pair in 'Scotland' hatched two young, and a feral pair in Dumbarton reared one), and Dumbarton in 1980 (a female from a 1979 feral pair and a wild male reared two young). Since 1980 one or two probably feral pairs have bred, or attempted to breed, in most years (RBBP reports). Recolonization is possible in view of the current trend towards cooler springs and summers, the present tendency of some northern species to spread to Scotland, and the recent range extensions of this swan in Fenno-Scandia. Since the late 1950s and early 1960s for example, the bird has become established on northern coasts of Norway and southern Sweden (Cramp *et al.*, 1970).

The bird is widespread in Britain in winter, mainly north of a line from the Wirral to the Humber; in recent years a flock of up to 500 has regularly wintered at the Ouse Washes (Cambridgeshire/Norfolk). The population counts in January appear stable, with about 16,700 birds counted in Britain and Ireland in 1986—of which about a third are found in Britain (Salmon & Black, 1986; Salmon *et al.*, 1987).

THREATS TO SURVIVAL

Threats include human disturbance and poisoning by lead and agricultural chemicals.

There is an increase in the risk of human disturbance to nesting birds with the spread of tourism to remoter parts of Scotland and the tendency for lochs to be used for boating, fishing and camping. Similar recreational pressures may cause disturbance to wintering birds.

Poisoning due to the ingestion of lead gunshot has become serious at several wintering sites. Incidents of mass mortality after the eating of grain still carrying quantities of toxic seed-dressing are recorded from time to time (Badenoch, 1980).

Deaths have been caused by birds flying into transmission lines, but there is no evidence that this affects populations.

CONSERVATION

Possible breeding areas, where pairs are seen in summer, should not be publicized, and when nesting is attempted, liaison with the landowners may be desirable to discuss ways of reducing the risk of disturbance.

Important wintering sites should receive statutory protection, and disturbance should be minimized.

Proposed land drainage improvements at wintering sites must be carefully assessed as they could reduce the carrying capacity of the area for Whoopers.

Further research into preventing poisoning incidents is recommended. The bird would benefit from the replacement of lead gunshot by a non-toxic alternative. In the case of seed dressing, clearer instructions about the risk to wildlife when planting in certain frosty conditions when the soil is loose may prevent some incidents.

Attachments to power-lines—to make them more visible—can help to reduce collisions in well-used areas. Consideration might be given to routing new power-lines underground in particularly sensitive areas.

REFERENCES

BADENOCH, C.O. 1980. A report on the wintering and one mortality incident among Whooper Swans (*Cygnus cygnus*) on the River Teviot, Roxburgh. Hist. Berwickshire. Nat. Club 41: 221–226.

BLACK, J.M. & REES, E.C. 1984. The structure and behaviour of the Whooper Swan population wintering at Caerlaverock, Dumfries and Galloway, Scotland: an introductory study. Wildfowl 35: 21–36.
CAMPBELL, B. & FERGUSON-LEES, J. 1972. A field guide to birds' nests. London: Constable.
SALMON, D.G. & BLACK, J.M. 1986. The January 1986 Whooper Swan census in Britain, Ireland and Iceland. Wildfowl 37: 172–174.
SALMON, D.G., MOSER, M.E. & KIRBY, J.S. 1987. Wildfowl and Wader Counts 1985–86. The Wildfowl Trust, Slimbridge.
THOM, V.M. 1986. Birds in Scotland. Calton: Poyser.

Bean Goose

Anser fabalis

The Bean Goose is a rare and localized winter visitor to Britain. Of the two sub-species that occur in Europe only the nominate *A. f. fabalis* occurs regularly in Britain, with a peak of about 400 birds in recent years. The species was formerly commoner, but a widespread decline began in the 1860s and continued until the early part of this century. The Bean Goose is now confined to two regular wintering sites, with small groups infrequently recorded elsewhere. The main site in the Yare valley, Norfolk, is only partially protected, and threats from changing land-use practices, and competition from Wigeon, need to be addressed.

LEGAL STATUS

Protected under WCA 1981; Annex II/I of EC Birds Directive; Appendix III of the Berne Convention.

ECOLOGY

In Britain winters regularly only on grasslands. In the Yare valley the flock selects cattle-grazed swards for feeding where the main food plant is the grass *Poa pratensis/trivialis*. Recently-improved swards, dominated by *Lolium* spp., are rarely used. Away from the Yare valley, birds are associated with relatively poor-quality grazing marshes and grassland. For roosting, the birds prefer small undisturbed waters of about 5 ha, often those surrounded by trees. In both Britain and the Netherlands, birds are very site-faithful, small flocks often returning to the same fields from year to year.

DISTRIBUTION AND POPULATION

North Palearctic. Five races have been identified throughout the range (Cramp *et al.*, 1977). The British wintering population is of the nominate race found breeding in the taiga of northern Europe, from Scandinavia east to the Urals. The bird winters in eastern Europe, the southern Baltic region and the Low Countries, the main wintering sites being in Sweden and East Germany.

The total population estimates vary due to problems with the identification of the subspecies. The nominate *A. f. fabalis* and the west Siberian race *A. f. rossicus* winter in varying numbers in the Low Countries (Van den Bergh, 1985) and the southern Baltic areas. Huyskens (1986) found that the *A. f. fabalis* population was around 100,000 birds and was declining.

The main wintering site in Britain is in the Yare valley, Norfolk, where the birds arrive from late October to December. Up to 300 birds winter through to early March, with occasional influxes in periods of prolonged bad weather. The peak winter count has been increasing since the mid-1960s, with the maximum to date being 420 in winter 1987/88.

In the 1950s, another wintering population in the Dee valley, Kirkudbright-shire, was 200 strong, but this gradually declined from 1958/9 to the present day, with only a few recent records, all of less than 50 birds. There were no records in the winter of 1986/87 (Watson, 1986 and pers. comm.).

It is possible that the increase in the Yare valley population has been made at the expense of the Dee population. However, in the period 1958/59 to 1965/66 both populations underwent a decline; the Dee has not recovered, but the Yare valley flock has, and is now at its strongest since 1940 when regular records began (Seago, 1977).

In 1981 around 70 birds were found in the Carron valley, west Stirling. These birds have been seen regularly since, arriving in September and moving in late October or early November to Slammanan in the Avon valley, 15 miles to the south-east. A maximum of 122 birds was counted at these sites in the winter of 1987/88.

THREATS TO SURVIVAL

Threats include alterations to habitat. Much of the area previously favoured in the Dee valley has now been re-seeded or converted to barley (Watson, 1986). In the Yare valley, re-seeding, deep drainage, conversion to arable land, the introduction of sheep grazing, and increasing competition from Wigeon have caused the birds to shift feeding sites over the last 10 years. Although some areas continue to remain suitable, the population is potentially vulnerable, as Wigeon numbers are rapidly increasing and there may not be sufficient areas for both species.

At the Carron valley reservoir, in central Scotland, Bean Geese feed on the bank exposed by low water levels. Work on the dam will result in raised water levels which will presumably deny this site to Bean Geese.

CONSERVATION

No specific action is being taken for the conservation of Bean Geese in Britain, except in the Yare valley. Even here the birds now spend only a proportion of their time on the SSSI notified for their protection. The revision of the ESA management prescription to secure the correct management of unimproved grazing marshes for the geese should be undertaken at the earliest opportunity.

The RSPB, in conjunction with the University of East Anglia, are currently conducting research which is monitoring the management of farmland in the Yare valley and its effects on the numbers of Bean Geese and other wildfowl. Long-term monitoring of this population will be maintained by the RSPB after the completion of this current initiative in 1989.

Preliminary analysis suggests that the maintenance of unimproved cattle-grazed marshes, and the minimization of disturbance by human activities, are important factors in securing the appropriate management for this species.

REFERENCES

HUYSKENS, P.R.G. 1986. Het Europese rietgangenprobleem *Anser fabalis* [The Bean Goose problem in Europe]. Oriolus 52: 105–256.
SEAGO, M.J. 1977. Birds of Norfolk. Norwich: Jarrold.
VAN DEN BERGH, L.M.J. 1985. Occurrence of the European Bean Goose *Anser fabalis fabalis* in the Netherlands. Limosa 58: 17–22 (Dutch with English summary).
WATSON, A.D. 1986. Bean Geese in south-west Scotland. Scot. Birds 14: 17–24.

Consultant: G. Allport.

Pink-footed Goose
Anser brachyrhynchus

This species winters in Britain in internationally important numbers. The world population is divided between two discrete breeding regions, one in Spitsbergen, the other in Greenland and Iceland. Birds from Spitsbergen winter almost entirely in Denmark, the Netherlands and Belgium, while the much larger population from Greenland and Iceland (about 80% of the world total) winters in Scotland and England. Disturbance at established wintering areas in Britain is a problem which must be resolved.

LEGAL STATUS

Protected under Schedule 2 of WCA 1981 (protected in the close season); Annex 1 of EC Birds Directive; Appendix III of the Berne Convention.

ECOLOGY

In winter Pink-footed Geese frequent arable fields and pasture within 30 km of nocturnal roosts, which are mainly on estuarine flats and sandbanks, freshwater lakes and reservoirs. Food in winter varies with availability, but consists mainly of the grass *Puccinellia* and short herb swards on saltmarshes, meadows and pastures, and also cereal grains from stubble fields (mainly barley), potatoes, carrots and growing cereals. In autumn, cereal stubble is now the preferred food source, with grass becoming progressively important later in the winter; waste potatoes and spring cereals are a minor source of food (Bell, 1988).

Holarctic. Counts on the breeding grounds are incomplete, so the best estimates of the population are based on regular counts in the wintering areas. In Scotland and England, where birds from the Greenland/Icelandic population begin to arrive during September and October, counts have been carried out by the Wildfowl and Wetlands Trust under contract to NCC since 1960 in November (and in spring in some years), when the birds are relatively concentrated. The total has risen steadily, with about 30,000 in 1950, 76,000 in 1966, an average peak of over 82,000 during 1977–82 increasing to 101,000 in November 1983, and a new peak of 176,000 in 1988 (Salmon *et al.*, 1989). Possible factors for this increase include lower adult mortality (which has declined from 22% in 1960–64 to 10% in the late 1970s), increased winter food supply (in terms of quantity and quality) and more statutory refuges on the winter roosting grounds. Birds disperse from the arrival areas through the winter, and in early spring they gather at traditional pre-migration gathering areas; of these the most important are the Solway Firth in southern Scotland, with about 20,000 in March, and the south Lancashire marshes. Estimates of the Spitsbergen population wintering in Belgium and the Netherlands, which has also increased, are less complete: 7,000–10,000 in the late 1950s, 12,000–15,000 in the early 1970s, and over 30,000 in the 1980s (Ebbinge *et al.*, 1986).

This century, due to habitat changes, the species' adaptability and opportunism, Pink-footed Geese have become almost entirely dependent upon farmland for foraging through the winter period. This has led to a major shift in the distribution and movements of these birds in Britain, influenced directly by agricultural practices and feeding opportunities.

In the 1950s and 1960s east central Scotland held 50% or more of the total population during November, when the geese concentrated on barley stubble; however, by the late 1970s and 1980s there was a rapid decline there in favour of more southerly and northerly haunts. Since the early 1960s the numbers of Pink-footed Geese at two traditional sites in north-east Scotland (Loch of Strathbeg and Meikle Loch) have greatly increased, and up to 30% (40,000 birds) now regularly roost there (Bell *et al.*, 1988). These shifts have been linked to the early ploughing of barley stubble because of increased preference for autumn-sown (winter) barley as opposed to spring-sown cereals, and a change from oats to increased barley and wheat production (see also Bell, 1988).

In contrast to the situation in Scotland, the Wash—and, more especially in recent winters—north Norfolk, now has five times the number of Pink-footed Geese in midwinter compared with the late 1960s; in the winter of 1985/86 this figure was 8,288. Lancashire also regularly holds more geese now than it did in the 1960s (average 3,600), with a current average of over 24,000 (1981–1986). An influx into Lancashire occurred in 1976 when a particularly 'clean' harvest left little stubble grain in Scotland; Lancashire then held approximately 40% of the British population. The Pink-footed Goose is therefore adept at exploiting a patchy, rapidly changing food source.

Disturbance at principal roosts on estuaries and lochs also plays a significant role in goose distribution. Intensive wildfowling at the Montrose Basin in the

1970s led to a virtual abandonment of the area; since the establishment of a refuge—a local Nature Reserve—in 1982 the numbers have substantially recovered (35,000 November, 1987). Pink-footed Geese also show marked cold-weather movement patterns; for example, in January, 1987, the population in eastern England moved west to Lancashire at the onset of severe weather.

THREATS TO SURVIVAL

Threats include disturbance at wintering areas. Disturbance at established wintering areas, principally at roost sites, is a problem which needs to be resolved as it is widely recognized that the bird is susceptible to continued interference in its use of traditional sites (Owen *et al.*, 1986; Forshaw, 1983).

Potentially more serious are the threats that may affect the breeding grounds in central Iceland: the Thjorsaver valley and Vatnajökull areas, which hold a substantial proportion of the Icelandic breeding population, could be flooded and developed for hydroelectricity schemes. Should these schemes go ahead it is not entirely clear whether the displaced birds would breed.

CONSERVATION

Although there are no serious threats to the survival of Pink-footed Geese in Britain, conservation of the existing feeding grounds, the spring migration staging areas, and protection at roost sites is important for the continued presence of the currently healthy population; undoubtedly the species would be further safe-guarded by the creation of more statutory no-shooting refuges, or by the minimiz-ation of disturbance in areas frequented by significant numbers. Further censuses to identify movements, distribution and population turnover of geese during spring migration are being continued by the Wildfowl and Wetlands Trust under contract to NCC. The Wildfowl and Wetlands Trust has also recently begun a winter ringing programme of Pink-footed Geese wintering in the Martin Mere area of south Lancashire, and has followed this up with summer visits to Iceland and Greenland to mark birds on the breeding grounds. Further research is being carried out into inter-site movements and feeding preference movements of flocks and individuals on the wintering grounds.

REFERENCES

BELL, M.V. 1988. Feeding behaviour of wintering Pink-Footed and Greylag Geese in north-east Scotland. Wildfowl 39: 43–53.

BELL, M.V., DUNBAR, J. & PARKIN, J. 1988. Numbers of wintering Pink-footed and Greylag Geese in north-east Scotland 1950–1986. Scot. Birds 15: 49–60.

EBBINGE, B., VAN DEN BERGH, L., VAN HAPEREN, A. *et al.* 1986. Numbers and distribution of wild geese in The Netherlands. Wildfowl 37: 28–34.

FORSHAW, W.D. 1983. Numbers, distribution and behaviour of Pink-footed Geese in Lancashire. Wildfowl 34: 64–76.

OWEN, M., ATKINSON-WILLES, G.L. & SALMON, D.G. 1986. Wildfowl in Great Britain (2nd edition). Cambridge: Cambridge University Press.

SALMON, D.G., PRYS-JONES, R.P. & KIRBY, J.S. 1989. Wildfowl and Wader counts 1988–89. The Results of the National Wildfowl Counts and Birds of Estuaries Enquiry in the United Kingdom. Slimbridge: The Wildfowl Trust.

Greenland White-fronted Goose

Anser albifrons flavirostris

The Greenland White-fronted Goose is a localized winter visitor which is found in Britain in internationally important numbers. It is a distinctive subspecies of the White-fronted Goose which breeds in west Greenland and winters exclusively in Ireland, western Scotland and central Wales. At all ages this race is distinguished from the nominate Eurasian race (*A. a. albifrons*) by its slightly larger size and longer orange (not pink) bill and generally darker plumage. Approximately 50% (13,000) of the world population of this race winters in Britain. The safeguarding of traditional wintering areas is important for its conservation.

LEGAL STATUS

Protected under Schedule 2 of WCA 1981 (small population in Wales protected in the close season as it would be in England; protected at all times in Scotland where the majority of this subspecies can occur); Annex 1 of EC Birds Directive; Appendix III of the Berne Convention.

ECOLOGY

In winter, traditionally prefers peatlands and freshwater marshes rather than the flat grazing land frequented by the Eurasian race, but in a few areas during the early 1970s it successfully adapted to feeding on newly available arable land for at least part of the winter.

Food in winter consists mainly of autumn stubble, poor agricultural grasses, and a range of plant roots, stem bases and bulbils; white-beaked sedge (*Rhyncospora alba*) and common cotton-grass (*Eriophorum angustifolium*) are important bog food plants.

DISTRIBUTION AND POPULATION

North Holarctic. White-fronted Geese breed across North America and northern Russia and in Greenland, involving four or five subspecies. About 240,000 of the nominate Eurasian race, *albifrons*, mainly from the western part of its north Russian breeding range, winter in the Baltic–North Sea region, including southern

England. The distinctive Greenland race, *flavirostris*, breeds only in west Green-land and winters exclusively in Ireland, north and west Scotland and at two sites in mid-Wales.

From winter counts at all sites, the world population of *flavirostris* was estimated at about 27,000 in the late 1980s (a recovery from a low point of about 16,000 in the 1970s). 7,000–10,000 of these birds winter at the Wexford Slobs in south-east Ireland.

The most important British wintering site is the island of Islay, Argyll, with 7,000–8,000 (over 27% of the world population); others are found on Kintyre, Strathclyde (about 2,100), Islands of Tiree (about 700) and Coll (about 550), Loch Ken, Dumfries and Galloway (about 300) (Owen *et al.*, 1986 and Salmon *et al.*, 1989), and in Caithness, which holds about 300—all of which are above the 1% population level of international importance set at 220 in 1989. Smaller flocks (less than 100) are regularly found at two sites in mid-Wales, a number of localities in northern and western Scotland, and most of the larger Hebridean islands, as well as on Orkney.

THREATS TO SURVIVAL

Threats include disturbance to wintering areas and (possibly) adverse weather.

Ringing has shown that birds are very faithful to particular sites, so that disturbance or persecution in important traditional wintering areas can be especially damaging (Wilson *et al.*, in press). Unlike many other geese, Greenland White-fronts usually tend to feed in small flocks at low densities, and over most of the wintering range they are unlikely to conflict with agricultural interests. Many of these smaller flocks are sensitive to disturbance and have declined in some areas or disappeared in others in recent years (Norriss & Wilson, 1988); up to 200 have deserted a wintering area in Anglesey, and between 550 and 600 have abandoned Cors Caron, Dyfed, following the severe winter of 1962/63 (Fox & Stroud, 1986).

Active scaring from agricultural areas has resulted in larger flocks being formed.

Whilst previously using only peatlands for feeding and roosting, birds in some areas have adapted to poorer agricultural land, especially poorly drained, low-intensity grassland. However, birds return to peatlands to roost, and here a considerable amount of feeding also takes place; the conservation of these areas is therefore important.

Consistently low reproduction rates are the result of only a small proportion of mature Greenland White-fronts breeding successfully. In 1983 only an estimated 725 pairs produced young out of a breeding population of 15,700 birds. Such a level of productivity makes it unsuitable as a quarry species, being slow to recover from any significant population loss (Greenland White-fronted Goose Study, 1985).

CONSERVATION

Conservation of the existing feeding grounds and traditional roost sites is essential, especially at sites used by large numbers. On Islay, creation of statutory refuges free from shooting and disturbance are essential. This is best achieved through the establishment of suitable SPAs. The maintenance of the traditional system of low-intensity agriculture (promoted by the ESA scheme), conservation of peatlands (increasingly under threat from afforestation), and protection from

from disturbance and illegal shooting, would certainly benefit the population throughout much of its range.

As Britain supports such a high proportion of the world population in winter, and breeding productivity is poor, it is vital that the population is monitored constantly to ensure that no new factors arise unnoticed which could adversely affect its future conservation.

REFERENCES

Fox, A.D. & Stroud, D.A. 1986. The Greenland White-fronted Goose in Wales. Nature in Wales 4: 20–27.
Greenland White-fronted Goose Study. 1985. A conspectus of information relevant to the conservation of the Greenland White-fronted Goose (*A. a. flavirostris*) in Britain and Ireland. Greenland White-fronted Goose Study Research Report No. 4.
Norriss, D.W. & Wilson, H.J. (1988). Disturbance and flock size changes in Greenland White-fronted Geese wintering in Ireland. Wildfowl 39: 63–70.
Owen, M., Atkinson-Willes, G.L. & Salmon, D.S. 1986. Wildfowl in Great Britain, 2nd edition. Cambridge: Cambridge University Press.
Salmon, D.G., Prys-Jones, R.P. & Kirby, J.S. 1989. Wildfowl and Wader Counts 1988–89. The results of the National Wildfowl Counts and Birds of Estuaries Enquiry in the United Kingdom. Slimbridge: The Wildfowl Trust.
Wilson, H.J., Norriss, D.W., Walsh, A., Fox, A.D. & Stroud, D.A. (in press). Winter site fidelity in Greenland White-fronted Geese: implications for conservation and management. *In* Proceedings of International Symposium on the Conservation of Western Palearctic Geese, Kleve, 1989. International Waterfowl Research Bureau.

Consultant: D.A. Stroud

Greylag Goose
Anser anser

The Greylag Goose winters in Britain in internationally important numbers. A small, wild population also breeds in Scotland, and there is a rapidly increasing, ie introduced, population, mostly in England. In the 1970s Britain held about 60% to 70% of the western European wintering population, including almost the whole breeding population from Iceland; since then numbers have steadily increased. There are no major threats to the wintering population but site safeguard measures are needed for the resident wild population in Scotland.

LEGAL STATUS

Protected under Schedule 2 of WCA 1981 (protected in the close season); in Outer Hebrides, Caithness, Sutherland and Wester Ross, on Schedule 1 part II of

WCA 1981 (protected by special penalties in the close season); EC Birds Directive; Appendix III of the Berne Convention.

ECOLOGY

The Scottish population nests on the ground in moorland and blanket bogs, in isolated marshy areas, in reed beds or on tussocks at the edge of lochs, islands in lochs or in streams, some under overhanging stunted trees or bushes. Nest: a loose construction of vegetation with a shallow cup, usually of twigs, heather, reeds and grass, lined with some down. Eggs: laid at the end of March to the end of April (mostly mid-April). Clutch: 4–6 (3–12); one brood. The young fledge from mid-July.

Food in winter varies according to seasonal and local availability, being mainly grass, aquatic vegetation, cereal grains (the main food in autumn), potatoes and other vegetable crops and growing cereals.

In winter the feeding grounds are mainly arable fields, grassland and shallow water areas with nearby (mostly within 5 km) secluded nocturnal roost sites on estuaries, freshwater lakes and reservoirs.

DISTRIBUTION AND POPULATION

Palearctic. Breeds in Iceland, Britain, northern and eastern Europe and in a broad range across the whole of Asia between 30°N and the Arctic Circle, a breeding distribution which extends much further south than that of other grey geese.

The Icelandic breeding population is increasing, with an estimated 3,500 pairs in 1960, 12,000 pairs in 1966, 18,900 pairs in 1969, 15,000 pairs in 1971 and 18,600 pairs in 1973 (Boyd & Ogilvie, 1972), and although no recent counts have been made the increase has apparently continued. The Icelandic population migrates to winter almost exclusively in Britain, mainly Scotland and northern England, 80% of this population arriving during the second half of October and early November and departing during March and April.

During the 1970s the total population wintering in western Europe was between about 80,000 and 110,000, with about 65,000 (60%–70%) in Britain; since then the numbers wintering in Britain have increased to an average of 81,200 during 1977–82 with peaks of 96,000 in 1981–82 and a new record count of 110,000 in November 1985 (Owen *et al.*, 1986; Salmon *et al.*, 1987). The current winter population of western Europe (including Spain) is estimated at 236,000 (Madsen, *in litt.*).

As with the Pink-footed Goose, agricultural and other land-use practices strongly influence the winter distribution of Greylag Geese. Since 1960 there has been a major re-distribution with fewer geese now present in east-central Scotland. North-east Scotland holds the largest concentrations, up to 40,000 (Bell *et al.*, 1988)—at least until early January where there has been an increase in available barley stubble. Unlike the Pink-footed Goose, Greylag Geese tend not to re-distribute southwards as the amount of available cereal declines, or undertake substantial cold-weather movements. The species appears to be more adaptable at exploiting alternative feeding areas locally.

There has been a similar increase in the numbers wintering in Ireland, from around 700 in the late 1960s and early 1970s to approximately 3,000+ in March 1986 (Merne, 1986).

Virtually all Greylag Geese wintering in Britain and Ireland are from Iceland, whereas the population wintering in the remainder of western Europe is drawn almost entirely from the northern parts of the European breeding range.

Britain retains a small remnant of its former widespread native breeding population (East Anglia, Lancashire and the Lake District), which is now confined to the peatlands of northern Scotland and the Western Isles. The Uist (Outer Hebrides) population is thought to represent about two-thirds of the British (non-feral) breeding population, which is estimated at 1,500–2,000 birds; another 300 pairs are found in Caithness and Sutherland. Re-introductions and escapes from parks and collections have resulted in a rapidly increasing feral population, especially in England—mainly in central, eastern and south-eastern counties—and south-west Scotland (which has probably in the region of 14,000 birds, not all of which breed); apart from localized concentrations in winter, British breeders appear to be mainly sedentary, although they often congregate in large flocks to moult in late summer.

THREATS TO SURVIVAL

Threats include disturbance and shooting, while potential threats include alterations to habitat.

In winter, Greylag Geese are not seriously threatened, but disturbance or persistent shooting in established winter feeding and roost sites can cause problems.

Changes in habitat in existing feeding areas, especially alteration of the existing grass or arable farming procedures, may present a potential threat, but Greylag Geese are quite adaptable. The widescale afforestation of Caithness and Sutherland peatlands is a threat to an important component of the native British stock.

CONSERVATION

The well-being of the sizeable Icelandic breeding population is almost entirely dependent on the welfare of the birds in their British wintering grounds and also during the spring. Recent increases in the size of the Icelandic population are probably due largely to improved protection, changes in agricultural practices, and freedom from persecution in statutory refuges in Britain. Continued protection of birds and habitats is the main conservation requirement, especially at sites supporting in excess of 1,000 birds. Further research into the native British birds has been commissioned by NCC to establish breeding/wintering site fidelity, mortality, movement patterns etc. which could reveal much more information on the ecology of the British stock in view of its 'pure' status.

REFERENCES

BELL, M.V., DUNBAR, J. & PARKIN, J. 1988. Numbers of wintering Pink-footed and Greylag Geese in north-east Scotland 1950–1986. Scot. Birds 15: 49–60.
BOYD, H. & OGILVIE, M.A. 1972. Icelandic Greylag Geese wintering in Britain in 1960–1971. Wildfowl 23: 64–82.
MERNE, O.J. 1986. Greylag Geese in Ireland, March 1986. Irish Birds 3: 207–214.
OWEN, M., ATKINSON-WILLES, G.L. & SALMON, D.G. 1986. Wildfowl in Great Britain, 2nd edition. Cambridge: Cambridge University Press.
SALMON, D.G., MOSER, M.E. & KIRBY, J.S. 1987. Wildfowl and Wader Counts 1985–86. Results of the National Wildfowl Counts and Birds of Estuaries Enquiry in the United Kingdom. Slimbridge: The Wildfowl Trust.

Consultant: I.J. Patterson

Barnacle Goose
Branta leucopsis

The Barnacle Goose winters in Britain in internationally important numbers but limited to a few important sites. All Barnacle Geese winter in western Europe, about 33,000 (30%) of them in Britain. Site protection measures must be maintained to ensure the integrity of the Islay flocks.

LEGAL STATUS

Protected under WCA 1981; Annex 1 of EC Birds Directive; Appendix II of the Berne Convention.

ECOLOGY

The feeding grounds in winter are mainly pasture, coastal saltmarshes and '*Plantago* sward' on low rocky islands, but the bird increasingly uses agricultural pasture sown for cattle-feeding.

Food in winter consists mainly of grasses and other pasture and marsh plants and seeds; occasionally (when available) cereal grains from stubble fields are eaten. This is a highly gregarious species which feeds and roosts in large flocks.

DISTRIBUTION AND POPULATION

Holarctic. The world breeding population of Barnacle Geese is confined to four areas: coastal north-east Greenland, Spitsbergen, southern Sweden (Gotland) and southern Novaya Zemlya/Vaigach Island in northern Russia. Each of the three populations migrates to winter in discrete areas: the Greenland population goes to western Scotland and Ireland, the Spitsbergen population goes to the Inner Solway Firth on the England/Scotland border, and the Siberian or Russian population goes to the Netherlands—very small numbers occasionally reaching eastern and south-eastern England, although in extremely severe weather large numbers may temporarily move across the North Sea. The wintering range is at traditional sites and is much more restricted than that of any other goose or duck species (Lack, 1986).

The world population has increased steadily with about 93,000 in the mid-1980s, apparently a result of the availability of better feeding and improved statutory protection on the wintering grounds (Lack, 1986; Owen *et al.*, 1986).

The wintering population from Greenland has averaged about 30,000 during 1977–82, with peaks of 33,800 in 1977–78 and 34,500 in March 1988. By far the most important site for this population is on Islay (Strathclyde) with a peak of 24,000 (1976–77) and an average of 21,400 during the period 1984/85 to 1988/89. The birds arrive in western Scotland during the second half of October; spring departure is from mid-April to mid-May, the birds stopping for up to three weeks in the valleys of northern Iceland.

The Spitsbergen population has increased steadily from about 400 in the late 1940s to an average of about 11,000 during 1984–89, with peaks of 11,400 in March 1988 and 12,100 in October 1988 (Salmon *et al.*, 1989). This population arrives on the Solway during late September and October using Bear Island (700 km south of the breeding area) as a staging post when weather conditions are favourable. Spring departure occurs mainly in the second half of April, the birds stopping for two to three weeks on staging islands just south of the Arctic Circle, in Helgoland and north Norway, before continuing on to Svalbard (Spitsbergen). On its wintering grounds in the Netherlands, the Russian population has increased from about 19,700 in 1959 to 45,000 in 1973–74, and to over 60,000 by the mid-1980s; the increase has been due largely to better protection and newly available feeding grounds on recently reclaimed polders.

THREATS TO SURVIVAL

Threats include disturbance and alterations to habitat. Disturbance or persecution in established feeding areas and roost sites presents a slight threat to the integrity of the wintering flocks on Islay.

Alteration of habitats or existing farming practices in main wintering areas and spring staging areas could cause future problems.

CONSERVATION

The well-being of both the Greenland and Spitsbergen breeding populations is almost entirely dependent upon the welfare of the wintering flocks in Britain and Ireland. Measures have recently been taken on the Greenland population's main winter site on Islay, where the creation of special refuges (notified as SSSI), which provide good feeding free from persecution and disturbance, have been established to lessen conflict with farming interests on the island. These areas have also been designated Special Protection Areas. The establishment of a reserve by the RSPB in 1983 and NCC management agreements on SSSIs are helping considerably to hold the greater proportion of the Barnacle Geese population away from other areas of grass sown for cattle-feeding. The management regime for this is still being refined.

Goose grazing on improved grassland and cereals has an impact on the grass yields in some areas, thus affecting the early bite for cattle. Special licences to shoot the otherwise fully protected Barnacle Goose have been issued for Islay by the Department of Agriculture and Fisheries for Scotland, in consultation with the Nature Conservancy Council, 'to prevent serious agricultural damage'. In some cases, however, the licences have apparently been used by land owners for purely 'sporting' purposes; this calls for greater care over the issuing or renewal of these licences.

The Spitsbergen population wintering on the Solway Firth uses established refuges at the Caerlaverock NNR, established by the NCC, with additional disturbance-free refuges managed by the Wildfowl and Wetlands Trust, and on the inner Solway at the proposed NNR at Rockcliffe Marsh on the southern side of the estuary.

REFERENCES

OWEN, M., ATKINSON-WILLES, G.L. & SALMON, D.G. 1986. Wildfowl in Great Britain, 2nd edition. Cambridge: Cambridge University Press.

SALMON, D.G., PRYS-JONES, R.P. & KIRBY, J.S. 1989. Wildfowl and Wader counts 1988–89. The results of the National Wildfowl Counts and Birds of Estuaries Enquiry in the United Kingdom. Slimbridge: The Wildfowl Trust.

Consultant: M.J. Nugent

Brent Goose
Branta bernicla

The Brent Goose winters in Britain in internationally important numbers. There are two distinct races in the Palearctic which require separate consideration. The dark-bellied Brent Goose (*B. b. bernicla*) breeds in northern Russia and winters entirely in western Europe, with about half the population in Britain. The pale-bellied Brent Goose (*B. b. hrota*) has two discrete populations, one breeding in north-eastern Canada and Greenland and wintering on the eastern seaboard of North America and (in Europe) almost entirely in Ireland; the other population breeds mainly in Svalbard, Spitsbergen and winters in Denmark and in variable numbers on Lindisfarne, Northumberland. Discussion of *bernicla* and of the Svalbard population of *hrota* is relevant to Britain. The former requires the establishment of alternative feeding areas where the geese can feed without causing agricultural damage; *hrota* requires strict site protection.

LEGAL STATUS

Protected under WCA 1981; Annex II/2 of EC Birds Directive; Appendix III of the Berne Convention.

ECOLOGY

Since the mid-1930s the winter habitat of the dark-bellied race was confined to coastal and estuarine mudflats, but with the rapidly increasing population during the 1970s and early 1980s the birds have tended to feed on coastal arable farmland and pasture, when food supplies on the mudflats have been largely depleted. In addition to various saltmarsh plants and grass, food on mudflats consists mainly of two species of eel-grass, chiefly *Zostera noltii* but also *Z. marina*, and green seaweeds,

seaweeds, especially *Enteromorpha* and *Ulva*, the choice much depending on availability; on farmland, food consists mainly of emerging winter cereals and grass. The birds roost communally on sheltered coastal and estuarine waters.

DISTRIBUTION AND POPULATION

Holarctic. The dark-bellied Brent Goose (*B. b. bernicla*) breeds in arctic Russia east to Taimyr and winters exclusively in north-western Europe, almost entirely in the Netherlands, western France and south-east England. Arrival in England begins at the end of September, with the main arrival in November, and peak numbers during December–February. There is a steady decline in numbers as the birds depart towards breeding grounds during March, and relatively small numbers are left in April and May. The birds use staging areas across the Netherlands and Germany as they do not return to the ice-free breeding grounds until late May.

During the 1930s the world population probably declined by at least 75%, apparently due mainly to disease restricting the main winter food plant, *Zostera*, and poor weather in the breeding grounds. The population remained at about 16,500 up to about 1955–57; subsequently, there has been at first a gradual general increase, and then a dramatic increase during the 1970s, with a peak in 1982–83 (Owen *et al.*, 1986). These changes in population are shown below.

Dark-bellied Brent Goose (*B. b. bernicla*) world population between 1960 and 1987

1960/61	1970/71	1973/74	1979/80	1982/83	1984/85	1986/87	1988/89
22,000	41,000	85,000	167,000	203,000	150,000	169,000	235,000

Within this trend of increase there are marked annual fluctuations in numbers, largely the result of breeding success or failure—resulting in winter flocks containing no young in some winters, and as many as 50% young in other winters. The main reason for the recent increases is thought to be a long series of very successful nesting seasons due to favourable climatic conditions on the Russian breeding grounds. However, other factors are important—for example, improved protection on the wintering grounds; this includes a ban on shooting in most continental European countries (France, UK and the Netherlands in the 1950s and 1960s, Denmark in 1972). Other factors include feeding on farmland, and the recent recovery of the *Zostera* beds (Ogilvie & St Joseph, 1976).

The numbers wintering in England have increased roughly in proportion to the world population, with an average maximum of 57,300 during 1976–81 and 94,300 during 1985–89; this represents 50% of the world population during each period. In England, the first main arrivals during October concentrate in two main areas: the Wash, and at Foulness–Leigh on Sea, Essex. During November–January, these birds and later arrivals disperse to other major sites in East Anglia, north Kent and onto the English south coast. Examples of recent peak counts (up to 1988–89) at individual sites are: 27,612 at the Wash; 8,640 at Langstone Harbour, Hampshire; 13,410 at the Blackwater Estuary, Essex; 10,000 at Hamford Water, Essex; and 5,250 at Leigh/Canvey, Essex (Salmon *et al.*, 1987; Salmon *et al.*, 1989).

The pale-bellied Brent Goose (*B. b. hrota*) in the Western Palearctic breeds on Svalbard and Franz Josef Land. From the few counts available, the total population has apparently declined from about 4–5,000 in the 1950s to less than 3,500 in recent years. The whole population arrives at its Danish wintering areas in October, and from there a variable number (averaging about 1,000) move later in the winter to their only regular British site at Lindisfarne, Northumberland. The variation in numbers at Lindisfarne results largely from the severity of the weather in Denmark, with as few as 300 (1974–75) to virtually the whole population in the severe winters of 1979–80 (2,170), 1982–83 and 1985–86 (3,100), when smaller groups were also seen in several other places, principally in coastal south-east England.

A third race, *B. b. nigricans*, breeding in Alaska, north-west Canada and north-east Siberia winters in California and Mexico but occurs in Britain and Europe as a vagrant.

THREATS TO SURVIVAL

Threats to *B. b. bernicla* include shooting in wintering areas, habitat changes, and disturbance by man; threats to *B. b. hrota* include disturbance and, possibly, competition from the Barnacle Goose.

B. b. bernicla. The present high population of this race could presumably be (quickly) reduced by a reversal of the factors which have brought about the increases of recent years, particularly a series of poor breeding seasons.

Other threats which could limit the current population increase are uncontrolled shooting in the important wintering areas, any widespread changes to existing arable land-use in the present coastal feeding areas, land-claims or other developments which would destroy or cause disturbance in those estuaries and mudflats which at present provide feeding areas for significant numbers, and the increasing recreational use of the foreshore and tidal waters, eg, for wind surfing, power boating, yachting, and light aircraft.

B. b. hrota (Svalbard population). The main threats are disturbance or persecution at the present stronghold at Holy Island, or developments or changes which adversely affect the main feeding areas there. Increasing competition with the expanding Barnacle Goose (*B. leucopsis*) population, which now nests on many of the Brent Goose's former breeding islands, has been suggested (Owen *et al.*, 1986).

CONSERVATION

B. b. bernicla. The present high population provides a vital buffer against any future drastic failure in breeding or food supply. The main conservation need is for measures which will maintain the current satisfactory population level. Most important among these are measures for the conservation of habitats at present used by significant numbers; freedom from persecution and disturbance at these sites is also important. There is a need for continued assessment and monitoring of the problems in areas where the current increased tendency for the geese to feed on arable land and pasture leads to conflict with farming interests. The establishment of strategically sited refuges or alternative feeding areas is an important management requirement which will provide safety and good feeding for birds driven from nearby farmland where crop protection measures are being practised. In this connection it should be noted that licences to shoot Brent Geese are issued by the Ministry of Agriculture Fisheries and Food in consultation with the NCC to protect crops from serious damage. The establishment of alternative feeding areas should be considered through the 'set-aside' scheme for farmland.

B. b. hrota (Svalbard population). Conservation of the existing feeding areas in the vicinity of Lindisfarne is essential; these areas provide not only the sole regular

British site for large numbers, but occasionally the only established alternative site for the whole Svalbard breeding population when forced to evacuate their only other European sites in Denmark during severe weather. Disturbance at this site should be monitored and, if necessary, controlled.

REFERENCES

OGILVIE, M.A. & ST JOSEPH, A.K.M. 1976. Dark-bellied Brent Geese in Britain and Europe, 1955–76. Birds 69: 422–439.
OWEN, M., ATKINSON-WILLES, G.L. & SALMON, D.G. 1986. Wildfowl in Great Britain, 2nd edition. Cambridge: Cambridge University Press.
SALMON, D.G., MOSER, M.E. & KIRBY, J.S. 1987. Wildfowl and Wader Counts 1985–86. Results of the National Wildfowl Count and Birds of Estuaries Enquiry in the United Kingdom. Slimbridge: The Wildfowl Trust.
SALMON, D.G., PRYS-JONES, P.R. & KIRBY, J.S. 1989. Wildfowl and Wader Counts 1988–89. Results of the National Wildfowl Count and Birds of Estuaries Enquiry in the United Kingdom. Slimbridge: The Wildfowl Trust.

Consultant: A.J. Prater

Shelduck
Tadorna tadorna

The wintering population of this bird in Britain is localized and is of international importance. The total flyway population in north-west Europe is increasing, and was estimated at 250,000 birds in the 1980s, with about 10,000 pairs nesting in Britain. In winter, although variable with weather conditions, the British population may be between 30,000 and 38,000, but 75,000 (30% of the north-west European flyway population) were counted in January 1986. No specific conservation measures are needed other than habitat protection and maintenance for this currently healthy population.

LEGAL STATUS

Protected under WCA 1981; EC Birds Directive; Appendix III of the Berne Convention.

ECOLOGY

The bird breeds on coastal marshes, farmland or other mainly open habitats close to feeding areas. In recent years a few pairs have bred inland, as far as 100 km from the coast, and this trend appears to be increasing (Owen *et al.*, 1986). Nest: in a hole or cavity, or occasionally in a tunnel under dense vegetation. Eggs: laid May–June. Clutch: 8–10 (3–12); one brood. The young fledge by August and often gather into crèches of up to 100. Shelducks may breed in colonies or solitarily. The latter tend to have better success as activities in colonies such as nest parasitism and egg dumping leading to desertions, loss of chicks by predators whilst adults are fighting and the gathering of young into crèches depress duckling survival (Evans & Pienkowski, 1982; Pienkowski & Evans, 1982a,b).

Food consists mainly of invertebrates, especially molluscs and worms obtained from wet sand or mud, with smaller amounts of green seaweeds; insects and plant material (especially grasses and seeds) from dry-land habitats are also eaten.

Shelduck first breed in at least their third calendar-year, so that a large part of the population consists of non-breeding birds.

The winter feeding habitats in Britain and north-western Europe are almost exclusively shallow coastal and estuarine waters with extensive low-tide areas of sand and mudflats and inland shallow waters near the coast.

DISTRIBUTION AND POPULATION

Palearctic. The birds breed in three separate regions: coastal north-western Europe (Britain, Ireland, Scandinavia and the Baltic and North Sea coasts); western Mediterranean (southern France, Italy, Tunisia, Algeria and Spain); and in a narrow belt from extreme south-eastern Europe (the Balkans, Black Sea coasts, Greece and Turkey) across central Asia, mainly between 40°N and 60°N, to western China (Rüger *et al.*, 1986).

The north-west European population is increasing; it was estimated as 120,000–130,000 during the 1970s, and about 250,000 in 1980–81, about half being non-breeding immatures. In mid-July the majority of adults and non-breeding immatures migrate from Britain and other north-west European breeding areas to form huge concentrations at traditional sites on the extensive mudflats of the German Waddensee (mainly on the Grosser Knechtsand between the Weser and Elbe estuaries) where they become flightless during their complete autumn moult. Another moulting ground for 3,000–4,000, perhaps Irish breeders, in Bridgwater Bay, Somerset, was used in the late 1950s and early 1960s, but counts in the mid-1970s showed that numbers had substantially declined — 1,270 in July 1985. In recent years several other moulting flocks have been discovered in Britain: at the Firth of Forth 300–800 by 1977, increasing to 2,500–3,000 in 1979 and 1980; at the Wash (Norfolk side) 1,000–1,500 by 1980, and 1,057 in 1984; in the Humber up to 200 in 1978 and 1979, and a smaller moulting flock on the Dee estuary, Cheshire (Owen *et al.*, 1986). Birds staying to moult within these areas are probably of local origin, many in the first or second year of life. These sites may have been in use for some time prior to their discovery, but it is more likely that they are related to the population increase and abundant food supply in these areas whilst the birds are flightless. During the moult period, only juveniles (which do not moult flight feathers in their first autumn) and those adults which have stayed with the young, or which moult locally, remain in Britain. After completion of the moult, the birds return from the Waddensee to Britain from September onwards, but many delay until November or early December, along with an apparently small number of wintering birds mainly from Scandinavian breeding grounds.

Shelduck are particularly affected by severe weather, and they undertake cold-weather movements of considerable distances, eg, a hard-weather influx following severe freezing temperatures in north-west Europe in 1978–79 increased the total wintering population in Britain from 38,000 in December to 68,000 in January (Owen *et al.*, 1986). The Shelduck is also one of the species most frequently found dead during or after severe weather, and the increase in the British population is due not least to the benefits of the long run of mild winters from 1963–64 to 1980–81. The largest concentrations in Britain occur during January and February when there are (currently) 8 sites which regularly hold internationally important concentrations (ie, flocks of over 2,500 birds) prior to the dispersal of adults to their breeding territories.

In Britain, the population has increased steadily since the 1930s, with perhaps 40,000–70,000 in winter (75,000 in January 1986) and 10,000–12,000 breeding pairs. Shelduck are common on most British estuaries and coasts which have suitable low-tide feeding areas, and the following table shows the numbers of Shelduck on those sites of international importance regularly holding 2,000 or more (Salmon *et al.*, 1987).

Shelduck: average seasonal maxima during the period 1984/85–1988/89 at principal sites	
The Wash	17,800
Dee Estuary	5,600
Humber Estuary	4,000
Ribble Estuary	4,000
Mersey Estuary	3,757
Morecambe Bay	3,700
Medway Estuary	3,700
Chichester Harbour	2,800

This table excludes the large moulting flock in Bridgwater Bay, Somerset, which — although not counted in recent years — has been known to be in excess of 2,000 birds.

THREATS TO SURVIVAL

Threats, at some sites, include changes in habitat. Increased statutory protection in Britain and Europe, especially on the German moulting grounds, is the main factor affecting recent general population increases, and any reversal of these protective measures would be a major threat; such threats would include, eg, disturbance, persecution, or reclamation of sites which at present hold significant numbers.

Apart from the main winter haunt at the Wash, other important estuary sites are under threat: eg, the barrage on the Mersey, the infrastructure and recreation developments on the Dee, the Humber, and elsewhere. Breeding sites are similarly threatened.

CONSERVATION

The main conservation need is for measures which will maintain or improve the current satisfactory healthy population: habitat conservation at sites with high breeding productivity and those sites currently used by significant numbers in winter is the most important. Sites such as the Mersey, Humber and Morecambe

Bay urgently require designation as Special Protection Areas and Ramsar sites. Even sites which already have this protection face problems and require better conservation. Better integration of the activities of statutory authorities is required, and a greater awareness of the responsibilities under both designations is needed. It is also very important to prevent oil spills at sites holding moulting flocks.

REFERENCES

EVANS, P.R. & PIENKOWSKI, M.W. 1982. Behaviour of Shelducks *Tadorna tadorna* in a winter flock: does regulation occur? J. Anim. Ecol. 51: 241–262.
OWEN, M., ATKINSON-WILLES, G.L. & SALMON, D.G. 1986. Wildfowl in Great Britain, 2nd edition. Cambridge: Cambridge University Press.
PIENKOWSKI, M.W. & EVANS, P.R. 1982a. Breeding behaviour, productivity and survival of colonial and non-colonial Shelducks *Tadorna tadorna*. Ornis Scand. 13: 101–116.
PIENKOWSKI, M.W. & EVANS, P.R. 1982b. Clutch parasitism and nesting interference between Shelducks at Aberludy Bay. Wildfowl 33: 159–163.
RÜGER, A., PRENTICE, C. & OWEN, M. 1986. Results of the IWRB International Waterfowl Census 1967–1983. Slimbridge: IWRB.
SALMON, D.G., MOSER, M.E. & KIRBY, J.S. 1987. Wildfowl and Wader counts 1985–86. Results of the National Wildfowl Count and Birds of Estuaries Enquiry in the United Kingdom. Slimbridge: The Wildfowl Trust.

Wigeon

Anas penelope

The Wigeon winters in Britain in internationally important and localized numbers, over 70% of which occur on nine sites. About 750,000 winter in western Europe, originating from the western part of the species' northern Palearctic breeding range. The component wintering in Britain is about 200,000, about 30% of the north-west European wintering population. Less than 500 pairs breed in Britain. Currently there are no major threats, and all the major wintering sites are established as SSSI.

LEGAL STATUS

Protected under Schedule 2, Part I of WCA 1981 (protected in the close season); Annex II/1 of EC Birds Directive; Appendix III of the Berne Convention.

ECOLOGY

Nest: a shallow depression, lined with grass and down, on the ground in thick cover, often under overhanging vegetation on a grass tussock or scrub. Eggs: laid in mid-April to the main period, May. Clutch: 8–9 (6–12); one brood. The young fledge in July.

Unlike other ducks, the Wigeon is almost entirely vegetarian; its diet and feeding behaviour, in dense grazing flocks, more resembles that of geese. On coastal mudflats, food consists mainly of eel-grass (*Zostera*) and green seaweeds, including *Enteromorpha* and *Ulva*; coastal and inland flooded grassland and saltmarsh pasture feeding areas are equally important where the main food is marsh foxtail (*Alopecurus geniculatus*), flote grass (*Glyceria fluitans*) and creeping bent-grass (*Agrostis stolonifera*). The bird also feeds on stubble grain and on sprouting winter wheat; its use of inland habitats for grazing may have originated during the 1930s when *Zostera* was reduced by disease (Thomas, 1982).

In winter the Wigeon frequents mudflats, mainly coastal flooded grassland and saltmarsh pastures. About 20% of British wintering Wigeon are found on inland flooded grassland.

DISTRIBUTION AND POPULATION

Palearctic. Breeds in Iceland, in Britain (about 500 pairs, mainly in Scotland), in Scandinavia and eastwards across sub-Arctic northern Russia to the Pacific coast. About 1.35 million of the birds winter in Europe and western Asia, from the western part of the breeding range, including western Siberia, with about 750,000 in western Europe.

The average maximum British total during the Wildfowl and Wetlands Trust's annual wildfowl counts during 1960–82 was about 200,000, 30% of the west European population. Ten sites in Britain are internationally important for Wigeon, holding at least 1% of the north-west European population; among these sites the Ouse Washes, Cambridgeshire/Norfolk (with an average of over 28,000 during 1976–83) and Lindisfarne, Northumberland (with an average of over 24,000 in November) are particularly outstanding. The table below gives those sites which support 1% or more of the north-west European wintering population.

Wigeon: maximum counts from the ten internationally important sites for Wigeon in Britain, 1984–89

	1984/85	1985/86	1986/87	1987/88	1988/89	(Mth)	Average
Ouse Washes	23,755	34,495	42,175	38,672	30,968	(Mar)	34,013
Ribble Estuary	17,600	24,150	24,462	35,000	41,809	(Nov)	28,604
Lindisfarne	10,000	12,495	18,000	22,000	28,000	(Oct)	18,099
Lough Foyle	26,310	12,262	12,220	11,997	22,000	(Oct)	16,959
Abberton Reservoir	35,000	10,180	10,000	2,453	5,704	(Jan)	12,667
Dornoch Firth	8,310	14,925	15,029	14,194	10,299	(Oct)	12,551
Elmley, Swale	19,500	5,610	10,714	9,125	5,931	(Feb)	10,176
Cromarty Firth	9,705	12,364	8,871	8,392	8,158	(Oct)	9,498
Mersey Estuary	9,300	11,650	12,000	6,000	4,630	(Dec)	8,710
Severn Estuary	14,072	9,264	9,256	5,359	4,557	(Jan)	8,501

The population wintering in Britain and north-west Europe—along with that wintering in the Black Sea–Mediterranean region—has been increasing steadily since the early 1970s though there has been some fluctuation to slow the overall increase. The north-west European population was estimated at 400,000 in 1974 and 500,000 in 1980 (Atkinson-Willes, 1976; Scott, 1980); since then this figure has, from recent counts, been revised to 750,000 (Rüger *et al.*, 1986). Wigeon arrive in Britain generally from September onwards but maximum numbers are not reached until January, following a mid-winter influx from the continent, and the recent total of 300,000 in 1987 reflects the increase in the north-west European population as a whole (Salmon *et al.*, 1987). This increase is also reflected by the number of inland sites now regularly used, and increasing use is made of the rising amount of suitable habitat available, such as reservoirs and gravel pits, which offer safe roosts within the proximity of good feeding areas.

Wigeon seem particularly vulnerable to severe winter weather, and this is one of the first species of duck to move south and west when prolonged severe weather threatens. in the winters of 1978/9 and 1981/2 the January totals were considerably reduced in Britain and the Netherlands whilst numbers correspondingly increased in southern Spain.

In 1971, between 300 and 500 pairs were estimated to have bred in Britain, at least 75% of them in Scotland. The majority of nesting pairs are found on the north Pennine moors, northwards through central Borders (Selkirk), east and central Tayside (Perthshire) to Highland (central and east Sutherland, Caithness) and Orkney; other sites are scattered in East Anglia, the south Midlands and southeast England. In winter these birds are largely sedentary, making only local or coastal movements.

THREATS TO SURVIVAL

Threats (actual or potential) include disturbance and changes to habitat, although the population has been steadily increasing and there are no major threats.

Large-scale disturbance or persecution in the important wintering areas and secondary areas of importance in south-west England (which are visited by large numbers in times of severe winter weather) can affect the integrity of flocks, but the relative importance of this to the population is not known.

Land-claim, or other developments which destroy intertidal areas or cause disturbance, and drainage or other changes of land-use in flooded pasture areas which at present provide feeding areas for significant numbers, are potential threats.

CONSERVATION

The main requirement is for measures which will ensure the continued presence of undisturbed estuarine, coastal and inland habitats which at present provide feeding areas for significant numbers, ie, notification as SSSI of the key wintering sites. Approximately 70% of the population wintering in Britain feed and roost on reserves (or on other sites which enjoy some degree of protection) which are disturbance-free and which are not used by wildfowlers. In some areas the number of Wigeon using these 'refuges' has increased as a direct result of the decrease in disturbance and the management of the habitat; the Ouse Washes prior to 1970 held less than 10,000 birds in mid-winter, but since the creation of refuge areas on the site—and management to provide winter flooding (though wildfowling still takes place in some areas within the site)—the numbers have risen dramatically (see table).

REFERENCES

ATKINSON-WILLES, G.L. 1976. The numerical distribution of ducks, swans and Coots as a guide in assessing the importance of wetlands in mid-winter. Proc. Int. Conf. Cons. Wetlands and Waterfowl, Heiligenhafen. 1974: 199–271.

OWEN, M., ATKINSON-WILLES, G.L. & SALMON, D.G. 1986. Wildfowl in Great Britain, 2nd edition. Cambridge: Cambridge University Press.

RÜGER, A., PRENTICE, C. & OWEN, M. 1986. Results of the IWRB International Waterfowl Census 1967–1983. Slimbridge: International Waterfowl Research Bureau.

SALMON, D.G., MOSER, M.E. & KIRBY, J.S. 1987. Wildfowl and Wader counts 1985–86. Results of the National Wildfowl Counts and Birds of Estuaries Enquiry in the United Kingdom. Slimbridge: The Wildfowl Trust.

SCOTT, D.A. 1980. A preliminary inventory of wetlands of international importance for waterfowl in western Europe and north-west Africa. International Waterfowl Research Bureau special pub. No. 2, Slimbridge.

THOMAS, G.J. 1982. Autumn and winter feeding ecology of waterfowl at the Ouse Washes, England. J. Zool., Lond. 197: 131–172.

Gadwall
Anas strepera

The Gadwall winters in Britain in internationally important and localized numbers. It is a local and scarce breeder (originating largely from introductions) with an estimated breeding population of between 500 and 600 pairs. The bird was introduced into England in about 1850, with marked increases occurring during the late 19th and mid-20th centuries; it colonized Scotland in 1909, and is still increasing locally, especially in south-western counties. The Gadwall is increasing as a winter visitor in Britain and much of western Europe (where the breeding range is also expanding), and in 1985/86 a new high of over 5,000 was recorded in Britain and Ireland. No special conservation measures are deemed to be necessary.

LEGAL STATUS

Protected under Schedule 2, Part 1 of WCA 1981 (protected in the close season); Annex II/1 of EC Birds Directive; Appendix III of the Berne Convention.

ECOLOGY

The bird breeds close to water on the shores or islets of lakes and slow rivers, or in marshes with reeds (*Phragmites* or *Glyceria*) on open pools; it is solitary, or social on islets. In winter, Gadwall are primarily found on inland waters—mainly gravel pits and reservoirs. Apart from the Ouse Washes, flood meadows are not used as frequently as by other dabbling ducks. Nest: made of grasses, leaves and down, and well-hidden in or under grass-tussocks, rushes (*Juncus*), nettles (*Urtica*), brambles (*Rubus*), bushes or other thick cover. Eggs: laid in late April to the end of June. Clutch: 8–12 (6–16); one brood. The young fledge by mid-August.

Food consists of water plants, such as pondweeds (*Potamogeton*), sedges (*Carex*), club-rushes (*Scirpus*), rushes (*Juncus*) and sweet-grasses (*Glyceria*), obtained by dabbling; the bird is less inclined to leave the water to graze in the manner of Wigeon.

DISTRIBUTION AND POPULATION

Holarctic. The Gadwall breeds locally in Iceland, Britain, Ireland and eastwards from France, north to south Sweden and Estonia, and south to Spain and the Balkans; it is much more numerous in Russia. It winters in western Europe, Mediterranean areas, southern Asia and the United States south to Mexico.

The first Gadwalls in Britain were introduced into Norfolk in about 1850 and, possibly reinforced by wild immigrants, have subsequently spread to other parts of East Anglia. Smaller concentrations have similarly (though generally more recently) built up elsewhere in England. Scotland was colonized (possibly from Iceland) in 1909, and the bird has since become established in Tayside (Kinross and Perth) and Fife, although it is found irregularly elsewhere.

The English population was firmly based in the Brecklands of East Anglia before the end of the 19th century, but it did not spread to eastern Suffolk until the 1930s or become established in the Norfolk Broads until the 1950s; smaller groups, often originating from introductions or escapes, gradually became settled in other parts of England—especially since the 1950s, and particularly in Essex, Kent, Surrey, the Isles of Scilly, Somerset, Gloucestershire, north Lancashire, the Lake District and Yorkshire.

The Scottish centre remains Loch Leven, Tayside (Kinross), with smaller numbers nearby in Perth and Fife, but in recent years the species has bred irregularly elsewhere, notably in the Orkneys and Western Isles (Atkinson-Willes, 1970).

The total British breeding population has been variously estimated at about 200 pairs in 1967 and 100–200 pairs in 1968, and it is probably now in the region of 500 pairs (Owen *et al.*, 1986); there are 25–40 pairs on Loch Leven, and the feral concentrations include about 40 pairs at Minsmere (Suffolk), 25–30 at Chew Valley Lake (Avon) and 20–25 on the Ouse Washes (Cambridgeshire/Norfolk), while the Brecks and the Broads hold many more. Analysis of the National Wildfowl Counts over the period 1960–1985 showed an annual increase of 4.6% in the population with Britain (Salmon *et al.*, 1987). This increase varied from region to region, with increases of 9·5% in south-west England and 9% in the south-east. In eastern and central England the population was stable, and in south-east Scotland it had increased by 2% in the period 1973–1985 (Fox, 1988).

In winter, approximately a quarter of the British population moves south or south-east, and these are replaced by similar numbers from Iceland, Scandinavia and the Baltic countries (Owen *et al.*, 1986). Birds from Britain move to France, Spain, Italy, the Netherlands, Germany, Denmark, Sweden and the USSR. Annual wildfowl counts have shown a dramatic rise in the numbers wintering in Britain, from under 300 in 1967 to over 3,000 in 1983, and 6,600 in 1988. The total north-west European population in winter is estimated at 12,000 birds (Rüger *et al.*, 1986). Although Britain clearly holds an important part of this total, very few sites hold large numbers, and only one (Rutland Water) is of international importance (ie, it holds 1% of the north-west European population level: 120); those sites regularly holding concentrations of 200 or more in winter are given in the table below. The main wintering area in Britain, the inland southern lowlands, south east of a line from the Humber to the Severn (and excluding most of Devon and Cornwall), encompasses those areas where the initial introductions were made (Lack, 1986).

Gadwall: winter maxima at main sites, 1984–89

	1984/85	1985/86	1986/87	1987/88	1988/89	(Mth)	Average
Rutland Water	1,109	1,577	1,031	1,387	1,805	(Oct)	1,382
Aberton Reservoir	325	169	410	160	784	(Dec)	370
Gunton Park, Norfolk	144	327	266	389	461	(Sep)	317
Ouse Washes	284	255	356	277	229	(Feb)	280
Slimbridge	237	321	200	322	290	(Dec)	274
Loch Leven	210	195	250	140	154	(Sep)	190
Cheshunt GPs, Hertfordshire	145	215	105	185	200	(Dec)	170
Thrapston GPs, Northamptonshire	145	215	105	185	181	(Oct)	167
Stanford Meres, Norfolk	77	245	316	67	110	(Sep)	163
Hornsea Mere, Humberside	105	235	70	281	77	(Sep)	154

THREATS TO SURVIVAL

Threats (possible and potential) include disturbance and water pollution. At present there are probably no threats, though human disturbance from recreational activities and water pollution may pose problems on the Norfolk Broads and at other large bodies of water, principally inland reservoirs, which are important for the Gadwall.

CONSERVATION

No special measures are needed for the time being. Several of the centres, such as Loch Leven and Minsmere, are already reserves. While island-nesting groups in places with more human disturbance, like Chew Valley Reservoir, seem unaffected at present by numbers of people in the general area, notification of key areas as SSSIs (and Ramsar/SPA sites) are important measures which may help to regulate the effects of further increases in water-based recreation.

REFERENCES

ATKINSON-WILLES, G.L. 1970. Wildfowl situation in England, Scotland and Wales. Proc. Int. Reg. Meet. Conserv. Wildfowl Resources, Leningrad 1968: 101–107.

Fox, A.D. 1988. Breeding status of the Gadwall in Britain and Ireland. Brit. Birds 81: 51–66.

OWEN, M., ATKINSON-WILLES, G.L. & SALMON, D.G. 1986. Wildfowl in Great Britain, 2nd edition. Cambridge: Cambridge University Press.

RÜGER, A., PRENTICE, C. & OWEN, M. 1986. Results of the IWRB International Waterfowl Census 1967–1983. Slimbridge: International Waterfowl Research Bureau.

SALMON, D.G., MOSER, M.E. & KIRBY, J.S. 1987. Wildfowl and Wader counts 1985–86. Results of the National Wildfowl Count and Birds of Estuaries Enquiry in the United Kingdom. Slimbridge: The Wildfowl Trust.

Teal

Anas crecca

The Teal winters in Britain in internationally important numbers. In 1986 the wintering population was estimated to be about 100,000, between 25% and 30% of the population wintering in north-west Europe. An estimated 3,500 to 6,000 pairs breed in Britain and Ireland. This species is dependent on the conservation of freshwater wetlands and estuaries.

LEGAL STATUS

Protected under Schedule 2, Part 1 of WCA 1981 (protected in the close season); Annex II/1 of EC Birds Directive; Appendix III of the Berne Convention.

ECOLOGY

In winter, Teal frequent areas of shallow water on estuaries, coastal lagoons, coastal and inland marshes, flooded pasture and ponds; they breed in dense cover, usually (but not always) near water, both far inland and near coasts. Eggs: laid mid-April to early June. Clutch: 8–11 (7–15); one brood. The young fledge in July.

Food consists mainly of seeds of aquatic plants, chiefly *Polygonum* sp., *Eleocharis* and *Ranunculus* in freshwater, and *Salicornia* and *Atriplex* in seawater, especially in autumn and winter, and various small invertebrates—principally Chironomid larvae and snails. Some Teals also feed on winter stubble.

DISTRIBUTION AND POPULATION

Holarctic. The Green-winged Teal (*A. c. carolinensis*) breeds and winters in North America; the nominate *A. c. crecca* breeds in Europe and Asia. Within Europe, the Teal breeds mainly in the north, the range becoming discontinuous in France and central Europe; it is virtually absent from southern Europe and the Mediterranean. Breeding areas in northern Europe and western Russia become entirely vacated for the mainly south and west European wintering areas. British breeders are largely sedentary (except in severe weather), with winter immigrants arriving here from Iceland, Scandinavia, and the Baltic countries across to north-west Siberia.

The widespread inland and coastal distribution in all seasons prevents accurate counting of breeding and wintering populations. An estimated 400,000 of the birds winter in north-west Europe (Rüger *et al.*, 1986) (mainly Britain, the Netherlands and western France) with 100,000 (between 25% and 30%) of these in Britain, where peak numbers occur in December; the maximum number ever counted was 102,000 in December, 1981 (Owen *et al.*, 1986). Approximately another 1 million of the birds winter around the Mediterranean, from Spain to Turkey (the Black Sea coast of the USSR), and from Israel to Tunisia (Rüger *et al.*, 1986).

The most important site in Britain is the Mersey Estuary, with an average wintering population of over 17,000 in the mid-1980s (1981/2–1986/7). However, this site is quite exceptional, as the other localities of international importance (1% level or more of the north-west European population) — the Ribble Estuary along with Hamford Water (Essex) and Martin Mere (Lancashire) — hold between 4,000 and 4,500 each on average; there are a further 11 sites supporting between 2,000 and 3,000 (on average) each winter (Salmon *et al.*, 1987). Elsewhere in Britain, Teal are widely distributed both on inland and coastal sites, with a large number of smaller flocks (each less than 200 birds) making up nearly 40% of the British wintering population. The winter population has increased in Britain (as has the north-west European population) since the early 1960s, due perhaps to a series of mild (or less severe) winters. In the mid-1950s two severe winters took a drastic toll of the population from which it is now recovering. The numbers wintering on the Mersey Estuary reflect this increase, with between 2,000 and 3,000 there in the winters of the mid-1960s increasing to 13,700 in 1973, 25,850 in 1980/1 and a peak of 35,000 in 1981/2. Since then the numbers have declined to around 9,000 on average, but this is probably due to the birds being more dispersed in the area as numbers on the neighbouring Dee and Ribble Estuaries have increased in recent years. This pattern may well be the norm, with declines followed by gradual recovery, but it is clear that the bird, being a dabbling feeder and dependent on open water or ice-free muddy areas, is particularly vulnerable to severe changes in the weather—even changes of the shortest duration. In winters which have spells of harsh or severe weather, large numbers of Teal quickly depart to Ireland, France or southern Spain (Owen *et al.*, 1986).

The breeding population in north-west Europe (excluding Fenno-Scandia, where about 80,000 pairs breed in Finland) is estimated at between about 6,370 and 9,370 pairs, with an estimated 3,500 to 6,000 pairs in Britain (mainly in the north and west) and Ireland.

THREATS TO SURVIVAL

Threats include those associated with the vulnerability of the habitat, together with the hazards of severe weather.

There is no single serious threat to the population as a whole, but dependence on shallow water areas puts local concentrations at risk from habitat loss—mainly from drainage and estuarine land-claim/barrage schemes such as those proposed at clearly crucial sites such as the Mersey Estuary.

Severe weather in winter probably has the greatest effect on the population.

The need for voluntary and statutory wildfowling bans is clearly demonstrated not only in this country but also in those areas receiving birds coming in seach of ice-free feeding and recuperation. Shooting or wildfowling is not a problem affecting the whole population, but in countries where the shooting levels are much higher than they are in the UK the additional mortality of birds moving south in front of severe weather is consequently greater, and is an unnecessary hazard.

CONSERVATION

The permanent presence of the current relatively abundant population is entirely dependent on measures which conserve all wetland areas. See also under 'Threats' for comments on severe weather.

REFERENCES

OWEN, M., ATKINSON-WILLES, G.L. & SALMON, D.G. 1986. Wildfowl in Great Britain, 2nd edition. Cambridge: Cambridge University Press.

RÜGER, A., PRENTICE, C. & OWEN, M. 1986. Results of the IWRB International Waterfowl Census 1967–1983. Slimbridge: International Waterfowl Research Bureau.

SALMON, D.G., MOSER, M.E. & KIRBY, J.S. 1987. Wildfowl and Wader counts 1985–86. Results of the National Wildfowl Counts and Birds of Estuaries Enquiry in the United Kingdom. Slimbridge: The Wildfowl Trust.

Pintail

Anas acuta

The Pintail is a rare breeder and a localized winter visitor in internationally important numbers. It first bred in central Scotland in the latter part of the 19th century and in south-east England in the early 20th century. It has nested in 28 or more counties, though usually in no more than 5–10 in any one year; the total breeding population in Britain is probably well under 50 pairs. Approximately 25,000 winter in Britain, a little over a third of the numbers wintering in north-west Europe. The protection of estuaries from land-claim reclamation is vital if the internationally important wintering numbers are to be maintained. The main threat to breeding birds is late flooding of the low-lying marshy breeding sites.

LEGAL STATUS

Protected under Schedule 1, Part II of WCA 1981 (specially protected in the close season); Annex II/1 of EC Birds Directive; Appendix III of the Berne Convention.

ECOLOGY

In winter the Pintail occurs mainly on estuaries, but it is also found on inland flood plains; on estuaries its most important food is the mollusc *Hydrobia*.

The bird typically breeds close to water, in diverse habitats ranging from shallow, dry-shored lowland lakes and extensive marshes to upland lochs and moorland pools; it is solitary, or social on lake islets. Nest: made of grass, leaves and down, and more exposed than those of most ducks, usually in short grass, low heather (*Calluna*), scattered rushes (*Juncus*) or marram (*Ammophila*), even in the open on almost bare ground. Eggs: laid mid-April to late June. Clutch: 7–9 (6–12); one brood. The young fledge by early August.

Food consists mainly of cereals and seeds—principally common spike-rush, *Eleocharis palustris*; various water-plants, insects, larvae, crustaceans, leeches and tadpoles are also eaten.

DISTRIBUTION AND POPULATION

Mainly Holarctic. Breeds locally in Iceland, Britain, Ireland and nearly all Continental countries largely north of a line from north-east France to Hungary, but only widespread and common in Fenno-Scandia and north Russia. It winters mainly in coastal areas of west Europe, the Mediterranean, Black and Caspian Seas, and also inland in northern tropical Africa, southern Asia, the United States and Central America.

Breeding in Scotland (Inverness-shire) was first recorded in 1869; subsequently the bird spread to the Northern Isles and to the chiefly eastern parts of the mainland and to England (Kent) in 1910. Numbers continued to increase during the first half of the 20th century. The bird has nested in at least 28 counties, but there has apparently been a recent decrease—nesting occurring now in only a handful of widely scattered areas, and often only sporadically. The bird is otherwise widespread, but as a local winter visitor, particularly in estuaries and on adjacent marshes and lakes. The nesting pattern in Britain has always been erratic, with usually no more than 5–10 counties involved in any one year. By the late 1930s the species was regarded as breeding fairly consistently in Shetland,

Orkney and the Moray, Dee and Forth basins, especially Tayside (Kinross), Fife and Grampian (Aberdeen), but only irregularly elsewhere in Scotland, northern England, East Anglia and southern Kent. By the mid-1960s the main centres seemed to be in the Highland Region (Caithness, Inverness-shire), Grampian (Aberdeen), Cambridgeshire/Norfolk and north Kent; nesting had become sporadic in Orkney, and had ceased in Shetland.

During the 1968–72 'Atlas' survey, breeding was confirmed or probable in 44 10-km squares widely scattered in Scotland, northern England, East Anglia and Kent; however, breeding was no longer an annual event in any of the north Scottish mainland counties. East Anglia and Kent accounted for almost one-third of the recorded instances of breeding and provided the main evidence of regularity. Even in these centres, the numbers are small: in the Ouse Washes three to seven pairs are usual (though there were 20 in 1969–70), and in north Kent not more than two (rarely five to six). Recently the largest concentrations have been in Orkney (13–16 pairs in 1975–77, against one to three in 1968–74, and less than 10 pairs in the years 1978–1985); elsewhere in Scotland, since 1974, odd pairs have been found in Highland (Caithness, Inverness-shire), Grampian (Aberdeen), Tayside (Angus, Perthshire), Strathclyde (Argyll) and Dumfries and Galloway (Kirkcudbright). Since the 1960s the population has been put at about 50 pairs, with fluctuations up to 100, but in the years 1974–88 the maximum total was only 32 pairs (1982 and 1983).

Pintails arrive in Britain from mid-September onwards, but the main arrival is not until December; about 25,000 of the birds winter in Britain, approximtely 35% of the population wintering in north-west Europe (Rüger *et al.*, 1986). Birds from western Siberia, Scandinavia and Iceland make up the bulk of this population, whilst others from further south and east winter around the Mediterranean/Black Sea coasts (currently estimated at about a quarter of a million); the origin of those wintering in North and West Africa (approximately 200,000) is unknown, but it is likely to be the USSR (Owen *et al.*, 1986). The wintering areas of those breeding within Britain are also unknown. The wintering population in Britain has increased steadily since the early 1970s with twice as many now remaining to winter than previously. The reasons for this are not clear but it is considered more likely to be good breeding seasons than any change in mortality factors. Although widespread in winter, between November and January, about 80% of the total are found on only nine sites, all (given in the table below) being above the 1% level of international importance (Salmon *et al.*, 1989).

Pintail: average winter maxima during the period 1984/85 to 1988/89 at principal sites	
Mersey Estuary	8,700
Dee Estuary	7,100
The Wash	5,200
Morecambe Bay	2,300
Burry Inlet	1,900
Martin Mere	1,500
Ouse Washes	1,200
Duddon Estuary	1,200
Medway Estuary	700

Threats to wintering birds include actual or potential changes to habitat, while breeding birds may be at risk from disturbance and flooding of nesting sites.

The most severe threat to wintering birds is land-claim on estuaries, particularly through the construction of barrages. The future of the entire Mersey stronghold is threatened by the proposed tidal barrage there, and the next most important site at the Dee faces a range of development and recreational threats.

Arguably there are no threats in the breeding season other than possibly climatic factors and the species' nomadic or opportunistic behaviour. Human disturbance must always be a risk, but there is little or no evidence that the desertion of any regularly used sites have been due to this, or that the small population of recent years has suffered much interference. Birds in low-lying marshes may occasionally be prevented from breeding by late floods, but disappearance from one site can mean no more than movement elsewhere. The pattern, in fact, is not untypical of a species that is on the fringe of its breeding range and an opportunist nester when conditions are right.

CONSERVATION

This duck will breed in a wide variety of wetland habitats (though the two main English sites are areas of low-lying marshland and rough pasture intersected by ditches) and will often occupy a locality for only one or a few years at a time. Conservation measures should therefore include the modification of agricultural policies to favour the maintenance or re-establishment of marshland. Fortunately, some of the more regular breeding sites, and most of the wintering sites, are either reserves, SSSIs or areas with established conservation policies. Nevertheless, some estuaries, notably the Mersey in the case of the Pintail, are threatened by barrage schemes, the development of which should be resisted as this would have a severe effect on the internationally important wintering population. The creation of further inland wetland reserves might help to spread the wintering population and thus make it less susceptible to threat at any one site. Sites such as the Mersey, Morecambe Bay and Burry Inlet urgently require designation as Special Protection Areas and Ramsar sites. Even sites which already have this protection face problems and require better conservation. Better integration of the activities of statutory authorities is required, together with a wider awareness of the responsibilities under both designations.

REFERENCES

ATKINSON-WILLES, G.L. 1970. Wildfowl situation in England, Scotland and Wales. Proc. Int. Reg. Meet. Conserv. Wildfowl Resources, Leningrad 1968: 101–107.
BERRY, J. 1939. The status and distribution of wild geese and wild duck in Scotland. International Wildfowl Inquiry, Vol. 2. Cambridge: Cambridge University Press.
OWEN, M., ATKINSON-WILLES, G.L. & SALMON, D.G. 1986. Wildfowl in Great Britain, 2nd edition. Cambridge: Cambridge University Press.
RÜGER, A., PRENTICE, C. & OWEN, M. 1986. Results of the IWRB International Waterfowl Census 1967–1983. Slimbridge: International Waterfowl Research Bureau.

SALMON, D.G., PRYS-JONES, R.P. & KIRBY, J.S. 1989. Wildfowl and Wader counts 1988–89. Results of the National Wildfowl Counts and Birds of Estuaries Enquiry in the United Kingdom. Slimbridge: The Wildfowl Trust.

Garganey

Anas querquedula

The Garganey is a rare breeding summer visitor. Britain lies on the north-western edge of the Garganey's breeding range, and although never common, there were 100 or more breeding pairs in ten English counties in the first half of the 20th century, and occasional breeding took place in 13 others. The population has declined and retreated since the early 1950s, and now less than 50 pairs breed annually—but occasional fluctuations occur, and possibly as many as 94 pairs bred in 1982. Drainage and agricultural changes to breeding habitats have left little room for any likely change in the future.

LEGAL STATUS

Protected under Schedule 1 of WCA 1981; EC Birds Directive; Appendix III of the Berne Convention.

ECOLOGY

The Garganey breeds in water meadows, grasslands with intersecting ditches, and rushy marshes, or in other shallow freshwaters often edged with reeds (*Phragmites*); it is solitary. Nest: made of leaves, grass and down, well concealed in long grass or in a tussock of rushes (*Juncus*), usually within 50 m of water. Eggs: laid at the end of April to late June. Clutch: 8–11 (6–14); one brood. The young fledge by mid-August.

Food consists mainly of insects and larvae, small molluscs, crustaceans, leeches, worms, frog spawn, tadpoles, leaves and the seeds of many water-plants.

DISTRIBUTION AND POPULATION

A summer visitor to the Palearctic. It breeds in much of Europe north to England, southern Fenno-Scandia and northern Russia, but is generally scarce or local in the western third and only sporadic in Iberia, most of Italy and the southern Balkans; it winters in north tropical Africa and southern Asia. The Garganey has nested in over 25 English counties, and in Wales and Scotland (although rarely); during 1900–50 it slowly increased in numbers, but now it is confined largely to East Anglia and south-east England—apart from a few pairs west to Somerset and north to Yorkshire. The bird is entirely a summer visitor, arriving in mid-March to late May and leaving mainly by September. In the first half of the 20th century it gradually spread from regular breeding in five counties, and occasionally in four others, to regular breeding in 10 counties and occasional breeding in 13; however, the range has since retracted: despite a large influx in 1959, which resulted in temporary colonization of parts of south-west England and elsewhere, nesting was regular in only eight counties, and occasional in 10 more, during the 1960s and early 1970s (Atkinson-Willes, 1970).

Numbers also fluctuate from year to year, being largest in warm springs following wet winters, when shallow floods remain on water meadows and marshes. It seems likely that in the 1940s the population was commonly 100 or more pairs, but estimates in the 1960s fell in the range 50–100 pairs; it is probable that in 1968–69 there were 65–70 pairs and in 1970–72 barely 50. By 1980 there were a possible 54 breeding pairs in Britain, of which only four were confirmed as having bred. Since then there has been a slight rise in the number of pairs proven to breed: 10 in 1982 and 15 in 1983 (and a consequent rise in the number of possible pairs to 94 and 70 respectively) followed by a return to the 1980 level, with eight pairs confirmed breeding out of a possible total of 45 in 1987 (RBBP Reports). Figures from the Ouse Washes (Cambridgeshire/Norfolk) show the general decline, in one of the main areas, in the table below.

Garganey: numbers at Ouse Washes, 1952–1986

Year	1952	1968/69	1970	1972	1973	1975	1976	1978	1981	1982	1985	1986
Pairs	25–35	23–24	12–15	7	0	9	0	6	4	14	0	5

THREATS TO SURVIVAL

Threats include climatic changes and the effects of drainage.

The increase and spread in the first half of the 20th century, which reflected a north-west range-extension in Fenno-Scandia in the 1930s–40s, coincided with the period of climatic amelioration, while the more recent decline has occurred at a time of generally drier winters, resulting in less spring flooding, and cold Aprils. The size of the March–April influx varies from year to year, and whether or not the birds stay to breed depends on favourable weather and on the availability of suitable habitat; in some years it may be mostly the later arrivals, in May, that remain to nest (Harrison & Harrison, 1970). Like the Pintail, this species is something of a nomadic opportunist on the fringe of its range, but its more limited habitat requirements make it even more vulnerable. In parts of East Anglia, Kent and Sussex drainage has contributed to—if not accelerated—the decline; regular breeding ceased in Lincolnshire with the drainage of the Welland Washes in the early 1960s, and this and the similar loss of washland habitat seriously reduced the Fenland population.

The fluctuating population breeding in Britain reflects a typical edge-of-range distribution with a fragile dependency on climate and the availability of prime habitat; the latter has drastically declined in recent years. The population on the continent is clearly very stable: 5,000 pairs in the Netherlands, 1,100 pairs in West Germany, approximately 2,000 pairs in Finland and thousands in Czechoslovakia. On a European—or even world—scale the species is not under any threat. In West Africa it is one of the most abundant wintering Palearctic species, with January concentrations of about 94,000 on the Senegal delta and up to 480,000 on the Niger delta in Mali (Scott, 1980).

CONSERVATION

Protection and sympathetic habitat management of inland shallow wetlands and grazing marshes is crucial to maintain a nucleus of breeding pairs in Britain.

REFERENCES

ATKINSON-WILLES, G.L. 1970. Wildfowl situation in England, Scotland and Wales. Proc. Int. Reg. Meet. Conserv. Wildfowl Resources, Leningrad 1968: 101–107.
HARRISON, J.M. & HARRISON, J.G. 1970. Mid-summer movements of duck in southeast England. Wildfowlers' Association of Great Britain and Ireland. Rep. and Year Book 1969–70: 64–68.
SCOTT, D.A. 1980. A Preliminary Inventory of Wetlands of International Importance for Waterfowl in West Europe and Northwest Africa. International Waterfowl Research Bureau Special Publication No. 2, Slimbridge.

Shoveler
Anas clypeata

The Shoveler winters in Britain in localized concentrations. About 40,000 of these birds winter in north-west Europe, with an average of about 7,000 (17%) wintering in Britain; thus the bird does not qualify for inclusion on grounds of international importance. Between 1,000 and 1,500 pairs breed in Britain. The conservation of shallow freshwater wetlands is important to maintain both wintering and breeding populations.

LEGAL STATUS

Protected under Schedule 2, Part 1 of WCA 1981 (protected in the close season); Annex II/1 of EC Birds Directive; Appendix III of the Berne Convention.

ECOLOGY

The Shoveler breeds in or near wetland areas. Nest: on the ground in grass, sedges or other vegetation, but often in the open, usually near water. Eggs: laid mid-April to early June. Clutch: 9–11 (6–14); one brood. The young fledge in July.

Food consists of small crustaceans, molluscs, insects and their larvae, together with plant material—especially seeds (commonly *Eleocharis* spp.)—from the surface or mud; the bird filters its food through a specially adapted spatulate edge to the bill.

In winter the Shoveler frequents shallow freshwater areas on marshes, flooded pasture, reservoirs and lakes with plentiful marginal reeds or emergent vegetation.

DISTRIBUTION AND POPULATION

Holarctic. Breeds in northern and eastern Europe including Finland, and southern Sweden, and in Britain, Denmark, the Netherlands and (sporadically) across southern Germany and France; it also breeds in Asia and in western North America. Between 1,000 and 1,500 pairs breed in Britain; they are well dispersed, mainly in the central and eastern counties of England, with the Ouse Washes (Cambridgeshire/Norfolk) holding between 80 and 300 pairs in the 1970s and 1980s, and the Nene Washes (Cambridgeshire) holding up to 350 pairs in the 1980s. These latter sites are the two most important breeding sites, but many nests are disrupted due to spring/summer flooding. About 40,000 of the birds winter in north-western Europe, mostly in the Netherlands, Britain and Ireland, mainly from breeding grounds in Iceland, Fenno-Scandia, eastern Europe and Russia, but it is estimated that about 100,000 breed, winter or migrate through north-west Europe (Rüger *et al.*, 1986). British breeding birds depart in the autumn to winter in southern France and Spain.

Immigrants to Britain reach a peak in November of around 9,000, declining thereafter to between 5,000 and 7,000 in February and March. In the late 1960s the highest winter numbers were recorded in late winter, presumably comprising returning birds, but the migration pattern has apparently shifted to the east, with most birds now avoiding the British Isles (Owen *et al.*, 1986). In winter, the Shoveler is fairly well-distributed throughout Britain, though over 50% of the population occurs at less than ten sites, given in the table below.

Shoveler: maxima at main localities, 1984–89

	1984/85	1985/86	1986/87	1987/88	1988/89	(Mth)	Average
Ouse Washes	403	505	445	1,443	523	(Mar)	664
Rutland Water	612	655	525	285	729	(Sep)	561
Loch Leven	595	177	780	391	540	(Sep)	497
Elmley, Swale	428	397	253	532	303	(Nov)	383
Abberton Reservoir	313	379	522	240	418	(Aug)	374
Woolston Eyes	427	510	475	230	167	(Sep)	362
Chew Valley Lake	275	190	390	440	475	(Sep)	354
Thames Estuary	404	631	178	207	258	(Nov)	336
King George VI Reservoir, Surrey	219	365	270	361	333	(Sep)	310
Staines Reservoir, Surrey	564	275	252	187	212	(Oct)	298

THREATS TO SURVIVAL

Threats to individual populations may include disruption of habitats due eg, to drainage or flooding.

The bird's fairly widespread but localized distribution, both in summer and winter, provides a natural safeguard against any single serious threat to the population as a whole, but dependence on shallow eutrophic water areas puts local concentrations at risk from drainage and reclamation schemes. Land drainage is known to have seriously affected breeding birds in at least one key area—the North Kent Marshes (Williams *et al.*, 1983).

Spring/summer flooding has disrupted breeding at the Ouse Washes.

CONSERVATION

The permanent presence of large numbers of wintering Shoveler in Britain is entirely dependent on freshwater wetland conservation measures. Conservation of habitats, and the provision of disturbance-free zones at sites which regularly attract important concentrations, are vital.

REFERENCES

OWEN, M., ATKINSON-WILLES, G.L. & SALMON, D.G. 1986. Wildfowl in Great Britain, 2nd edition. Cambridge: Cambridge University Press.

RÜGER, A., PRENTICE, C. & OWEN, M. 1986. Results of the IWRB International Waterfowl Census 1967–1983. Slimbridge: International Waterfowl Research Bureau.

WILLIAMS, G., HENDERSON, A., GOLDSMITH, L. & SPREADBOROUGH, A. 1983. The effects on birds of land drainage improvements in the North Kent Marshes. Wildfowl 34: 33–47.

Pochard

Aythya ferina

The Pochard is a rare breeding bird in Britain. Between 375 and 395 pairs breed mainly in southern and eastern counties, with some evidence that the population is slowly increasing. Considerable numbers gather at several sites in south-east England to moult in late summer and early autumn. The wintering population increased dramatically until the mid 1970s peaking at about 35,000 (10% of the north-west European wintering population) though the actual population was estimated to be nearer 50,000. Since then there has been a stabilization and a slight decline in overall numbers wintering in Britain and western Europe. The breeding population is not subject to any major threats.

LEGAL STATUS

Protected under Schedule 2, Part 1 of the WCA 1981 (protected in the close season); EC Birds Directive; Appendix III of the Berne Convention.

ECOLOGY

The Pochard breeds on large pools, lakes or slow-moving streams in Britain; 'fleet' type habitat is favoured in reclaimed coastal marshes. Nest: a platform of reeds, leaves, or other vegetation with a shallow cup, on the ground or floating in dense reeds or similar cover. Eggs: laid in early May to the end of July, mainly in June. Clutch: 8–10 (4–15); one brood. The young fledge by mid-August.

Food consists chiefly of plants—including seeds, shoots and tubers—and also crustaceans, molluscs, insects (and larvae), fish, frogs and tadpoles.

In winter the bird occurs in lowland freshwater reservoirs, lakes, ponds, gravel pits etc., usually with a good growth of submerged aquatic plants and small animals (molluscs) etc.

DISTRIBUTION AND POPULATION

Palearctic. Breeds in mainly northern Europe east to central Siberia and south to southern Hungary; small numbers breed in southern Spain and central Turkey. In Europe the bird breeds mainly in the USSR, Finland, Czechoslovakia, West Germany and France. In Britain it is widely scattered from the southern counties of England to northern Scotland, with some concentration in the south-east of England: the overall population probably between 375–395 pairs.

There is some evidence of an increase in numbers in Scotland and England at a few sites; this is balanced by a decline due to drainage of the habitat in one of the former strongholds in north Kent (Williams et al., 1983). In the 19th century the population was restricted to East Anglia; there was a slow expansion to Yorkshire and Hertfordshire by 1850, to Scotland in 1871, and to Caithness by 1921. There was a slow increase in numbers mainly along the eastern side of Britain and the London Area by mid-1950s—where possibly some recruitment resulted from full-winged birds in the Royal Parks. The North Kent marshes, Essex coastal marshes and the Norfolk Broads have the highest concentration, with between 30 and 50 pairs at each, although numbers at the former site have declined due to land reclamation works. The Pochard is also a passage migrant and common winter visitor, mainly from September to April, to large inland lakes and reservoirs.

In late summer and early autumn the post-breeding moulting flock at Abberton Reservoir, Essex, is usually between 2,000 and 3,000 birds. Smaller numbers are also found at other sites in south-east England, including several of the London reservoirs. These moulting flocks consist of British breeding birds together with others from the Netherlands and Germany (Owen et al., 1986; Salmon et al., 1987; Fox & Salmon, 1988).

Wintering birds arrive in October. Although widely distributed throughout Britain, mainly in flocks of less than 200, there are two sites which hold internationally important (1% of the north-west European population) wintering concentrations: the Ouse Washes (Norfolk/Cambridgeshire) and the Loch of Harray (Orkney).

THREATS TO SURVIVAL

Threats may include disturbance, changes to habitat, and water pollution.

There are no major threats, though breeding birds can be affected by human disturbance and by drainage and reclamation of suitable breeding habitat.

Water pollution can be a problem in areas such as the Norfolk Broads.

CONSERVATION

No special measures are needed. The creation and management of wetland reserves will help to protect breeding birds, especially those in fairly high concentrations.

REFERENCES

Fox, A.D. & Salmon, D.G. 1988. Changes in the non-breeding Distribution and Habitat of Pochard *Aythya Ferina* in Britain. Biological Conservation. 46: 303–316.

Owen, M., Atkinson-Willes, G.L. & Salmon, D.G. 1986. Wildfowl in Great Britain, 2nd edition. Cambridge: Cambridge University Press.

Rüger, A., Prentice, C. & Owen, M. 1986. Results of the International Waterfowl Research Bureau International Waterfowl Census 1967–1983. Slimbridge: The Wildfowl Trust.

Salmon, D.G., Moser, M.E. & Kirby, J.S. 1987. Wildfowl and wader counts 1985–86. Results of the National Wildfowl Counts and Birds of Estuaries Enquiry in the United Kingdom. Slimbridge: The Wildfowl Trust.

Williams, G., Henderson, A., Goldsmith, L. & Spreadborough, A. 1983. The effects on birds of land drainage improvements in the North Kent marshes. Wildfowl. 34: 33—47.

Scaup
Aythya marila

The Scaup is an occasional breeder and a winter visitor in localized concentrations. It has been a sporadic nester since the end of the 19th century—originally in the Western Isles, but more recently in Orkney. Occasional breeding has occurred on the Scottish mainland and unexpectedly, once in Wales and once in eastern England. Conservation efforts should be directed towards safeguarding the main winter flocks through greater controls over oil pollution, and the extension of land-based site safeguard measures (eg, SSSI or SPA) to offshore areas.

Protected under Schedule 1 of the WCA 1981; Annex II/2 of EC Birds Directive; Appendix III of the Berne Convention.

ECOLOGY

In winter the bird occurs mainly in coastal or estuarine areas, where a strong attraction to sewage outfalls has been noted in Britain, food in winter consists of mussels and also items in, or prey benefiting from, sewage effluent.

Breeding occurs on islets or shores of moorland lochs and rivers. Nest: built of grasses, rushes (*Juncus*) and down, usually hidden in long grass, heather (*Calluna*), reeds (*Phragmites*) or other thick cover, sometimes more in the open or in a tussock growing in water. Eggs: laid in May to early July. Clutch: 8–11 (6–15); one brood. The young fledge by mid-August.

Food in the breeding season consists mainly of insects and larvae, fish eggs, molluscs, crustaceans and the leaves and seeds of water plants.

DISTRIBUTION AND POPULATION

North Holarctic. Breeds in Iceland, Fenno-Scandia and north Russia, locally in Estonia, and irregularly in Britain, Denmark and elsewhere; it winters along the coasts of western Europe, the Adriatic, Black and Caspian Seas, southern and eastern Asia and North America. The bird was first recorded nesting in Scotland in 1897, and nesting has been observed at irregular intervals since: South Uist (Western Isles) 1–3 pairs, 1897–1902, irregularly to 1913; Orkney 1–3 pairs, 1954–1959, and at intervals to 1978. There are odd records of nesting from North Uist (Western Isles) in 1969, Sutherland in 1899, Caithness in 1939, Ross in 1946 (all Highland), and from Angus in 1971 and Perth in 1970 (3 pairs) (both Tayside) although this last record is possibly suspect (Andrew, 1968; Thom, 1986; Walker, 1967). A pair bred in Lincolnshire in 1944 (Brown, 1945) and an unpaired female laid infertile clutches in Suffolk during 1967–71. In 1988 three pairs bred: two in Scotland, one in Wales.

The bird is a regular and quite common winter visitor around coasts and in the estuaries of Scotland as well as north-west and east England. The current population is between 6,000 and 7,500, a small proportion of the total north-western European population of 150,000 (Salmon, 1988). The main concentrations are in the Firth of Forth (2,000), Islay (1,000), and the Solway (1,500). Former wintering concentrations of 20,000–30,000 in the Firth of Forth no longer occur, mainly as a result of improved sewage disposal (Campbell, 1978, 1984).

THREATS TO SURVIVAL

Threats to individual pairs may include disturbance and the loss of eggs to collectors, while threats to the wintering birds may include oil pollution and loss or reduction in food supplies.

The continued breeding or spread of Scaup in Britain seems to be outwith the control of man. Individual breeding pairs may be particularly threatened by disturbance or by egg collectors, but such threats are unpredictable.

Wintering flocks may be threatened by oil pollution (eg, Campbell *et al.*, 1978) or by the commercial exploitation of their preferred food, mussels. Flocks in the Firth of Forth and in Islay are closely associated with effluent discharges and are unlikely to remain if these effluents are removed (Campbell, 1984).

CONSERVATION

The locations of sites with summering pairs or possible breeders should not be publicized. The threats from oil pollution can be reduced by effective legislative control measures. Commercial exploitation of mussels should be restricted to areas not used by feeding flocks. Efforts should be made to ensure that offshore flocks are included in site designations such as SSSI or marine SPAs.

REFERENCES

ANDREW, D.G. 1968. Scaup breeding in Orkney. Scot. Birds 5: 23–24.

BROWN, P.E. 1945. Observations on a Scaup-Duck and brood on the Lincolnshire coast. Brit. Birds 38: 192–193.

CAMPBELL, L.H. 1978. Patterns of distribution and behaviour of flocks of seaducks wintering at Leith and Musselburgh, Scotland. Biol. Conserv. 14: 111–123.

CAMPBELL, L.H. 1984. The impact of changes in sewage treatment on seaducks wintering in the Firth of Forth, Scotland. Biol. Conserv. 28: 173–180.

CAMPBELL, L.H., STANDRING, K.T. & CADBURY, C.J. 1978. Firth of Forth oil pollution incident, February 1978. Mar. Pollut. Bull. 9: 335–339.

SALMON, D.G. 1988. The numbers and distribution of Scaup Aythya marila in Britain and Ireland. Biol. Conserv. 43: 267–278.

THOM, V.M. 1986. Birds in Scotland. Calton: Poyser.

WALKER, K.G. 1967. Scaup breeding in Orkney. Scot. Birds 4: 503–504.

Consultant: L.H. Campbell

Long-tailed Duck

Clangula hyemalis

The Long-tailed Duck winters in Britain in localized concentrations. The peak population in Britain is probably regularly in excess of 20,000, over half being within the Moray Firth. The bird has bred in Britain occasionally in the past, but not since 1926. The main threats to the large flocks are oil pollution and food reduction through commercial dredging for mussels.

LEGAL STATUS

Protected under Schedule 1 of WCA 1981; Annex II/2 of EC Birds Directive; Appendix III of the Berne Convention.

ECOLOGY

The main winter flocks occur on open coastal waters, along the east coast of mainland Scotland and the northern isles. Shallow, sandy areas within the Moray Firth are particularly favoured, although small flocks may also occur off rocky coasts, within smaller estuaries or on brackish coastal lochs.

The type of food taken by these birds in Britain is poorly known, but elsewhere the wintering diet is predominantly of molluscs, crustaceans and small fish. Unlike other British wintering seaducks, Long-tailed Ducks may feed several kilometres offshore and are often difficult to see from the land. Night-time roosting aggregations in areas distinct from those used by day have been recorded in both Orkney and the Moray Firth (Campbell et al., 1986; Hope Jones, 1979).

DISTRIBUTION AND POPULATION

Breeds continually from southern-central Norway through Fenno-Scandia (also in isolated areas to Finland) through northern USSR to Bering Sea, Alaska, northern Canada, south to the Hudson Bay and Newfoundland; Greenland Iceland and Spitsbergen. Part of the breeding population in Greenland is known to winter in Iceland, and possibly in Britain, but most of the British wintering population is believed to come from northern Norway and northern Russia. The wintering population in western Europe (mainly concentrated in the Baltic region) has recently been estimated to be about 500,000 (Owen et al., 1986).

Long-tailed Ducks are found scattered in small numbers off much of the northern and eastern coastline of Britain. Flocks of a few hundred have been regularly recorded at several sites in Shetland, Orkney, Aberdeenshire, St Andrews Bay and the Firth of Forth, but in the last 10 years it has become clear that the Moray Firth has regularly held peak numbers of between 10,000 and 20,000 (Campbell et al., 1986; Prater, 1981; Thom, 1986).

Several major feeding areas have been identified on the south shore between Whiteness Point and Spey Bay, and further north between Dornoch and Helmsdale, but the true size of the wintering population has been evident only when counting birds flighting into roost areas off Brora and in Burghead Bay. Orkney holds a peak population of 6,000, but the total population elsewhere in the British Isles probably does not exceed a further 5,000. The total British wintering population is probably between 20,000 and 30,000.

THREATS TO SURVIVAL

The main threats to the wintering population include marine pollution, commercial exploitation of invertebrate food resources, and disturbance from increased recreational activities.

Wintering Long-tailed Ducks are at risk from the effects of oil-spillage, particularly in Orkney where roosting flocks gather in the vicinity of fixed-point oil terminals in Scapa Flow.

Recent proposals within the Moray Firth to dredge commercially for mussels may also present a considerable potential threat to Long-tailed Duck food resources, and flocks may also be threatened by any expansion of recreational activities, such as sailing or power-boats.

CONSERVATION

Threats from oil pollution can be reduced only by the effective implementation of legislative control measures.

Further research is needed to assess the extent of the threat posed to food resources by mussel dredging, and permission for such schemes should be witheld until such work has been undertaken.

Steps may also need to be taken to restrict winter recreational activities in and close to areas used by feeding and roosting birds. As with other seaducks there is a need for marine SPAs.

REFERENCES

CAMPBELL, L.H., BARRETT, J. & BARRETT, C.F. 1986. Seaducks in the Moray Firth: a review of their current status and distribution. Proceedings of the Royal Society of Edinburgh 91B: 105–112.
HOPE JONES, P. 1979. Roosting behaviour of Long-tailed Ducks in relation to possible oil pollution. Wildfowl 30: 155–158.
OWEN, M., ATKINSON-WILLES, G.L. & SALMON, D.G. 1986. Wildfowl in Great Britain, 2nd edition. Cambridge: Cambridge University Press.
PRATER, A.J. 1981. Estuary Birds of Britain and Ireland. Calton: Poyser.
THOM, V.M. 1986. Birds in Scotland. Calton: Poyser.

Consultant: L.H. Campbell

Common Scoter
Melanitta nigra

This is a rare breeding bird in Britain and a localized winter visitor; in the mid-19th century it colonized the north Scottish mainland, spreading north and south to Shetland, Strathclyde (Argyll) and the Central Region. There are no reliable data on population trends, but the current breeding population is believed to exceed 100 pairs. More work is needed on its basic ecology before detailed conservation plans can be drawn up. Winters in large but localized numbers where oil pollution and commercial exploitation of food resources are the main threats.

LEGAL STATUS

Protected under Schedule 1 of WCA 1981; Annex II/2 of EC Birds Directive; Appendix III of the Berne Convention.

ECOLOGY

In the north, small moorland lochs are used for breeding; pairs may be solitary, nesting well away from water, but further south nesting occurs on wooded islands on larger lochs where several pairs may nest close together. Nest: made of grasses, moss, lichens and down, well-hidden in heather, brambles or other thick vegetation, and usually close to water on shores, promontories or islands. Eggs: laid in late May to mid-July. Clutch: 6–8 (4–12); one brood. Most of the young fledge by the end of August.

In the breeding season, food consists mainly of insects, fish eggs, cladocerans, molluscs and the seeds of water plants.

Some young are reared to fledging on the loch to which they were brought after hatching, but others may be moved rapidly to the sea, or perhaps to other lochs nearby. When moulting and wintering on the sea, the birds eat a range of sand-dwelling invertebrates and small fish.

DISTRIBUTION AND POPULATION

Holarctic. Breeds in Fenno-Scandia and northern Russia, in Iceland, Scotland, and north-west Ireland. It winters mainly along Atlantic coasts south to north-west Africa and Pacific coasts of the southern United States of America and China. Although breeding was probably established earlier, it was first proved only in 1855, in Sutherland and spread slowly to Inverness and Argyll (1880s), Shetland (1911), Ross (1913), Perth (1921), Dumbarton/Stirlingshire (1971) and Dumfries and Galloway (1986). Nesting has also been recorded in Orkney and in Fife.

No systematic surveys have been undertaken, and there are insufficient data for any trends in population to be detected. Thom (1986) estimated that the population was around 100 pairs for much of the 1970s, well in excess of Sharrock's (1976) estimate of 30–50 pairs. A recent review (Partridge, 1987) suggested a minimum population of 100–114 pairs, the main strongholds being Caithness and Sutherland (more than 50 pairs), Inverness-shire (30 pairs), Islay (seven pairs) and Loch Lomond (4 to 6 pairs), with scattered pairs elsewhere in north Perthshire, Ross and Cromarty and Shetland.

Late-summer moulting flocks, sometimes exceeding 1,000, regularly occur off sandy coastal areas along the east coast of Scotland, especially in the Moray Firth, near Aberdeen, Montrose, Tentsmuir, and in the Firth of Forth. Smaller numbers may occur off sandy shores elsewhere in the east and west, and there is a regular flock of a few hundred in Harris.

Large wintering flocks are regular in the Moray Firth (5,000–10,000), St Andrews Bay, the Firth of Forth and Lindisfarne, and over 25,000 (regularly much fewer) have been counted in Carmarthen Bay (Prater, 1981). Small numbers may be found off many other sandy shores, and large passage movements have been recorded off the southern coasts of England. The wintering population in western Europe and north Africa is believed to exceed 1 million.

THREATS TO SURVIVAL

Threats include predation, freshwater and marine pollution, commercial exploitation of food resources and afforestation.

No detailed studies have been carried out in Scotland, and there are no data on breeding performance or on the relative importance of different causes of breeding failure. Nutrient enrichment of Lough Erne in Northern Ireland is believed to be the main reason for a dramatic decline in the breeding population there, although predation, probably by mink, may be an important contributory factor. Crows (*Corvus* spp.) and Magpies (*Pica pica*) have also been suggested as damaging predators.

Afforestation is likely to be the main threat to the Scottish population, particularly within its main stronghold in Caithness and Sutherland, where the majority of nesting pairs are found in or close to areas of recent, planned or potential forestry opertions. Loss of nesting habitat and increased predator numbers close to nesting areas may pose direct threats, but changes in water quality, as a result of acid run-off or fertilizer application, may have a wider and more general effect through reduced or changed potential food sources.

Although disturbance and egg collecting are at present not a major problem, improved access through forestry roads and increased angling activity could present more of a threat. Disturbance associated with agricultural intensification and peat extraction may also be a threat.

Outside the breeding season, moulting and wintering scoters are at risk from the effects of oil-spillage, and may be threatened by proposals to commercially exploit mussels or other shellfish upon which they feed.

Moulting flocks, which occur off sandy shores, may also be threatened by any expansion of recreational activities, such as sailing or power-boats.

CONSERVATION

Basic data on population size, breeding performance and causes of failure are needed for the main stronghold areas and, with such a small population, a regular monitoring programme should be established. Partridge (1987) estimated that up to 30% of the population was included within existing SSSI, although it is unlikely that these fully encompassed the areas required and used by breeding scoters.

Further measures may be needed to ensure that scoters are adequately protected from afforestation in northern Scotland. Consideration should also be given to restricting access along forest roads which traverse areas used by breeding scoters.

Marine pollution, the main threat to moulting and wintering flocks, can be limited only by the effective implementation of legislative controls and up-to-date oil-spill contingency plans.

Permission to commercially exploit beds of shellfish should not be given in areas holding large flocks, and it is important that site designation measures, similar to SSSI and SPAs, should be developed to include offshore areas.

REFERENCES

PARTRIDGE, K. 1987. The Common Scoter *Melanitta nigra* in Ireland and Britain—a review of the breeding population with special reference to Lough Erne. Unpublished RSPB report.

PRATER, A.J. 1981. Estuary birds of Britain and Ireland. Calton: Poyser.
THOM, V.M. 1986. Birds in Scotland. Calton: Poyser.

Consultant: L.H. Campbell

Velvet Scoter

Melanitta fusca

The Velvet Scoter winters in Britain in localized concentrations. The peak population is regularly 2,500–5,000, occasionally up to 10,000, and is largely restricted to the Moray Firth. The bird is also a passage visitor, with small numbers moulting in late summer. Breeding has occasionally been suspected, but has never been proved. The main threats are oil pollution and commercial exploitation of food resources. There is a need for effective pollution controls and the development of site designations that include offshore areas.

LEGAL STATUS

Protected under Schedule 1 of WCA 1981; Annex II/2 of EC Birds Directive; Appendix III of the Berne Convention.

ECOLOGY

Winter, passage and moulting flocks all occur on open coastal waters, mainly along the east coast of Scotland, where shallow, sandy areas are particularly favoured. Small numbers may occur within smaller estuaries or on freshwater sites inland. Food in Britain is poorly known, but elsewhere the wintering diet is predominantly of molluscs, crustaceans and small fish.

DISTRIBUTION AND POPULATION

Holarctic. Breeds in Fenno-Scandia and in northern Russia as far south as 50°N. Winters mainly along Atlantic coasts south to north-west Africa and Pacific coasts of the southern United States of America and China.

Velvet Scoter are usually found in mixed flocks with Common Scoter (*M. nigra*), the latter normally being much more abundant. Accurate counts are difficult to obtain, but few sites hold more than a hundred birds each winter. Over the last 10 years the Moray Firth (in particular Burghead Bay and Spey Bay) has regularly held peak numbers of between 1,000 and 2,000, 8,000 being present in March 1983. The total population elsewhere in the British Isles probably does not exceed 1,000, the most important secondary sites, holding more than 100 birds, being in Orkney, St Andrews Bay and the Firth of Forth (Campbell *et al.*, 1986; Owen *et al.*, 1986; Prater, 1981; Thom, 1986).

Late summer flocks of moulting scoter regularly occur off sandy coastal areas along the east coasts of Scotland, especially in the Moray Firth, near Aberdeen, Montrose, Tentsmuir and in the Firth of Forth, and Velvet Scoter are normally present amongst these in small numbers.

The large passage movements of Common Scoters recorded off the southern coasts of England also include small numbers of Velvet Scoters.

THREATS TO SURVIVAL

Threats include marine pollution, commercial exploitation of invertebrate food resources and disturbance from increased recreational activities.

Moulting and wintering scoter are particularly at risk from the effects of oil-spillage.

Recent proposals to dredge commercially for mussels within the Moray Firth present a considerable potential threat to food resources, and flocks may also be threatened by any expansion of recreational activities, such as sailing or power-boats.

CONSERVATION

Threats from oil pollution can be reduced only by the effective implementation of legislative control measures.

Further research is needed to assess the extent of the threat posed to food resources by mussel dredging, and permission for such schemes should be withheld until such work has been undertaken.

Steps should also be taken to restrict winter recreational activities in and close to the scoter feeding and roosting areas. Site designation measures should be developed to include offshore areas used by seaduck flocks.

REFERENCES

CAMPBELL, L.H., BARRETT, J. & BARRETT, C.F. 1986. Seaducks in the Moray Firth: a review of their current status and distribution. Proceedings of the Royal Society of Edinburgh 91B: 105–112.

OWEN, M., ATKINSON-WILLES, G.L. & SALMON, D.G. 1986. Wildfowl in Great Britain, 2nd edition. Cambridge: Cambridge University Press.

PRATER, A.J. 1981. Estuary Birds of Britain and Ireland. Calton: Poyser.

THOM, V.M. 1986. Birds in Scotland. Calton: Poyser.

Consultant: L.H. Campbell

Goldeneye
Bucephala clangula

The Goldeneye is a rare breeding bird. This common winter visitor to the British Isles from Scandinavia has also nested regularly in the central Highlands of Scotland since 1970. The population has increased annually to at least 85 occupied nests in 1989. Breeding in Scotland has been stimulated by the provision of nest boxes which are still used by most of the breeding population. The provision and maintenance of nest boxes in suitable nesting areas is still important for this species.

LEGAL STATUS

Protected under Schedule 1, Part II of WCA 1981; Annex II/2 of EC Birds Directive; Appendix III of the Berne Convention.

ECOLOGY

Breeds in coniferous forests close to water. Nest: can be up to 1 km from water in adjacent forests, in natural tree holes or woodpecker holes, readily uses nesting boxes, but rarely in burrows or under rocks and logs. Eggs: laid from early April. Clutch: 8–11 eggs. Extra eggs may be 'dumped' in nests by other females, probably young birds; large clutches in Scotland have included two of 20 eggs each, and there have been single clutches of 22, 23, 26 and 28 eggs. Once complete, the female lines the nest with down and starts incubation. Some clutches are not incubated; in fact between 25% and 33% of clutches are not incubated. The ducklings are taken to the water soon after hatching, and they may be moved up to 10 km to rearing areas. Fledging success in Scotland has been encouraging, with over a third of the young hatched fledging.

Food is obtained by diving and consists mainly of invertebrates (especially molluscs) and crustaceans obtained largely from lochs with stony bottoms, and rivers.

In winter, the birds occur in fresh and salt water, sometimes in large concentrations, especially at waste outfalls.

DISTRIBUTION AND POPULATION

North Holarctic. The Goldeneye breeds in Fenno-Scandia, the Baltic States, USSR and North America, and locally in Scotland, Germany, Poland and Czechoslovakia. It winters along unfrozen coasts and inland waters south to France, the Balkans, central Asia, China and the southern United States.

In winter occurs throughout the British Isles, larger numbers being found principally in the north. Most of the birds arrive in October, departing from March to early May, and there is much display and pairing in the winter quarters. Late displaying birds were often observed in the Scottish Highlands in the 1950s and 1960s, and, as a consequence, nest boxes similar to those used in Scandinavia were erected.

The first evidence of breeding in Britain was a female with four young in the Spey Valley in 1970 (MacMillan, 1970). Goldeneyes nested again in 1971–72, with three females laying eggs in 1973 (Dennis & Dow, 1974). The population subsequently increased to 12 nests in 1978, 41 in 1981, 54 in 1984 and at least 85 in 1989. The number of broods has been correspondingly good, with over 3,300 ducklings hatched in Scotland up to 1989. In recent years, some pairs have been located in natural holes, and it is now believed that extra pairs are nesting in unknown natural sites. In 1984 two pairs nested and subsequently attempted to nest to the north of the original area of colonization (Dennis, 1987). There is no other documented breeding of Goldeneyes in Britain except for a report of nesting in Cheshire in 1931–32.

Some of the breeding birds remain all year near the nesting areas, but a number move away. A build-up in recent years of moulting birds in summer at Inverness and in the Beauly Firth probably comprises non-breeders and moulting drakes from the breeding population.

Large numbers of Goldeneyes breed in Scandinavia, where it is common in Sweden and Finland (an estimated 50,000 pairs breed in Finland). The estimated winter population for northern and central Europe is 200,000 birds (Cramp *et al.*, 1977).

THREATS TO SURVIVAL

Threats include a scarcity of nesting holes, predation, and competition (by fish) for food.

Modern forestry has been recognized as causing a shortage of natural nest holes in Scandinavia, but this has been offset by the provision of a large number of nest boxes. Natural nest holes appear scarce in Scotland, and the added disadvantage in this region is that the absence of Black Woodpecker means that available woodpecker holes are too small.

Although birds shot in winter have included one Scottish ringed breeding female, the Goldeneye is rarely shot deliberately—although it is still legal to do so in Britain in winter.

Eggs are illegally taken by collectors, and probably also for wildfowl collections, though not in large numbers.

Nests are taken over by Jackdaws and, more rarely, by pine martens; problems with the latter are likely to increase as the ducks colonize areas used by pine martens—which are now re-colonizing the Spey Valley.

Occasionally, nests have been deserted because of disturbance by fishermen inadvertently spending too much time close to occupied boxes and not allowing females to get back to their eggs.

Heavy stocking of lochs with rainbow trout may deplete invertebrates on which the Goldeneye feeds; the poisoning of lochs to remove unwanted fish species before restocking may also present problems.

In the long term the species would benefit from the increase and retention of deciduous trees along rivers and near lochs to provide natural nest holes.

CONSERVATION

At present nearly half the Scottish breeding population nests on nature reserves or SSSIs. The Goldeneye has fared well in Scotland since its colonization, with much interest and encouragement shown to it from the owners and managers of the land on which it breeds. In consequence, site safeguard is not a high priority. Management has centred round the provision of nest boxes in many areas of Scotland and northern England. The RSPB Highland Office pioneered this work and encouraged others to become involved. The Forestry Commission responded very positively with the provision of nest boxes in the four northern conservancies. Management guidelines for the construction, erection and monitoring of boxes have been produced. Roving wardens have protected the breeding population, and the RSPB has carefully monitored the population each year. Annual newsletters have been produced and circulated to all people involved with the project.

The Goldeneye's population is increasing rapidly; the bird does not appear to be competing with any other species and it should eventually colonize a large area of northern Britain. The main requirement is the continued provision of boxes. Patience is also needed, for it does take a long time for birds to colonize new areas.

Finally, whilst the effects of acidification are unknown, there is the potential for this to affect invertebrates on which the Goldeneye feeds. The monitoring of invertebrate levels in Scottish lochs is therefore seen as a high priority for this and other invertebrate feeders.

REFERENCES

DENNIS, R.H. 1987. Boxes for Goldeneyes: a success story. RSPB Conservation Review 1: 85.
DENNIS, R.H. & Dow, H. 1974. The establishment of a population of Goldeneye *Bucephala clangula* breeding in Scotland. Bird Study 34: 217–222.
MacMILLAN, A.T. 1970. Goldeneye breeding in East Inverness-shire. Scot. Birds 6: 197–198.

Consultant: R.H. Dennis.

Honey Buzzard
Pernis apivorus

The Honey Buzzard is a rare summer visitor. Its numbers decreased in Britain through persecution in the 18th and 19th centuries, but it was probably always scarce. Since at least the 1930s, some pairs have nested in Hampshire and others less regularly elsewhere, mainly in the southern half of England, although more recently also in Scotland. The total population is possibly about 30 pairs. The more important conservation objectives are the management of regular breeding woods, to retain tall, mature trees.

LEGAL STATUS

Protected under Schedule 1 of WCA 1981; Annex 1 of EC Birds Directive; Appendix II of the Berne Convention.

ECOLOGY

The Honey Buzzard usually arrives in Britain between mid to late May. In the breeding season it requires mature woodland with open areas for feeding. The home range may be as large as 34–36 km², with birds flying up to 3·5 km from the nest to feed (Thiollay, 1967). In Britain the preferred breeding areas are usually on light or sandy soils. Nest: made of sticks, sometimes placed on top of an old corvid or raptor nest (Glutz *et al.*, 1971), built at a height of 10–25 m in tall, mature beech, oak or other broadleaved tree, less often in conifer, at the edge of a wood, or near a ride or clearing. The bird is generally solitary, but sometimes a few pairs occur in the same tract of woodland. The same nest may be used in successive years. Eggs: laid June–July. Clutch: 2 (1–3); one brood. The young fledge by mid-September.

The food from mid-June to autumn departure, and in winter quarters, consists largely of wasp larvae, pupae and adults obtained by digging out ground nests. Before June, other insects (particularly beetles), earthworms, small mammals and amphibians are taken (Chapin & Eisentraut in Glutz *et al.*, 1971; Thiollay, 1969). Wasp larvae/pupae appear to be essential for the early stages of chick develop-ment.

The young are dependent on adults in the immediate post-fledging period, but adults may leave for the winter quarters before the young.

DISTRIBUTION AND POPULATION

West Palearctic. Breeds over much of Europe north to southern Fenno-Scandia and north-central Russia, though it is local in much of the western Mediterranean area, Iberia and Britain. In central Europe there has apparently been a small decline in recent years (Glutz *et al.*, 1971); elsewhere: France 8,000–12,000 pairs (Fonds D'Intervention pour les Rapaces, 1984), Belgium 200–400 pairs, Luxem-burg 70–90 pairs and the Netherlands 150–200 pairs (Cramp *et al.*, 1980). Winters in tropical and southern Africa. In Britain, it was thought to have become almost extinct early in the 20th century following a decrease through shooting and collecting in the 18th and 19th centuries (Parslow, 1973). A small population has now been established. The bird occurs regularly in Hampshire, and pairs occur and breed during most years in three to six other counties in England and Scotland, but most records are not published because of the risk to nest sites. The Honey Buzzard is otherwise a scarce passage-migrant found largely in eastern counties. In the 19th century nesting was known west to Herefordshire and north to Cleveland, Grampian and Highland, but since the 1930s published records have referred mainly to the southern half of England, apart from Nottinghamshire, Yorkshire and, in 1949, probably Fife (Hollom, 1957).

The documented population is now considered to be fairly stable at 8–15 pairs, but confidential, unpublished information indicates that the population may be as high as 30 pairs—summering but not necessarily breeding—per year. Established pairs may not breed each year if climatic conditions reduce food availability. Productivity was perceived to have been good in the 1970s, when wasp popu-lations were high, but lower in the 1980s when summers were, on average, wetter and wasps scarcer.

THREATS TO SURVIVAL

The main threats are currently the shooting of migrant birds in southern Europe, habitat clearance, and possibly climatic factors which will affect food supplies.

The scant information available suggests that productivity may not be high with young dying in the nest, possibly as a result of food shortage caused by inclement weather which reduces the availability of wasps and bees.

The true level of the breeding population and the effects of interference are not fully known. However, Honey Buzzards are affected by disturbance (Voous, 1977). Tolerance of disturbance varies between individuals although on one occasion in Britain felling of trees at a distance of 100 m led to desertion. In some areas birdwatchers have certainly caused disturbance to nesting birds, as well as problems with landowners, by trespassing in search of Honey Buzzards.

Although persecution was heavy in the past, only very occasionally in recent years have nests been robbed by collectors and/or birds shot.

On the Continent the population is apparently also affected by climatic factors and food supply, being less numerous and less successful in wet summers.

CONSERVATION

As Honey Buzzards show great site fidelity (although progeny generally return to a new potential breeding area) all regular nesting woods should be managed to maintain tall, mature trees. There needs to be a cessation of forestry operations within at least 200 m of any occupied nest. The provision of artificial nest platforms may attract breeding pairs to new or more secure areas of woodland. As this species is on the edge of its range in Britain, any attempts to increase the population may not prove successful.

International efforts should be made to reduce or eradicate the traditional (but now illegal) shooting of Honey Buzzards in southern Europe.

Birdwatchers who travel to see the species must watch from a distance and never approach or enter the woodland breeding area. Furthermore, breeding sites should not be publicized; liaison with landowners and keepers is clearly important.

The monitoring of breeding Honey Buzzards and their productivity is severely hampered because those studying them rarely make their information available to the Rare Breeding Birds Panel or to any conservation body. This has prevented rational consideration of measures to assist the species.

REFERENCES

FONDS D'INTERVENTION POUR LES RAPACES. 1984. Estimation des Effectifs de Rapaces Nicheurs Diurnes et non Rupestres en France. Enquete FIR/UNAO 1979–82.
GLUTZ VON BLOTZHEIM, V.N., BAUER, K. & BEZZEL, E. 1971. Handbuch der Vögel Mitteleuropas, Vol. 4. Frankfurt am main: Akademische Verlagsgesellschaft.
HOLLOM, P.A.D. 1957. The rarer birds of prey: their present status in the British Isles. Honey Buzzard. Brit. Birds 50: 141–142.
PARSLOW, J.L.F. 1973. Breeding birds of Britain and Ireland. Calton: Poyser.
THIOLLAY, J.M. 1967. Ecologie d'une population de Rapaces diurnes en Lorraine Terre et Vie 21. 116–183.
VOOUS, K.H. 1977. Three lines of thought for consideration and eventual action. Proc. ICBP World Conference on Birds of Prey, Vienna, 1975, 343–347.

Consultant: G. Sweet

Red Kite
Milvus milvus

The Red Kite is a rare breeding resident in Britain. The bird was once widespread but its persecution led to near-extinction by the late 19th century. Protection in Wales from the end of the 19th century helped to maintain a tiny population of 3–4 pairs (at lowest), which has shown steady but slow increase since the Second World War to 52 nesting pairs in 1989. Wardening of nests to protect them from disturbance and egg collecting has been essential to safeguard the slow increase and will continue to be required. The species is still limited to a restricted area of Wales and a re-introduction programme to establish populations elsewhere in Britain has recently started.

LEGAL STATUS

Protected under Schedule 1 of WCA 1981; Annex 1 of EC Birds Directive; Appendix II of the Berne Convention.

ECOLOGY

The Red Kite breeds in Wales in mature woodland, often on the steep sides of valleys; it is a solitary or loosely grouped bird (Walters-Davies & Davis, 1973). Nest: made of sticks and turf lined with wool, occasionally rags and other rubbish, usually high in the main fork of a broadleaved tree. [In Wales nests are built mostly 12–15 m above the ground in oaks (*Quercus*)]. Eggs: laid late March to May. Clutch: 2–3 (1–4); one brood. The young fledge by mid-July. Breeding success is, however, generally poor in Wales, with an average of 1·34 young per successful nest with many nests unsuccessful. This is significantly lower than the breeding success of birds on the Continent (Cramp & Simmons, 1980). Food shortage and wet climate are considered to be the most important reasons for nesting failure (Davis & Newton, 1981).

Food consists of carrion, small mammals, birds, occasionally frogs, and also earthworms, beetles and other invertebrates. The bird also scavenges at refuse tips and around abattoirs (Davis & Davis, 1981).

DISTRIBUTION AND POPULATION

West Palearctic. Almost the entire breeding range of this bird occurs within Europe (where it is decreasing), from Iberia and the Caucasus north to central France, northern Germany, southern Scandinavia and the Baltic States, with an isolated remnant population in Wales, where breeding birds are resident but some juveniles disperse widely after fledging. The Red Kite otherwise winters mainly in southern Europe with a few crossing to north-west Africa. The bird was formerly widespread throughout Britain, but intense persecution led to a massive decline and eventual extermination in the 19th century — the bird becoming finally extinct in England by 1870 and in Scotland by 1890. Subsequently, only isolated pairs nested in Devon in 1913, Cornwall in 1920 and Cumbria in 1978.

Organized protection in Wales began in 1903, when there were believed to be only a dozen birds left, including four nesting pairs. Early figures are unreliable, but the total probably never exceeded 10–12 pairs before the 1940s and usually only three to five nests were known. A small increase during the 1939–45 war was possibly due to reduced persecution. From 1951 onwards much more accurate figures are known (Salmon, 1970; Davis & Newton, 1981). Until the 1960s the population remained precariously low at less than 20 pairs, but from then on a slow increase began which has been maintained at approximately 5% per annum.

Recent wing tagging indicates high rates of survival over the last 10 years. A minimum of 41% of the young survive to enter the breeding population between their 2nd to 7th years of life, and about 95% of breeders survive from one year to the next (Newton, Davis & Davis 1989). The improved survival of adults in the past two decades is believed to be responsible for much of the recent increase, since the production of young has not greatly improved.

The bird is a rare wanderer outside the breeding season. Ringing recoveries and increased occurrences confirm it to be a passage migrant, particularly in counties of eastern England, mainly in March and April.

THREATS TO SURVIVAL

Threats include indifferent breeding success and the persecution of full-grown birds. Human disturbance and egg collecting, by exacerbating the low breeding success, also pose a significant problem.

The likely impacts of land-use changes in Wales are not well understood although afforestation has not yet been shown to be a serious problem (Newton, Davis & Moss, 1981); some temporary benefit accrues after the establishment of conifer forests, eg, increased availability of voles — but once the forests have grown up they are abandoned by Kites. There is, however, no evidence that afforestation has so far limited the number of Kites in Wales as there is still much available habitat which could be colonized.

Many Welsh sites are vulnerable to disturbance and, with the spread of tourism and the understandable interest of birdwatchers, it is only rigorous protection that has limited this. The localities of such sites — and even the counties involved — are rightly not publicized, but many of the general areas are well known to ornithologists and collectors alike. Despite wardening, some nests are robbed of eggs each year. However, the main factors limiting breeding success appear to be poor weather in spring and low food supplies resulting in the loss of all or some of the chicks.

A serious problem for the resident population is the traditional, though long-illegal, practice of laying out bait injected with strychnine and other poisons for foxes (*Vulpes vulpes*) and carrion crows (*Corvus corone*): almost half the dead kites examined in recent years have been poisoned (Davis & Newton, 1981). This illegal poisoning and its occurrence in many Welsh and border areas is probably a major reason for the lack of natural spread in the distribution of the population.

Although one juvenile Red Kite ringed in Germany has been recovered in

Wales, there is no other evidence of immigration into the breeding population from outside, nor are there ringing recoveries of Welsh birds on the Continent. The possibility of inbreeding is being investigated by DNA finger-printing. Early results indicate reduced genetic variation of Welsh birds compared with those in Germany, but this has not yet been linked to low breeding success or survival.

CONSERVATION

Although much time and money has been spent on the protection of this species over the last 75 years, it is only since the 1960s that intensive research has been undertaken. Recent programmes are greatly improving our knowledge of the species' requirements, but more still needs to be known about the reasons for poor breeding, the causes of mortality among immature birds, ranging behaviour, home range requirements in relation to land-use, food availability, movements, and longevity. At the same time, as the population grows it will become increasingly difficult to monitor it closely and to give the protection from disturbance that has been possible in the past. However, there must be continuing close liaison between the conservation bodies, land managers, planning authorities, the Agriculture Departments and the Forestry Commission to ensure that developments do not seriously affect the habitats of this species in some 5,000 km² of central Wales. A new road may destroy an essential nesting woodland, or a change from farming to forestry may remove an essential source of sheep carrion. It is a wide-ranging bird, foraging over large areas, and a network of reserves can never be adequate to maintain this small but important portion of the European population.

The understandable enthusiasm of birdwatchers and tourists who wish to see Welsh Kites needs to be channelled, perhaps by giving publicity to roads and other locations from which flying birds can readily be seen and the provision of well controlled public viewing facilities. Visitors need to be encouraged further to look for kites outside the breeding season, when they are in any case much easier to see. Greater publicity needs to be given in the public and game-interest media to ensure a wider sympathy and understanding of this species so that wandering immatures are left unmolested (Walters-Davies & Davis, 1973). Dialogue with the rural communities of central Wales and increased vigilance by the general public and enforcement agencies will help to deter the deplorable and illegal poisoning of these birds.

Red Kites have been very slow to colonize new parts of Wales, and they are still restricted to a small area. To secure their future an experimental project by NCC and RSPB is already underway to re-establish new core populations elsewhere in Britain where breeding success may approach continental levels.

REFERENCES

CRAMP, S. & SIMMONS, K.E.L. 1980. Handbook of the Birds of Europe the Middle East and North Africa vol. II. Oxford: Oxford University Press.
DAVIS, P.E. & DAVIS, J.E. 1981. The food of the Red Kite in Wales. Bird Study 28: 33–39.
DAVIS, P.E. & NEWTON, I. 1981. Population and breeding of Red Kites in Wales over a 30 years period. J. Anim. Ecol. 50: 759–772.
NEWTON, I., DAVIS, P.E. & DAVIS, J.E. 1989. The age of first breeding dispersal and survival of Red Kites in Wales. Ibis. 131: 16–21.

Newton, I., Davis, P.E. & Moss, D. 1981. Distribution and breeding of Red Kites in relation to land-use in Wales. J. Appl. Ecol. 18: 173–186.

Salmon, H.M 1970. The Red Kites of Wales: the story of their preservation. In Lacey, W.S. (ed.), Welsh wildlife in trust. 67–79. North Wales Naturalists Trust, Bangor.

Walters-Davies, P. & Davis, P.E. 1973. The ecology and conservation of the Red Kite in Wales. Brit. Birds 66: 183–224, 241–270.

Consultants: P.E. Davis and K.W. Smith

White-tailed Eagle

Haliaeetus albicilla

The White-tailed Eagle is a rare breeding resident (re-introduced) and one of only three British breeding species which are endangered on a world scale. It became extinct as a breeding bird in Britain in 1916, prior to which there were at least 100 known breeding sites in Scotland and at least 50 pairs in Ireland. Re-introductions were attempted in 1959, 1968 and again in 1975 when a large-scale programme involving new releases in each of the following 10 years was initiated by NCC. One pair raised one young in 1985 and two young in 1986; two pairs raised three young in 1987, one pair raised two young in 1988 and three pairs raised five young in 1989. Protection of nesting sites and prevention of illegal poisoning are the most important conservation objectives.

LEGAL STATUS

Protected under Schedule 1 of WCA 1981; Annex 1 of EC Birds Directive; Appendix II of the Berne Convention.

ECOLOGY

Breeding largely confined to coastal areas. Nest: a bulky structure of branches, twigs, and driftwood lined with grass, lichens or seaweed; in trees, ledges or cliff tops or on slopes, and often used and added to in successive years. Eggs: laid March–May. Clutch: 2 (1–3); one brood, which takes five years to reach maturity. The young fledge from mid-July.

Food consists mainly of seabirds and fish, but also includes mammals such as sheep, goats, hares, together with a considerable amount of carrion.

DISTRIBUTION AND POPULATION

Palearctic, but also the south-west coast of Greenland. The White-tailed Eagle is widespread in eastern Europe and across the USSR, but is rather scarce and is a local breeder; it is mostly resident, but some northern European immatures and non-breeding birds move south in winter—particularly to the Baltic and Black Sea coasts. Breeding birds in the coastal districts of Sweden, Norway (including North Cape), Iceland and south-west Greenland are sedentary. In Britain, the bird formerly inhabited coastal cliffs and islands, as well as freshwater and sea-lochs, estuaries and rivers—often some way inland.

Increased disturbance, poisoning of sheep carcasses, shooting and destruction of eyries by farmers, shepherds and gamekeepers, together with the collection of skins and eggs in the 19th century, drastically reduced the population of White-tailed Eagles until only a few pairs remained by 1900. The species last bred in England and Wales in the 1830s and in Ireland in 1898, but without protection the last birds succumbed in Scotland in 1916, and the last British-bred bird was shot in Shetland in 1918. Smaller declines have taken place across the entire range, but since the inception of protection measures considerable recovery has been noticeable. Persecution abroad was never as heavy as it was in Britain, but in some countries, eg, Norway, a bounty was paid in the earlier part of this century for every White-tailed Eagle shot. Other countries have seen declines due to poisoning (through the use of poisoned baits) and habitat destruction, and around the Baltic poisoning by organochlorine pesticides has affected breeding success through egg-shell thinning. Since the introduction of protection measures the population is now stable in most countries, and is even increasing in some.

In recent years (mid-1980s) a few immature birds from the Baltic have wandered to southern England, and one bearing an East German ring was found shot. Re-colonization from such vagrancy is unlikely.

Small-scale re-introductions in Scotland were attempted in 1959 and 1968, but the seven birds released disappeared, presumably wandering away within their first year of freedom. In 1975 a 10-year programme of releasing young birds from Norwegian nests was initiated by NCC on Rhum; 82 birds had been released by 1985, over three-quarters of them surviving around Rhum and on the adjacent Hebridean islands (Love, 1983). Several pairs attempted nesting in the early 1980s, and in 1985 the first juvenile was fledged, followed by two the following year. In 1987 two pairs raised three young to the flying stage, and one pair raised two young in 1988, though six pairs attempted to nest. In 1989 five young fledged from three successful nests.

THREATS TO SURVIVAL

Threats include illegal poisoning (two birds were found poisoned in the early years), shooting, collisions with over-head power cables, egg-collectors, Fulmar oiling and human disturbance; all of these present potential hazards to the species' tenuous foothold in Britain but there is no evidence that any are critical.

The unity of the re-introduced population is important in ensuring pairing, so that one of the main threats is that of birds wandering away from the nucleus.

CONSERVATION

It is crucial that the re-introduction programme is a success as it is unlikly to be repeated in full again because of the high cost. However, the option to release more

Norwegian birds in the area in the next few years remains open at present. The location of all nest sites should continue to be witheld to discourage the undesirable attention of birdwatchers, tourists etc, and round-the-clock protection is necessary for vulnerable nests.

The education of the general public and maintenance of better dialogue with the rural communities in the vicinity may help to prevent unnecessary and illegal poisoning or shooting.

REFERENCES

Love, J.A. 1983. The return of the sea-eagle. Cambridge: Cambridge University Press.

Consultant: J.A. Love

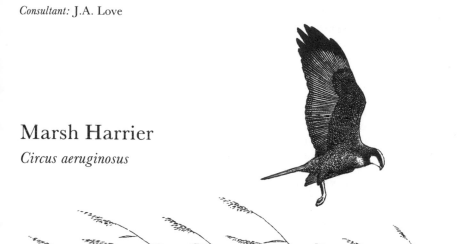

Marsh Harrier

Circus aeruginosus

The Marsh Harrier is a scarce or locally common summer visitor, although small numbers winter in Britain. It breeds almost entirely in reed beds (*Phragmites australis*). It was once widespread in Britain, but declined due to the effects of drainage on its habitat, and persecution, and ceased to breed by the end of the 19th century. The bird re-established itself in Britain by the late 1920s and slowly increased in numbers up to the late 1950s. There was a rapid decline during the 1960s but a swift recovery from the early 1970s; by 1988 over 75 nests were, between them, raising about 130 young. The population is largely protected in nature reserves and elsewhere by protection schemes.

LEGAL STATUS

Protected under Schedule 1 of WCA 1981; Annex 1 of EC Birds Directive; Appendix II of the Berne Convention.

ECOLOGY

Breeding birds arrive at suitable habitat during late March and April. Breeding takes place amongst reeds or sedges, usually within extensive reed beds. In recent years small numbers of birds have nested in cereal fields or in small patches of reed surrounded by arable land or saltmarsh. Nest: usually constructed of grass, reeds and small sticks placed on the ground, or occasionally in plants growing in shallow water within thick beds of reed or sedge. Eggs: laid usually during late April and early May. Clutch: 4–5 (2–8). Most broods of 2–4 (1–6) are fledged by the end of July. The birds tend to hunt over open country dominated by aquatic vegetation; where this is not available, hunting takes place over agricultural land.

Food consists mostly of birds, rabbits and small mammals (Underhill-Day, 1985).

DISTRIBUTION AND POPULATION

Palearctic; the nominate race from Britain ranges east to northern Mongolia and Lake Baikal. Six further races are found in north-west Africa, New Guinea, Australia, the Pacific region and the Indian Ocean region. Winters in western and southern Europe to tropical Africa and southern Asia (Cramp *et al.*, 1980). In Britain it breeds mainly in East Anglia, but occurs on passage on the south and east coasts as far north as Scotland and occasionally, in the west, in Wales and Ireland. The Marsh Harrier winters in small numbers in East Anglia, Kent and south Wales, with scattered records elsewhere (Lack, 1986).

The bird was widespread in Britain, but a scarce breeder, during the last century, but it declined in numbers due to the effects of drainage on its habitat and to heavy persecution, and it had become extinct as a breeding bird in Britain by 1900. Sporadic breeding has been recorded from 1911, but regular breeding started from 1927, with between one and five pairs to 1947 in East Anglia. The population subsequently increased to 15 nests by 1958, with records from Norfolk, Suffolk and Dorset and with occasional nesting in four other English counties and two areas in Wales. A decline in numbers occurred from 1959 to 1971, when there was only a single nesting pair. A rapid recovery followed from 1972, and by 1989 there were over 75 nests, more than at any time this century (Underhill-Day, 1984, and *pers. comm.*). The British population of the Marsh Harrier is small by comparison with many other western European countries (eg, the Netherlands has 800–900 pairs, Denmark has 500 pairs, Sweden 520 pairs, West Germany 725–850 pairs, France 700–1,000 pairs and Spain 500 pairs), being 1–2% of the total of about 4,100 pairs (Gensbol, 1984). Populations in north-west Europe have generally been increasing over the last 10–15 years.

The population and breeding success are monitored annually, and a summary is provided by the Rare Birds Breeding Panel.

THREATS TO SURVIVAL

Threats include the deliberate disturbance of nesting sites, the loss of eggs to collectors, and predation, eg, by foxes.

There is no evidence that the Marsh Harrier population in Britain has been affected by habitat loss this century, although the small size of many breeding sites may result in greater susceptibility to disturbance. Compared to other north-west European populations, the average sizes of fledged broods in Britain have been low. The pattern of decline during the 1960s was mirrored elsewhere in north-west

Europe, and it accords with that recorded for other birds of prey affected by pesticides. Marsh Harrier egg shells became 10% thinner after 1947, when DDT became commonly used, showing that the birds had been affected by organochlorines. In recent years, analysis of egg contents has shown that toxic chemicals were present only in low concentrations, although thin-shelled eggs were still being laid (Underhill-Day, 1984).

Persecution still occurs in Britain, and in recent years it has included deliberate disturbance of nesting sites (to discourage breeding) and illegal poisoning (though not necessarily directed at Marsh Harriers).

Marsh Harriers have suffered from the attentions of egg collectors, though this has not been a significant factor for some time.

Accidental disturbance could affect breeding success since Marsh Harriers are particularly susceptible, although tolerance levels vary widely between individuals.

Agricultural operations seem to be accepted by the birds.

The main natural predator of Marsh Harriers' eggs and young in Britain is the fox.

CONSERVATION

Of 32 nests in 1986, 18 were on nature reserves, five were subject to protection schemes, and the remaining nine were unprotected, although at some of these the birds were kept undisturbed by sympathetic landowners. Of 23 breeding sites in 1986, 12 were within SSSIs, holding 19 nests.

Little management for Marsh Harriers can be carried out, although the prevention of scrub encroachment and maintenance of water levels within reed beds, particularly on smaller sites, would benefit the species by maintaining suitable habitat and deterring foxes.

Protection from human disturbance, and the encouragement of sympathetic management practices by farmers and landowners on unprotected sites, is the most important element in a strategy for encouraging a continuing increase and spread in the population.

Research into the breeding biology, food, and hunting behaviour of the Marsh Harrier has taken place in recent years both in Britain and the Netherlands. Little is known however, of population dynamics.

Pesticide levels should continue to be monitored since this is one of the few large British birds of prey which breeds in close association with intensive agriculture.

REFERENCES

Gensbol, B. 1984. Collins guide to the birds of prey of Britain and Europe, North Africa and the Middle East. London: Collins.

Underhill-Day, J.C. 1984. Population and breeding biology of Marsh Harriers in Britain since 1900. J. Appl. Ecol. 21: 773–787.

Underhill-Day, J.C. 1985. The food of breeding Marsh Harrier *Circus aeruginosus* in East Anglia. Bird Study 32: 199–206.

Consultant: J.C. U-Day

Hen Harrier

Circus cyaneus

After a marked decrease in the numbers of Hen Harriers during 19th century, apparently due largely to human persecution, there was an increase and spread, starting in the 1930s, to at least 300–400 pairs in the 1960s and 1970s—mainly in Scotland, but also in northern England and Wales. Recently (in the 1980s) there has been some contraction of range and a perceived decline in numbers; the population in 1989 was considered to be in the order of 500 pairs. The retention of mature heather moorland and a reduction in persecution are considered to be the most important conservation objectives.

LEGAL STATUS

Protected under Schedule 1 of WCA 1981; Annex I of EC Birds Directive; Appendix II of the Berne Convention.

ECOLOGY

The Hen Harrier breeds on moorland, especially where there is old, deep heather (*Calluna vulgaris*); it also breeds in heather in young conifer plantations. Nest: a shallow-cupped pile of vegetation sited in deep cover, always on the ground or in low scrub. Eggs: laid May–June. Clutch: 4–6; one brood. The young fledge from the end of June.

Food consists of small birds, grouse, rodents, young rabbits and young hares.

DISTRIBUTION AND POPULATION

Holarctic. *C. c. cyaneus* breeds in a broad zone across Europe and Asia, between 40°N and 70°N, east to the Kamchatka peninsula, and winters mainly in southern Asia and western and southern Europe; *C. c. hudsonius* breeds in North America. The nominate race was formerly a widespread breeder in Britain, but numbers and range have been reduced dramatically through loss of heath and scrubland, and through persecution on grouse moors and on wintering areas on southern English farmland. By the beginning of this century, and until the 1930s, the Hen Harrier was confined, as a breeding bird, to Orkney and the Outer Hebrides, but since then it has increased and spread south across the Scottish mainland; since 1968 it has spread to northern England and Wales.

The initial re-establishment and spread on the mainland was associated largely with new afforestation from the 1930s onwards; such afforestation provided suitable, unkeepered nesting areas. In 1968–72 the British and Irish breeding population was estimated at 500 to 600 pairs, of which the British component was probably 300–400 pairs. The British population of Hen Harriers may have been above 500 pairs during the period 1973–75 (Watson, 1977) since when a decline has been perceived. However, this may not be general, although declines have definitely occurred in certain areas. A comprehensive survey in Scotland in 1988/89 indicated a population of about 500 pairs, despite the intensity of coverage.

Elsewhere in western Europe, the Hen Harrier breeds in significant numbers in France, where recent estimates indicate a population in the order of 2,800 to 3,800 pairs (Fonds D'Intervention pour les Rapaces, 1984), in the Netherlands, where the population increased from 10 to 15 pairs in the 1950s to over 100 pairs in 1975–77, and in Sweden, 1,000–2,000 pairs, Spain 500 pairs, Norway 10 pairs, and West Germany 200 pairs (Gensbol, 1984).

A report in the late 1970s indicated a marked decline in many areas in Ireland associated with the loss of feeding areas on marginal hill ground and the maturation of coniferous plantations previously used (in their younger stages) for nesting.

THREATS TO SURVIVAL

Threats include persecution and the loss of habitat through afforestation.

Persecution on grouse moors during the breeding season, and possibly at winter roosts, is considered to be the main threat. In 1988/89 breeding success on managed grouse moors was significantly lower than on unmanaged moors or afforested areas although clutch size and successful brood size were similar in all three areas.

Afforestation may be of limited benefit in some areas initially, since removal of sheep and deer, together with other forestry management, increases heather growth and provides suitable nesting habitat, an increase in prey (small birds and mammals) and a decline in persecution. However, in the longer term, afforestation destroys moorland—so denying harriers suitable areas for nesting and feeding. The loss of heather moor to re-seeding, reclamation and overgrazing remains an important threat in the long term. Increased afforestation of moorland also results in increased numbers of foxes and crows—which are believed to be major predators of harrier nests.

CONSERVATION

The problem of the harrier's predation on grouse needs to be addressed, and the conflicting interests of moor owners and conservationists should somehow be reconciled. Until then, continued vigilance against shooting and nest destruction will be needed.

Afforestation schemes, and the conversion of moorland to improved grass swards, is also a direct threat; the Government afforestation target of 33,000 ha/annum is nearly all destined for areas suitable for Hen Harriers. Evidence from Ireland (O'Flynn, 1983) suggests that the loss of marginal farmland in the uplands, due to either agricultural intensification or afforestation, can severely affect breeding success in the long term.

Programmes (eg, SSSI designation) to conserve extensive tracts of moorland are also important to maintain viable Hen Harrier populations. Key areas should also be declared as SPAs. Hen Harriers can nest at quite high densities, have overlapping ranges, and are not really territorial.

The Hen Harrier is polygynous, the incidence of polygyny probably being associated with food availability and habitat quality (Picozzi, 1978). Thus, if suitable nesting cover is available, it is likely that food availability will limit the breeding numbers and breeding success. The availability of prey especially small birds and mammals, eg, Meadow Pipits, could be maintained through policies which sustain traditional forms of agriculture in the hills.

Since harriers roost communally it is important that roost sites are protected. In this context drainage of key marshes should be opposed as this could remove winter roosts and reduce areas for winter feeding.

REFERENCES

Fonds D'Intervention pour les Rapaces. 1984. Estimation des Effectifs de Rapaces Nicheurs Diurnes et non Rupestres en France. Enquete FIR/UNAO 1979–1982.
Gensbol, B. 1984. Collins guide to the birds of prey of Britain and Europe, North Africa and the Middle East. London: Collins.
O'Flynn, W.J. 1983. Population changes of the Hen Harrier in Ireland. Irish Birds 2: 337–343.
Picozzi, N. 1978. Dispersion, breeding and prey of the Hen harrier *Circus cyaneus* in Glen Dye, Kincardineshire. Ibis 120: 498–509.
Watson, D. 1977. The Hen Harrier. Berkhampstead: Poyser.

Consultants: I. Newton, P.J. Hudson and S. Redpath

Montagu's Harrier
Circus pygargus

Montagu's Harrier is a rare summer visitor. It breeds largely in cereal crops, although it has previously been found nesting in a much wider range of grassland habitats. Following a rapid decline from high numbers in the early 1950s, and a brief partial recovery, the bird has become very scarce in Britain since about 1970, with a maximum of eight nests in 1988. Breeding pairs have been threatened by disturbance from birdwatchers and by the destruction of nests by agricultural machinery. Each year, protection schemes are mounted to ensure that nests are not disturbed or destroyed accidentally by harvesting operations.

LEGAL STATUS

Protected under Schedule 1 of WCA 1981; Annex 1 of EC Birds Directive; Appendix II of the Berne Convention.

ECOLOGY

Arrival in Britain occurs from late April to early June. Nesting has traditionally taken place in reed beds, rough grassland, young conifer plantations and on heathland and moorland; in recent years, however, most nests have been made in cereal crops. Eggs: laid mid to late May in most years. Clutch: 4 (2–10); one brood. Fledging occurs between late July and early August. Polygamy is unusual and only then involves two females.

Food consists mainly of small birds and mammals; the bird hunts over open country, sometimes some distance from the nest site.

DISTRIBUTION AND POPULATION

Palearctic. Montagu's Harriers breed between about 35°N and 60°N across southern and central Europe, and in Asia east to about 100°E. A summer migrant to breeding areas, wintering mainly in Africa and India. The European population was believed to be about 5,500–6,000 pairs (Gensbol, 1984), with the majority of these birds in Spain 3,000 pairs, Portugal 1,000 pairs, and France 300–400 pairs. Elsewhere, smaller numbers were recorded in West Germany 80–90 pairs, the Netherlands 15–25 pairs, Belgium 3–5 pairs, Sweden 55 pairs and Denmark 50 pairs (Gensbol, 1984).

In Britain, Montagu's Harriers were heavily persecuted during the 19th century and the early part of the 20th century, with no more than seven pairs being recorded in any year between 1850 and 1920. Thereafter the population increased steadily to a maximum of 30 nests in 1953. At this time birds were widely distributed, the main centres of population being in East Anglia and the South West. Montagu's Harriers have bred in 18 counties in England, four in Wales and two each in Scotland and Ireland. The population declined between 1953 and 1962, when only seven pairs bred; it partially recovered to 19 nests in 1967, but declined again until not a single pair was confirmed breeding in 1974 and 1975. Breeding recommenced in 1976 and since then the population has fluctuated between two and eight breeding females. The underlying trend shows a slow increase; the number of young reared each year reached a maximum in 1989 when 18 young fledged (Elliott, 1988). A similar recent decline has been apparent in most of north-west Europe—with the exception of Sweden and Denmark, where numbers are increasing slowly.

The population and breeding success are monitored annually by the RSPB, and the results summarized for the Rare Breeding Birds Panel.

THREATS TO SURVIVAL

Threats include the effects of toxic sprays and of harvesting machinery when nesting occurs in cereal fields, predation by foxes, and possible disturbance by birdwatchers.

Persecution is not a current threat in Britain, although in the past the population received much attention from egg collectors.

The decline in the 1950s was probably due to pesticides, since the pattern matches that of other species similarly affected. Analysis of egg contents in recent years shows only low levels of contamination by toxic residues.

Montagu's Harriers although as sensitive are possibly more tolerant of disturbance than are Marsh Harriers, but by breeding later in the season their young are at risk from toxic sprays—and later from harvesting machinery when nests are in cereals. Some predation by foxes also occurs.

Due to their rarity, nesting Montagu's Harriers arouse intense interest among birdwatchers who visit known nesting areas in large numbers. Apart from the risk of disturbance, this could cause problems to landowners who might then seek to discourage breeding by harriers. That this has not yet happened is due largely to wardening schemes in breeding areas with which farmers have co-operated.

CONSERVATION

No recent nesting of Montagu's Harriers in Britain has been within an SSSI, ESA or SPA. Other than protection through wardening schemes little can be done to encourage Montagu's Harriers. For example, they are unlikely to respond to habitat management, and many of the former reed bed and heathland breeding sites are now reserves.

It is important that nests on arable land are located and brought to the attention of landowners to prevent destruction of the nest by agricultural operations. In tall crops, young can be lost during high winds and heavy rain if the crop smothers the nest. This can be avoided by pruning or tying back the surrounding vegetation.

Recent research has concentrated on breeding biology, food and population status, and trends in Britain. Little is known of the population dynamics, of the total populations and trends in Europe, and of the threats which the species might face on its African wintering grounds.

REFERENCES

ELLIOTT, G.D. 1988. Montagu's Harrier Conservation. In RSPB Conservation Review 1988. Sandy: Royal Society for the Protection of Birds.
GENSBOL, B. 1984. Birds of prey of Britain and Europe. London: Collins.

Consultant: J.C. U-Day

Goshawk
Accipiter gentilis

The Goshawk is a rare breeding resident in Britain. As a result of deforestation and persecution, this bird had been largely exterminated by the late 19th century, with only occasional or sporadic breeding thereafter. From the late 1960s pairs became established in several areas to form the basis of the present population — which is estimated at 100–200 pairs. Although still scarce, Goshawks do not have stringent habitat requirements, and the main factors currently limiting their population expansion appears to be persecution and nest robbing.

LEGAL STATUS

Proteced under Schedule 1 of WCA 1981; EC Birds Directive; Appendix II of the Berne Convention.

ECOLOGY

Goshawks breed at relatively low densities, generally in areas of extensive woodland, both coniferous and broadleaved, but also (where there is little choice) in quite small woods. Nest: built of sticks in any tree that can provide support for the bulky structure; it is generally close to the main trunk and more than 12 m from the ground. One pair can have several nests, though usually only one is refurbished in any one year. Eggs: laid from late March to early May. Clutch: 3–4 (2–6, mean 3·8). The young usually fledge in July. From 1973 to 1980, at unmolested sites, 83% of nests produced young; the brood size averaged 3·0 (Marquiss & Newton, 1982). However, breeding attempts over 300 m above sea level tend to produce smaller clutches (mean 3·5) and fewer young (mean 2·6). If initial breeding fails at an early stage some pairs in areas of food abundance will attempt to breed again.

Food is obtained by hunting in both woodland and open country. In Britain, as elsewhere in Europe (Glutz von Blotzheim *et al.*, 1971; Opdam *et al.*, 1977), Goshawks take a variety of prey, even those as large as the brown hare (*Lepus capersus*) or as agile as the Sparrowhawk (*Accipiter nisus*), the proportion of various species in the diet being largely determined by their availability. In lowland Britain Goshawks feed especially on pigeons (*Columba* sp.), squirrels (*Sciurus*), rabbits (*Oryctolagus cuniculus*) and crows (*Corvidae* sp.), but no one species tends to be of over-riding importance. By contrast, in the uplands they feed on a smaller variety of mainly open-country species, particularly Red Grouse (*Lagopus lagopus scoticus*) and hares (*Lepus*) (Marquiss & Newton, 1982).

DISTRIBUTION AND POPULATION

Holarctic. Breeds almost throughout continental Europe in good numbers, though it is scarce in Britain. The Goshawk is largely resident, except in northern-most Fenno-Scandia and Russia where some birds apparently move south in some winters. The bird nested in England until the 18th century, and in the Scottish Highlands to about 1880. There was sporadic nesting in England to 1893 (last recorded in Yorkshire) and then up to three pairs nested regularly in Sussex from 1938 to 1951 (Hollom 1957; Newton, 1972). Since 1968 Goshawks have nested annually, the population increasing exponentially with particularly dramatic increases following the peaks in the importation of birds in 1973 and 1975 (Marquiss, 1981). By 1981 over 60 pairs were breeding in 14 dispersed areas of Britain. Thereafter the increase slowed, so that by 1988 there were at least 100 (but probably nearer 200 pairs), with well-established populations in four widely separated regions of Britain. As the Goshawk is resident in Britain, winter and breeding distributions are similar (Marquiss, 1986). Ringed juveniles have rarely been recovered more than 75 km from their birth place (Marquiss & Newton, 1982) so that the sparse records well away from breeding areas could be of continental vagrants now that Goshawks have become abundant in Western Europe (Kalchreuter, 1981; Thissen *et al.*, 1981; Link, 1981), though they could also be of birds recently escaped from captivity.

The current British population is probably derived entirely from imported birds which have escaped from hawk keepers or which have been deliberately released. Apart from the direct evidence of free-living nesting birds carrying leather anklets, jesses or bells, there is considerable circumstantial evidence. Both the geographical distribution and the timing of first breeding records are more consistent with the distribution of falconry activities and known releases than with natural colonization. Moreover, the majority of Goshawks breeding in Britain are larger than those continental birds which one would expect to colonize naturally by immigration. Populations established in Britain in the mid-1970s are of very large individuals compared with those established in the mid-1960s (Marquiss, 1981); this is consistent with a change in the source of imported Goshawks, from central Europe in the mid-1960s to north-eastern Europe (particularly Finland) in the 1970s.

THREATS TO SURVIVAL

Threats include persecution, nest-robbing, and infection by the protozoan parasite *Trichomonas gallinae.*

Goshawks do not have stringent habitat requirements. The only parts of Britain unlikely to support breeding Goshawks are extensive tracts of open country devoid of woodland. Many more areas of Britain are suitable for Goshawks than are occupied at present, and the main restraint on population increases is the rate at which new pairs are recruited. Few birds now escape, or are released to the wild, so that the main source of recruits must be young produced in the wild.

Goshawks in Britain are not adversely affected by persistent pollutants, and they could produce about two to five young per pair per year. This level of production has, however, never been attained because of robbing and persecution (Marquiss & Newton, 1982). Moreover, in some areas many Goshawks are persecuted by gamekeepers (Marquiss, 1981). These birds are not easy to breed in captivity, and the success rate is probably less than that claimed. As demands exceed supply, the prices of these birds become inflated, and this makes nest robbing lucrative and the full protection of wild Goshawks very difficult.

One population of Goshawks in Britain has been found to be prone to the protozoan parasite *Trichomonas gallinae*, which can infect nestlings and usually results in their death from stomatitis around the time of fledging (Cooper & Petty, in press).

CONSERVATION

Despite nest-robbing and persecution, the Goshawk has become firmly established and appears to be spreading. No national conservation measures appear to be necessary. Nesting localities that become well known have to be protected otherwise they are likely to be robbed either by those wanting the young or by egg collectors. Even organized wardening and liaison with landowners, though desirable, can be almost totally ineffective. Breeding sites should therefore be kept secret for as long as possible. More effort should be put into areas where breeding success is low in order to resolve whether this is due to robbing, persecution or poor food supply.

The large, maturing conifer forests in the uplands are likely to offer the security needed by this species, and these forests may well become the stronghold of this species in the future. In this latter habitat, Goshawks commence nesting around the time that the trees are harvestable and due for felling. To avoid continually restricting the felling of nesting areas, it is advisable to identify nest sites, and to retain 4·5 ha of mature timber surrounding them. Goshawks will also readily take to artificial platforms, and these can be used to either attract birds into areas where they have seen prospecting, or to move birds from unsatisfactory sites into new areas. The high pruning of nest trees may also help to minimize disturbance and the theft of eggs and chicks.

REFERENCES

Cooper, J.E. & Petty, S.J. (in press). Trichomoniasis in free-living Goshawk *Accipiter gentilis gentilis* from Great Britain. J. Wildlife Dis.

Glutz von Blotzheim, U.N., Bauer, K. & Bezzel, E. 1971. Handbuch der Vogel Mitteleuropas, Vol. 4. Akademische Verlagsgesellschaft: Frankfurt am Main.

Hollom, P.A.D. 1957. The rare birds of prey, their present status in the British Isles: Goshawk. Brit. Birds 50: 135–136.

Kalchreuter, H. 1981. The Goshawk in Western Europe. *In* Kenward, R.E. & Lindsay, I. (eds). Understanding the Goshawk: 18–27. Oxford: International Association for Falconry and Conservation of Birds of Prey.

Link, H. 1981. Goshawk status in Bavaria. *In* Kenward, R.E. & Lindsay, I. (eds). Understanding the Goshawk: 57–68. Oxford: International Association for Falconry and Conservation of Birds of Prey.

Marquiss, M. 1981. The Goshawk in Britain—its provenance and current status. *In* Kenward, R.E. & Lindsay, I. (eds). Understanding the Goshawk: 43–56. Oxford: International Association for Falconry and Conservation of Birds of Prey.

Marquiss, M. 1986. Goshawk. *In* Lack, P. (ed.). The atlas of wintering birds in Britain and Ireland. Calton: Poyser.

Marquiss, M. & Newton, I. 1982. The Goshawk in Britain. Brit. Birds 75: 243–260.

Newton, I. 1972. Birds of prey in Scotland: some conservation problems. Scot. Birds 7: 5–23.

Opdam, P., Thissen, J., Verschuren, P. & Muskers, G. 1977. Feeding ecology of a population of Goshawks *Accipiter gentilis*. J. Orn. 118: 35–51.

Thissen, J., Muskers, G. & Opdam, P. 1981. Trends in the Dutch Goshawk population. *In* Kenward, R.E. & Lindsay, I. (eds). Understanding the Goshawk: 28–42. Oxford: International Association for Falconry and Conservation of Birds of Prey.

Consultants: M. Marquiss and S.J. Petty

Golden Eagle
Aquila chrysaetos

The Golden Eagle is a breeding resident in Britain in internationally important numbers. There was a marked decrease in numbers and a contraction in range during the 19th century, but there has been a gradual partial recovery since 1945 to an estimated 424 pairs in 1982. This represents about 20% of the total in western Europe. Continued vigilance against illegal killing, particularly by poisoning, is necessary—as well as restrictions on blanket forestry which destroys the Golden Eagle's hunting habitat.

LEGAL STATUS

Protected under Schedule 1 of WCA 1981; Annex 1 of EC Birds Directive; Appendix II of the Berne Convention.

ECOLOGY

In Britain the Golden Eagle is virtually restricted to Scotland where it inhabits hills, mountains, moorland and pine forests. Nest: a bulky platform of twigs and branches, often in a traditional site which is re-used in successive years, on a ledge in a steep cliff or crag, or occasionally in a large tree. Eggs: laid March to April. Clutch: 2 (1–3); one brood. The young fledge from the beginning of July.

Food consists mainly of mammals and birds. In Scotland it consists largely of grouse, hares, rabbits, young sheep and red deer; the last two are taken mainly as carrion. Dead adult sheep and deer are also eaten, especially in winter (Brown & Watson, 1964; Watson et al., 1987).

DISTRIBUTION AND POPULATION

Holarctic. The Golden Eagle is widespread, but rather rare and a local breeder, in much of mainly upland Europe, north-west Africa, Asia and North America. The bird vacates the northern-most parts of its breeding range in winter, but it is otherwise sedentary in Britain and elsewhere (Cramp et al., 1980). In Britain, Golden Eagles formerly occupied mountain areas of Scotland, England and Wales, but persecution connected with the spread of sheep farming, and the attentions of egg and specimen collectors, reduced the population drastically; the breeding population was exterminated in many areas, including all those in Wales and England, by the middle of the 19th century. A reduction in the activities of gamekeepers during the two wars apparently allowed some recovery, and former sites in the Hebrides and south-west Scotland have been recolonized since 1945. Since 1969 breeding has taken place in the Lake District, the first in England for over 100 years.

Estimates of the British population have increased from about 190 pairs in the early 1950s (Nicholson, 1957) and 300 pairs in 1968 (Everett, 1971), to a minimum of 424 pairs occupying home ranges in 1982 (Dennis *et al.*, 1984) — all in Scotland, except one breeding pair in the Lake District.

The 1982 survey revealed 598 known home ranges, and Dennis *et al.* (1984) suggested that in unmolested conditions, and assuming no competition with White-tailed Eagles, the population could reach 600 pairs in Scotland.

THREATS TO SURVIVAL

Threats include poisoning, egg-collection, disturbance by man, and the continuing loss of habitat.

There are substantial and suitable areas where eagles do not breed — especially around the grouse moors of eastern Scotland. Illegal killing, usually by poisoning, still continues on some hunting estates and sheep rearing areas, and this may well account for some of these anomalies.

Egg collecting also remains a problem in some areas, together with desertion of nests due to disturbance by tourists, including bird-watchers.

Chlorinated hydrocarbons, used in sheep dips, caused a serious decline in breeding success in the early 1960s, but this threat has now diminished (Lockie & Ratcliffe, 1964; Lockie *et al.*, 1969).

The major threat now is continuing habitat loss and degradation, due to overgrazing, excessive burning, and blanket forestry resulting in prey scarcity. afforestation in the west and extreme north of Scotland (Watson *et al.*, 1987). Some pairs on the western seaboard presently occupying traditional White-tailed Eagle nest sites may be displaced if numbers of the latter build up, although precise levels cannot yet be predicted.

CONSERVATION

A reduction in grazing levels and the control of burning would help the native upland vegetation recover and support more wild prey for Golden Eagles. Although numbers of eagles may decline if carrion levels decrease following improved husbandry, the anticipated improved breeding success consequent upon recovery of wild prey populations should be welcomed and would lead to a more stable population structure across the range (Watson *et al.*, 1987).

Moves towards an integrated land-use policy in the uplands, and away from massive changes — such as wholesale conversion of sheep walk to blanket-forestry — are essential if the long-term health of the population is to be sustained. In localized areas a sensitive approach towards new tourist developments will be needed if individual pairs are not to be lost. Site safeguard (SSSIs, SPAs) helps, but does not cater adequately for the needs of such widely dispersed species with large hunting ranges. Land-use policy shifts and the use of mechanisms such as ESAs will therefore be especially important.

As with several other birds of prey, continued vigilance against illegal killing and egg collecting, and the imposition of suitably deterring fines when offenders are caught, are vital; a continuation of the existing programmes of education to point out the benefits and desirability of healthy bird-of-prey populations is important.

REFERENCES

Brown, L.H. & Watson, A. 1964. The Golden Eagle in relation to its food supply. Ibis 106: 78–100.
Dennis, R.H., Ellis, P.M., Broad, R.A. & Langslow, D.R. 1984. The status of the Golden Eagle in Britain. Brit. Birds 77: 592–607.
Everett, M.J. 1971. The Golden Eagle survey in Scotland 1964–68. Brit. Birds 64: 49–56.
Lockie, J.D. & Ratcliffe, D.A. 1964. Insecticides and Scottish Golden Eagles. Brit. Birds 57: 89–102.
Lockie, J.D., Ratcliffe, D.A. & Balharry, R. 1969. Breeding success and organo-chlorine residues in Golden Eagles. J. Appl. Ecol. 6: 381–389.
Nicholson, E.M. 1957. The rarer birds of prey, their present status in the British Isles. Brit. Birds 50: 131–135.
Watson, J., Langslow, D.R. & Rae, S.R. 1987. The impact of land-use changes on Golden Eagles in the Scottish Highlands. CSD Report No. 720. Peterborough: Nature Conservancy Council.

Consultant: J. Watson

Osprey
Pandion haliaetus

The Osprey is a rare breeding summer visitor to Britain. It formerly bred throughout Britain but declined through persecution in the 18th and 19th centuries, with the last pair reported breeding in 1916. A small population—53 pairs in 1988—has become established in Scotland since recolonization in 1954 by immigrants from Scandinavia. Encouraging Ospreys to nest in new sites by the provision of artificial nests is considered to be the best way of helping the population to increase.

LEGAL STATUS

Protected under Schedule 1 of WCA 1981; Annex I of EC Birds Directive; Appendix II of the Berne Convention.

ECOLOGY

The Osprey is a migrant breeding species which arrives from Africa in late March to early April and departs between mid-August and mid-September. The typical breeding area in Britain is the Spey Valley of the Highland Region where native Scots Pine forests, freshwater lochs and rivers provide nesting and feeding sites similar to those in Scandinavia. Ospreys now breed in a large part of Scotland, sometimes reasonably close to human habitation, in both freshwater and estuarine areas. Nest: a bulky platform of sticks typically in the crown of a live or dead Scots Pine or conifer tree, rarely a deciduous tree; nesting sites can be occupied for a long period—for example, 30 years in the case of Loch Garten. Eggs: laid mid-April to mid-May. Clutch: 2–3 (1–4); single brood. The young fledge from mid-July to August. The annual production of young has varied between 0·65 and 1·71 fledged young per occupied nest, with an average of 1·31 young per nest. This compares favourably with Scandinavian and North American studies, and is sufficient to ensure an increase in the population.

Out of 397 ringed young, 39 have been recovered dead—principally on the migration route from Scotland to the West African wintering grounds in Senegal, Gambia and Mauritania. Extralimital recoveries of ringed birds have come from Iceland, the Faeroes and Yugoslavia. In the 1970s recoveries were due principally to shooting, but in the recent decade collisions with overhead wires have featured more prominently.

Food consists of live fish of up to 1 kg in weight, caught during the breeding season by the male. Inland prey comprises brown trout, pike, perch and very rarely eels, together with rainbow trout from fish farms; in estuaries the prey consists principally of flounder and occasionally of sea trout—rarely of grey mullet. On migration, Ospreys take a wider range of species.

DISTRIBUTION AND POPULATION

Cosmopolitan. The nominate race, *haliaetus*, breeds in the Palearctic, from Scotland to southern China and Japan, with isolated populations in the Mediterranean, in islands off north-west Africa and in the Red Sea region; other races occur in North America, the Caribbean, south-east Asia and Australia. The bird winters principally in Africa, south and south-east Asia and South America. It was formerly quite common in Scotland, and probably in England—where it last nested in 1840 (Gloucestershire).

The number of Ospreys decreased considerably in the 18th and 19th centuries as a result of interference by man, particularly persecution. After years of shooting and collecting, the population became extinct in 1916 despite landowners' attempts to protect a few remaining nest sites. Then, after a long absence, migrants appeared in Scotland with more regularity in the early 1950s, and a pair nested successfully in 1954 at Loch Garten, rearing two young (Brown & Waterston, 1962). Egg-collecting and disturbance resulted in breeding failures until 1959 since when intensive wardening by the RSPB has produced almost annual success. The population in Scotland was slow to increase (Dennis, 1983). Two pairs nested in 1963, and three in 1966, but the subsequent increase was more rapid: 7 pairs in 1969, 13 in 1972, 20 in 1977, 30 in 1982, 53 in 1988 and 54 in 1989. Not all pairs lay eggs each year, and some pairs are notably more successful than others at producing fledged young.

In Europe there were similar population declines in the last century followed by recolonization in recent decades. The European population is principally in Scandinavia, with about 2,000 pairs in Sweden and 1,000 pairs in Finland. At least two Swedish ringed birds have been identified breeding in Scotland, and recolonization is presumed to have been due to birds of Scandinavian origin. The British population winters in West Africa, with some birds wintering further north on the Mediterranean coast.

In Scotland breeding Ospreys are annually monitored by the RSPB and other ornithologists; details of the breeding biology are collected, as well as behavioural data at Loch Garten, and young Ospreys are ringed and have individually marked colour rings. Annual data are presented in the 'Osprey Newsletter' (produced by the RSPB) and in the Rare Breeding Birds Panel reports.

THREATS TO SURVIVAL

Threats include egg collection, disturbance by man, obstructions (such as power lines), and depletion of fish.

There is no apparent shortage of nest sites, although large areas of commercial plantations rarely have suitably-shaped potential nesting trees.

Fish stocks are probably insufficient in some areas, in quantity and variety of species, to allow Ospreys to breed successfully. This may be part of the reason why they have not yet recolonized the north-west Highlands.

The taking of clutches of eggs by collectors is still a problem, and is one of the principal reasons for nest failures; 6·9% of clutches were illegally taken between 1954 and 1986.

A few nests have been deserted through human disturbance, such as forestry operations, and on at least two occasions by photographers acting illegally. Disturbance can be cumulative, and people should keep well away from occupied Osprey nests.

Natural nesting failures have been due to bad weather: storms and high winds damage or destroy some nests, especially in winter; 2·4% of clutches/broods failed in this way.

Interference by other Ospreys (including bigamy in two cases) can cause failures.

Analysis of addled eggs have generally shown low levels of toxic chemicals, and at present this is not thought to be a problem in Scottish Ospreys.

Collisions with overhead wires have resulted in Ospreys being killed or injured, especially on migration. Birds have also been injured or killed at fish farms by colliding with overhead wires and netting erected to protect the fish from predation. There have been complaints from fish farmers, principally those operating freshwater trout farms, and it is recommended that all fish farms in Osprey areas should be adequately bird-proofed with netting.

Shooting is no longer a threat in Scotland, but it was very disappointing that a young migrant Osprey was shot in Leicestershire in 1985.

As the Osprey is a fish-eating species, acidification of fresh waters—and the subsequent loss of fish stocks—is a potential threat in the future.

CONSERVATION

Public viewing of the Ospreys at Loch Garten has been extremely successful, and well over one million people have visited the RSPB observation post. A similar observation post has been in operation during some years at the Scottish Wildlife Trust reserve at Dunkeld in Perthshire. Public interest and enthusiasm has been a great boost to the conservation of the species; TV, radio, press coverage and the RSPB Osprey film have helped to keep Ospreys in the public eye. The original site at Loch Garten is now a nature reserve, and several pairs of Ospreys are on SSSIs/reserves designated for other purposes. Specific protection of nesting sites by SSSI designation would seem to be unnecessary. Protection has been enhanced by an Osprey guardian scheme organized by the RSPB Highland Office where land-owners, farmers, gamekeepers and naturalists have been encouraged to protect Ospreys in their areas, aided by RSPB staff. This has been backed up by an annual 'Osprey Newsletter' sent to all helpers.

The prevention of nest robberies is still a major task, and, in addition to rebuilding damaged nests, increasing effort (since 1974) has gone into building artificial eyries in safe locations. More effort has gone into these activities in recent years because it has been demonstrated that it can help to spread the range of an increasing population. It is an important way of establishing Ospreys in new areas, in safe locations away from public pressure and in places with good fish stocks. Hopefully these activities—as well as continuing high production of young—will lead to recolonization throughout the original range of the species.

A potential concern is the availability of wild fish stocks. In some areas it is suggested that wild brown trout stocks have declined for a variety of reasons, and this could lead to impoverished food supplies for Ospreys. Pike have been eradicated from at least one loch in the Loch Garten area, and this has led to a loss of choice to hunting Ospreys. Stocked lochs and fish farms are attractive to Ospreys, but it is considered important that fish farms be adequately bird-proofed and that no artificial eyries be erected in their vicinity. The major potential fishery for Ospreys is in estuarine and coastal waters where food supplies, especially flat fish in shallow waters, appear to be plentiful.

REFERENCES

BROWN, P. & WATERSTON, G. 1962. The return of the Osprey. London: Collins.
DENNIS, R.H. 1983. Population studies and conservation of Ospreys in Scotland. *In* Bird, D.M. (ed.) Biology and management of Bald Eagles and Ospreys: 207–214. Montreal: Macdonald Raptor Research Centre of McGill University and Raptor Research Foundation.
DENNIS, R.H. 1987. Osprey Recolonisation in RSPB. Conservation Rev. 1: 88–90.

Consultant: R.H. Dennis

Merlin
Falco columbarius

The Merlin is of special concern; it is one of the few raptors which are declining in numbers in Britain, locally to a considerable extent. Habitat loss is the major problem, but toxic chemical contamination may remain a threat. Conservation will be achieved mainly by promotion of mechanisms that protect heather-dominated moorland on a wide scale.

LEGAL STATUS

Protected under Schedule 1 of WCA 1981; Annex 1 of EC Birds Directive; Appendix II of the Berne Convention.

ECOLOGY

Merlins require open ground for hunting. Judged by nesting densities, dry heather moors are preferred to grass-dominated sheep walks (Bibby & Nattrass, 1986). In Wales, nesting success was also higher on heather moorland (Bibby, 1986). In Northumbria, however, this was not the case; tree nests which are more frequent on sheep walks were more successful (Newton et al., 1986).

Nest: may be a scrape on the ground in heather, or on rocky bluffs, or in old stick nests of crows in trees. Some pairs nest well into woodland, including conifer plantations, but always with open moorland nearby. There has been a recent trend towards more nesting in conifers in Wales and Northumbria. Eggs: laid late April or May. Clutch: 3–5, single brooded, but early egg losses are sometimes replaced.

Food consists almost exclusively of small birds from open country, though mammals and large insects are occasionally taken (Bibby, 1987; Newton et al., 1984; Watson, 1979).

In winter, birds move to lower ground where they hunt over open farmland and coastal habitats. Winter roosts may be communal and are often shared with Hen Harriers.

DISTRIBUTION AND POPULATION

Holarctic. The bird breeds in North America, Iceland, Ireland, Britain, Fenno-Scandia and the Baltic states eastwards across Russia. It is a resident or short-range migrant in the west, but Scandinavian and Russian populations move south to winter in southern Europe, North Africa and southern Asia.

In Britain, the Merlin is still widely but thinly scattered in moorland areas from the south-west to Wales, northern England and Scotland. Wintering birds from Britain are augmented by some from Iceland and are widely scattered throughout lowland Britain.

Merlins were formerly more numerous throughout the British range, but widespread declines throughout the present century accelerated from about 1950 and are still continuing, in some cases alarmingly. The first detailed enumeration of this bird in the period 1983–84 estimated a total of 550–650 pairs (Bibby & Nattrass, 1986). In the Peak District, nesting was quite common until the 1950s but had declined by 90% by the 1970s (Newton et al., 1981). Numbers in Wales roughly halved in the decade following the early 1970s (Bibby, 1986; Roberts & Green, 1983). In Northumbria, numbers of nests fell from 33 in 1974 to 15 in 1983. In Orkney, a drop from about 25 pairs to below 5 occurred from about 1975 (Newton et al., 1978, 1986).

Threats include loss of habitat, the effects of toxic chemicals, and disturbance by man.

Loss of habitat through conversion of heather moorland to grassland—by re-seeding, or heavy grazing by sheep—or to forestry are the main causes for concern. In parts of the range, such as the South West, south Wales, the southern Pennines or the Lake District, this process has gone far enough to bring the species close to local extinction.

Merlins were adversely affected by organochlorine contamination at the same time as the better documented Peregrine and Sparrowhawk (Newton, 1973). They show no signs of having recovered in numbers since, although contamination by these chemicals is probably now below a level which might cause high mortality or breeding failures (Newton et al., 1982).

Mercury contamination may be a problem in the northern islands, as eggs from Orkney, Shetland and possibly the Hebrides have high enough mercury loadings to be a cause for concern.

Nesting success in recent years has not been high, with failure rates commonly up to 50%. Causes of failure are poorly known. Predation has been suggested as a possibility, but there is also reason to suspect that toxic chemical contamination may be involved. The better success of tree nests in Northumbria suggests that predation may be an important factor for ground nesters.

Merlins can be disturbed by humans, and some nests are lost to egg collectors or falconers. Such factors might locally be limiting in accessible and well-known sites, but they are most unlikely to be sufficient to limit the population.

Moorland sites have been scheduled as SSSI, and a small number have been acquired as reserves, but only about 10% of the population is protected in this way. Some Merlins occur in ESAs, though at the moment none of these are in the best areas. Such measures cover only relatively few pairs, and only a small proportion of the population of a widely and thinly dispersed bird. Further consideration should be given to site scheduling to guard against future land-use changes, particularly in the Pennines and the Grampian Region.

Means of protecting heather moorland, especially in the more productive areas which coincide with the best grouse moors, are required. If protection on a wider scale from forestry, or from over-grazing, is to be achieved careful consideration will be needed to influence the future economics of forestry, upland agriculture, grouse shooting and recreation. As long as forestry and agriculture are determined principally by state support, they are susceptible to examination and possible change.

Curtailment of the use of persistent organochlorine pesticides was undoubtedly a successful measure for other birds of prey. Merlins must have benefitted too, but they still face other threats. Further investigation and appropriate subsequent action is needed on toxic chemical contamination, especially with respect to mercury in the north.

A few pairs have been encouraged to breed in artificial stick nests which might restrict losses to human and natural predators and locally allow sites to be protected against hazards such as felling in forests.

The Merlin has until recently been rather little studied and monitored, and continued attention is needed.

REFERENCES

BIBBY, C.J. 1986. Merlins in Wales: site occupancy and breeding in relation to vegetation. J. Appl. Ecol. 23: 1–12.

BIBBY, C.J. 1987. Foods of breeding Merlins *Falco columbarius* in Wales. Bird Study 34: 64–70.

BIBBY, C.J. & NATTRASS, M. 1986. Breeding status of the merlin in Britain. Brit. Birds 79: 170–185.

NEWTON, I. 1973. Egg breakage and breeding failure in British Merlins. Bird Study 20: 241–244.

NEWTON, I., MEEK, E.R. & LITTLE, B. 1978. Breeding ecology of the Merlin in Northumberland. Brit. Birds 71: 378–398.

NEWTON, I., ROBSON, J.E. & YALDEN, D.W. 1981. Decline of the merlin in the Peak District. Bird Study 28: 225–234.

NEWTON, I., BOGAN, J., MEEK, E.R. & LITTLE, B. 1982. Organochlorine compounds and shell thinning in British Merlins *Falco columbarius*. Ibis 124: 328–335.

NEWTON, I., MEEK, E.R. & LITTLE, B. 1984. Breeding season foods of merlins *Falco columbarius* in Northumbria. Bird Study 31: 49–56.

NEWTON, I., MEEK, E.R. & LITTLE, B. 1986. Population and breeding of Northumbrian merlins. Brit. Birds 79: 155–170.

ROBERTS, J.L. & GREEN, D. 1983. Breeding failure and decline of merlins on a north Wales moor. Bird Study 30: 193–200.

WATSON, J. 1979. Food of merlins nesting in young conifer forests. Bird Study 26: 253–258.

Peregrine

Falco peregrinus

The Peregrine is a breeding resident which is found in Britain in internationally important numbers. The fortunes of the Peregrine have fluctuated in the last 50 years, with the major decline in the population occurring in 1957–1963 through the use of persistent organochlorine pesticides in agriculture. Following controls over pesticide use, and a campaign of protection and education, numbers have risen to over 900 pairs—which is at, or above, the pre-war level. This represents about 25–30% of the breeding population in western Europe. Threats from pesticides are now mostly over, but the problems of illegal killing and the theft of eggs and chicks still continue.

LEGAL STATUS

Protected under Schedule 1 of WCA 1981; Annex 1 of EC Birds Directive; Appendix II of the Berne Convention; Annex 1 of CITES.

ECOLOGY

The Peregrine breeds mainly in coastal, moorland or mountain terrain with undisturbed cliffs or crags which provide a nest site. Nest: a shallow scrape in the earth, or the nest of another species, on a ledge or mountain crag, quarry or sea cliff, occasionally on ruins, other man-made structures, or even on the ground; tree nesting has occurred twice recently. Eggs: laid from mid-March to May. Clutch: 3–4 (2–6); one brood. The young fledge from the end of May.

Food consists mainly of birds, especially domestic (including feral) pigeons also starlings, crows, thrushes, waders, auks, gulls, terns, ducks and grouse (Cramp *et al.*, 1980).

DISTRIBUTION AND POPULATION

Cosmopolitan. In the west Palearctic the Peregrine breeds in suitable habitats from the North African coasts of the western Mediterranean north to Scandinavia—but not in the Faeroes, Iceland or the Arctic islands; it vacates northern parts of its breeding range in the winter, but is otherwise sedentary (including in Britain) or a partial migrant.

Limited evidence suggests that human persecution in Britain during the 19th and 20th centuries had no serious effect on the population as a whole and that, because of habitat limitation, numbers were probably never much higher, even in pre-history, than the almost 900 pairs in the UK (including 54 pairs in Northern Ireland) estimated during 1930–39. The military use of homing pigeons during the 1939–45 war prompted a programme of Peregrine control by the Air Ministry, and over 600 adults were shot and many nests and eggs destroyed. By 1945 the English Peregrine population had been reduced to about 48% of the 1939 level. Numbers were virtually restored by 1955, except in a few parts of southern England (Ratcliffe, 1980).

During the late 1950s and the early 1960s, surveys revealed a rapid and alarming decline in the numbers of Peregrines in Britain, combined with a marked reduction in breeding success among the population which remained. The cause was traced to the agricultural use of organochlorine pesticides which had accumulated in Peregrines via their prey. By 1963 the situation was at its worst, with numbers down to about 360 pairs (44% of the 1939 level) and only 16% of pre-war territories producing young. Voluntary bans on the use of these chemicals resulted in a marked recovery: by 1971 numbers were at 54% of the 1939 figure, with 25% rearing young, and a sample census in 1975 suggested a further increase to about 420 pairs, 60% of the 1939 level (Ratcliffe, 1972). By 1981 the population had recovered to within 90% of the 1930–39 level, with approximately 730 breeding pairs (Ratcliffe, 1984), and by 1985 it had exceeded that level—with an estimated 880–900 pairs breeding. Similar declines in the 1960s, attributable to organochlorine pesticides, were noted elsewhere—especially in Europe and North America. For example, in western Europe there were only about 150 pairs in France in 1983 (formerly 300–500), 40–50 pairs in West Germany (formerly 380–410) and none in Belgium (formerly about 35 pairs) (Newton & Chancellor, 1985). Since then, in parallel to the situation in Britain, numbers have increased. In the case of some countries (eg, France) this is to their former levels, while in others (eg, Germany) to less than half the previous levels (Newton & Chancellor, 1985); in some regions (eg, Scandinavia) the Peregrine continues to be a very rare bird.

THREATS TO SURVIVAL

Threats include the continuing effects of toxic chemicals, egg collection and persecution.

The serious dangers associated with the use of organochlorine pesticides have been reduced, and legislation has been introduced, giving statutory control on their use. However, there appears to be a residual marine pollution effect (expressed notably in PCB levels but possibly involving other pollutant residues) preventing the recovery of Peregrines in coastal areas of northern Scotland and associated islands (Ratcliffe, 1980).

Other threats to local populations include the continuing desire among many to keep birds of prey in captivity (which results in both egg and chick taking); egg collecting; shooting or nest destruction on some grouse moors; persecution by racing pigeon fanciers; and occasionally disturbance by rock climbers. Monitoring by the RSPB has shown that an average of 45 Peregrine eyries are known to have been robbed (of eggs or young) in each of the last nine years. The figures are given in the table below.

Peregrine: number of thefts from eyries between 1980 and 1988

1980	1981	1982	1983	1984	1985	1986	1987	1988
28	34	44	76	85	32	27	42	41

In some areas, eg, western Scotland, the lack of wild prey caused by habitat degradation is reflected in low breeding density. However, many areas are now 'saturated', and nesting habitat demands are becoming less specialized, resulting in the use of 'walk-in' ground nests and trees.

CONSERVATION

Regular surveys (for occupancy and productivity) and analysis of addled or deserted eggs are necessary to monitor the population status and any continuing effects of chemical pollutants. Appropriate action could then be pursued via the Food and Environment Protection Act or the Pesticide Safety Precaution Scheme (PSPS). Censuses of the whole population should continue at 10-year intervals under the aegis of the NCC, BTO and RSPB.

Continued vigilance against illegal killing and the taking of eggs and young is important, as is the imposition of suitably deterrent fines when offenders are caught. As Peregrines are one of the most favoured birds for falconry, and can fetch high prices, enforcement to prevent illegal trading and smuggling is essential. In this respect the registration of Birds of Prey in captivity (a statutory requirement under the Wildlife and Countryside Act, 1981) has an important role to play, but the regulations must be enforced to prevent wild birds being filtered into the system as 'captive-bred'.

Site safeguard action, such as the provision of reserves, cannot ensure the conservation of the bird. It is considered unwise to publish nest sites unless they are extremely well known or are guarded full time (such as at a public-viewing project). The need for widespread protection by guarding some nest sites is still considered to be necessary in certain districts in order to discourage systematic robbing of eyries.

The continuation of education programmes to increase awareness of the wildlife heritage value of Peregrines, and the desirability of maintaining healthy bird-of-prey populations, should continue to be a long-term objective.

REFERENCES

NEWTON, I. & CHANCELLOR, R.D. (eds) 1985. Conservation studies on raptors. ICBP technical publication No. 55.
RATCLIFFE, D.A. 1972. The Peregrine population in 1971. Bird Study 19: 117–156.
RATCLIFFE, D.A. 1980. The Peregrine Falcon. Calton: Poyser.
RATCLIFFE, D.A. 1984. The Peregrine breeding population of the United Kingdom in 1981. Bird Study 31: 1–18.

Consultant: D.A. Ratcliffe

Red Grouse
Lagopus lagopus

The Red Grouse was once classed as a separate species, *L. scoticus*, but is now classified as a distinct endemic sub-species of the Willow Grouse—and is therefore of international importance. The bird has declined in Britain since the 1930s, and the population in 1976 was estimated to be less than 500,000 pairs. Further sharp declines in the late 1970s have been attributed to unusually low cyclic troughs following years of high breeding success. The loss of preferred habitat to agricultural intensification, afforestation and poor (or lack of) moorland management have exacerbated the problem. Recent evidence shows that high parasitic burdens are also responsible for reduced breeding success in some areas.

LEGAL STATUS

Protected under the Game Acts (open season: 12 August–10 December); Annex III/1 of EC Birds Directive; Appendix III of the Berne Convention.

ECOLOGY

The Red Grouse breeds on open, treeless moorland dominated by heather (*Calluna vulgaris*), or by crowberry (*Empetrum nigrum*) and bilberry (*Vaccinicum myrtillus*) if heather is scarce or absent. Nest: a shallow scrape lined with vegetation or peat, usually concealed in old heather. Eggs: laid between March and early June, but mostly in late April or early May. Clutch: 6–9 (2–17); one brood, but readily re-lays if the first clutch is lost early in incubation. An average of 0–4 young fledge per pair; the young are independent by early August. Breeding success is very variable between years.

Food consists mostly of the young growth of heather and bilberry, but inflorescences of cotton grass (*Eriophorum vaginatum*) are also taken in the spring, while berries, grass and sedge seeds are eaten in the summer and autumn. Young chicks eat protein-rich insects and *Polytrichum* moss capsules in their first 10 days of life.

In Britain Red Grouse males compete for territory from September–October onwards. The number of territories established then determines the density of the breeding population in the following season. Most of the males which fail to obtain or hold a territory disappear over winter. There is evidence that such birds are forced into marginal habitats where they die of starvation, disease or predation (Jenkins, Watson & Miller, 1967).

DISTRIBUTION AND POPULATION

Holarctic. The distinct sub-species *L. l. scoticus* is confined to Scotland, northern and south-west England, Wales and Ireland. Other sub-species are found eastwards across Scandinavia (except southern Sweden) and Estonia, through most of northern USSR, and south, in Asia, to Kazakhstan, the Kirgiz steppes and Mongolia; there are also sub-species in the Aleutian Islands, in Alaska and in northern Canada. Sixteen sub-species are recognized. *L. l. scoticus* is resident, but some sub-species from the northern tundra move south to winter within the range.

In Britain and Ireland, the birds are sedentary, rarely moving more than a few kilometres; males attempt to establish territories on the same ground they were reared upon (Lance, 1978).

The highest densities of these birds occur in northern England and eastern Scotland; densities decline further north and west. Population densities vary from two to three pairs per square kilometre in western Ireland and Scotland to about 100 pairs per square kilometre in the east (Watson, 1986).

The Red Grouse was re-introduced to Dartmoor and Exmoor in 1915–16 after an earlier attempt in 1820 had failed. The Devon population has never been high, and in the mid-1980s numbers on Exmoor were down to a few pairs; on Dartmoor it breeds in small numbers and is regularly seen in about 20 localities.

In Wales, northern England and Scotland, long-term population trends have been estimated by shooting-bag returns and by research carried out by ITE and the Game Conservancy. In 1911 the number of birds shot in mainland Britain was approximately 2,500,000 (Leslie, 1911). In 1983 this figure was estimated at 260,000–660,000 (Harradine, 1983). The number of birds fluctuates considerably, and many populations show periodic cycles of abundance every six to seven years (though the cycle can be as short as four to five years) (Watson, 1986; Hudson, 1986).

Annual shooting-bag returns have indicated several phased declines since the mid-1930s, with only one period of sustained increase throughout Britain as a whole. By 1985 the third sharp decline in the last 20 years had halted, and numbers increased on many moors—but bag returns were still below the level of 30 years ago (Rands & Tapper, 1986). In Scotland a gradual and continuing decline was noted in the early 1900s, and by the early 1970s shooting bags were 10% of what they had been in the early 1900s (Thom, 1985); however, there were signs of an upturn in numbers in the early 1980s. Similar population fluctuations are known to occur across the entire range. In north Norway, peak spring densities of between 54 and 116 birds per square kilometre have been recorded (Jenkins, Watson & Miller, 1967), whilst, in July, densities of up to 750 adults and first-year birds per square kilometre are not unknown (Hudson & Watson, 1985).

There are a few estimates of populations for other countries—eg, Sweden has approximately 200,000 pairs, while in Finland the population is about 110,000 pairs, but is known to be declining.

THREATS TO SURVIVAL

The principal threat is the loss of suitable moorland due to agricultural intensification, afforestation and a decline in the traditional methods of moorland management associated with shooting. In the 19th century, strip burning of heather (to promote young growth and to prevent invasion of scrub) and keepering (to minimize predation) resulted in huge increases in grouse numbers. Nowadays, afforestation of moorlands with non-native conifers, promoted by government grants and (formerly) tax concessions, has become more economically attractive than game management. Elsewhere, high stocking levels of sheep, or grazing by red deer, have converted heather to grass moorlands which are unsuitable for Red Grouse. Moorland has also been lost due to agricultural improvement to provide pasture, usually for sheep.

Predation of incubating birds and nests by foxes and crows can reduce breeding productivity if it is not controlled. Winter predation of full-grown birds may be unimportant if the majority of birds taken are non-territorial and therefore not likely to breed the following season. The impact of predators on grouse populations at different densities is unclear.

CONSERVATION

The main conservation requirement is a reduction in grazing pressure, especially to prevent sheep from congregating on local areas where trampling results in total destruction of heather and leads to replacement by grasses.

Maintenance of a mosaic, predominantly of heather with some grassland by controlled rotational burning to provide areas of both old and new heather, and action to prevent the spread of bracken and grass, would benefit not only Red Grouse but also other upland breeding birds such as the Golden Plover and Merlin.

Currently, much management effort goes into predator control by legal and illegal methods. The full effects of this are unknown, but several ground-nesting species could benefit, while some legally protected species may be adversely affected. Steps should be taken to find legal and acceptable ways of controlling crows and foxes without harming protected birds of prey in particular.

Curtailment of afforestation on key moorland areas would enable more habitat to survive.

The treatment of birds suffering from parasitic worms and tick-borne diseases may be helpful in some localities.

Several large areas of grouse moorland lie within SSSIs and NNRs which were established for reasons other than their grouse populations. Other areas lie within National Parks—eg, the North Yorkshire Moors, the Derbyshire Dales and the Yorkshire Dales. However, such designation may not in itself prevent adverse changes in the vegetation, due to lack of proper management. Bringing the rateable treatment of grouse moors into line with land used for agricultural or forestry purposes may help to stem the loss of heather moorland.

Continuing research, in this country and abroad, into the causes of the fluctuations, aimed at the development of conservation methods, should shed more light on the factors influencing the population of Red Grouse.

REFERENCES

HARRADINE, J. 1983. Sport in the United Kingdom. *In* Leeuwenberg, F. & Hepburn, I. (eds). Proceedings of the International Union of Game Biologists Working Group on Game Statistics 63–83. Zoetermeer, the Netherlands.
HUDSON, P. 1986. Red Grouse: the biology and management of a wild game bird. Fordingbridge: The Game Conservancy.
HUDSON, P. & WATSON, A. 1985. The Red Grouse. Biologist 32: 13–18.
JENKINS, D., WATSON, A. & MILLER, G.R. 1967. Population fluctuations in the Red Grouse *Lagopus lagopus scoticus*. J. Anim. Ecol. 36: 97–122.
LANCE, A.N. 1978. Survival and recruitment success of individual young cock Red Grouse *Lagopus l. scoticus* tracked by radio-telemetry. Ibis 120: 369–378.
LESLIE, A.S. (ed.) 1911. The value of grouse shootings in Great Britain. The grouse in health and in disease, 491–502. London: Smith, Elder & Co.
RANDS, M. & TAPPER, S. 1986. The National Game Census: 1985/6 season. The Game Conservancy Annual Review No. 17 (1985).
THOM, V. 1985. Birds in Scotland. Calton: Poyser.

Consultant: P.J. Hudson

Black Grouse

Tetrao tetrix

The Black Grouse is declining over much of its range in Europe, but it is relatively stable in Scotland and Wales, though threatened in England. Loss of habitat, resulting in fragmentation of populations, represents a serious threat. Black Grouse would be favoured by the preservation of existing habitat and by the sympathetic management of forestry plantations and adjacent moorland. Research is needed to identify the species requirements in non-forest habitats in northern England.

LEGAL STATUS

Protected under the Game Acts (close season: 11 December–19 August); Annex II/2 of EC Directive; Appendix III of the Berne Convention.

ECOLOGY

The Black Grouse is a sedentary bird which occupies a mosaic of vegetation types of which birch (*Betula*) scrub, heather (*Calluna vulgaris*) and bilberry (*Vaccinium myrtillus*) are the most important. Groups of males indulge in complex communal displays (leks) in the early morning (to establish a hierarchy) at traditional sites. Nest: a shallow scrape lined with grass or moss, usually concealed by rushes, bracken, bilberry or heather or by a low branch or a young tree; exceptionally, it makes use of an old nest of other birds. Several females may nest in the vicinity of the lek. Eggs: laid in late April to early June. Clutch: 6–11 (4–15, varies latitudinally); usually one brood. The young are precocial; they can fly at two weeks, but are not fully independent for two to three months (Johnsgard, 1983).

Food consists predominantly of plants, but is geographically and seasonally variable—depending on availability or accessibility (snow cover); heather, bilberry and birch dominate. In spring, food consists almost exclusively of the flowering tips of cotton grass or the buds of pines and larch. In summer and autumn berries of bilberry and crowberry are taken, while in winter it lives mostly on the shoots of heather and bilberry. The bird may also take grain from stock feed, or from artificial feeders placed near leks. During the first few weeks of life the chicks are mainly fed on invertebrates (Picozzi, 1986; Cayford, Tyler & Macintosh-Williams, 1989).

DISTRIBUTION AND POPULATION

Palearctic. In Britain, breeds locally in northern England; it is widespread in Scotland but scattered in Wales. Outside Britain breeding occurs in Scandinavia and Poland east through the USSR, north of 50°N to the Kirgiz steppes, in the Tien Shan range, including north-western Mongolia and the Chinese Turkestan mountains, and north to the Kolyma, Lena and Ussuriland (Vaurie, 1965). The bird occurs in fragmented areas throughout Europe. It is all but extinct in Luxembourg and Rumania, and there are less than 100 birds in Denmark. Populations are declining in the French and Austrian lowlands, in Poland, in East and West Germany, and in the Netherlands—where numbers have fallen from about 5,000 males in the 1940s to 77 males in 1986. Populations are relatively stable in the Franco-Austrian alpine area, in Scotland and in Fenno-Scandia where densities are highest [Cayford, in press (a)]. It is mainly resident in Europe though seasonal migrations of up to 300 km have been recorded in the USSR. Males are more site faithful than females. Little is known about the dispersal of immatures. Chicks may move several hundred metres in their first few days in search of food.

The Black Grouse has declined considerably in England over the last 100 years.

It was formerly widespread in south-west England and in the east to Lincolnshire and Norfolk. It is now virtually extinct in Devon, Cornwall and Somerset, and less than 20 males remain in the Peak District (Yalden, 1986). In northern England, from north Yorkshire to Cumbria, the population is resident and has undergone some fluctuation; at present it is thought to be stable in the east whilst declining again in the west.

The population in Wales has partially recovered from the decline in the early years of this century when it became extinct in Hereford, Glamorgan, Monmouth and Flint; the number of males estimated in 1986 was 264–300 (Grove *et al.*, 1988), with numbers remaining stable in the core area (Cayford, Tyler & Macintosh-Williams, 1989). The bird has increased since the late 1940s, and has established itself in most of central and northern Wales largely through expansion into young conifer plantations (Cayford & Hope Jones, 1989).

In Scotland populations have shown both short- and long-term fluctuations (on the continent short-term population fluctuations parallel those of small mammals which represent alternative prey for the main predatory species), but are now relatively stable. A considerable decline has been seen during the first half of this century, but since the mid-1950s there have been local increases. Recolonization is apparent in recently afforested areas and may account for local population increases in Caithness and Sutherland and in the Inner Hebrides (Thom, 1986).

The British population was estimated by Parslow to be between 10,000 and 100,000 pairs. Sharrock (1976) and Picozzi (1986) considered the true figure to lie well within the lower half of this range.

THREATS TO SURVIVAL

Threats include loss of habitat, fragmentation of habitat with resulting isolation of populations, egg and chick predation, disturbance, shooting pressure, and cold, wet weather during the fledging period. Reasons for declines are not well understood or documented, but predation, human interference, hunting and particularly loss of habitat have been implicated.

In Britain and Europe, intensification of agriculture has drastically altered habitats formerly occupied by the Black Grouse. Sheep-grazing at high stocking densities has been a major contributor to the destruction of birch scrub and heather moorland which are the favoured habitats. Agricultural subsidies have encouraged the switch from rough-grazing to 'improved' pasture in the uplands, through drainage, re-seeding and the use of fertilizers. In Britain, where upland afforestation has expanded as a result of Government policy, Black Grouse utilize young plantations and clear-felled areas with a well-developed shrub layer that includes heather and bilberry for the period (10–20 years) prior to canopy closure (Cayford, Tyler & Macintosh-Williams, 1989). Dense forest stands are avoided, which suggests that the Black Grouse will benefit from afforestation in the long term only if efforts are made to preserve areas of suitable habitat within or close to plantations (Cayford & Bayes, 1989; Cayford & Hope Jones, 1989).

Displaying cocks are shot on leks in central Europe. Shooting dominant males could alter the social structure on leks and adversely affect breeding success. The effects of hunting need urgent review.

Changes in land-use can result in a shift in the relative abundances of predators and prey. The contribution which predators make to egg and chick losses needs to be researched in Britain.

The disturbance of males at leks, and of incubating hens, could be locally important, but it is probably not a serious threat in Britain at present.

CONSERVATION

Black Grouse would be favoured by the preservation and creation of suitable habitat, controls on hunting and predators, management agreements with land-owners (particularly foresters), and an active programme of research to produce realistic management proposals and to monitor the effectiveness of experimental manipulations [Cayford, in press (a & b)].

Only in the last five years have conservation organizations focused on the status of the Black Grouse in Britain. Its rapid decline in England, the contraction of its range northwards, and the lack of information on its numbers, distribution and general biology have brought about this change.

Enough is known about the general habitat requirements of the Black Grouse to make some well-informed recommendations for management in areas where populations are declining. Any habitat manipulations must be carefully moni-tored, and comparisons must be made with controls to measure the effectiveness of individual treatments.

In the short term, a reduction in grazing pressure and the use of herbicides, promoting young growth of heather and bilberry by mowing or burning, preser-vation of damp insect-rich flushes close to leks, placing a voluntary ban on shooting, and limiting public access to leking areas in spring, may prove beneficial.

In the longer term, more research is needed on the detailed habitat require-ments of these birds, their minimum area requirements, the relationship between productivity and recruitment, and the effects of predation and shooting on population dynamics.

In commercial forests, emphasis must be placed on maintaining numbers by making Black Grouse management an integral part of forestry practice. This would entail preservation of semi-natural habitats within forests, maintaining wide open stream margins, unplanted rocky outcrops, rides and road-side verges, and planting clumps of larch or rowan along the edge of forests while encouraging the growth of bilberry and heather in clear-felled areas and young plantations (Cayford & Bayes, 1989; Cayford, Tyler & Macintosh-Williams, 1989).

In Scotland, the high densities of Black Grouse in certain areas provide an opportunity for some large-scale experimental trials and research aimed at quantifying the factors which both limit and regulate population density. A detailed statistical analysis of game-bag records in relation to land-use has been proposed (Picozzi, 1986), but this remains to be carried out. A similar use of forestry records and other vegetation and land-use data could help to identify the critical factors which limit the birds' distribution and density, and provide an alternative route into management.

For populations in decline, the emphasis must be on the maintenance of numbers through a co-ordinated programme of research and habitat manage-ment. In some cases, biological solutions may prove to be less effective than tackling the socio-economic/political factors which are the cause of changes in habitat; both approaches must have their place in a coherent and effective conservation strategy.

REFERENCES

CAYFORD, J.T. (in press) (a). Summary of an international workshop on black grouse: Lam 1987. *In* Hudson, P.J. & Lovel, T.W.I. (eds). Proceedings of the IVth International Grouse Symposium, 1987. Reading: World Pheasant Association.

CAYFORD, J.T. (in press) (b). Developing a management programme for the conservation of black grouse (*Tetrao tetrix*) in commercial forests in Wales. *In* Hudson, P.J. & Lovel, T.W.I. (eds). Proceedings of the IVth International Grouse Symposium, 1987. Reading: World Pheasant Association.

CAYFORD, J.T. & BAYES, K. (1989). Black Grouse and Forestry. RSPB Advisory Literature. Sandy: RSPB.

CAYFORD, J.T. & HOPE JONES, P. (1989). Black grouse in Wales. RSPB Conservation Review 1989. Sandy: RSPB.

CAYFORD, J.T., TYLER, G. & MACINTOSH-WILLIAMS, L. (1989). The ecology and management of black grouse in conifer forests in Wales. RSPB Research Report. Sandy: RSPB.

GROVE, S.J., HOPE JONES, P., MALKINSON, A.R., THOMAS, D.H. & WILLIAMS, I. (1988). Black grouse in Wales, spring 1986. Brit. Birds 81: 2–9.

JOHNSGARD, P.A. (1983). Grouse of the World. London: Croom Helm.

PICOZZI, N. (1986). Black grouse research in N.E. Scotland. ITE Report to the World Pheasant Association.

THOM, V.M. (1986). Birds in Scotland. Calton: Poyser.

VAURIE, C. (1965). The birds of the palearctic fauna (non-passeriformes). London: Witherby.

YALDEN, D.W. (1986). The further decline of the black grouse in the Peak District 1975–1985. Naturalist 111: 3–8.

Consultant: J.T. Cayford

Capercaillie

Tetrao urogallus

The Capercaillie is a localized breeder which is markedly decreasing in numbers. The original population in Britain was restricted to Scotland and northern England, and the bird eventually became extinct in the mid-18th century;

however, it was successfully re-introduced into Perthshire in 1837–38, and subsequently into five other counties. It has since spread throughout east and central Scotland. It has undergone some fluctuations: decreases in the early 20th century, in inter-war years, and more recently—and markedly—in the late 1970s/early 1980s; this has been balanced by a slight increase in some areas since 1950. Loss of habitat through the felling of old Scots Pine forests, over-shooting, and adverse climatic conditions, are probably the main reasons for the population decline.

LEGAL STATUS

Protected under Schedule 2, Part 1 of WCA 1981 (close season: 1 February–30 September); Annex 1 of EC Birds Directive; Appendix III of the Berne Convention.

ECOLOGY

The Capercaillie is a bird of open mature pinewoods on hills and valleys with an undergrowth of heather (*Calluna vulgaris* and *Erica* sp.) and bilberry (*Vaccinium myrtillus*). Nest: a shallow, lined scrape, usually in thick cover at the foot of a tree between exposed roots; those in new plantations are often exposed, frequently in mature heather or bilberry, or, exceptionally, in the old nests of other birds some 3–5 m up in a tree. Although the bird is solitary, several males gather at traditional sites to communally display (lek) to females and several females may lay within the general vicinity of the lek. Eggs: laid mid-April to early July. Clutch: 7–11 (4–15); one brood. The young fledge by mid-June to late July; they are full-grown at 3 months, but are capable of flight after 2–3 weeks.

Food in winter consists almost entirely of needles and shoots of the Scots Pine (*Pinus sylvestris*), whilst in summer and autumn the bird may take leaves, stems and berries of the bilberry, crowberry (*Empetrum nigrum*), cow-wheat (*Melampyrum* sp.), cloudberry (*Rubus chamaemorus*), sedges (*Scirpus* sp.), horsetails (*Equisetum* sp.), cottongrass (*Eriophorum* sp.), moss, and of deciduous trees, as well as grain lying about in fields. Insects are taken by the young chicks during their first few weeks of life.

DISTRIBUTION AND POPULATION

Palearctic. Capercaillies breed locally in Scotland (though the numbers here make up only a small part of the world population), in the Cantabrian mountains of northern Spain, in Aragon and Navarre, in the Catalan Pyrenees of Spain and France, and discontinuously through eastern France, Luxembourg, Belgium, Germany, Poland, Czechoslovakia and Hungary; birds are continuously distributed through the Alps, from the Jura and Vosges ranges through Switzerland, Austria and south-east through central Yugoslavia to northern Albania and western and central Bulgaria, and there are further isolated populations in central Rumania and northern Poland. Also occurs in Scandinavia from western and central Norway east to Finland and the USSR south of 20°N and north of about 52°N to the ranges south and east of Lake Baikal, a distribution that closely matches the range of the Scots Pine. Capercaillies are resident and virtually sedentary in Scotland; the birds in Europe and the USSR commonly move up to 25 km (Koivisto, 1956, 1963). The Capercaillie is not usually affected by heavy winter snowfalls as food in the treetops is largely unaffected, but some long-distance movements of 1,000 km have been recorded in Sweden (Cramp *et al.*, 1980).

In England, the Capercaillie became extinct in the 17th century, and in Scotland and Ireland the last of the indigenous stock died out about a hundred years later. There is little available information on the bird's distribution in England prior to its demise, and it may have been restricted to the older pinewoods of the borders possibly as far south as Teesdale (County Durham). In Scotland, the decline continued until the last of these birds had been confined to the ancient pinewoods of Inverness-shire and Aberdeenshire where they became extinct in about 1770 (though a few may have survived until 1785 on upper Deeside).

The Capercaillie was re-introduced into Perthshire in 1837 and 1838, and within 25 years it had spread into the surrounding counties. Further releases of the birds—also from stock imported from Sweden—took place in Angus, Kincardineshire, Morayshire (1862–1883) and in Inverness-shire, and these, with one or two supplementary releases elsewhere, have helped the species to recolonize much of its former Scottish range; it is now present throughout much of the eastern Highlands. The spread following re-introduction reached a peak just prior to the First World War but was severely affected by the felling of timber on forested estates. The creation of the Forestry Commission in 1919, with its subsequent forestry plantations, was of immense benefit as new feeding areas took over previously inhospitable habitat and encouraged further advances; this has slowed—if not ceased altogether— in recent years as the extensive forests in the west, especially Argyll, have yet to be colonized (Sharrock, 1976; Thom, 1986). Lone females, well outside the normal distribution (and perhaps the first indications of range expansion), have been sighted in Caithness, Ayr and Kirkcudbright from 1972 to 1982 (Thom, 1986). The Capercaillie has been known to breed with Black Grouse and has produced hybrids. In 1971, 35 birds were released into Grizedale Forest, Cumbria, and a nest (unsuccessful) was found in 1973; subsequently, numbers have dwindled, and none have been seen since 1978.

In 1973, Parslow put the population for Scotland within the range 1,000–10,000 pairs, but 'pair' is an inappropriate unit to use for a polygamous species. Sharrock (1976) did not give a population estimate but gave instances of high breeding density—eg, 17–20 birds per square kilometre in the Black Wood of Rannoch (Perthshire). He recorded the presence of Capercaillies in 182 10-km squares, with breeding confirmed in 116. In winter, densities in some forests of the Highlands have ranged from 5 to over 30 birds per square kilometre, but numbers fluctuate yearly. The most recent peak in Capercaillie numbers was in the late 1960s and early 1970s; by the mid-1980s the population in eastern Scotland was lower than it was in the period 1968–72 (Thom, 1986).

A survey of Forestry Commission forests in northern Scotland (north of the Grampians) by the RSPB and the FC in 1986 found that there had been a major decline since the mid-1960s, and 80% of the woods which had previously held Capercaillies recorded a decrease within the past five years. The Scottish population is now believed to be between 1,000 and 2,000 individuals.

Similar declines have been noted across the species range. In Norway, the population was estimated in 1960 to be between 300,000 and 400,000 birds when the annual shooting bag was 40,000 birds; in 1981 this figure was down to 13,000 birds shot. In West Germany, the total population is under 2,000 males, and hunting has been banned since 1973. In Finland, the population during the late 1960s was estimated at about 600,000 birds when the annual shooting bag between 1959 and 1967 was from 47,000 to 104,000 birds; by 1969–76 this had dropped to

14,500 birds. The population is also declining in Austria, Bulgaria, Czechoslovakia, East Germany (population under 200), and Switzerland. In Spain there were 582 displaying males in the Cantabrian mountains in 1982 (from only 475 displaying males in 1979, when hunting of Capercaillies was banned), and the population in the French Pyrenees is probably about 5,000 birds (Johnsgard, 1983; Anon., 1984).

THREATS TO SURVIVAL

Threats implicated in the population decline in Britain have included loss of habitat, over-shooting and adverse climatic conditions. These have contributed towards the poor reproductive success and poor chick survival.

The felling of ancient and mature Scots Pine in Scotland has been the most important factor in habitat loss throughout the Capercaillies' range. Earlier declines in Britain were directly related to extensive felling. Underplanting with non-native softwoods must now represent the greatest threat.

The extermination of the original British race in the mid-1770s was largely attributed to the felling of the natural pine forest, but it is unlikely that this was the sole cause; sufficient forest remained to enable birds such as the Crested Tit and the Scottish Crossbill (which are similarly dependent on large stands of ancient Pinewoods) to survive, and it seems more probable that the bird—having become scarce by the depletion of its habitat—was finally wiped out by hunting.

In the 1950s and 1960s, the Capercaillie was regarded as a pest by foresters and farmers, and both birds and eggs were destroyed. Sport shooting became a source of revenue on many estates, but continuing declines have led to a ban on shooting in order to safeguard the population. Since 1982, the rights for Capercaillie shooting have not been let on Forestry Commission land.

In addition to the felling of old pine forests and over-shooting, the RSPB/Forestry Commission survey in 1986 suggested nine other possible reasons for the decline; these reasons included increased pine marten and fox predation as well as agricultural changes, spraying, and lack of food.

CONSERVATION

The first priority must be to safeguard large parts of the ancient Caledonian pinewood and other mature Scots Pine forests with shrubby understory, (particularly bilberry) as well as oak (*Quercus* sp.) and juniper (*Juniperus communis*) woodlands (Moss *et al.*, 1979). Such habitat protection should be through SSSI designation, Management Agreements and reserve acquisition, all of which are crucial in the core areas of the birds' distribution. The areas where management should be first directed are those with known lek sites. Here, rotations of Scots Pines should be extended beyond their economic maturity. As pine plantations set down 50–60 years ago mature, they also offer new boughs for perching, a source of food, and—perhaps only temporarily—nesting sites before the canopy closes out daylight. Continuity of suitable habitat may be important if losses from emigration are high, as suggested by Moss (1987, a & b). In such situations, felling small clearings but retaining old pines is an important habitat management practice. When areas of scots pine are clear-felled for commercial reasons they should be re-stocked with scots pines and native deciduous trees.

In all areas where the Capercaillie occurs, forestry operations should ideally be kept to a minimum, especially during the breeding season. The opening up of forest areas for tourism should take into account the need to keep lek sites free from disturbance. Because of the difficulty of assessing Capercaillie populations, regular monitoring should be established as a matter of urgency.

REFERENCES

ANON. European News. 1984. Brit. Birds 77: 233–243.
JOHNSGARD, P.A. 1983. The grouse of the World. London: Croom Helm.
KOIVISTO, I. 1956. Suom. Rusta 10: 179–184.
KOIVISTO, I. 1963. Vogelwarter. 22: 75–9.
Moss, R. 1987a. Demography of capercaillie *Tetrao urogallus* in north-east Scotland. II. Age and sex distribution. Ornis Scand. 18: 135–140.
Moss, R. 1987b. Demography of capercaillie *Tetrao urogallus* in north-east Scotland. III. Production and recruitment of young. Ornis Scand. 18: 141–145.
Moss, R., WEIR, D. & JONES, A. 1979. Capercaillie management in Scotland. Proceedings of the International Symposium on Woodland Grouse, Inverness 1978, 140–155. Bures: World Pheasant Association.
PARSLOW, J. 1973. Breeding birds of Britain and Ireland. Berkhampstead: Poyser.
THOM, V.M. 1986. Birds in Scotland. Calton: Poyser.

Consultants: J. Cayford, R.H. Dennis and R. Moss

Grey Partridge
Perdix perdix

Although still a widespread bird of arable farmland and associated hedgerows, the Grey Partridge has undergone a dramatic decline since about 1950; this has been largely attributed to the widespread use of chemical sprays. By the early 1980s the population was estimated to be about a quarter of the pre-Second World War total. Conservation headlands, a technique enabling cereals to be grown at field margins without the use of damaging agrochemicals, would go some way to reversing the downward trend.

LEGAL STATUS

Protected by the Game Acts (open season: 1 September–1 February); Annex III/1 of EC Birds Directive; Appendix III of the Berne Convention.

ECOLOGY

The Grey Partridge is a resident in open arable farmland with hedgerows. Nest: a depression on the ground lined with plant material, usually at the edge of a field, at the foot of a hedge, on a bank or in long grass. Eggs: laid from the end of April to early June, with repeat clutches into August. Clutch: 15 (4–29), size increasing in Europe from south to north, and from south-west to north-east; one brood. The young hatch from mid-June onwards and fly after 10–11 days. There is a high rate of mortality among chicks due to the lack of insect food; this is intensified by the use of herbicides and insecticides.

Food for adults consists chiefly of plant material, notably leaves and seeds of grasses, cereals, clover, grain and weed seeds; seed-heads of chickweed are particularly favoured, and occasionally ants are taken. Early in life the chicks feed principally on insects, especially diurnal carabid, chronsomelid and curculionid beetles, sawfly, lepidopteran larva, plant bugs and aphids. As the chicks grow, grass seeds, leaves and eventually cereal grain are taken. By three weeks of age plant material forms most of the diet (Southwood & Cross, 1969; Green, 1984).

The bird winters in family groups: coveys.

DISTRIBUTION AND POPULATION

Palearctic, also introduced into northern America. The Grey Partridge breeds almost continuously from the British Isles, east to the Kirgiz Steppes and Kazakhstan in eastern USSR. The northern limit of population in Finland was reached at 65°N; the bird also breeds in southern Norway and southern Sweden. Isolated races occur in Spain, Portugal, Italy and Turkey and in the Caucasus.

In Britain the Grey Partridge occurs everywhere except in the uplands of Wales and the Scottish Highlands; it is most abundant in cereal-growing areas in the east.

Between the middle and late 19th century the Grey Partridge population increased dramatically in Britain following the agricultural revolution which provided an increased amount of cereal production, field boundary enclosures with planted hedgerows, and gamekeepers who controlled potential predators. At the turn of the century partridge shooting had become an important resource, affording a viable financial return on large estates. Prior to 1940, it is estimated that approximately two million Grey Partridges were shot annually. From the bag returns kept by the estates, the population was maintained at a high level until the outbreak of the Second World War. In the years following the end of the war, partridge management continued (the largest number ever shot in one day in Britain—2,069 on the north Lincolnshire wolds—was taken in October, 1952) before collapsing due to changing agricultural practices (Potts, 1986).

The application of herbicides and insecticides, which became widely used, quickly eradicated most of the staple food of young birds. In the early 1960s it was shown that the chick survival rate had been declining during the 1950s and that herbicides removed the food plants for insects on which chick survival was dependent.

Other factors have contributed to the decline—principally a fall in the level of gamekeeping consequent on the lower population size, the break-up of large estates, and the reduction of hedgerows as field boundaries became larger. At the start of the NCC/BTO Common Birds Census the Grey Partridge index for farmland was 194 in 1962, dropping to 82 by 1970, 63 by 1981 and 42 by 1987, though there were short-lived reversals of the trend in 1971 and 1976–77.

The decline of the Grey Partridge in Britain is reflected in the game bags of at least 20 other countries, and the same pattern of events is being repeated on a similar scale throughout its range. Prior to the Second World War there were approximtely 21 million birds shot annually, whereas in recent years this has dropped to less than three million (Tapper, *pers. comm.*).

THREATS TO SURVIVAL

Threats include a decline in suitable habitat and the effects of agricultural chemicals on the supply of chick food.

It is principally the continuation of agriculturally related threats that have caused the decline of the Grey Partridge population in the last 30–40 years, namely, loss of habitat and the use of herbicides and pesticides. The latter have caused high chick mortality because of the loss of insects either directly, through pesticides, or indirectly through the loss of insect food plants.

Shooting is not considered a threat to the Grey Partridge population. It should also be noted that partridge shooting in Britain nowadays relies very much on the large-scale introduction of commercially bred Red-legged and Chukar Partridge hybrids.

CONSERVATION

A change to less intensive agricultural practices is needed before any reversal in the current downward trend is likely. The conservation of field margins is crucial for the survival of chicks, especially in the first two weeks of life—a width of up to 6 m left unsprayed would enhance the growth of plant species on which insects feed: conservation headlands (Rands, 1985).

REFERENCES

GREEN, R.E. 1984. The feeding ecology and survival of Partridge chicks (*Alectoris rufa* and *Perdix perdix*) on arable farmland in East Anglia. J. Appl. Ecol. 21: 817–830.

POTTS, G.R. 1980. The effects of modern agriculture, nest predation and game management on the population ecology of partridges (*Perdix perdix* and *Alectoris rufa*). Adv. Ecol. Res. 11: 1–79.

POTTS, G.R. 1986. The Partridge: pesticides, predation and conservation. London: Collins.

RANDS, M.R.W. 1985. Pesticide use on cereals and the survival of Grey Partridge chicks: a field experiment. J. Appl. Ecol. 22: 49–54.

SOUTHWOOD, T.R.E. & CROSS, D.J. 1969. The ecology of the Partridge: 3. Breeding success and the abundance of insects in natural habitats. J. Anim. Ecol. 38: 497–509.

TAPPER, S. & BOND, P. 1987. The National Game Census—1986/87. Game Cons. Ann. Rev. 18: 167–173.

TAPPER, S. & COOK, S. 1988. The National Game Census—1987/88. Game Cons. Ann. Rev. 19: 179–186.

Consultant: G.R. Potts

Quail
Coturnix coturnix

The Quail is a rare breeding summer visitor to Britain. Prior to the end of the 18th century it was a common breeding bird, but since about 1865 the population has declined, although there are occasional years of comparatively high numbers, mostly since 1947. Decreases in numbers are attributed mainly to changes in agricultural practices, eg, the earlier cutting of grass, and the increased use of firearms, with indiscriminate shooting of migrant birds in southern Europe.

LEGAL STATUS

Protected under Schedule 1 of WCA 1981; Annex II/2 of EC Birds Directive; Appendix III of the Berne Convention.

ECOLOGY

In Britain the Quail inhabits cereal and hay fields; it is solitary or loosely social. Nest: a shallow scrape on the ground, sparsely lined and well hidden in a dense cover of crops or rough grass. Eggs: laid from mid-May to the end of July, but repeat or second clutches may be laid to late August. Clutch: 8–10 (7–18), larger numbers apparently being due to two females laying in the same nest; normally one brood, but a second is sometimes suspected. The young fledge from mid-June to the end of August.

Food consists of seeds (principally those of agricultural weeds), some grain, insects (chiefly ground-dwelling insects and larvae), and (rarely) plant material.

DISTRIBUTION AND POPULATION

Palearctic, Afro-tropical and Oriental. In the Palearctic the Quail breeds east to Lake Baikal (USSR), north to about 60°N and south through the Kirgiz Steppes, avoiding most of the desert areas of Soviet Central Asia. West Palearctic birds winter in coastal north-west Africa, but most cross the Sahara to winter in the Sahel region.

In Britain it is now a scarce summer migrant, regularly occurring in only about 12 counties in England. It was apparently a common breeding bird up to the late 18th century, but since the mid-19th century it has undergone a considerable decline in numbers, with only a slight revival since the early 1940s; however, the population has never regained its apparent earlier levels of abundance. In 1947 about 300 calling birds were recorded, twice as many as in any other previous year this century (Moreau, 1951). An enquiry in 1953 coincided with another good year, when twice as many of the birds occurred as in 1947. The period 1968–1972 also included a 'good year' (1970—probably one of the best this century), and so the 'Atlas' recorded breeding Quail as 'confirmed or probable' in 328 10-km squares. This probably considerably overstates the normal situation, particularly given the problems of carrying out a census for this species (see below). Since 1953, other good years (based on calling birds) have been 1960, 1961, 1963–1965 (1964 alone produced well over 600 calling birds), 1979 and 1983. Similar declines, punctuated by occasional good years, have also been noted in north-west Europe (Sharrock & Hilden, 1983).

A survey of county bird reports in England and Wales, and Regional Bird Reports in Scotland, for the years 1973–1987 (not all years' reports are available for some counties) suggests that the population in Britain still fluctuates markedly from year to year (see accompanying graph). Birds can be present in an area for

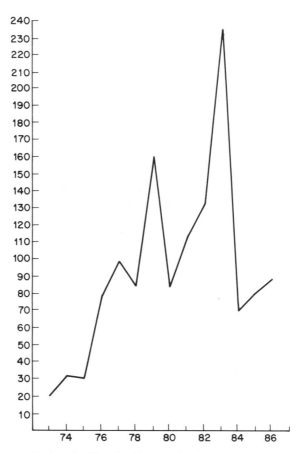

Number of calling Quail recorded in Britain, 1973–87

several years, often in increasing numbers, only to fail to appear in the subsequent season, even though the habitat has not changed noticeably. In years of high abundance, eg, 1983 (236) and 1979 (160), birds were present in areas where they had not been recorded before or, at least, not recorded since previous years of high abundance. Conversely, in some areas, birds either did not increase in number dramatically or they disappeared altogether.

Carrying out a census of breeding Quail is beset with difficulties since some birds arrive early and begin calling whilst still on migration, while others arrive late (many records refer to birds on territory in late May or early June) and begin calling only to fall silent when presumably paired and nesting. Moreover, the significance and status of birds which call throughout the summer is uncertain: they could either be unmated (but perhaps indicative of the presence of (silent) pairs that are breeding) or failed breeders that resume calling from time to time.

THREATS TO SURVIVAL

Threats appear to include the shooting of considerable numbers of the birds on migration (particularly in the poorer areas of southern Europe) for food and sport, and, in Britain, the early mowing of grass for crops at critical stages of nesting or fledging of young. Moreover, climatic factors may influence the numbers arriving in this country.

CONSERVATION

Pressure on the EC and enforcement of laws designed to prevent indiscriminate shooting in the southern areas of Europe would help to reduce the numbers shot illegally. In Britain, delaying the mowing of crops or rough grass where Quail are known to be present (but this is often hard for the non-ornithologist to determine) until later in the breeding season, eg, to mid-August or the end of August, would reduce losses of nests and young. In this respect, the potential benefits of ESAs and set-aside should be explored. The second Breeding Atlas (1988–90) should go some way towards establishing the current status of Quail in Britain. However, research is needed into the relationship between calling birds and breeding activity. Until this is understood, no meaningful monitoring programme can be devised. The relationships, if any, between 'good' Quail years and climatic factors also warrants investigation.

REFERENCES

Moreau, R.E. 1951. The British status of the Quail and some problems of its biology. Brit. Birds 44: 257–276.
Sharrock, J.T.R. & Hilden, O. 1983. Survey of some of Europe's breeding birds. Brit. Birds 76: 118–123.

Spotted Crake

Porzana porzana

The Spotted Crake is a rare breeding summer visitor to Britain. Formerly more numerous, it decreased in the 18th and early 19th centuries, and has been regarded as only a sporadic breeder for much of the 20th century. There were up to 12 singing males at up to six sites annually during 1973–85, though there was much fluctuation. SSSI notification should be considered for those few sites where the bird is regularly recorded in summer.

LEGAL STATUS

Protected under Schedule 1 of WCA 1981; Annex 1 of EC Birds Directive; Appendix II of the Berne Convention.

ECOLOGY

The Spotted Crake breeds in lowland swamps and fens, in overgrown edges of lakes and rivers with adjacent carr, and in upland bogs. Nest: of sedges, rushes and dead leaves, usually well hidden in sedge or in a grass tussock. Eggs: laid mid-May to early August. Clutch: 8–12 (6–15); one or two broods. The last young fledge by mid-September.

Food consists of small molluscs, insects and seeds.

DISTRIBUTION AND POPULATION

Palearctic. Breeds widely, but locally, in Europe north to southern Fenno-Scandia, except most of Iberia, the Mediterranean islands and south Balkans, but is rare in Britain. It winters in the Mediterranean area, in north and east Africa, and in south-west Asia. After decreasing in numbers in the 18th and early 19th centuries, probably mainly because of drainage but influenced by range fluctuations, the Spotted Crake apparently became only a sporadic nester in Britain in the first half of the 20th century—though it is probably often overlooked; however, there has been evidence of more regular breeding in widely scattered counties during 1926–37, and again since about 1963. Otherwise widespread, but a scarce passage-migrant and an occasional winter visitor. During 1926–37 it probably nested at least once in about 10 counties of England and Wales, with four or five pairs in Somerset alone in 1930 (Lewis, 1952); during 1963–81 breeding was

135

regarded as probable at least once in some 25 counties from Kent, Devon and Dyfed north to Shetland, Highland (Sutherland) and the Western Isles. In some instances several males have been heard at a single site, and in a few areas, such as Highland (Sutherland) and south-west Scotland, nesting has been suspected in various years. Population figures are impossible to estimate, but in 1978 a total of six males were heard at six sites, in 1983 12 males in six localities, in 1984 10 males at four localities, in 1985 three males at two localities, in 1986 four males at three localities, in 1987 18 males in seven localities and in 1988 ten males in six localities.

All breeding season records are summarized annually by the Rare Breeding Birds Panel.

THREATS TO SURVIVAL

Threats include loss of habitat and disturbance by man.

Being restricted to swamps and bogs with extensive sedges and rushes, the species must always be vulnerable to the effects of drainage and habitat destruction, particularly in lowland areas. There is some risk of disturbance, mainly from over-enthusiastic birdwatchers trying to glimpse such a scarce and elusive bird.

CONSERVATION

Generally, breeding or suspected breeding is too sporadic for any special measures to be effective, but the provision and maintenance of suitable habitat would be a worthwhile aim on reserves in likely areas. Serious consideration should be given to SSSI notification to those few localities where the species is regularly recorded in summer. Possible breeding sites should not be publicized while they are occupied.

REFERENCES

Buxton, A. 1948. Travelling Naturalist. London: Collins.
Lewis, S. 1955. The breeding birds of Somerset and their eggs. Ilfracombe: Stockwell.

Corncrake
Crex crex

The Corncrake is a rapidly declining summer visitor. It was once widespread in Britain, but a marked decrease in numbers began towards the end of the 19th century, especially since 1900, and it is still continuing. The population is confined almost entirely to north and west Scotland; there were less than 750 calling birds (males) by 1978/79, and the number in 1988 has been estimated at 550–600. The conservation measures required are complicated, but retention of hay meadows and special methods of cutting hay are of paramount importance as is the maintenance of traditional farming and crofting leading to small scale habitat mosaics.

LEGAL STATUS

Protected under Schedule 1 of WCA 1981; Annex 1 of EC Birds Directive; Appendix II of the Berne Convention.

ECOLOGY

At all times the Corncrake requires grass or herb cover; herbs are especially important early in the season when cover is in short supply. Nest: on the ground, in a shallow cup lined with grasses or leaves, mostly in meadows, clumps of nettles (*Urtica*) or other tall vegetation, sometimes in *Iris* or *Phragmites* in wet meadows and marshes, but rarely in cereal crops. The bird is probably social, though it is also solitary, and is sometimes polygynous. Eggs: laid May to mid-August, mostly mid-May to early July. Clutch: 8–12 (4–14); sometimes two broods. The average brood size appears to fall quickly after hatching. The young fledge from late July to September.

Food consists mainly of insects taken from the ground or from plants.

The bird does not appear to be site-faithful in Britain, sites being occupied annually but by different individuals (Stowe & Hudson, 1988).

DISTRIBUTION AND POPULATION

Palearctic. The breeding range of the Corncrake formerly extended over much of northern and central Europe between about 44°N and 63°N, extending to Siberia, 120°E. It is absent from Iceland, Fenno-Scandia (except sub-arctic coastal Norway and southern Sweden) and northern Russia. Its distribution is now much restricted within its former range, and is disjunct and fragmentary.

The Corncrake winters mainly in south-eastern Africa, from southern Tanzania to northern South Africa. Southward movement through Africa lasts from September to December and is linked to the occurrence of rainfall and the growth of cover in which to hide (Stowe & Becker, in press). The spring migration route to Europe is concentrated through Morocco; autumn migration passes through Egypt.

Formerly widespread throughout much of Britain. Its decline began in the south and east of England in the latter part of the 19th century, becoming more marked from the early 1900s, and most noticeable since the 1950s (Norris, 1945, 1947). Breeding is now confined almost entirely to north and west Scotland. The Corncrake is a scarce passage migrant from mid-April to early June, and from late July to early October in some counties.

The Corncrake is now numerous only in the Outer Hebrides and Inner Hebrides (principally Tiree), which, together, accounted for about 90% of the British total of these birds in 1988. Numbers have declined in Orkney (102–105 in 1979 to 29–38 in 1988). A few birds are still present in Highland (north-west

Sutherland), but are scarce elsewhere on the Scottish islands and mainland; they have almost disappeared from northern England, and are absent in Wales. In 1968–72 the British and Irish population was estimated at 5,500–6,500 pairs (=calling males; Sharrock, 1976), probably under 2,600 of these in Britain (Cadbury, 1980). A survey in Britain during 1978–79 indicated a population of 730–750 calling males. A survey of the Uists and Benbecula, in the Western Isles, showed the following fluctuations between 1978 and 1988: 191 calling birds in 1978, 145–167 in 1983, 137–151 in 1986, 167–186 in 1987, and 169–182 in 1988. On Canna, there was a decline from the average of about 10 males in 1969–82 to 2–5 males in 1983–1985 (Swann, 1986). There was no evidence of a decline on Tiree (1969–87) where numbers have fluctuated between about 50 and 100 calling birds (99–103 in 1988).

Declines have taken place since the late 19th and early 20th centuries in other parts of Europe. The population in Ireland was estimated at 1,200–1,500 calling birds in 1978 (O'Meara, 1979), but numbers in seven small study areas declined from 114 in 1978 to 4 in 1985 (O'Meara, 1986). The Irish population in 1988 was estimated as 900–930 calling birds (Mayes & Stowe, 1989). Populations elsewhere have been estimated at 2,000 calling birds in France (Broyer, 1985), 2,600–2,750 in Poland (ICBP, unpublished), 10 in Belgium, 50 in Luxembourg, 100–360 in the Netherlands (Osieck, 1986), 200–500 in Sweden, 10–30 in Denmark, 100–200 in Norway (Roalkvam, 1984), and several hundred in Finland (O. Hilden, *pers. comm.*, 1980). No total count for West Germany is available, but the population is probably in the range 200–1,000. Britain holds about 10% of the western European population.

THREATS TO SURVIVAL

Threats include loss of suitable habitat, early harvesting of meadows (causing destruction of nests, adults and particularly young), the risk of collisions with wires, predation by domestic and feral cats, the apparent lack of site-faithfulness, the hazards of migration across the Sahara and Sahel, and climatically induced population fluctuations.

The cause of the continuing decline in Britain and Europe is not fully understood. In Britain the pattern of decline has proceeded in a north-westerly direction, away from intensive cultivation with its earlier harvesting dates, loss of hay meadows, loss of herb vegetation at field margins, and amalgamation of small fields. Although birds survive today in areas of mechanical cutting, the earlier and rapid completion of harvest (which machines allow) has increased deaths. Early-growing hay meadows are especially attractive to birds at a time when other cover is scarce. Such meadows are usually cut earlier, increasing the risk of death. The increase in silage cultivation is not responsible for the long-term decline since the practice did not become widespread until the 1950s and 1960s, although it is likely to have accelerated the decline in some areas and may continue to do so in the future.

Reduction in available habitat and low-intensity farming and crofting, as well as the loss of hayfields to permanent sheep pasture, or earlier harvesting of meadows (as a result of sowing earlier-growing grasses or a change to early silage) threaten survival in remaining strongholds. The loss of young at harvest can be total in individual broods, though this is uncommon. Brood size appears to decline rapidly in the first two weeks (cause unknown, but not due to mowing).

Domestic and feral cats are common in many Corncrake habitats, and are known to capture and kill adults.

Apparent mobility and the lack of site-faithfulness in adults suggests that the protection of small areas would be inadequate to maintain the survival of these birds, which, in successive years, appear to use breeding areas that are well dispersed.

The migration routes of Corncrakes are poorly known. Concentrations occur in Egypt (especially in the autumn) and Morocco (especially in the spring), but not in the intervening countries—suggesting two main migration pathways. The available evidence indicates that the birds winter in south-eastern Africa. The increasing desertification of the Sahel, with attendant loss of cover, must make any such journey more hazardous.

There is no evidence of pesticide problems in birds in Britain or abroad, though few birds have been examined; however, the future use of pesticides on breeding grounds may affect food supply. The reversion of some agricultural areas to the uncultivated state, including the loss of hay meadows, may pose almost as great a threat as conversion of meadows to permanent pasture. Birds in the Hebrides nest in and use recently re-seeded meadows as well as meadows with higher floristic diversity.

CONSERVATION

Corncrakes breed mainly on agricultural land which is not farmed by intensive methods. Much of it is crofting land and is not readily available for purchase by conservation bodies. The low-intensity farming practice of crofting is largely sympathetic to the needs of Corncrakes (and other wildlife). Conservation of their breeding grounds is thus closely linked to the maintenance of low-intensity farming, crop rotation systems producing diverse habitat mosaics based on small field sizes, boundary features and widespread hay production. Site protection should aim to prevent intensification of agricultural production which would have adverse effects, and particularly the conversion of hay meadows and cereals to permanent sheep pasture. At the same time, the retention of sites with current agricultural practices should be encouraged since derelict crofting land eventually becomes unsuitable breeding habitat. Maintenance of marshy and rushy fields is also important especially for use by the birds early in the season.

On the breeding grounds, Corncrakes are known to range over large areas (up to 100 ha), their ranges overlapping those of their neighbours. Many adults move from *Iris* beds occupied in May and early June to meadows in late June and July. A network of large well-spread sites within the Corncrake's range needs to be maintained. Small-scale site protection is unlikely to be adequate.

Probably less than one-quarter of the population breeds on existing SSSIs. SSSI protection may not be ideal in the light of the need to promote and maintain the existing agricultural system. ESA designations may be more appropriate provided that the incentives offered are sufficient to outweigh any gains from alternative intensive uses of the land.

Within Corncrake breeding areas cattle should be favoured rather than sheep, especially to promote the use of hay as a winter feed, and to discourage any further increase in sheep farming where it involves conversion of crofting land to permanent pasture. Enclosure by fencing of common land should be discouraged, since this is frequently the first step in the change of land-use leading to intensification.

Fewer young birds would be killed if meadows were cut from the centre outwards, or from side to side rather than from the edge inwards. This method involves little extra work on the part of the farmer. Leaving uncut patches along the perimeter of the field, or in corners, provides refuge for the young during harvest.

Late harvesting of hay causes fewer deaths among young Corncrakes, but control of the dates of hay cutting is unwise because of the likelihood that hay production would suffer and be abandoned.

Corncrakes may nest near houses and ruins, often in patches of rank vegetation. Conventional protection of such nesting areas is not practicable, but persuasion of the local community to leave such patches undisturbed during the breeding season (April–August) would be of benefit.

The understandable enthusiasm of birdwatchers and other visitors to see Corncrakes needs to be directed to suitable places where birds can be viewed without disturbance. With the cooperation of individual farmers, such activities could be beneficial to the islands' tourist-related economy.

A reduction in the numbers of feral and domestic cats is desirable, though probably impractical. The extermination (or prevention of spread) of mink should be a high priority.

REFERENCES

BROYER, J. 1985. Le rale de genets en France. Union Nationale des Associations Ornithologiques, Centre Ornithologique Rhone-Alpes.

CADBURY, C.J. 1980. The status and habitats of the Corncrake in Britain 1978–79. Bird Study 27: 203–218.

MAYES, E. & STOWE, T.J. (1989). The status and distribution of Corncrakes in Ireland in 1988. Irish Birds 4: 1–12.

NORRIS, C.A. 1945. Summary of a report on the distribution and status of the Corncrake (Crex crex). Brit. Birds 38: 142–148, 162–168.

NORRIS, C.A. 1947. Report on the distribution and status of the Corncrake. Brit. Birds 40: 226–244.

O'MEARA, M. 1979. Distribution and numbers of Corncrakes in Ireland in 1978. Irish Birds 1: 381–405.

O'MEARA, M. 1986. Corncrake declines in seven areas, 1978–1985. Irish Birds 3: 237–244.

OSIECK, E.R. 1986. Bedreigde en karakteristieke vogels in Nederland. NVV, Zeist.

ROALKVAM, R. 1984. Akerriska Crex crex i Rogaland og Norge. Var Fuglefauna 7: 87–90.

STOWE, T.J. & BECKER, D. (in press). Status and conservation of Corncrakes outside their breeding grounds. Tauraco.

STOWE, T.J. & HUDSON, A.V. 1988. Corncrake studies in the Western Isles. RSPB Conserv. Rev. 2: 38–42.

SWANN, R.J. 1986. The recent decline of the Corncrake Crex crex on the Isle of Canna. Bird Study 33: 201–205.

Consultants: T.J. Stowe and A.V. Hudson

Crane
Grus grus

The Crane is a rare breeding resident in Britain. It formerly bred in East Anglia until about 1600 when it became extinct, possibly due to hunting. At least one pair has bred or attempted to breed every year since 1981, a total of four young being raised up to 1988. Due to the need for large, undisturbed wetlands, Cranes will at best always be scarce as a breeding bird in Britain. Protection from disturbance and ground predators is essential if a colony is to be established. The breeding of Cranes in Britain has not been publicized in the past as adequate arrangements for their protection were not then in existence.

LEGAL STATUS

Protected under WCA 1981; Annex 1 of EC Birds Directive; Appendix II of the Berne Convention.

ECOLOGY

The Crane breeds in widely spaced territories in reedy wetlands with adjacent farm land for foraging, but forms flocks in winter and on migration. Nest: a large pile of vegetation in an area of low marsh, added to through the nesting period to make a structure of about 1 m wide rising well above the water level. In Britain the nest site is normally adjacent to open areas, and is always situated where the birds can see long distances; the nest site is usually within a few hundred metres of a feeding area. Eggs: laid from mid-April, but re-laid as late as mid-June. Clutch: 2 (1–3); single brood; incubation 28–31 days. The young are precocial, walking or swimming from the nest site within a few days of hatching. In Britain the breeding success has averaged one young fledged every two years; there is no comparative data from elsewhere. The young are highly vulnerable to disturbance and predation for at least ten weeks from hatching; the first flight is not achieved until then, and parental attention must be constant if the young are to fledge. The young are dependent on one or both parents until at least their first autumn.

Food consists of a wide range of vegetable and animal matter. In Britain feeds especially on potatoes (tubers still in the ground are preferred), but also on grain and grass-shoots; insects and other invertebrates are taken, as are frogs. Cranes often dig for grubs and worms as well as vegetable matter.

DISTRIBUTION AND POPULATION

Palearctic. The Crane breeds from Germany and Scandinavia to eastern Siberia. The British breeding birds are the most western of the nominate race

G. g. grus. The main European population breeds in the bogs of Scandinavia and the USSR but also in reed and sedge beds in Germany and eastern Europe. In Britain a single pair bred in East Anglia during the period 1981–1988 and two pairs attempted to breed in 1989. By 1988 a total of four young had been raised.

Persecution in the Norfolk Broads was probably the reason for its extinction in about 1600; at that time substantial wetlands remained but Cranes often featured on the menu in East Anglian banquets.

Apart from the 'recolonization' of Britain, the range has contracted in Europe — having previously bred in Spain, Italy, Austria, Hungary and possibly Ireland. Numbers declined in West Germany earlier this century due to habitat destruction but rigorous protection in recent years has allowed the population to increase to around 50 pairs, the most significant population in the EC (Grimmett & Jones, 1989). Elsewhere in western Europe important populations of Cranes are located in Norway, 1,000 pairs, Sweden 11,000 pairs, and Finland 8,000 pairs. East Germany, Poland and the Soviet Union also hold important numbers (Cramp *et al.*, 1980).

Cranes are essentially migratory in northern Europe, occurring in flocks sometimes numbering thousands on passage, with the main movement south in September–October and north in March–April. Part of the Scandinavian population, the Baltic and some USSR birds take a south-western route to winter in Iberia, while some go to North Africa. Finnish, Soviet and some Swedish Cranes take a south-easterly route to winter from the Middle East south to Ethiopia.

The small British population winters regularly in East Anglia; otherwise it is an annual migrant which occurs in both spring and autumn and occasionally overwinters elsewhere in the UK.

THREATS TO SURVIVAL

Threats include predation, egg collection, disturbance by man, and changes in habitat.

Although nest flooding has been the cause of failure on occasions, predation of both eggs and young especially by foxes, is the main reason for nesting failure in Britain. The adult birds are not good at defending their nests against predators though they are usually effective against foxes in open feeding areas.

Egg collecting must remain a potential threat.

Disturbance by humans is a problem, especially on the Crane's scarce feeding areas in winter. Birdwatchers that try to get too near to the birds often cause considerable distress especially if the birds continually have to move from one area to another.

Crane's need a choice of undisturbed areas, its vigilance in the nest area, and its observed sensitivity underline the birds vulnerability. Any disturbance is likely to inhibit any spread away from the core area.

The loss of wetlands would be damaging but is unlikely in the forseeable future in the area they are attempting to colonize. A lack of sympathetic management could also be a problem if low-growing species of marsh vegetation became replaced by taller species, for example, a reed, *Phragmites*, that restricted nesting birds' visibility.

Agricultural changes in the wintering area could also be damaging. In addition to sufficiently large areas of grazing marsh, a supply of root crops seems to be essential, enabling survival even in hard winters.

CONSERVATION

For the Cranes in Britain at present the highest priority is the provision of disturbance-free areas for breeding and feeding. Because Cranes are popular birds with birdwatchers this is likely to require the continuing appointment of protection wardens (especially if the numbers of Cranes increases), the co-operation of land owners and managers, and much care about secrecy. The monitoring of breeding success, the effects of disturbance, and feeding requirements should continue.

More detailed research entailing nest visits (for example for ringing) will need to be done with great care due to the sensitivity of this species to disturbance. There are potential opportunities for encouraging the maintenance and re-establishment of reed beds in a mosaic of arable and grazed land. These should be explored to enhance the prospect for the increase of the colonists in Britain.

The provision of food in the wintering area may be needed if cropping patterns change.

REFERENCE

GRIMMETT, R.F.A. & JONES, T.A. 1989. Important Bird Areas in Europe. International Council for Bird Preservation, Cambridge.

Oystercatcher
Haematopus ostralegus

The wintering population of the Oystercatcher in Britain is localized and of international importance. A resident, in Britain, with numbers supplemented by many north-west European birds arriving in the autumn and remaining through to late winter. Of the 280,000 Oystercatchers wintering in Britain, 65,500 (23%) occur away from estuaries. About 38,000 pairs breed in Britain. Pressures on the species come from estuarine land-claim and persecution due to claims of damage to commercial beds of cockles (*Cerastoderma edule*), one of its main foods.

LEGAL STATUS

Protected under WCA 1981; Annex II/2 of EC Birds Directive; Appendix III of the Berne Convention.

ECOLOGY

Outside the breeding season the Oystercatcher is associated mainly with sandy estuaries, beds of cockles and mussels (*Mytilus edulis*), and rocky coasts; a small number feed on coastal pastures. The bird is gregarious.

Most breeding Oystercatchers occur on coastal habitats of Britain, especially in the north and west, but increasingly they are breeding inland, along river valleys in northern Britain (Heppleston, 1972). Eggs: laid from mid-April to mid-July. Clutch: 3 (1–4); one brood. The adults carry food to the young. The Oystercatcher has a low fledging rate in many areas, but this is balanced by the high survival rate of adults, with birds of up to 26 years old being reported.

Food consists mainly of the lamellibranch molluscs (*Cerastoderma edule*, *Mytilus edulis* and *Scrobicularia plana*); the bird will also take the ragworm *Nereis diversicolor*. There can be major changes in the distribution of *Cerastoderma* between years, so that numbers of Oystercatchers can vary greatly both within and between estuaries over short time-scales. In winter, adult birds exploit the best feeding areas, and immatures are displaced to the less favourable habitats (Goss-Custard *et al.*, 1982). On rocky coasts, many limpets (*Patella vulgaris*) are taken and, when on pasture inland the birds also take a variety of invertebrates including earthworms, larvae of butterflies and moths, beetles, flies, adult moths and earwigs.

DISTRIBUTION AND POPULATION

Palearctic. The Oystercatcher breeds over a wide latitude from 37°N to 72°N; in Western Europe most of these birds are north of 50°N. The range extends from Iceland and the north-west USSR to the British Isles, but with only scattered colonies south to the north Mediterranean coasts. All West European birds belong to the race *H. o. ostralegus*, the population of which is about 218,000 pairs. In Britain 33,000–43,000 pairs breed, this being approximately 17% of the European total. Oystercatchers have increased at least in range, and almost certainly in numbers, since the 1940s; in the early 1960s it was estimated that there were 19,000–35,000 pairs.

The largest West European breeding population is in the Netherlands, where numbers have increased from 8,000–12,000 pairs in 1955 to 50,000–60,000 pairs in 1976–77, and an estimated 90,000 pairs in the mid-1980s. Many of the British-bred juveniles move south to winter in France (a few to Iberia) but the majority of adults remain in Britain. They are augmented by large numbers which arrive here from Iceland, the Faeroes and Norway in August and September and depart in February–March. Small numbers from Denmark to the Netherlands winter on the south coast (Anderson & Minton, 1978).

In winter, Britain supports about 280,000 birds, 37% of the European population. From 1973 to 1980 there was a steady increase, totalling 40%, in numbers wintering in Europe. The large sandy estuaries support very large numbers: the average winter peak population over the period 1984–89 on Morecambe Bay was 54,126, on the Dee it was 29,577, on the Solway 32,270, on the Wash 32,102, on Burry Inlet 18,334, and on the Thames Estuary 13,752. These top six sites support over 50% of British wintering Oystercatchers.

THREATS TO SURVIVAL

Threats include those which generally affect birds using an estuarine habitat (see page 308); in addition to these threats there are also four special factors which are considered below.

The first concerns the dynamic nature of the distribution and numbers of the bird's main food, *Cerastoderma*; means that a protection strategy is required not only for areas which are used at present but also for areas which are potentially suitable and on which the bird will depend on in other years.

The second factor is that both *Cerastoderma* and *Mytilus* are susceptible to major changes in sediment deposition; significant variations in littoral erosion and accretion patterns, especially where fine, muddy sediment is deposited, can result in the smothering of these species.

The third is the perceived competition between commercial shell-fisheries and the Oystercatcher's predation on, principally, second-winter cockles. Since 1956, two 'culls' have been carried out under licence: one in Morecambe Bay, where, from 1956 to 1969, about 16,300 birds were killed, and one in 1973–74, in the Burry Inlet, where 11,000 were shot. Subsequent to the latter cull it was shown that there was no evidence that Oystercatchers materially reduced the landings of cockles, and that other factors are much more important (Horwood & Goss-Custard, 1977). The emotional response will always be part of human nature and, while no licences have yet been issued to kill Oystercatchers for this purpose under the Wildlife and Countryside Act 1981, the threat remains.

The fourth factor is the changing methods of cockle gathering—from the relatively benign hand-gathering to modern suction-dredging techniques. The potential is there for significant damage to, or reduction in, cockle stocks—as well as incidental damage to other intertidal invertebrates.

CONSERVATION

General conservation measures that are required for those birds, including the Oystercatcher, which are associated with an estuarine habitat are given on pages 317–327.

In view of the Oystercatcher's mobility between years, there is a need to consider potential as well as actual sites of value for this species; changes in sediment deposition which may occur as part of a development—and affect the bird's food—could have a major impact.

In view of research findings, no licences should be issued under Section 16.1 (k) of the Wildlife and Countryside Act, 1981, to kill Oystercatchers because of their alleged damage to shellfish. Detailed research is required to assess the impact of changing techniques for the commercial gathering of cockles.

REFERENCES

ANDERSON, K.R. & MINTON, C.D.T. 1978. Origins and movements of Oystercatchers on the Wash. Brit. Birds 71: 439—447.
GOSS-CUSTARD, J.D., DURELL, S.E.A., McGRORTY, S. & READING, C.J. 1982. Use of mussel, *Mytilus edulis*, beds by Oystercatchers, *Haematopus ostralegus*, according to age and population size. J. Anim. Ecol. 51: 543–554.
HEPPLESTON, P.B. 1972. The comparative breeding ecology of Oystercatchers (*Haematopus ostralegus* L.) in inland and coastal habitats. J. Anim. Ecol. 41: 23–51.
HORWOOD, J.W. & GOSS-CUSTARD, J.D. 1977. Predation by the Oystercatcher, *Haematopus ostralegus* (L.), in relation to the cockle, *Cerastoderma edule* (L.), fishery in the Burry Inlet, South Wales. J. Appl. Ecol. 14: 139–158.

Consultant: A.J. Prater

Black-winged Stilt

Himantopus himantopus

The Black-winged Stilt is an occasional breeding summer visitor. Three isolated instances of nesting in Britain have been recorded during the last 50 years; otherwise it is a rare but annual visitor. Breeding pairs require full-time protection.

LEGAL STATUS

Protected under Schedule 1 of WCA 1981; Annex 1 of EC Birds Directive; Appendix II of the Berne Convention.

ECOLOGY

The Black-winged Stilt breeds on or near shallow fresh or brackish water which has high biological productivity. Stilts are opportunist breeders which can quickly move onto areas of flash-flooding and will often utilize man-made sites such as saltpans, rice fields and sewage farms, etc. They can tolerate close human presence. In Britain, breeding sites have included an old-style sewage farm, a flooded arable field, and a small brackish coastal lagoon. Nest: can vary from a simple scrape to a more substantial structure built of available vegetation, depending on site conditions. Eggs: laid from late April to early June. Clutch: 4 (3–5); incubation period: 22–25 days. The fledging period is 28–32 days.

Food consists mainly of invertebrates, especially aquatic insects, but larger items such as fish fry and tadpoles are also taken (Cramp *et al.*, 1983).

DISTRIBUTION AND POPULATION

Global distribution involving several races. Within the western Palearctic the nominate race, *himantopus*, breeds from central and southern Europe across to Asia and south to North Africa. European birds move south in the winter, but they are not thought to cross the Equator (Cramp *et al.*, 1983; Marchant *et al.*, 1986).

A rare, annual visitor to Britain, with small influxes in some years, mainly during the spring migration. In recent years it has bred on three occasions: in 1945, when two (possibly three) pairs nested in Nottinghamshire [one pair of which raised young (Staton, 1945)]; in 1983, when one pair nested in Cambridgeshire but failed to raise young; and lastly, in 1987, when a pair successfully raised two young in Norfolk. Some evidence of recent increases on the near-Continent, as well as an upsurge of sightings in Britain, has prompted discussion of possible colonization here. In western Europe the bird breeds regularly only in Spain (20,000 pairs), France (1,000 pairs—mainly in the Camargue), and Portugal, with occasional breeding recorded from Belgium and the Netherlands.

THREATS TO SURVIVAL

In Britain the main threat is probably from egg collectors and mammalian predators. The 1983 flooded field site suffered from rapid drying out which made the area available to ground predators, especially foxes. Attention from bird-watchers may be a problem even when the birds have settled down to incubation unless proper control is exercised.

CONSERVATION

The presence of this striking and highly vocal wader can often be difficult to keep quiet. Once a pair is located they will require twenty-four-hour protection by a team of watchers in order to deter human intruders.

If the birds are nesting in an area of flash flooding, efforts should be made to keep the area wet during incubation. The variety of existing wetland reserves in Britain should provide a suitable range of nest sites for this sporadic breeder.

REFERENCES

MARCHANT, J., PRATER, T. & HAYMAN, P. 1986. Shorebirds. London & Sydney: Croom Helm.
STATON, J. 1945. The breeding of Black-winged Stilts in Nottinghamshire in 1945. Brit. Birds 38: 322–328.

Consultant: S. Rooke

Avocet
Recurvirostra avosetta

In Britain, the Avocet breeds and winters locally in small numbers. Formerly, the bird bred regularly along the coasts of east and south-east England, but it became extinct by the early 1840s. Following isolated breeding attempts, it recolonized Suffolk in 1947. There was then a general increase in the population, and in 1988 nearly 400 pairs bred at 17 sites in East Anglia and south-east England, 80% of these on reserves. Since regular wintering began in 1947 the overwintering population has increased to about 680 birds—most of them on estuaries on the south coasts of Devon and Cornwall, and in East Anglia. The main conservation requirement is correct management of existing reserves, but colonization of new areas is likely if protection and appropriate management is afforded to potential breeding sites.

LEGAL STATUS

Protected under Schedule 1 of WCA 1981; Annex 1 of EC Birds Directive; Appendix II of the Berne Convention.

ECOLOGY

The Avocet breeds on banks or islets of shallow brackish lagoons; a social to loosely colonial bird. Nest: a scrape in open dry mud or sand, or among sparse vegetation. Eggs: laid mid-April to the end of June. Clutch: 4 (3–5); one brood. Most of the young fledge by late July.

At the two main breeding sites in Britain, Havergate (1947–86) and Minsmere (1963–86), egg loss averaged 24% and 55%, respectively. Breeding success tended to decrease as the number of pairs increased (Cadbury & Olney, 1978; Hill, 1988) due to increasing rates of egg loss at both sites and the rate of chick loss at Havergate. At Havergate the number of chicks reared per pair each year varied from 1·3 to 3·0 during 1964–1971, from 0·1 to 0·7 during 1972–78, and from 0·04 to 0·9 during 1979–86. Most of the chick loss was attributed to starvation and predation; only one young fledged in 1977. Success at Minsmere has generally been higher, but again, only three young were raised in 1977. At both sites chick loss explained over 80% of the year-to-year variation in total losses to the Avocet populations, and it was therefore identified as the key factor affecting population fluctuations.

Most Avocets return to breed after two years, and the loss between the autumn population in one year (ie, adults and fledged young) and the breeding population two years later was greater when autumn populations were high for both sites. This was particularly so in later years when the populations were no longer increasing—suggesting that breeding populations are limited through intraspecific competition for nesting and feeding habitat during the breeding season (Hill, 1988).

Food consists of aquatic insects and their larvae, crustaceans, and worms, obtained from shallow water or surface mud by sweeping movements of the bill or by picking up individual items. At Havergate, hypersaline conditions (above 65 g l^{-1} NaCl) reduce the availability of invertebrate food for chicks.

DISTRIBUTION AND POPULATION

Palearctic and Ethiopian. In the western Palearctic Avocets breed locally, mainly in coastal areas, from south Sweden, Denmark, Estonia, north Germany, the Low Countries and south-east England, round western and Mediterranean Europe, to the Black and Caspian seas—as well as far inland in Czechoslovakia, Austria, Hungary and turkey. Birds winter in western and southern Europe, Africa and southern Asia.

In Britain, the Avocet was formerly widespread on the east coast, from the Humber to south-east Sussex, but it had become extinct in most of England by 1820–40 due largely to land-claim and disturbance (Williams, 1986), and possibly also to shooting and egg-collecting. The last proven breeding was in Kent, in 1842.

After a gap of 100 years the Avocet nested in Norfolk in 1941, and in Essex in 1944; it recolonized Suffolk in 1947 (Brown, 1950) following huge increases in numbers in the Low Countries and Denmark. The initial recolonization in 1947 was achieved by four pairs at both Havergate and Minsmere. Numbers at the former site increased to 21 pairs by 1950 and to 97 by 1957; the numbers then fluctuated between 48 and 90 pairs during 1958–67, and between 84 and 132 pairs during 1968–86. At Minsmere, regular breeding began in 1963, after which the population increased to 15 pairs by 1970, 41 pairs by 1975, and 44–69 pairs during 1977–86. A third colony was established at Cley, in Norfolk, in 1977, with 4, 5, 8, 20 and 28 breeding pairs, respectively, in the five years to 1981. The maximum number of breeding pairs in Britain has increased steadily over recent years, as is shown in the following table.

Avocet: maximum number of breeding pairs in Britain, 1978–1988

1978	1979	1980	1981	1982	1983	1984	1985	1986	1987	1988
149	158	166	208	203	239	237	269	321	342	385

In 1988, 182 pairs nested in Suffolk, 153 pairs in Norfolk, about 19 pairs in Essex, 30 pairs in Kent, and possibly one or two pairs elsewhere.

Otherwise, the Avocet is a scarce passage-migrant, found mainly in south-east and southern England, and a local winter visitor, chiefly to south-west England and north Kent.

Regular wintering started in 1947; initially this was virtually restricted to the Tamar and Tavy estuaries (Devon/Cornwall) and the Exe estuary (Devon). There is a good deal of interchange between these estuaries, and the combined total of Avocets has been over 250 in recent winters (1986–87, 1988–89). Wintering flocks have gradually become established elsewhere on the south and east coasts: Poole Harbour, Dorset (from 1964/65); Pagham Harbour, Sussex (from 1965/66); the Alde, Suffolk (from 1968/69), where 357 were recorded in 1986–87; the Thames, Essex and Kent from 1975/76), and Hamford Water, Essex (from 1982/83). The total wintering population in 1988–89 was about 890.

THREATS TO SURVIVAL

Threats include disturbance and predation during breeding, and the shooting of birds wintering abroad; as 80% of Avocets breed on reserves, correct management of breeding habitat is also vital.

At Havergate, the availability of aquatic invertebrates varies between years and is reduced by high or fluctuating salinity levels due to drought conditions (eg, during the summer of 1976) or cold springs and wet summers (eg, 1977).

Inclement weather also causes high mortality among newly-hatched chicks by increasing the amount of time they need to be brooded, and so reducing the time available for feeding.

Kestrels (*Falco tinnunculus*) take the young of Avocets at Havergate, and high numbers of breeding Black-headed Gulls (*Larus ridibundus*) increase the losses of Avocet chicks and compete with Avocets for nest-sites.

A number of Avocets are shot in wintering areas in France and Iberia. One death due to lead poisoning, following ingestion of spent shot, has been reported from Suffolk.

CONSERVATION

Ecological studies and habitat management have been priorities at the RSPB reserves of Havergate and Minsmere (Axell, 1974), but the relationships between salinity, invertebrate food supply and Avocet numbers and breeding success, are still imprecisely known. Avocet populations on these two reserves have probably reached saturation level, but there is an opportunity to encourage further colonization of new areas. Recent analyses (Hill, 1988) suggest that population expansion would ensue if density-dependent competition for nest-sites and food was reduced by the creation of further suitable nesting island/lagoon complexes to enable new colonies to become established. Provided that both Havergate and Minsmere continue to produce more fledged young than is necessary to sustain their populations, then potential recruits will be available to colonize suitable habitat elsewhere on the south and east coasts. However, without protection from human disturbance and ground predators, these highly conspicuous birds may find successful colonization difficult. New reserves should be established, or management advice provided, at potential sites, or suitable lagoons created on existing coastal reserves—as has been done successfully at the RSPB reserves at Minsmere, Elmley and Titchwell.

The disappearance of Avocets from Britain in the 1840s coincided with the building of sea walls and extensive land-claim, both of which reduced the area of land temporarily inundated with brackish water (Williams, 1986).

REFERENCES

AXELL, H.E. 1974. Minsmere (part 2). Establishment and management of an artificial brackish lake with nest island ('The Scrape'). IUCN/IWRB Manual of wetland management. Slimbridge: IWRB.
BROWN, P.E. 1950. Avocets in England. London: RSPB.
CADBURY, C.J. & OLNEY, P.J.S. 1978. Avocet population dynamics in England. Brit. Birds 71: 102–121.
HILL, D.A. 1988. Population dynamics of the Avocet (*Recurvirostra avosetta*) breeding in Britain. J. Anim. Ecol. 57: 669–683.
WILLIAMS, G.W. 1986. The impact of land drainage on the birds of the North Kent Marshes and a strategy for pasture management. MPhil Thesis, University of London.

Consultant: D.A. Hill

Stone Curlew
Burhinus oedicnemus

The Stone Curlew is a rare breeding summer visitor to Britain with a rapidly declining population. Not more than 160 pairs breed; the range has contracted, now being confined to a few counties south-east of a line from Dorset to the Wash. The future maintenance of a Stone Curlew population in Britain is dependent upon the immediate safeguarding, and management through grazing, of semi-natural grasslands where the bird breeds. The protection of nests from farming operations is also important.

LEGAL STATUS

Protected under Schedule 1 of WCA 1981; Annex 1 of EC Birds Directive; Appendix II of the Berne Convention.

ECOLOGY

The Stone Curlew breeds on open stony ground with sparse or short vegetation. In Britain it is clearly associated with free-draining stony soils, mainly overlying chalk. Approximately equal numbers of pairs nest on semi-natural grassland, chalk downland and Breckland grass-heaths as well as on arable land. On semi-natural grassland, grazing by sheep (and especially rabbits) is important to maintain a sward short enough for the birds. On farmland, most spring-sown crops are suitable for nesting in early spring, but by mid-May some become too tall and dense for Stone Curlews. Spring cereal crops are suitable only in April and early May, and the birds must move to grassland or other, less dense, crops with their chicks—or if they re-nest after failure of their first attempt. By contrast, sugar-beet, carrots, onions, maize and spring field beans remain open enough for Stone Curlews until June. Nest: a scrape on open, bare ground. Eggs: laid April to August. Clutch: 2 (1–3); two broods are occasionally reared within a season. Clutches of three eggs are rare and may be attributable to two females. Most first clutches are started in late April, and replacement nesting occurs after the loss of eggs or chicks. Up to four successive clutches may be laid.

Food, which is hunted for mainly at night, plover-fashion, consists of invertebrates and occasional small mammals and birds, taken from the soil surface. Earthworms, woodlice, millipedes and beetles are important items.

Preferred feeding habitats are tightly grazed semi-natural and improved grassland, pig fields, manured arable fields, the edges of arable fields and manure heaps. During incubation, birds may move 2–3 km from the nest to feed. The young are fed by their parents but often remain near the nest, food being brought to them by the parents.

DISTRIBUTION AND POPULATION

South Palearctic and Oriental. The nominate race, *oedicnemus*, breeds discontinuously from southern England east to southern Russia, south to Iberia, southern France, Italy, the Balkans and the Caucasus. The European Stone Curlew winters in Iberia, North Africa and the southern edge of the Sahara. British Stone Curlews winter in southern Spain, south-western France and north-western Africa. There has been one ringing recovery of a first-winter bird in West Africa south of the Sahara, but a dearth of mid-winter recoveries of first-winter birds suggests that many young birds may move to this area—where they have a slim chance of being reported.

The Stone Curlew is present in Britain from March to October. It was formerly widespread on free-draining soils north to the Cotswolds, East Midlands and Yorkshire, but it became extinct there early in the twentieth century. It is now found mainly in Norfolk, Suffolk, Cambridgeshire, Hertfordshire, Essex, Berkshire, Wiltshire, Hampshire and Dorset. A long-term range contraction and a decrease in population have taken place since the mid-nineteenth century. In the late 1930s the population was thought to be 1,000–2,000 pairs. Parslow (1967) estimated the population at 200–400 pairs, and Sharrock (1976) estimated 300–500 pairs. Thorough surveys in the mid-to-late 1980s have located only 135–155 pairs, and regular breeding no longer occurs in areas occupied in the 1970s (Kent and Sussex).

In Europe, population declines and range contractions have also been recorded, especially in the north. The species has become extinct in the Netherlands, the Federal Republic of Germany, and perhaps the German Democratic Republic.

THREATS TO SURVIVAL

Threats include a decline in suitable habitat, egg collection, predation, and disturbance by man.

Conversion of semi-natural chalk grassland to arable farmland has been a major cause of population decline. The decimation of rabbits by myxomatosis, and a reduction of grazing with livestock, have made much of the remaining grassland too lightly grazed for Stone Curlews. Many areas are protected from development by NNR or SSSI status, or use as military training areas, but maintenance of Stone Curlew populations will depend on management to increase grazing pressure on many of them.

On farmland, agricultural change is the main threat. The birds depend for nesting on crops such as sugar-beet or maize, which remain open until mid-summer, close to feeding grounds on manured land and pasture. The decline in mixed farming in southern England (O'Connor & Shrubb, 1986) has already restricted the area suitable for farmland-nesting Stone Curlews. Future changes in farm support and prices may have further adverse effects, though moves to reduce cereal production have potential benefits for Stone Curlews. Improved crop husbandry has resulted in more rapid and uniform crop growth. Patches of bare ground or sparse growth within crops, which are favoured by Stone Curlews, have become rarer as crop nutrition and pest control have improved. In particular, the control of nematode diseases of sugar-beet on sandy soils by pesticides introduced in the mid-1970s have resulted in much denser crops in some of the Stone Curlew's strongholds.

Egg collectors pose a direct threat to breeding success, particularly at well-known grass-heathland sites, and disturbance from leisure activities, including birdwatching, is a potential problem.

Nests and young chicks of farmland-nesting pairs are at risk from agricultural operations such as rolling, tractor-hoeing and irrigation. Replacment of mechanical weed control in row crops by herbicide application has resulted in some reduction of this threat, but new weed problems such as that of weed-beet in sugar-beet crops have delayed the phasing out of mechanical control. Faster tractors and wider hoes have made it more difficult for sympathetic farm workers to spot and avoid nests and chicks.

Stone Curlews are capable of defending their nests and chicks from many predators, but foxes appear to cause heavy egg and chick losses, particularly on semi-natural grassland. The recent increase in fox numbers in southern Britain, particularly in East Anglia where gamekeepers formerly kept populations at a low level, may seriously reduce Stone Curlew productivity.

CONSERVATION

Most semi-natural grassland Stone Curlew sites are now protected by SSSI or NNR status or by military use. However, careful management of many of these areas is required if they are not to become unsuitable for Stone Curlews. Maintenance of grazing by sheep, and particularly rabbits, is required. One Breckland reserve—where rabbit grazing has been encouraged by enclosing the area with a rabbit-proof fence—has a conspicuously dense and successful Stone Curlew population. Further fencing of this kind should be carried out, and grazing with livestock encouraged where appropriate. The recent designation of Breckland as an Environmentally Sensitive Area offers a mechanism by which this type of management could be supported.

When conservation agencies are consulted about the effects of changes in agricultural policy on Stone Curlews they should argue for arable farming systems which result in sparse, open areas of cropped land close to pig fields or tightly grazed pasture.

Farmers with Stone Curlews on their land should be made aware of the rarity of the bird—and the effects of farming practice on it—and encouraged to protect nests and chicks in field crops from damage by agricultural operations. There is almost always considerable willingness to do this, but time is required to locate nests and broods so that they can be avoided. NCC grant-aided RSPB protection wardens and birdwatchers have recently shown that collaboration with farmers in finding and temporarily marking nests can produce an increase in breeding success (Green, 1988). This work should be continued and expanded.

REFERENCES

GREEN, R.E. 1988. Stone Curlew conservation. RSPB Conservation Review. 2: 30–33.
O'CONNOR, R.J. & SHRUBB, M. 1986. Farming and birds. Cambridge: Cambridge University Press.
PARSLOW, J.L.F. 1967. Breeding birds of Britain and Ireland. Berkhamsted: Poyser.

Consultant: R.E. Green

Ringed Plover
Charadrius hiaticula

The British wintering population of the Ringed Plover is localized and is internationally important; about 23,000 are present in winter, representing some 64% of the European total. The Ringed Plover is widely dispersed, mostly in small flocks, along the sandier coasts, but there are some concentrations of 200–1,000 in a few estuaries or coastal systems. It also breeds throughout Britain, but mainly coastally, with the majority occurring on the islands off north and west Scotland. The greatest threat to the wintering population comes from estuarine land-claim.

LEGAL STATUS

Protected under WCA 1981; Annex II of EC Birds Directive; Appendix II of the Berne Convention.

ECOLOGY

During the winter, and in periods of passage, the Ringed Plover occurs mainly on sandy, upper-shore zones where, using visual clues, it takes a wide variety of invertebrates, principally small polychaete worms and Crustacea. Birds form small to medium-sized roosting flocks at high tide on small sand or shingle bars, often separated from the large flocks of estuarine waders.

In the breeding season, most of the birds are found on sandy or shingle beaches, but in 1983 a uniquely high total and density involving 2,224 pairs were discovered to breed on the machair of the Western Isles of Scotland (Fuller *et al.*, 1986). Small numbers nest inland. The Ringed Plover has an extended breeding season from late March to late August, being apparently double-brooded in the south but single-brooded in the north; however, many nests are lost, and repeat clutches are frequently produced.

DISTRIBUTION AND POPULATION

Palearctic and marginally Nearctic. The Ringed Plover breeds on tundra from north-east Canada east to the eastern USSR, and mostly in coastal western Europe south to about 50°N. Britain supports the most southerly breeding population, apart from a very few in northern France. Between 8,400 and 8,800 pairs of Ringed Plovers breed in Britain; this is about 9% of the north-western European population of nearly 100,000 pairs, with at least 5,800 (69%) in Scotland, 2,400 (28%) in England and 225 (3%) in Wales. By far the most important areas are the machair of the Western Isles (2,224 pairs, 26%), Shetland (900 pairs, 11%), Orkney (552 pairs, 7%), Norfolk (541 pairs, 6%) and the Inner Hebrides (500+ pairs, 6%) (Prater, 1989). A slight increase in breeding numbers occurred in Britain between 1974 and 1984; in England the increase was 19%, and in Wales it was 21%, but in Scotland and Northern Ireland numbers hardly changed.

The total western European breeding population is about 13,100 pairs, with other much larger populations (with different migration patterns) in Iceland (50,000 pairs) and north Scandinavia (36,500 pairs), the latter belonging to the race *C. h. tundrae*.

During the late autumn there is a movement of breeding birds from eastern Britain to western and southern Britain and continental coasts to north Spain, but most of the western birds are resident. In winter, 23,000 birds are present in Britain, 71% of which are on the non-estuarine coast. This British total represents about 64% of European wintering birds. By far the largest numbers are on the non-estuarine coasts of the Uists (4,150, 18%), Strathclyde (3,850, 17%) and Orkney (1,600, 7%).

Throughout Europe, wintering numbers increased substantially during the 1970s, perhaps doubling.

Large movements from Iceland/Greenland/north-east Canada pass through Britain in autumn (mid-August to September) and spring (May). A much smaller movement of northern Scandinavian birds is seen in eastern England in the autumn, with even fewer in spring. During the autumn migration, peak numbers occur in late August to early September; these birds are seen widely over Britain, with up to 3,800 on the Severn and over 2,000 on Morecambe Bay and the Dee. In spring most of the movement takes place in western Britain: up to 7,280 have been seen in Morecambe Bay, 2,100 on the Dee, and over 1,000 on the Severn and Solway. Due to the rate of turnover of populations, it is not yet possible to assess accurately the total number of birds involved at this time (Moser & Carrier, 1983).

THREATS TO SURVIVAL

Threats include those which generally affect birds using an estuarine habitat (see page 308); in addition to these threats, two other factors could affect breeding Ringed Plover populations, and these factors are considered below.

Throughout its British range there is an increasing problem of disturbance. It has been shown that frequent, innocent, disturbance results in a very poor (<2%) nest survival, and hence recruitment rate, but where disturbance is minimal nest survival increases to about 50% (Pienkowski, 1984 a & b). Access by people and dogs has probably been the main problem in the past, but off-road vehicles could potentially become a major factor.

A very large percentage (27% +) of British Ringed Plovers breed on the Hebridean machairs. This habitat has remained ideal due to the traditional, low intensity, rotational farming system operated there. The potential exists for more intensive methods, including sheep monoculture, which could have a major deleterious impact on the waders which breed there in extremely high densities.

CONSERVATION

General conservation measures that are required for those birds, including the Ringed Plover, which are associated with an intertidal habitat are given on pages 317–27.

It should be noted that Ringed Plovers feed in relatively discrete, sandy, high-level sites and are thus potentially vulnerable to even small, upper-shore land-claim.

Special measures that should be considered for breeding birds are efforts to minimize substantial increases in disturbance through the insensitive siting of caravan sites, car parks, footpaths, etc, and the prevention of access by motorized vehicles.

The maintenance of viable farming operations at a low intensity on the machair is vital. On the dry machair land of the Uists and Benbecula, an Environmentally Sensitive Area (ESA) was introduced in 1988; this provides financial support for traditional farming there to the benefit of breeding waders, including the Ringed Plover. It is essential to monitor the effectiveness of the ESA management prescription in maintaining the special quality of the machair. There are, however, smaller areas of machair elsewhere in north-west Scotland where no support through ESA payments is available; special measures need to be considered for these sites as well.

REFERENCES

FULLER, R.M., REED, T.M., BUXTON, N.E., WEBB, A., WILLIAMS, T.D. & PIENKOWSKI, M.W. 1986. Populations of breeding waders *Charadrii* and their habitats on crofting lands of the Outer Hebrides, Scotland. Biol. Conserv. 37: 333–361.

MOSER, M.E. & CARRIER, M. 1983. Patterns of population turnover in Ringed Plovers and Turnstones during their spring passage through the Solway Firth in 1983. Wader Study Group Bull. 39: 37–41.

PIENKOWSKI, M.W. 1984a. Breeding biology and population dynamics of Ringed Plovers *Charadrius hiaticula* in Britain and Greenland: nest predation as a possible factor limiting distribution and timing of breeding. J. Zool. Lond. 202: 83–114.

PIENKOWSKI, M.W. 1984b. Behaviour of young Ringed Plovers *Charadrius hiaticula* and its relationship to growth and survival to reproductive age. Ibis 126: 133–155.

PRATER, A.J. 1989. Ringed Plover *Charadrius hiaticula* breeding population in the United Kingdom in 1984. Bird Study 36: 154–160.

Consultant: A.J. Prater

Kentish Plover

Charadrius alexandrinus

The Kentish Plover is an occasional breeding summer visitor. It was formerly a regular breeder in south-east England, but since 1956 it has become a scarce passage-migrant with only one record of nesting. Conservation measures in Britain are unlikely to improve this situation while the population on the adjacent coasts of Europe remains low.

LEGAL STATUS

Protected under Schedule 1 of WCA 1981; EC Birds Directive; Appendix II of the Berne Convention.

ECOLOGY

Breeding in Britain has been primarily along sea-coasts on shell banks, sand, or exposed mud by estuaries and salt or brackish lagoons. Nest: a bare or sparsely lined scrape. Usually solitary, although locally dense populations may build up in suitable locations elsewhere in the range. Eggs: laid (in northern Europe) in May–July. Clutch: 3 (2–4); occasionally two broods. The young fledge by late August, but mostly earlier.

Food consists mainly of insects, crustaceans, worms and molluscs (Cramp *et al.*, 1983).

DISTRIBUTION AND POPULATION

Cosmopolitan, occurring in Eurasia, North Africa and parts of North and South America. In Europe the bird breeds mainly in coastal areas of continental Europe north to France, the Low Countries, Denmark, Germany and south Sweden — and also inland in Austria and Hungary. Birds of European origin winter in the Mediterranean area and Africa south to the equator (Cramp *et al.*, 1983).

In the early part of this century, up to 40 or more pairs bred in south-east England, mainly west Kent and east Sussex, but numbers declined in the 1920s and breeding became sporadic after the last regular nesting in 1935. One or two pairs nested in east Sussex during 1949–56, and one pair nested in Suffolk in 1952 (Parslow, 1973), but there were no further records until 1979 when one pair hatched two young in Lincolnshire/south Humberside (Sharrock *et al.*, 1981). Otherwise it is a scarce passage-migrant in late March–May and August–October, mainly in East Anglia and south-east England, with frequent records in recent years, for example, up to 40 in Kent in 1980 (Taylor *et al.*, 1981).

The species has also declined and become generally scarce to rare on adjacent coasts of France, Belgium and the Netherlands, although small numbers do still regularly breed there.

THREATS TO SURVIVAL

Threats include disturbance by man and the possibility of predation. The main reason for the decline in Britain and north-west Europe is believed to be disturbance resulting from increased human usage of coastal areas. It would now be difficult for the species to breed in some of its former natural haunts in south-east England. As with other ground-nesting birds in coastal habitats, ground and avian predators could have a significant effect on any attempts at recolonization.

CONSERVATION

In adjacent areas of Europe, breeding occurs successfully each year in sandy areas within fenced industrial enclosures, where disturbance is low, and on sandy spots on islands created by infilling and excavation of ballast lagoons. The chance or intentional creation of similar habitat in south-east England, in areas where Kentish Plovers occur regularly in spring, may improve the prospects of recolonization. Areas protected for other species, such as terns, may also provide suitable disturbance-free areas for breeding. In the event of future breeding attempts, the areas should not be publicized (to keep disturbance to a minimum), and measures such as the use of electric fences should be considered to deter mammalian predation.

REFERENCES

PARSLOW, J. 1973. Breeding birds of Britain and Ireland. Berkhamsted: Poyser.
SHARROCK, J.T.R. and the RARE BREEDING BIRDS PANEL. 1981. Rare breeding birds in the United Kingdom in 1979. Brit. Birds 74: 17–36.
TAYLOR, D.W., DAVENPORT, D.L. & FLEGG, J.J.M. 1981. The birds of Kent. Kent Ornithological Society, Meopham.

Dotterel
Charadrius morinellus

The Dotterel is a breeding summer visitor to Britain which was until recently either rare or overlooked; it is confined almost entirely to the Scottish Highlands. Its numbers declined in the late 19th and early 20th centuries, but some increase in the population became evident following the Second World War when between 60 and 80 pairs were considered to have bred annually between 1945 and 1969. In the 1970s the population increased to between 100 and 150 pairs; since then it has risen again, and an NCC survey of the entire breeding habitat in 1987 and 1988 put the population in excess of 450 pairs. The opening up of the Scottish mountains for tourism and recreation, and widespread grazing, present the main threats to Dotterel breeding in Britain.

Protected under Schedule 1 of WCA 1981; Annex 1 of EC Birds Directive; Appendix II of the Berne Convention.

ECOLOGY

The Dotterel is a summer visitor which breeds in Britain in the montane (arctic–alpine) zone, with concentrations particularly on the high plateaux over 900 m (Thom, 1986). In Fenno-Scandia the bird breeds on tundra at lower altitudes, whilst in the Netherlands it has bred very locally on newly drained polders. The Dotterel is a solitary or loosely social bird. Nest: a scrape which is either bare or lined with lichens or moss, on bare ground or in an open patch of short vegetation, often among scattered boulders. Eggs: laid from mid-May to late July. Clutch: 3 (rarely 2–4); one brood. The male bird does almost all of the incubating (the Dotterel is one of only 22 polyandrous species in the world). Most of the young fledge by early or mid-August. Because of the severe weather that these high tops can experience, even in summer, productivity is not high, and in years when there is snowfall or heavy rain in June or July few young are reared (Nethersole-Thompson & Watson, 1981).

Food in the breeding season consists chiefly of insects and larvae, also spiders. The rock-types on which the breeding sites occur vary considerably, and these in turn influence the nature of the vegetation and the density of invertebrates present.

The ratio of young to old birds is lowest on the bare granite summits, intermediate on the Moine gneisses, schists and quartzites of the central and western Grampians, and highest on the Dalradian schistose of the eastern Grampians (Nethersole-Thompson, 1973).

DISTRIBUTION AND POPULATION

North Palearctic. The Dotterel breeds in Fenno-Scandia, North Russia, locally in the uplands of northern Britain, Austria, Italy, Czechoslovakia and Romania, and (in the 1960s and 1970s) at sea-level on the Dutch polders; the species winters in the Mediterranean area (some ringed Scottish birds have been recovered in the North African mountains) and south-west Asia. The Dotterel was formerly (early to mid-19th century) more widespread and much more numerous, from Suther-land (Highland) south to the English Lake District (and even North Wales); however, its numbers decreased markedly during the second half of the 19th century, and the bird is now restricted largely to the central and eastern Scottish Highlands, with local breeding north to Sutherland and south to northern England and north Wales. The bird is otherwise scarce, but is a regular passage-migrant, mainly during April–May and September–October, being noted at traditional staging-posts—chiefly in Norfolk, Cambridgeshire, south-west England and Lancashire.

In the 19th century, flocks of up to 200 were seen regularly in northern England and southern Scotland, but shooting by collectors and for food, and to provide feathers for fishing flies, together with egg-collecting, probably reduced the population. The number of pairs was estimated at between 60 and 80 in the years 1945–1969 and at 56–74 in the early 1970s, whilst, in good years, the estimate was between 130 and 150 pairs in the early 1980s. The upper limit may be regularly exceeded, as in 1987 and 1988, when a thorough survey of all the Dotterel's breeding habitat revealed a total of over 450 pairs (1987) and 550+ pairs (1988). This may represent a genuine population increase (there were larger than usual numbers seen at migration staging posts in England in the spring of 1987) or may merely be the result of intensive searching by the survey team, with populations having been greatly underestimated in previous years.

THREATS TO SURVIVAL

Threats include human disturbance, egg collecting, increased predation, and habitat modification by grazing (Thompson *et al.*, 1987).

Possibly some of the birds are still illegally shot on passage, but serious shooting pressure stopped in Britain in the 19th century. More worrying now is the spread of tourism and the paraphernalia of winter sports in the Scottish Highlands—with the consequent opening-up of the higher ground by roads and ski-lifts. Fortunately, the Dotterel will sit tight and tolerate people passing quite close to its nest, but some disturbance is undoubtedly caused by birdwatchers who can also damage sensitive vegetation. Disturbance to newly-hatched chicks and consequent loss of feeding time is an adverse factor in some areas.

Some clutches are still taken by egg collectors, and there is evidence of others being eaten by Carrion or Hooded Crows (*Corvus corone*) or gulls (*Larus* spp.) attracted to the high tops by hill-walkers' or skiing enthusiasts' scraps.

The decline of the population in southern Scotland is considered to be due to overgrazing, particularly by sheep, resulting in a change from montane vegetation or moss and dwarf shrub to grass.

The effects of climate on the Dotterel population is not fully understood but it is possible that the present trend towards a more continental climate in the highlands is benefitting the species.

CONSERVATION

The main Dotterel breeding grounds in Britain are already SSSIs, encompassing over 60% of the population. Core areas are also in three proposed montane SPAs. Early consideration should be given to designating further SSSIs (and SPAs) in the light of the findings of the NCC surveys in 1987 and 1988.

Growing recreational impacts on the high tops of the Highlands need to be carefully monitored, and the possibility of discouraging access to certain Dotterel breeding areas should be considered. At the same time, a 'honey-pot' site where birdwatchers can see the Dotterel should be established; this will help to prevent disturbance to other areas.

Overgrazing by sheep, and in places by Red Deer, leading to habitat modification, is a particularly severe problem in some areas, and its spread should be monitored and discouraged where it is shown to be having an impact on vegetation.

Now that a full Dotterel survey has been undertaken for the first time in Britain, a monitoring programme should be established, centred on the main breeding areas.

REFERENCES

NETHERSOLE-THOMPSON, D. 1973. The Dotterel. London: Collins.

Nethersole-Thompson, D. & Watson, A. 1981. The Cairngorms: their natural history and scenery, 2nd edition. Perth: Melven Press.

Thom, V.M. 1986. Birds in Scotland. Calton: Poyser.

Thompson, D.B.A., Galbraith, H. & Horsfield, D. 1987. Ecology and resources of Britain's mountain plateaux: land-use conflicts and impacts. *In* Bell, M. & Bunce, R.G.H. (eds) Agriculture and conservation in the hills and uplands: 22–31. Grange-over-Sands: Institute of Terrestrial Ecology. (ITE Symposium No. 23).

Consultant: D.B.A. Thompson

Golden Plover
Pluvialis apricaria

The Golden Plover winters in Britain in internationally important numbers. Up to 300,000 are present in winter, being 30% of those in western Europe. Whilst the breeding population is below that of international importance it is declining as a result of severe threats to its upland habitat, particularly through afforestation. The winter population is not threatened.

LEGAL STATUS

Protected under Schedule 2, Part 1 of WCA 1981 (protected in close season: from 1 February to 31 August); Annex 1 of EC Birds Directive; Appendix III of the Berne Convention.

ECOLOGY

The geographical range of this species in Britain in the breeding season reflects the distribution of the major upland blocks, mainly between 240 and 600 m altitude, although down to sea-level in the extreme north-west of Scotland. Breeding occurs on a range of upland blanket bogs, wet-heaths, acidic grasslands and other sub-montane habitats. Grouse moor management can provide ideal breeding habitat (Reed, 1985). Marginal or low-intensity agricultural pastures are of importance for supplementary feeding during the summer (Ratcliffe, 1976). On suitable terrain there is a frequent relationship between breeding density and soil fertility—highest densities being recorded on Pennine limestone grassland: up to 16 pairs/km^2 (Ratcliffe, 1976). On the extensive Caithness and Sutherland blanket bogs there is an average of 1–2 (range 1–5) pairs/km^2 (Stroud *et al.*, 1987). The average density in the montane zone is 0.1–0.5 pairs/km^2. Nest: a shallow scrape, often hidden in moorland vegetation. Eggs: laid April to mid-May, although variable with altitude and season. Clutch: 4 (2–5); single brood.

Food consists of invertebrates, mainly beetles and earthworms, and also some plant material; the bird appears to have preferred feeding areas in summer which may be 2–5 km from the nest (Ratcliffe, 1976).

The winter distribution of the Golden Plover is markedly different. In autumn the birds move south and east to winter in a range of lowland agricultural habitats and estuaries. Wintering birds use traditional areas on a regular basis (Fuller & Youngman, 1979), with feeding occurring mainly on permanent pasture, probably a function of greater near-surface dwelling earthworm densities (Barnard & Thompson, 1985). Roosting occurs in winter on ploughed fields and winter cereals (Fuller & Lloyd, 1981). In very harsh winter conditions the birds move south and west, often out of Britain (Barnard & Thompson, 1985; Lack, 1986).

DISTRIBUTION AND POPULATION

Palearctic. Boreal/continental distribution includes Iceland, Britain, Ireland, Scandinavia and the USSR north of 65°N. Small outlying populations occur in Belgium, West Germany and the Netherlands. The population moves south in autumn to winter mainly in Britain, the Low Countries, France, Spain and the coastal regions of the Mediterranean; Britain is the major wintering ground for European and Icelandic Golden Plovers.

Breeding distribution is widespread throughout north and west Britain, with smaller populations in Wales and south-west England. There is evidence of a recent decline in the British breeding population. Sharrock (1976) estimated about 30,000 breeding pairs, whilst the most recent estimate is 22,600 pairs (in Stroud et al., 1987). In Wales the population has declined and is now about 200 pairs (R.R. Lovegrove, pers. comm.). Elsewhere in Europe declines have occurred in some countries. Populations, where known, are: Norway (130,000 pairs), Sweden (27,000–32,000 pairs), Denmark (10 pairs) and West Germany (25 pairs). The Icelandic population is not known but it is thought to be stable. The British breeding population is not likely therefore to exceed 10% of the western European population.

The wintering population in Britain — 200,000–300,000 birds — is internationally important, being at least 30% of those wintering in western Europe. Of these, some 32,000 winter in coastal habitats, with non-estuarine shores being of greater importance than estuaries (Moser & Summers, 1987) — although no British estuary regularly supports numbers of international significance.

THREATS TO SURVIVAL

Threats include the loss of upland breeding habitat due to coniferous afforestation of previously open moors, heaths and blanket bogs, and to intensification (eg, re-seeding) of rough grassland and moorland. On the blanket bogs of Caithness and Sutherland, an area originally holding at least 18% of the British population, afforestation has resulted in a 19% loss, substantially in the last decade. There have been further losses in Wales, the North Yorkshire Moors, the Cheviots, the southern Uplands and the eastern Highlands, probably amounting to at least 2,000 pairs (Stroud et al., 1987). The loss of Grouse moors to afforestation, and the deterioration of heather due to a decline in management, is clearly of particular concern to this and other upland bird species. Current afforestation is likely to have greater effects on the population in future years because of greater predation from foxes and crows, and competition for nesting sites in the smaller area available (Thompson *et al.*, 1988).

CONSERVATION

Whilst upland and moorland SSSIs currently protect a proportion of the breeding population, the majority remain unprotected by this means. Further SSSI and SPA designation should be considered urgently for those areas holding the highest densities. Already several such key areas have been identified for designation as SPAs; these have not yet been progressed.

Much new afforestation is being targetted at areas which support Golden Plovers, and there is an urgent need to contain the spread of afforestation of open upland habitats and, where possible, guide this away from the best areas for the species.

Over-grazing by sheep, and the conversion of heather to sheep pasture through re-seeding, can also cause a loss of preferred habitat.

Both forestry and upland farming are heavily dependent on Government support, and the balance of grants and incentives will be important determining factors as to which activities gain the ascendency. Furthermore, the establishment of ESAs to restrict damaging land-use practices and encourage the traditional management of upland vegetation could have an important role to play in safeguarding the breeding grounds of the Golden Plover and other dispersed upland species.

Wintering birds may be affected by the loss of permanent grasslands (which are preferred as a winter feeding habitat in some regions) through agricultural intensification, and this may have implications for winter feeding and survival. The monitoring of Golden Plover in winter and—particularly—in summer requires addressing (see Barnard & Thompson, 1985).

REFERENCES

BARNARD, C.J. & THOMPSON, D.B.A. 1985. Gulls and plovers: the ecology and behaviour of mixed-species feeding groups. London: Croom Helm.

FULLER, R.J. & LLOYD, D. 1981. The distribution and habitats of wintering Golden Plovers in Britain, 1977–1978. Bird Study 28: 169–185.

FULLER, R.J. & YOUNGMAN, R.E. 1979. The utilisation of farmland by Golden Plovers wintering in southern England. Bird Study 26: 37–46.

LACK, P. (ed.) 1986. The atlas of wintering birds in Britain and Ireland. Calton: Poyser.

MOSER, M.E. & SUMMERS, R.W. 1987. Wader populations on the non-estuarine coasts of Britain and northern Ireland: results of the 1984–85 Winter Shorebird count. Bird Study 34: 71–81.

RATCLIFFE, D.A. 1976. Observations on the breeding of Golden Plover in Great Britain. Bird Study 23: 63–116.

REED, T.M. 1985. Grouse moors and wading birds. Game Conservancy Ann. Rev. 16: 57–60.

STROUD, D.A., REED, T.M., PIENKOWSKI, M.W. & LINDSAY, R.A. 1987. Birds, Bogs and Forestry: the peatlands of Caithness and Sutherland. Peterborough: Nature Conservancy Council.

Thompson, D.B.A., Stroud, D.A. & Pienkowski, M.W. 1988. Effects of afforestation on upland birds: consequences for population ecology. *In* Usher, M.B. & Thompson, D.B.A. (eds), Ecological Change in the Uplands: 237–259. Oxford: Blackwell.

Consultant: D.A. Stroud

Grey Plover
Pluvialis squatarola

The Grey Plover is a localized winter visitor and a passage-migrant to Britain in internationally important numbers. Very few are found away from estuaries, where over 90% of the British wintering population of 40,000 occur. Numbers have increased substantially over the last 20 years but the distribution within Britain remains essentially in the south. As with most waders, estuarine land-claim for industrial and leisure development, or the creation of barrages, poses the greatest threat.

LEGAL STATUS

Protected under WCA 1981; Annex II/2 of EC Birds Directive; Appendix III of the Berne Convention.

ECOLOGY

The Grey Plover feeds mainly on the middle and upper shore levels on estuaries; it will take a wide range of food items, but polychaete worms (eg, *Nereis, Arenicola, Notomastus*) typically predominate. Gastropod and bivalve molluscs may be important in some areas. Feeds by sight. Individuals are usually well dispersed; many establish low-tide feeding territories (Townshend, 1985). Others feed in flocks, especially in severe weather. The Grey Plover is found in large roosting concentrations; it appears to require large, open mud-flats.

DISTRIBUTION AND POPULATION

North Holarctic. The Grey Plover breeds on arctic tundra from the western USSR east to eastern Canada, but it does not breed in Greenland or Scandinavia. Birds which use the East Atlantic Flyway breed in the USSR east to the Taimyr peninsula (Branson & Minton, 1976).

During the period 1980–85, an average of 80,000 wintered in western Europe, of which 21,000 (26%) were in Britain. In 1988–89 the western European population had reached 150,000 and that for Britain 40,000 (26%). This shows that there has been a very large increase in numbers since 1969–75, when there were 30,000 in western Europe and 10,000 (33%) in Britain. The reason for this increase is believed to be a series of highly successful breeding seasons in the Soviet Arctic during the 1970s (Moser, 1988).

In Britain, apart from the Ribble and Dee, all of the important estuaries for the species lie south-east of a line from the Humber to Hampshire; of particular importance are the Wash (average 6,570) and Chichester Harbour, Foulness and The Swale, each with 1,400–1,600. The top 10 estuaries for the species support over 60% of the total wintering population in Britain (Salmon *et al.*, 1989).

In most estuaries, numbers during August–October are slightly higher than they are in mid-winter, but full national count data are not (at present) available. During late March and April there is a steady movement away from Britain; these birds are thought to go to the Wadden Sea. Only the Wash and the Ribble support over 1,000 individuals until May. Birds which have wintered further south move north-eastwards to the Wadden Sea in May, small numbers of them stopping briefly in south-east Britain.

THREATS TO SURVIVAL

Threats include those which generally affect birds using an estuarine habitat (see page 308).

The dispersed nature of feeding birds is likely to mean that nearly all habitat loss will have a direct effect on this species. In the past, the Grey Plover was hunted extensively throughout Europe, and the relaxation of this pressure may have aided its recent rapid increase in numbers.

CONSERVATION

General conservation measures that are required for those waders, including the Grey Plover, which are associated with an estuarine habitat are given on pages 317–27. Few other measures are needed at present, except for the maintenance of the no-shooting restrictions.

REFERENCES

Branson, N.J.B.A. & Minton, C.D.T. 1976. Moult, measurements and migrations of the Grey Plover. Bird Study 23: 257–266.

Moser, M.E. 1988. Limits to the numbers of Grey Plovers *Pluvialis squatarola* wintering in British estuaries: an analysis of long-term population trends. J. Appl. Ecol. 25: 473–485.

Salmon, D.G., Prys-Jones, R.P. & Kirby, J.S. 1989. Wildfowl and Wader Counts 1988–89. The Results of the National Wildfowl Counts and Birds of Estuaries Enquiry in the United Kingdom. Slimbridge: The Wildfowl Trust.

Townshend, D.J. 1985. Decisions for a life-time: establishment of spatial defence and movement patterns by juvenile Grey Plovers (*Pluvialis squatarola*). J. Anim. Ecol. 54: 267–274.

Consultant: A.J. Prater

Knot

Calidris canutus

The Knot is a localized winter visitor and passage-migrant to Britain in internationally important numbers. It is almost entirely restricted (98% of total numbers) to estuaries, and is found in very large concentrations on a few sites. Small numbers occur on rocky coasts in east and north Scotland. It is the third most numerous of British estuarine waders, with an average population of 220,000. At present, the major threat comes from estuarine barrages and development involving land-claim.

LEGAL STATUS

Protected under WCA 1981; Annex II/2 of EC Bird Directive; Appendix III of the Berne Convention.

ECOLOGY

The Knot is a specialist feeder on marine bivalve molluscs, particularly *Macoma balthica*, *Mytilus edulis*, and *Cerastoderma* sp.; items in the length range 3–15 mm are taken. Knots are long distance migrants capable of covering over long distances in a single flight. During the pre-migration build-up of weight in Morecambe Bay and Iceland, spat of *Mytilus edulis* are especially prominent in the diet. Birds form very large, dense flocks both on feeding grounds and at roosts; they appear to require large, open mud-flats.

DISTRIBUTION AND POPULATION

North Holarctic; breeding distribution is discontinuous in the high Arctic above 60°N. There are four distinct races: *C. c. islandica* in the high arctic of northern Canada and Greenland; *C. c. rufa* in the low arctic in north-east Canada; *C. c. canutus* in the north-central Palearctic; and *C. c. rogersi* in the north-east Palearctic. The first and third of these winter in or migrate through Britain (Dick *et al.*, 1976). *C. c. islandica* winters in western Europe with possibly a few reaching West Africa.

The numbers in western Europe averaged 350,000 over the period 1980–88, a substantial decrease of 30% since 1969–75 when an average of 500,000 was estimated. A decrease of 27% has taken place in Britain where average numbers dropped from 300,000 (60% of the European wintering population) to 220,000 (63%). Although recent counts in Britain have shown a slight increase, which may only be a slight fluctuation or a reversal in the trend. A much larger percentage decrease has taken place towards the edge of the wintering range of *islandica* in France, where it fell from 110,000 in the late 1960s to fewer than 20,000 by 1976.

In Britain, the Wash is the most important wintering site (89,000), with Morecambe Bay, and the Alt, Ribble, Humber and Thames estuaries regularly supporting over 200,000. Elsewhere in Europe the Wadden Sea is of particular importance in winter.

During the autumn moulting period most *islandica* gather on the Wadden Sea (though some birds also moult on the Wash and at other main wintering sites). After moult, in November/December, many of these birds move west to Britain. In March, many *islandica* move back to the Wadden Sea before migrating—either via Iceland or Norway—to their breeding grounds (Davidson *et al.*, 1986). In Britain, Morecambe Bay, the Ribble and the Wash are of particular value as pre-migratory fattening grounds: birds leave Britain in early May, most migrating north via staging points in Iceland and a few via north Norway.

The race *canutus* from north-central and western Siberia migrates via the Wadden Sea to winter in West Africa and south to South Africa. These birds migrate via the west European coast (or reach it from an overland flight from Siberia) in July–September and return north along the same route (also via the Wadden Sea) in May. Relatively small numbers of this race occur in Britain on autumn passage (Dick *et al.*, 1987). It is thought that the Atlantic flyway population of this race totals about 512,000 individuals (Smit & Piersma, 1989).

The numbers of both races fluctuate considerably. This appears to be due to great variations in breeding success, as is typical of species nesting in the high Arctic.

THREATS TO SURVIVAL

Threats include those which generally affect birds using an estuarine habitat (see pages 302–16); site-specificity and a reduction in the availability of food are particularly important threats for this bird.

Of particular importance is the very large concentration of this species in a very few key estuaries at any one time. The use of only a few major spring staging or stop-over sites in Britain makes the species especially vulnerable to habitat loss or degradation. From these sites, Knots leave for their few 'refuelling' sites in Iceland and Norway; during this migration stage nearly all the body-reserves which have been gained are lost or severely depleted (Davidson & Evans, 1988). Any reduction in food availability in British sites is likely to prove a serious threat to the birds' ability to accumulate sufficient reserves. There is evidence from recent research which indicates that body-reserves gained at staging posts are vital to ensure arrival and survival on inhospitable breeding grounds and for successful breeding (Davidson & Evans, 1988; Morrison & Davidson, 1990).

Knots can be disturbed easily at their roosts; a major roost on the Dee which was abandoned in favour of an undisturbed site 20 km away appeared to be related to severe recreational disturbance (Mitchell *et al.*, 1988).

CONSERVATION

General conservation measures that are required for those birds, including the Knot, which are associated with an estuarine habitat are given on pages 317–27. The particular importance of ensuring that such measures within Britain effectively cover moulting, wintering, migration and staging sites cannot be emphasized too strongly for this species. In addition, the special role of certain sites outside Britain should be highlighted, especially the role of the Wadden Sea (in the

Federal Republic of Germany and Denmark) and of staging posts in Iceland and Norway. Consideration needs to be given to preventing excess disturbance to its roosts.

REFERENCES

DAVIDSON, N.C. & EVANS, P.R. 1988. Pre-breeding accumulation of fat and muscle protein by Arctic-breeding Shorebirds. Proc. XIX International Ornithological Congress, Ottawa.

DAVIDSON, N.C., STRANN, K-B., CROCKFORD, N.J., EVANS, P.R., RICHARDSON, J., STANDEN, L.J., TOWNSHEND, D.J., UTTLEY, J.D., WILSON, J.R. & WOOD, A.G. 1986. The origins of Knots (Calidric canutus) in arctic Norway in spring. Ornis Scandinavica 17: 175–179.

DAVIDSON, N.C. & WILSON, J. 1990. The migration system of the Nearctic Knot Calidris canutus islandica. Wader Study Group. Bull. Supplement. In press.

DICK, W.J.A., PIENKOWSKI, M.W., WALTNER, M. & MINTON, C.D.T. 1976. Distribution and geographical origins of Knot Calidris canutus wintering in Europe and Africa. Ardea 64: 22–47.

DICK, W.J.A., PIERSMA, T. & PROKOSCH, P. 1987. Spring migration of Siberian Knots Calidris canutus: results of a co-operative Wader Study Group project. Ornis Scand. 17: 5–16.

MITCHELL, J.R., MOSER, M.E. & KIRBY, J.S. 1988. Declines in midwinter counts of various waders roosting on the Dee estuary. Bird Study 35: 191–198.

MORRISON, R.I.G. & DAVIDSON, N.C. 1990. Migration, body condition and behaviour of Shorebirds during spring migration at Alert, Ellesmere Island, N.W.T. in Canada's Missing Dimension Science & History on the Canadian Arctic Islands. C.R. Harrington (ed.). Canadian Museum of Nature.

SMIT, C.J. & PIERSMA, T. 1989. Numbers, midwinter distribution and migration of wader populations using the East Atlantic Flyway. In Flyways and reserve networks for water birds. Boyd, H. and Pirot, J-Y. (eds) IWRB Special Publication No. 9.

UTTLEY, J.D., THOMAS, C.J., DAVIDSON, N.C., STRANN, K.B. & EVANS, P.R. 1987. The spring migration system of Nearctic Knots Calidris canutus islandica: a reappraisal. Wader Study Group Bull. 49, Suppl./IWRB Special Publ. 7: 80–84.

Consultants: A.J. Prater and N. Davidson

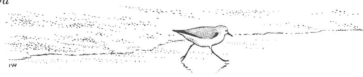

Sanderling
Calidris alba

The Sanderling is a localized winter visitor and a passage-migrant to Britain in internationally important numbers. It is entirely restricted to sandy coasts and estuaries. Of the total British wintering population of 14,000, 67% are found on open, non-estuarine coast. The major threat is from estuarine barrage development and land-claim which could especially affect the few critical spring migration sites.

LEGAL STATUS

Protected under WCA 1981; EC Birds Directive; Appendix II of the Berne Convention.

ECOLOGY

The Sanderling feeds almost exclusively in areas with sandy substrata; thus, where they occur in estuaries they are found on the outer, more sandy intertidal flats. A wide range of invertebrate food is taken, particularly small Crustacea. At times they feed high on the shore among the decaying algae of the high-tide mark. Here they probe vigorously and take mostly adult, pupal and larval Diptera. Birds are often tame. At high tide they form roosting flocks, often mixing with Dunlin and Ringed Plovers. They have a short breeding season in the Arctic; most leave western Europe in late May or early June and return between mid-July and late July.

DISTRIBUTION AND POPULATION

Holarctic. Breeds on the high Arctic tundra where it has a very discontinuous distribution, but most birds are found in two sectors of the Arctic—Greenland/north-east Canada and north-central USSR based on the Taimyr peninsula. A few pairs breed in other areas of the high Arctic, eg, Spitsbergen, the only Sanderling breeding site in the Palearctic.

Sanderling winter on coasts throughout the world's temperate and tropical regions. The details of their migration system are not yet fully understood but birds from both sectors migrate to and through Britain (Summers *et al.*, 1987). It is thought that most, but not all, British wintering birds originate in Siberia and that most of the Greenland/Canadian birds using the East Atlantic flyway winter in western Africa.

Britain supports about 14,000 Sanderling in winter (over 50% of those wintering in western Europe) (Smit & Piersma, 1989). Sanderling are widely dispersed in flocks of 20–300 (Prater & Davies, 1978), but major concentrations occur on the Ribble Estuary (2,207 average from 1984–1989, 16% of the British population) and on the west coast of the Uists (2,388 in 1984–85, 17·1%). On estuaries, where long-term population monitoring takes place, numbers have fluctuated considerably over the last 17 winters but no overall trend is discernible.

During the spring migration, Sanderling are particularly abundant in May on the major west coast estuaries, with up to 11,800 in Morecambe Bay, 9,000 on the Solway, 6,500 on both the Dee and Ribble, and 3,000 on the Duddon. These are birds which have wintered further south along the shores of western Europe and Africa from Mauritania south to eastern South Africa many of these are en route to Greenland/north-east Canada via staging points in Iceland (Salmon *et al.*, 1989).

THREATS TO SURVIVAL

Threats include those which generally affect birds using an estuarine habitat (see page 308).

Of particular importance are threats which may affect the critical migration stop-over sites in spring. Such sites are relatively few and small, and they are the final-stage feeding grounds where reserves of fat and muscle protein are put on to provide the resources for migration across the North Atlantic and to Siberia.

CONSERVATION

General conservation measures that are required for those birds, including the Sanderling, which are associated with an estuarine habitat are given on pages 317–27. The need to identify and target action on the migration stop-over sites should be emphasized.

REFERENCES

PRATER, A.J. & DAVIES, M. 1978. Wintering Sanderlings in Britain. Bird Study 25: 33–38.
SALMON, D.G., PRYS-JONES, R.P. & KIRBY, J.S. 1989. Wildfowl and Wader Counts 1988–89. The results of the National Wildfowl Counts and Birds of Estuaries Enquiry in the United Kingdom. Slimbridge: The Wildfowl Trust.
SMIT, C.J. & PIERSMA, T. 1989. In Boyd, H. & Pirot, J-Y. (eds). Flyways and reserve networks for water birds. IWRB Special Publication No. 9. Slimbridge.
SUMMERS, R.W., UNDERHILL, L.G., WALTNER, M. & WHITELAW, D.A. 1987. Population, biometrics and movements of the Sanderling Calidris alba in southern Africa. Ostrich 58: 24–39.

Consultant: A.J. Prater

Temminck's Stint
Calidris temninckii

This is a rare breeding summer visitor to Britain, and an uncommon passage-migrant. Its future as a breeding bird in Britain is probably mostly influenced by climate and the maintenance of suitable breeding habitat.

LEGAL STATUS

Protected under Schedule 1 of WCA 1981; EC Birds Directive; Appendix II of the Berne Convention.

ECOLOGY

The Temminck's Stint is a summer visitor to Europe which, in the breeding season, occurs in arctic, subarctic and boreal habitats from sea-level to montane plateaux; it breeds near tidal-waters and freshwater lakes, rivers and swamps. On passage, and in winter quarters, this bird can be found in tidal areas, but it prefers freshwater habitats, large and small—even those which are far inland.

In Britain the birds that form the tiny breeding population arrive on the breeding grounds from mid-May to June. Breeding strategies are complicated;

both sexes are successively bigamous, making it difficult to determine breeding pairs. In Scotland, where the British breeding population is found, it is difficult to establish how many of the adults are actually breeding. Nest: a scrape on the ground, sparingly lined with grasses, in short vegetation, generally near water. Eggs: laid June–July. Clutch: 4, very rarely 3; separate clutches/broods are cared for by the male and female. The young fledge in July–August.

Food consists of insects, small molluscs and crustaceans, earthworms and seeds (Hilden, 1975).

DISTRIBUTION AND POPULATION

North Palearctic. Temminck's Stints breed in Scotland, north Fenno-Scandia and Russia eastwards through Siberia to Pacific coasts. It winters in Africa and southern Asia. In Britain, Temminck's Stints attempted unsuccessfully to nest in Inverness-shire in 1934, 1936 and 1947 (two birds were present at a site in 1935, and one in 1947), and in Yorkshire in 1951. Birds were present at a suitable nesting site in the Scottish Highlands in 1969 and 1970, and breeding was recorded there in 1971 (Headlam, 1972). Since then, birds have been present every summer, with records from 11 sites in Scotland; however, nesting has been recorded only at four places. Only two sites have been regular: the 1969 site was used until 1980, and again from 1985, while a second site was used annually from 1974 to 1986. Nesting has been confirmed on at least 13 occasions, and with young on at least nine occasions. Because of the dangers of excessive disturbance, the nesting sites have not been systematically searched for nests or young. The numbers of adults recorded in Scotland rose from two to four annually in 1969–1973, and to five or six in 1974–1977, reaching a peak of nine in 1978–1980; since then it has fluctuated between two and eight.

Population estimates for northern Europe are 34,000 pairs in Norway, 20,000 pairs in Sweden and at least 2,000 pairs in Finland. Decreases have been recorded in some areas of all three countries, especially in western Finland (Cramp *et al.*, 1983).

THREATS TO SURVIVAL

Threats include disturbance by man, flooding of nesting sites, and the effects of afforestation.

Farming operations, human disturbance and flooding can cause problems during the breeding season, and afforestation is a potential threat.

Egg-collecting is also a threat with such a small proportion. It is important that the nesting sites are left undisturbed and their locations kept confidential.

CONSERVATION

One main site is already an SSSI for other species, and the other main site has been recommended as an SSSI and SPA/Ramsar site. Areas where the species is seen in summer should not be publicized.

Arrangements should be made with landowners to minimize the effects of farming and other activities. There may be opportunities for habitat management to enhance breeding success. The known breeding sites in Scotland have certain habitat features in common, although many other apparently suitable similar localities are not used. Its fortunes in this country are probably therefore most influenced by climatic conditions.

Consideration should be given to adding this species to Annex 1 of the EC Directive.

REFERENCES

HEADLAM, C.G. 1972. Temminck's Stints breeding in Scotland. Scot. Birds 7: 94.
HILDEN, P. 1975. Breeding system of Temminck's Stint *Calidris temminckii*. Orn. Fenn. 52: 117–146.

Consultant: R.H. Dennis

Purple Sandpiper
Calidris maritima

The Purple Sandpiper is a rare breeding bird that has bred successfully at one site in Scotland since 1978. Otherwise it is a passage-migrant and winter visitor, but not in internationally important numbers. No special conservation measures are considered necessary, other than the safeguarding of the Scottish breeding site.

LEGAL STATUS

Protected under Schedule 1 of WCA 1981; EC Birds Directive; Appendix II of the Berne Convention.

ECOLOGY

The Purple Sandpiper breeds on open ground on hillsides, mountains and arctic tundra. Nest: a deep scrape lined with dead leaves. Eggs: laid May–July. Clutch: 4 (3–4); one brood. The young fledge by July to mid-August.

Food in the breeding season consists of small leaves, seeds, algae, moss, insects, spiders, crustaceans, molluscs and worms (Bengtson, 1970; Bengtson & Fzellberg, 1975).

DISTRIBUTION AND POPULATION

North Holarctic. There are two groups, one breeding in western Greenland/eastern Canada and wintering in Greenland/North America, and the other breeding in east Greenland, Iceland, the Faeroes, Scandinavia, Spitsbergen and Arctic Russia and wintering in Europe.

In Britain, the Purple Sandpiper is a regular passage-migrant and winter visitor, from October to May or from July to May, depending on region, chiefly on rocky coasts of eastern and northern Britain. It is also a rare breeding bird. One pair hatched three young in Scotland in 1978, rearing at least one juvenile, and bred successfully at the same site from 1979 to 1988; in recent years there have been two to three nests. Although these are the only breeding records, the species has been recorded singing at one other area.

The wintering population in Britain is about 16,000 (Moser, 1987). Although no counts have been made of the European population it probably exceeds 200,000 individuals; thus, the British wintering component is not of international importance as it represents no more than 8% of the total European population.

THREATS TO SURVIVAL

Threats include human disturbance and egg-collecting. Fortunately though, this species sits very tightly on the nest and is easily overlooked.

CONSERVATION

In the hope that a regular breeding population will become established (and there seems to be plenty of suitable habitat in Scotland), disturbance in the nesting area should be kept to a minimum. Fortunately, the Scottish breeding site is now wardened.

Areas where the species is seen in summer should not be publicized, and, if breeding becomes regular, favoured sites will need special protection and freedom from winter-sport developments.

Consideration should be given to adding the Purple Sandpiper to Annex 1 of the EC Birds Directive.

REFERENCES

BENGTSON, S.-A. 1970. Breeding behaviour of the Purple Sandpiper *Calidris maritima* in west Spitsbergen. Ornis Scand. 1: 17–25.

BENGTSON, S.-A. & FZELLBERG, A. 1975. Summer food of the Purple Sandpiper (*Calidris maritima*) in Spitsbergen. Astarte 8: 1–6.

DENNIS, R.H. 1983. Purple Sandpipers breeding in Scotland. Brit. Birds 76: 563–566.

MOSER, M.E. 1987. A revision of population estimates for Waders (*Charadrii*) wintering on the coastline of Britain. Biol. Conserv. 39: 153–164.

NICOLL, M., SUMMERS, R.W., UNDERHILL, L.G., BROCKIE, K. & RAE, R. 1987. Regional, seasonal and annual differences in the population structure of Purple Sandpipers in Britain. Ibis (in press).

SUMMERS, R.W., COURSE, C.J. & WHITFIELD, D.P. 1987. Purple Sandpiper studies in North Iceland 1986. A report of the Tay, Orkney and Grampian Ringing Groups' expedition to the Melrakkasletta, north Iceland in summer 1986. Kirkwall.

TOMKOVICH, P.S. 1985. Sketch of the Purple Sandpiper (*Calidris maritima*) biology of Franz Josef Land. Ornithologiya 20: 3–17.

Dunlin
Calidris alpina

The British wintering population of this species is localized, and of international importance. The Dunlin is a species with a complex pattern in Britain; there are three sub-species which regularly occur on migration, one of them wintering in this country. An internationally important breeding population is present, particularly in north and west Scotland. It is the most numerous of the estuarine waders which winter in Britain: 430,000 occur, of which only 6% are on non-estuarine coasts. A significant decrease in numbers has been observed over the last 15 years. As with many other wading species, the major threat comes from estuarine barrages and developments involving land-claim; these activities are likely to reduce the wintering feeding habitat.

LEGAL STATUS

Protected under WCA 1981; EC Birds Directive; Appendix II of the Berne Convention.

ECOLOGY

In winter, and on passage, the Dunlin feeds over all shore levels, but especially on the middle shore. It takes a very wide range of small prey species, ragworms (*Nereis diversicolor*) and the spire-shell (*Hydrobia ulvae*) predominate in the diet, but many other small polychaete worms, gastropod and bivalve molluscs, and crustaceans are also taken. As it is the smallest of Britain's wintering waders, the Dunlin needs to feed for nearly all of the winter daylight hours in order to obtain enough food to satisfy its energy requirements.

Breeding birds are found in two main habitats: wet upland moorland, where there are pools and patches of very short vegetation, and in coastal zones, particularly the wet areas in the machair of the Western Isles. Nest: on the ground, concealed in vegetation. Eggs: laid mostly in late May to mid-July. Clutch: 3–4 (2–6); one brood. The Dunlin is a gregarious species which often forms very large flocks at roost, on passage and in winter.

During the breeding season, adult and larval insects form the diet—with most items being chironomid and tipulid flies. Items of food are located both by sight and by feel during probing.

DISTRIBUTION AND POPULATION

Holarctic. The Dunlin breeds in the tundra and upland zones mostly north of 60°N, and in south-western England, where the southernmost breeding population is found. Three races occur in Britain: *C. a. arctica* (which breeds in north-east Greenland), *C. a. schinzii* (which breeds in Iceland, Britain and western Europe north to southern Scandinavia), and *C. a. alpina* (which breeds in northern Scandinavia to the western USSR). Four other races are found from the central USSR to northern Canada.

In Britain, about 9,150 pairs breed, most being in the peatlands of Caithness and Sutherland (3,800 pairs, 41%), the peatlands of Lewis and the machair of the Western Isles (3,300 pairs, 36%). This forms a very high proportion (83%) of the 11,000 pairs of *schinzii* breeding in temperate Europe. Many of the breeding populations in southern Sweden, Finland and Poland have declined alarmingly in recent years in several cases to extinction.

About 300,000 pairs of the sub-arctic breeding race *schinzii* are found in Iceland, and 5,000 pairs of *arctica* are found in Greenland. Both *schinzii* and *arctica* occur throughout Britain as passage-migrants, moving through between mid-July and September in the autumn, and between mid-April and May in the spring; extremely few, if any, of these birds winter in Britain. Most winter on the Atlantic coast from the Mediterranean to 5°N. In spring, however, the movement is more concentrated, and then up to 150,000 birds are reported, mainly from the same estuaries where they are seen in the autumn.

Some *C. a. alpina* are present in the autumn. These moult in British estuaries, moving south and west after moult; however, the majority arrive during October–November (after completing their moult on the shores of the Wadden Sea) and return to the Wadden Sea during March (Pienkowski & Evans, 1984; Piersma *et al.*, 1987). The winter population in Britain averaged 430,000 birds during 1981–1986, 21% of the birds in the whole East Atlantic flyway, but about 38% of the *alpina* sub-species. The numbers of this sub-species wintering in Britain and Europe have decreased by 20–25% since the early 1970s. The largest numbers wintering are on the Severn (46,000), Morecambe Bay (43,000) and the Wash (65,000), but other estuaries with over 20,000 are the Thames, Medway, Langstone Harbour, the Humber, Chichester Harbour and the Mersey.

THREATS TO SURVIVAL

Threats include those which generally affect birds using an estuarine habitat (see pages 302–16). The Dunlin also faces a number of other major problems, related to change in habitat, both on the winter and the breeding habitats.

The decrease in winter numbers has been shown to correlate closely with the spread of *Spartina anglica* over the upper-shore zone. This plant has spread rapidly in many estuaries, often having been introduced by man. The loss of high-level flats through *Spartina* and land-claim is believed to have removed crucial winter feeding grounds for this species — which feeds for all the tidal cycle even in severe weather (Goss-Custard & Moser, 1988). The use of large west coast estuaries as staging posts, to put on body reserves for long flights (e.g. across the North Atlantic), highlights the vital role of those estuaries at a critical phase of the life cycle. Loss of these areas could pose a particular problem.

The main threats to breeding populations come from changes in land-use. Moorland breeders are under particular pressure from blanket afforestation by exotic species of conifers. These plantations mainly remove breeding grounds. They may also create edge effects on nearby moorland through changing microclimate, drainage patterns, and increasing predator numbers and species—but these effects are still being investigated. On the peatlands of Caithness and Sutherland, where 41% of British Dunlin breed, there is a major threat due to afforestation. It has been estimated that, already, 17% of the Dunlin of these flows have been lost, and more will be lost if further planting proceeds (Stroud et al., 1987). High numbers also occur on other peatland areas especially on the island of Lewis. The other major breeding area is the machair of the Western Isles; here, Dunlin are dependent on low-intensity, traditional farming, where they breed in exteremely high densities on wetter patches (Fuller et al., 1986). If changes took place in agricultural practices, then it could have a significant effect on this population.

CONSERVATION

General conservation measures that are required for those birds, including the Dunlin, which are associated with an estuarine habitat are given on pages 317–27.

Special measures are needed to halt the loss of the upper-shore feeding zone. The disproportionate effect of land-claim is clear, as is the need both to prevent the further spread of *Spartina anglica* and to contain existing beds of this grass. Studies are required to assess the impact of returning these areas to potential feeding grounds. Preliminary observations indicate that such areas are not as good as long-established upper-shore mudflats; if confirmed, this would emphasize the need to prevent the further spread of *Spartina*.

To prevent serious loss of breeding habitat in the peatlands, special protection measures are needed urgently. These include further changes to the system of forestry grants and tax reliefs, and an examination of the ways of enhancing public support for other enterprises compatible with the maintenance of traditional land-uses. The designation of the Caithness and Sutherland peatlands as an Environmentally Sensitive Area (ESA) could assist this process considerably.

The recent ESA designation of the machair should enable traditional low-intensity farming to continue there—and thus protect its important breeding populations of Dunlin, however the restricted boundary of the current ESA requires urgent revision. A long-term commitment to ensuring that the ESA works is vital.

REFERENCES

FULLER, R.J., REED, T.M., BUXTON, N.E., WEBB, A., WILLIAMS, T.D. & PIENKOWSKI, M.W. 1986. Populations of breeding waders *Charadrii* and their habitats on the crofting lands of the Outer Hebrides, Scotland. Biol. Conserv. 37: 333–361.

GOSS-CUSTARD, J.D. & MOSER, M.E. 1988. Rates of change in the numbers of Dunlin, *Calidris alpina alpina*, wintering in British estuaries in relation to the spread of *Spartina anglica*. J. Appl. Ecol. 25: 95–110.

HARDY, A.R. & MINTON, C.D.T. 1980. Dunlin migration in Britain and Ireland. Bird Study 27: 81–92.

PIENKOWSKI, M.W. & EVANS, P.R. 1984. Migratory behaviour of Shorebirds in the western Palearctic. *In* Burger, J. & Olla, B.H. Shorebirds: migration and foraging behaviour, 73–123. Plenum Publishing Co.

PIERSMA, T., BEINTEMA, A.J., DAVIDSON, N.C., MUNSTER, O.A.G. & PIENKOWSKI, M.W. 1987. Wader migration systems in the East Atlantic. Wader Study Group Bull. 49 Suppl./IWRB Special Publ. 7: 35–56.

SALMON, D.G., PRYS-JONES, R.P. & KIRBY, J.S. 1987. Wildfowl and Wader Counts 1988–89. The Results of the National Wildfowl Counts and Birds of Estuaries Enquiry in the United Kingdom. Slimbridge: The Wildfowl Trust.
STROUD, D.A., REED, T.M., PIENKOWSKI, M.W. & LINDSAY, R.A. 1987. Birds, Bogs and Forestry: the peatlands of Caithness and Sutherland. Peterborough: Report by Nature Conservancy Council.

Consultant: A.J. Prater

Ruff
Philomachus pugnax

The Ruff is a rare, localized breeding bird in Britain. It was formerly widespread in England, but the population declined to extinction during the 18th and 19th centuries. Breeding has occurred sporadically since regular breeding ceased in the 1870s—with regular lek displays by males since the 1960s, and regular nesting by females at some East Anglian sites. About 1,400 individuals winter on estuaries and at inland wetlands. Future breeding in Britain is dependent on correct wetland management.

LEGAL STATUS

Protected under Schedule 1 of WCA 1981; Annex 1 of EC Birds Directive; Appendix III of the Berne Convention.

ECOLOGY

Most Ruff breed on the arctic and sub-arctic tundra of Eurasia, but in Britain nesting occurs on inland wet meadowland, coastal grazing marshes and high saltmarsh. Nest: a scrape on the ground, hidden among grasses or sedges. Females visit the communal display areas (leks) of the males to mate, but they nest solitarily. Eggs: laid May to mid-June. Clutch: 4. Of the wet meadow breeding waders, the Ruff nests latest in the season, with most nests started in late May to early June (Cramp *et al.*, 1983). The breeding season is short, so that there is little opportunity for replacement nesting after breeding failure.

Food in the breeding season consists of invertebrates, mainly insects, gleaned from the surface of water, mud or vegetation, or located by probing in mud. The bird forages by wading rapidly through shallow water or walking over grassland. In winter, seeds may be taken in quantity (Cramp *et al.*, 1983).

DISTRIBUTION AND POPULATION

Palearctic. The vast majority of Ruffs breed in arctic and subarctic parts of the USSR, Finland, Sweden and Norway. Only about 2,700 females are estimated to nest in Europe south of Fenno-Scandia, with most of these breeding in the Netherlands, Germany, Denmark and Poland (Piersma, 1986). Small numbers (totalling less than 100) breed in England, France, the German Democratic Republic, Luxembourg and France.

The bird winters mainly in sub-Saharan Africa, with smaller numbers in the Indian sub-continent, around the Mediterranean and in north-western Europe, including Britain. Wintering Ruffs in Britain number about 1,400; they are found both at inland wetlands and estuaries and have increased in numbers since the 1930s (Sorensen, 1986). They are thought not to include the breeding population because breeding males arrive with their breeding plumage much more advanced than that of the wintering males. There has been a ringing recovery, during the breeding season, of a British wintering Ruff in Siberia.

The Ruff became extinct as a regular breeding bird in Britain in the 19th century because of the drainage of marshland and, finally, as a result of egg collecting and shooting. Regular breeding began again at the Ouse Washes (Cambridgeshire/ Norfolk) in the 1950s or 1960s (Cottier & Lea, 1969), and other sites in Kent and northern England have been used more recently. More sites have leks than are known to have breeding females. Since 1963, estimates of the numbers of females suspected of breeding have fluctuated markedly between 0 and 32, but the number of confirmed breeding attempts was usually less than ten.

THREATS TO SURVIVAL

Threats include the effects of agricultural land-use and loss of habitat through flooding.

The decline and current low breeding population of the Ruff in western Europe is almost certainly caused by the drainage and intensification of agricultural use of former wet grasslands. Pools and shallow flooded fields are important feeding habitats, and even small improvements to drainage are likely to result in these being absent in late spring and midsummer when Ruffs breed.

The Ruff's late breeding season also makes it especially susceptible to losses of nests and broods as a result of trampling by livestock, or through mowing (Beintema & Muskens, 1987). The short duration of the breeding season makes compensation for such losses by re-nesting unlikely.

On the main breeding site in England, the Ouse Washes, there has been a marked increase in the frequency of summer flooding; this may have destroyed nests or prevented nesting in at least five of the ten years 1975–84 (Green et al., 1987). This area acts as an emergency flood control reservoir, and hydrological changes and increased rainfall have caused a change in the flooding pattern.

CONSERVATION

Regular breeding sites are nature reserves or have SSSI or NNR status. However, habitat management is critically important. Populations of breeding Ruff can be expected to persist not only in areas of wet grassland in which the water table is maintained at a high level, but also in which summer flooding of nesting areas is prevented.

Grazing and mowing of breeding areas need to be restricted or prevented before midsummer. The disturbance of nesting females by humans is unlikely to occur, but leks do attract the attention of birdwatchers. Fortunately there are opportunities to watch displaying Ruffs from hides at a number of reserves.

REFERENCES

BEINTEMA, A.J. & MUSKENS, G.J.D.M. 1987. Nesting success of birds breeding on Dutch agricultural grasslands. J. Appl. Ecol. 24: 743–758.

COTTIER, E.J. & LEA, D. 1969. Black-tailed Godwits, Ruffs and Black Terns breeding on the Ouse Washes. Brit. Birds 62: 259–270.

GREEN, R.E., CADBURY, C.J. & WILLIAMS, G. 1987. Floods threaten black-tailed godwits breeding at the Ouse Washes. RSPB Conservation Rev. 1: 14–16.

PIERSMA, T. 1986. Breeding waders in Europe. Wader Study Group Bulletin 48, Supplement.

SORENSEN, J. 1986. Ruff. *In* Lack, P. (ed.), The atlas of wintering birds in Britain and Ireland. Calton: Poyser.

Consultant: R.E. Green

Black-tailed Godwit

Limosa limosa

The Black-tailed Godwit is a rare, localized breeding bird in Britain, with a separate, also localized, population wintering on estuaries. After being a widespread breeding bird in wetlands in eastern England it became extinct in Britain early in the 19th century. After sporadic nesting in the 1930s and 1940s, East Anglia was recolonized in 1952. A few pairs also breed in northern England and Scotland. After reaching a peak of 87 pairs in 1976, numbers have declined to about 50 pairs. About 4,800 winter in Britain (11% of the European population), the majority on eight estuaries. Protection and management of wet grassland is essential if it is to remain or prosper as a breeding bird in Britain.

LEGAL STATUS

Protected under Schedule 1 of WCA 1981; Annex II/2 of EC Birds Directive; Appendix III of the Berne Convention.

ECOLOGY

The Black-tailed Godwit breeds in wet meadows, coastal grazing marshes (in eastern England) and moorland bogs—well-grazed grassland being preferred.

Nest: moderately well concealed in a tussock. The bird is loosely colonial, with an effective communal defence of eggs and young against avian and mammalian predators. Eggs: laid mainly from late April to late May. Clutch: 4; replacement clutches are usually laid in Britain only after failure at the egg stage.

Food in the breeding season consists of earthworms and tipulid larvae, which are taken by probing damp grassland, together with insect larvae, molluscs and other benthic invertebrates which are obtained from the mud of pools and ditch edges. Females incubate by day while males feed on wet grassland, near the nest if possible, and defend the site against crows and other potential egg predators. Females feed mainly at night and are more likely to feed in pools. The chicks glean insects from grassland vegetation and shallow water, and they may move a considerable distance from the nest.

In winter, in Britain, invertebrates—particularly oligochaete and polychaete worms—are obtained by probing estuarine mud (Hale, 1980). Inland wet grassland, especially at the Ouse and Nene Washes (Cambridgeshire/Norfolk), is also used for staging areas by part of the wintering population in late winter–spring.

DISTRIBUTION AND POPULATION

Palearctic. One race, *L. l. islandica*, breeds in Iceland and occasionally in Britain and Ireland, whilst *L. l. limosa* occurs in northern Europe and the USSR, breeding locally in Norway, Finland, Britain, Austria and France. Small populations breed in Sweden, Denmark, Belgium, the Federal Republic of Germany, the German Democratic Republic, Czechoslovakia, Poland and Hungary, but the bulk of the European population of *L. l. limosa* is in the Netherlands and USSR (Piersma, 1986).

L. l. islandica winters in the British Isles, western France, Iberia and perhaps Morocco, while the west European *L. l. limosa* winters in tropical West Africa (Beintema & Drost, 1986).

The total breeding population of *L. l. limosa* in Europe (excluding the USSR) is put at 102,000–123,000 pairs, and that of *L. l. islandica* at 10,000–30,000 pairs (Piersma, 1986).

The average British wintering population of *L. l. islandica* for the years 1980–86 was 4,800, about 11% of the total wintering population of this sub-species. Eight estuaries hold most of the birds: the Ribble (1,587), Stour (1,131), Langstone Harbour (918), Colne (950), Chichester Harbour (627), Hamford Water (826), Exe (603) and Poole Harbour (803). The figures given are average monthly maxima for 1984–89 (Salmon et al., 1989). The British wintering population increased from the 1930s to the mid-1970s (Prater, 1975), but has declined substantially since then (Marchant, 1981).

There was no regular breeding of Black-tailed Godwits this century in Britain until 1952, when nesting by birds of the European race *L. l. limosa* began at the Ouse Washes (Cambridgeshire/Norfolk border) (Cottier & Lea, 1969). The breeding population at this site grew exponentially to 64 pairs in the early 1970s but has declined since then to about 20 pairs. Recent poor breeding success, due to the flooding of nests, which now occurs in most years, is probably the main cause, though the effects of drought on the suitability of the West African wintering grounds may also be involved (Green et al., 1987). The species also breeds at a few other sites in south-eastern England, where numbers are not declining. A few pairs breed annually in Somerset, northern England and in Shetland (where the birds are of the Icelandic race.) The total population in 1986–87 was about 50 pairs.

THREATS TO SURVIVAL

Threats include a decline in suitable habitat and the effects of flooding on nesting sites.

An important constraint on the size of the breeding population in southern Britain is the restricted area of suitable wet grassland available. The birds require well-grazed pastureland or hayfields with a high water table, and much of this has been drained and intensified or converted to arable land in the past twenty years.

Because of its colonial nesting habits, which are probably important for nest defence against predators, this species is unlikely to survive in isolated pairs on small patches of suitable habitat.

Although the main breeding site at the Ouse Washes is mainly a nature reserve, it functions as a floodwater storage facility, and its water regime is outside the control of the conservation bodies involved. A recent marked increase in the risk of summer flooding has reduced breeding success by direct disruption of nesting and has also hindered vegetation control by grazing and mowing.

The timing and intensity of grazing can also have an important influence on breeding success. High densities of livestock in April and May can substantially reduce nest success by trampling, and the early mowing of hay can cause chick losses (Beintema & Muskens, 1987).

Egg collecting and human disturbance are occasional problems, and enforcement or protection measures are necessary to prevent them.

Because of the concentration of the wintering population into a small number of estuaries, the Black-tailed Godwit is especially vulnerable among estuarine wintering waders to loss of intertidal feeding habitat, caused by development, and to disturbance of high-tide roosts (see section on threats to estuarine habitats on pages 302–16).

CONSERVATION

If this species is to remain or prosper as a breeding bird in Britain there is a need for large areas of well-grazed wet grassland where water tables are maintained at a high level but where widespread surface flooding is prevented after mid-April. Although considerable areas of damp meadowland have SSSI status, the management of water levels and grazing on them is often far from ideal for Black-tailed Godwits or other breeding waders. Relaxation of the standard of field drainage would be beneficial to these birds.

Grazing or mowing should aim to produce a predominantly short but varied sward in spring, but grazing animals should not be introduced too early in the spring (before late May) if trampling losses are to be avoided.

While all sites on which wintering and passage flocks occur are SSSIs, constant vigilance is required to ensure that feeding habitat and roosts are adequately protected from development and disturbance.

REFERENCES

BEINTEMA, A.J. & DROST, N. 1986. Migration of the Black-tailed Godwit. Gerfaut 76: 37–62.
BEINTEMA, A.J. & MUSKENS, G.J.D.M. 1987. Nesting success of birds breeding on Dutch agricultural grasslands. J. Appl. Ecol. 24: 743–758.

Cottier, E.J. & Lea, D. 1969. Black-tailed Godwits, Ruffs and Black Terns breeding on the Ouse Washes. Brit. Birds 62: 259–270.

Green, R.E., Cadbury, C.J. & Williams, G. 1987. Floods threaten black-tailed godwits breeding at the Ouse Washes. RSPB Conservation Rev. 1: 14–16.

Hale, W.G. 1980. Waders. London: Collins.

Marchant, J.H. 1981. Birds of estuaries enquiry 1976–77 to 1978–79. Tring: BTO.

Piersma, T. 1986. Breeding waders in Europe. Wader Study Group Bulletin 48, Supplement.

Prater, A.J. 1975. The wintering population of the Black-tailed Godwit. Bird Study 22: 169–176.

Salmon, D.G., Prys-Jones, R.P. & Kirby, J.S. 1989. Wildfowl and wader counts 1988–89. The Results of the National Wildfowl and Wader Counts of Estuaries Enquiry in the United Kingdom. Slimbridge: Wildfowl Trust.

Consultant: R.E. Green

Bar-tailed Godwit

Limosa lapponica

The Bar-tailed Godwit is a localized winter visitor and passage-migrant to Britain in internationally important numbers. It is almost entirely restricted to estuaries, and particularly to a few major sites. The 61,000 that winter here represents about 50% of the population wintering on the Atlantic coast of Europe. The major threat comes from estuarine land-claim arising from large developments.

LEGAL STATUS

Protected under WCA 1981; Annex II/2 of EC Birds Directive; Appendix III of the Berne Convention.

ECOLOGY

The Bar-tailed Godwit feeds mainly on the middle to low shore levels of relatively sandy estuaries. It will take a range of larger molluscs and polychaete worms, but its main food consists of the lugworm (*Arenicola marina*). The wetness of the surface of the intertidal flats is important; under dry conditions the worms cannot be detected or captured. There is a slight sexual separation in feeding areas: the longer-billed and longer-legged females are able to exploit sites in deeper water, while the smaller males forage on wet sand or in very shallow water (Smith & Evans, 1973). These birds form large roosts at high tide, choosing to remain as far from land as possible but coming inland on extreme high-water spring tides. The Bar-tailed Godwit is a nervous species which is easily disturbed.

DISTRIBUTION AND POPULATION

Palearctic and marginally Nearctic. Breeding occurs on arctic tundra from northern Scandinavia east to north-west Alaska. Birds migrating to and through Britain come from the nominate race in the western zone, east to the Taimyr peninsula (central USSR). The easternmost populations form the race *L. I. baueri*; they winter on Pacific coasts, especially in Australasia.

During 1980–85 an average of 61,000 birds wintered in Britain (50% of the European wintering birds; 11% of the East Atlantic flyway population). Between 1973 and 1980, numbers in Europe fluctuated but showed no clear trend; there is no reliable information prior to this period. There are two arrival periods in Britain. The first is in late August/early September; birds arriving during this period moult in a few major estuaries, particularly the Wash, Morecambe Bay and the Ribble. The rest arrive in November/December after having moulted on the Wadden Sea. In Britain, the top twenty estuaries support 70% of the British wintering population, other estuaries are important in maintaining their numbers and distribution.

A very rapid emigration takes place in late February/March, back to the Wadden Sea. Spring migrants from Africa pass through eastern Britain in late April/early May. They gather in the Wadden Sea in May before returning to the breeding grounds.

THREATS TO SURVIVAL

Threats include those which generally affect birds using an estuarine habitat (see pages 302–16); disturbance and bait-digging are particularly important threats.

Of special importance for this species is the problem of disturbance. In one case, a major roost site has become untenable, apparently due to an increase in general public access activity. Here, the roost at West Kirby (Cheshire, Dee) was forced to move to the Alt estuary, 20 km away, with a resulting loss of the energy expended in this flight (Mitchell *et al.*, 1988).

As lugworms form the bulk of the diet, excessive bait-digging can pose a particular problem for Bar-tailed Godwits, this threat being enhanced by mechanical techniques which are becoming more widely used in Europe.

CONSERVATION

General conservation measures that are required for those birds, including the Bar-tailed Godwit, which are associated with an estuarine habitat are given on pages 317–27.

Special measures may be required to minimize the impact of disturbance; these could include special sanctuary zones and action to prevent access to four-wheel drive vehicles/motor cycles.

Steps to educate the public about the problems caused by disturbance to this species would be beneficial. In certain areas, bye-laws and their enforcement will be necessary to prevent prey depletion by bait-diggers. The species was removed from the quarry list in Britain in 1982.

REFERENCES

MITCHELL, J.R., MOSER, M.E. & KIRBY, J.S. 1988. Declines in midwinter counts of waders roosting on the Dee estuary. Bird Study 35: 191–198.
SMITH, P.C. & EVANS, P.R. 1973. Studies of shorebirds at Lindisfarne, Northumberland. I. Feeding ecology and behaviour of the Bar-tailed godwit. Wildfowl 24: 135–139.

Consultant: A.J. Prater

Whimbrel
Numenius phaeopus

The Whimbrel is a species of special concern because of the marked decrease in the British breeding population in the late 19th and early 20th centuries; only recently has the population increased to over 300 pairs. Breeding is confined largely to Shetland (about 470 pairs), with a few pairs in Caithness, Orkney, the Outer Hebrides, and occasionally elsewhere in Scotland. Conservation of the main breeding areas in Shetland within SSSIs affords protection to over a third of the British breeding population. Further SSSIs and SPAs to conserve more of the breeding habitat are planned.

LEGAL STATUS

Protected under Schedule 1 of WCA 1981; Annex II/2 of EC Birds Directive; Appendix III of the Berne Convention.

ECOLOGY

The Whimbrel is a summer visitor which breeds on the ground on a low hummock or on rough pastures—usually on maritime heath with a predominant ground cover of *Calluna*, cotton-grass (*Eriophorum*) or long grasses. Nest: a scrape scantily lined with grass or moss. Pairs are usually solitary although loose aggregations may occur. Eggs: laid mid-May to mid-July. Clutch: 4 (3–5); one brood. The young fledge by mid-August.

Food consists of invertebrates—including crustaceans, molluscs, marine and annelid worms, grasshoppers, moths and millipedes, together with plant material such as the berries of *Eriophorum*, *Vaccinium* and *Rubus*, and some seeds.

DISTRIBUTION AND POPULATION

North Holarctic. Western Palearctic birds breed in Iceland, the Faeroes, northern Scotland, Fenno-Scandia, the Baltic States and northern Russia eastwards to the Taimyr peninsula; the European component winters mainly south of the Mediterranean, chiefly along the coasts of Africa. In Britain the Whimbrel nests in Shetland, with a few pairs in Caithness, Orkney, the Outer Hebrides (especially Lewis), and occasionally elsewhere on the Scottish mainland; otherwise it is a regular passage-migrant, between mid-April–mid-June and July–October, to all coasts—and occasionally in small numbers in winter at some estuaries in south-west England and Wales.

The population decreased markedly in Britain during 1880–1930, when it ceased to nest in Orkney and numbers were reduced to a handful in Shetland; however, since then it has increased steadily. The number of pairs in Shetland was put at 50–55 in the early 1950s, rising to 150 in the early 1970s and a maximum of 471 pairs in the mid-1980s; outside Shetland there were probably only about 25 pairs in Britain (mid-1980s), half of which were in Caithness and Orkney (Richardson, 1990). Elsewhere in northern Europe the breeding population has been estimated as: Iceland 200,000 pairs, the Faeroes 2,800 pairs, Norway 10,000 pairs, Sweden 5,000 pairs and Finland 30,000 pairs (Piersma, 1986).

THREATS TO SURVIVAL

Threats include the reclamation of moorland and maritime heaths for agriculture and forestry, and possibly egg collecting—and other forms of human disturbance.

The earlier decrease may well have been due largely to climatic amelioration, the recent trend towards colder springs and cooler summers having favoured this northern species.

Egg collecting and human disturbance probably played their part in contributing to the earlier decline, and some clutches are still taken in most years. The development of Shetland in connection with North Sea oil is increasing the problem of disturbance.

CONSERVATION

The main nesting areas should be protected from agricultural intensification or forestry through management planning, reserve acquisition, SSSI and SPA protection. Existing SSSIs already include 30–40% of the Shetland breeding population, most of which is in core areas comprising groups of six or more pairs. Further extensions to existing SSSIs, and the designation of currently proposed sites, will increase the population breeding within SSSIs to about 50%. Many of the smaller, more remote, groups of breeding Whimbrels are unlikely to be affected by man-induced changes, and provided that stringent protection can be given to those within SSSIs the future of the Whimbrel as a breeding bird within Britain should be secure.

Egg collecting must be strongly discouraged, and areas where the species is seen in summer on the Scottish mainland should not be publicized.

REFERENCES

PIERSMA, T. 1986. Breeding Waders in Europe. Wader Study Group Bulletin 48, supplement.
RICHARDSON, M.G. 1990. The distribution and status of Whimbrel *Numenius p. phaeopus* in Shetland and Britain. Bird Study 37: 61–68.

Consultant: M.G. Richardson

Curlew

Numenius arquata

The Curlew breeds and winters in Britain in internationally important numbers. The breeding population of about 35,000 pairs is some 28% of the European total, whilst the 91,000 wintering birds represent 30% of the East Atlantic flyway population. Of those present in winter, 47% are found on non-estuarine coasts and adjacent farmland. Land-use changes — particularly re-seeding, over-grazing and afforestation — represent the major threat to the breeding population which requires moist, poorly drained moors and heaths and rough grassland. In winter the main threat is from estuarine land-claim.

LEGAL STATUS

Protected under WCA 1981; Annex II/2 of EC Birds Directive; Appendix III of the Berne Convention.

ECOLOGY

In Britain the Curlew breeds typically in upland areas, favouring moist, poorly drained moors and heaths; it also breeds on rough grassland. Nest: on the ground, often on a tussock. Eggs: laid mostly between late April and late June. Clutch: 4 (2–5); one brood.

The bird feeds in a wide range of habitats and on a similarly wide range of medium–large invertebrates. On intertidal areas Curlews take most of the commoner bivalve molluscs, polychaete worms and crustacea, including crabs (*Carcinus*). Inland, adult and larval insects — and especially earthworms — form the bulk of the diet, although some berries are eaten on the breeding grounds.

The birds are typically well spread out when feeding, but even so, there is a substantial amount of intraspecific aggression over food items. Curlews form large roosting flocks. They tend to be wary and are easily disturbed.

DISTRIBUTION AND POPULATION

Palearctic. Breeding occurs mostly in the latitude band 45°N–65°N. In Britain, most breed in western and northern regions where poorly drained, unimproved, grazed pasture occurs in river valleys to lower moorland up to an altitude of 550 m.

Between 33,000 and 38,000 pairs breed in Britain, about 28% of the European total; most of the rest are in Scandinavia.

Following a general spread in Europe in the first half of the 20th century, there have been decreases reported subsequently from many countries, although the scale of decrease in Britain is uncertain. Many of those breeding in Scotland winter in Ireland or western Britain, while of those in southern England many move to France or Iberia.

Over much of Britain the wintering birds originate from Scandinavia, especially Finland and Sweden. They arrive from August onwards and depart in February/March (Bainbridge & Minton, 1978). The 91,000 birds which winter in Britain comprise about 30% of the East Atlantic flyway population. While they are spread quite widely, they concentrate in some areas; of particular note are the 17,700 on Orkney, 9,800 in Strathclyde, 10,000 in Morecambe Bay, 7,000 on the Solway but other estuaries are also important in maintaining their distribution. Between 1973 and 1981 there was little change in the numbers recorded wintering in Europe.

THREATS TO SURVIVAL

Threats include those which generally affect birds using an estuarine habitat (see pages 302–16). Land-use change affecting breeding populations is of particular concern; in this respect three trends are apparent: (i) the intensification of agriculture (improved drainage, intensive grass management in valleys), (ii) changes in agricultural practice, and (iii) afforestation of the lower moorland.

With pressure on the species in its breeding and wintering grounds, any increased mortality from hunting could pose an additional problem (Meltofte, 1986).

CONSERVATION

General conservation measures that are required for those birds, including the Curlew, which are associated with an intertidal habitat are given on pages 317–27.

Land-use changes—particularly agricultural intensification, over-grazing and afforestation—pose the major threat to breeding populations. Thus, imaginative steps need to be incorporated into measures to decrease agricultural production—and particularly to maintain the grazing systems and wetter fields in zones between the fertile lowlands and the uplands. Environmentally Sensitive Areas should help in the few places where they affect Curlew breeding areas, but the great majority of birds are not within these designated zones.

The bird was removed from the quarry list of species in 1982.

REFERENCES

BAINBRIDGE, I.P. & MINTON, C.D.T. 1978. The migration and mortality of the Curlew in Britain and Ireland. Bird Study 25: 39–50.

MELTOFTE, H. 1986. Hunting as a possible factor in the decline of Fenno-Scandian populations of Curlews *Numenius arquata*. Var Fagelv., Suppl. 11: 135–140.

Consultant: A.J. Prater

Redshank

Tringa totanus

The British wintering population of Redshanks is localized and is internationally important. About 75,000 winter in Britain; this is about 60% of the number wintering in Europe. There has been a 25% decline in British wintering numbers since 1975/76—although high numbers were again recorded in 1987/88. About 30,000 pairs breed in Britain (18% of the European total), with the majority nesting on saltmarshes. Inland breeding has declined markedly, especially in the lowlands of southern Britain. Though many of the main wintering or breeding sites receive some protection through SSSI status, few have so far been designated as SPAs or Ramsar Sites.

LEGAL STATUS

Protected under WCA 1981; Annex II/2 of EC Birds Directive; Appendix III of the Berne Convention.

ECOLOGY

Outside the breeding season the Redshank frequents mainly coastal habitats; three-quarters of those wintering in Britain are on estuaries, but flat rocky shores support many in north-east Britain (Moser, 1987; Moser & Summers, 1987). The feeding range extends higher up the shore than it does for most waders, and in winter some birds continue feeding in pastures at high tide. Few winter inland, but birds begin returning to breeding areas in the early spring.

The Redshank breeds mainly on the coast, with the highest densities (50 to 100 pairs/km^2) on the middle and upper parts of saltmarshes (Cadbury *et al.*, 1987), and locally on coastal grazing marshes (Smith, 1983) and damp machair (Fuller *et al.*, 1986). Breeding inland occurs in damp pastures, particularly those which are flooded regularly in winter, in lowland river valleys and on rough grazing land in upland valleys; it achieves densities which are usually below 10 pairs/km^2 (Smith, 1983; Galbraith *et al.*, 1985). Flooded gravel pits and wet depressions caused by mining subsidence also provide breeding habitat inland. Small numbers nest on lowland heaths, moorland and even in cereal crops. For nesting, the Redshank favours taller vegetation than that preferred by the Lapwing, but shorter than that in which Snipe usually nest. Nest: usually a deeply cupped depression hidden among grass or sedge tussocks. Eggs: early April to the end of June with the peak in May, but replacement nests (within a week to ten days) are frequent.

The Redshank first breeds in its first summer but some delay into their second. Males are highly site-faithful to the nesting areas; females are much less so. Access to shallow water (estuarine creeks, pools and flooded ditches) within 1 km of the nest is important for adults and young—which probably feed mostly on small insects and aquatic invertebrates (Green, 1985).

Feeding takes place by day and by night, and occurs throughout the tidal cycle on neap tides in winter. Winter food consists principally of estuarine invertebrates such as *Nereis diversicolor*, *Hydrobia ulvae* and *Corophium volutator* (Cramp & Simmons, 1983). Birds form small to medium-sized flocks; roosting usually occurs on sparsely vegetated islets, spits and the banks of pools and creeks, but also among *Spartina* grass and, on the highest spring tides, on bare arable fields.

DISTRIBUTION AND POPULATION

Northern Palearctic and Asia. The nominate race, *totanus*, breeds in Europe from Britain and Ireland east to the USSR; *robusta* breeds in Iceland and the Faeroes, British breeders being partially migratory, but most of these birds winter in Britain, and 40% move less than 100 km from the breeding site. The Icelandic population is migratory, wintering mainly in the British Isles and the Low Countries. In severe winters, some move to Britain and Ireland from the Continent (Cramp *et al.*, 1983).

The British breeding population was estimated to be of the order of 30,000 pairs (Reed, 1985). The numbers on saltmarshes, mainly in East Anglia and north-west England, have been cautiously estimated to be 17,500 pairs (nearly 60% of the total); a few breed on saltmarshes in south-west England, South Wales, and on the west coast of mainland Scotland (Cadbury *et al.*, 1987). There are local concentrations on coastal grazing marshes in eastern and south-east England (Smith, 1983) and on machair marshes of the southern Outer Hebrides, with an estimated 2,650 pairs (Fuller *et al.*, 1986), and also on Tiree, Inner Hebrides, where there are an estimated 550 pairs (Shepherd *et al.*, 1988).

In inland Britain there was a huge population decrease and contraction of breeding range in the first 70 or so years of the 19th century, coincident with the Victorian boom in drainage. With the decline in drainage efficiency in the 1880s, the population began to recover. By the 1930s breeding Redshanks were again common in East Anglia and had spread into western and south-west England (Thomas, 1942; Parslow, 1973). With the resurgence of intensive field drainage in the 1940s there was again a contraction in range and a marked decline in numbers breeding in lowlands, particularly inland in eastern and southern England (Sharrock, 1976).

Only 2,482 pairs were recorded (3,000 pairs estimated) on damp grasslands in lowland England and Wales in 1982/83. Apart from concentrations at a few sites, such as the washlands of the Cambridgeshire and Norfolk Fens, and the Derwent Ings (North Yorkshire), Redshanks are now sparsely distributed inland (Smith, 1983), but they are still apparently widespread in damp pastures and meadows in upland valleys in northern England.

In Scotland, an estimated 3,000 pairs occur on farmland mostly on rough grazing below 300 m (Galbraith *et al.*, 1985).

Most of the 550 pairs in Northern Ireland are inland in the Lough Neagh basins (Partridge, 1988).

The European breeding population (nominate race) is estimated to be 164,000–172,000 pairs, mostly in Norway (about one-third the total), Britain (18%), the Netherlands (17%), Sweden (12%) and West Germany (8%). Some 100,000 pairs of *robusta* breed in Iceland (Piersma, 1986).

The total wintering population in Britain is estimated to be 75,400 birds, with 21,100 (rather over a quarter) on non-estuarine coasts (Moser, 1987). Between 1984 and 1989, 21 estuaries (13 on the east coast) had an average winter maximum exceeding 1,500 (ie, in excess of 1% of the European wintering population) (Salmon *et al.*, 1989). Over the period 1975/76 to 1986/87 there was a 25% decrease in the numbers wintering in Britain, although higher numbers were counted in the winters of 1987/88 and 1988/89. Of 127,000 birds wintering in Europe, three-quarters do so in Britain and Ireland (Hale, 1986). Autumn numbers on certain estuaries, particularly on the east coast, may greatly exceed those in winter.

THREATS TO SURVIVAL

Threats include those which generally affect birds using an estuarine habitat (see pages 302–16); particular problems for the Redshank include loss of habitat through the spread of *Spartina* grass, severe weather, and agricultural encroachment.

Since the Redshank feeds a good deal in the upper zones of the intertidal areas, it is deprived of feeding habitat by *Spartina* encroachment (Goss-Custard & Moser, 1988).

Redshanks are particularly vulnerable when mudflats and saltmarshes are frozen, and several large winter mortality incidents have occurred on the east coast of Britain in severe weather (Davidson, 1981; Clarke, 1982).

A considerable amount of former breeding habitat in the higher saltmarshes has been reclaimed for agriculture (see the section (pages 302–16) on threats to breeding waders on lowland damp grassland).

Many inland sites have lost their breeding Redshank as a result of land drainage and flood alleviation works. In such circumstances, shallow pools and flooded ditches—so important as feeding areas for adults and young—are no longer available. Many coastal grazing marshes in south-east England, if they have not been converted to arable land, are too dry to support breeding Redshanks.

CONSERVATION

General conservation measures that are required for those birds, including the Redshank, which are associated with an intertidal habitat, and with lowland damp grasslands, are given on pages 317–27.

Of the factors which influence nesting densities of Redshanks on saltmarshes, grazing is one of the most practicable to manipulate. Highest densities of Redshanks are associated with vegetation subjected to medium grazing pressure by livestock, preferably cattle; ungrazed swards with rank vegetation, or those closely cropped by sheep, are unsuitable for nesting (Cadbury *et al.*, 1987). Inland wet grasslands are important for this species and need protection from drainage.

The creation of pools or shallow flooded areas on coastal grazing marshes and upper saltmarsh has locally greatly boosted breeding densities of Redshanks (Everett, 1987).

REFERENCES

CADBURY, C.J., GREEN, R.E. & ALLPORT, G. 1987. Redshanks and other breeding Waders of British saltmarshes. RSPB Conserv. Rev. 1: 37–40.
CLARKE, N.A. 1982. The effects of the severe weather in December 1981 and January 1982. Wader Study Group Buil. 34: 5–7.
DAVIDSON, N.C. 1981. Survival of shorebirds (*Charadrii*) during severe weather: the role of nutritional reserves. *In* Jones, N.V. & Wolff, W.J. (eds), Feeding and survival strategies of estuarine organisms. New York: Plenum Press.
EVERETT, M.J. 1987. The Elmley experiment. RSPB Conserv. Rev. 1: 31–33.
FULLER, R.J., REED, T.M., BUXTON, N.E., WEBB, A., WILLIAMS, T.D. & PIENKOWSKI, M.W. 1986. Populations of breeding waders *Charadrii* and their habitats on the crofting lands of the Outer Hebrides, Scotland. Biol. Conserv. 37: 333–361.
GALBRAITH, H., FURNESS, R.W. & FULLER, R.J. 1985. Habitats and distribution of waders breeding on Scottish agricultural land. Scot. Birds 13: 96–107.
GOSS-CUSTARD, J. & MOSER, M.E. 1988. Rates of change in the numbers of Dunlin *Calidris alpina* wintering in British estuaries in relation to the spread of *Spartina anglica*. J. Appl. Ecol. 25: 95–109.
GREEN, R.E. 1985. The management of lowland wet grassland for breeding waders. Unpublished handbook. Sandy: RSPB.
HALE, W.G. 1986. *In* Lack, P. (ed.), The atlas of wintering birds in Britain and Ireland. p. 218. Calton: Poyser.
MOSER, M.E. 1987. A revision of population estimates for Waders (*Charadrii*) wintering on the coastline of Britain. Biol. Conserv. 39: 153–164.
MOSER, M.E. & SUMMERS, R.W. 1987. Wader populations on the non-estuarine coasts of Britain and Northern Ireland: results of the 1984–85 Winter Shorebird Count. Bird Study 34: 71–81.
PARSLOW, J.L.F. 1973. Breeding birds of Britain and Ireland. Berkhamsted: Poyser.
PARTRIDGE, J.K. 1988. Breeding Waders in Northern Ireland. RSPB Conserv. Rev. 2: 69–71.
PIERSMA, T. 1986. Breeding waders in Europe. Wader Study Group Bull. 48: (supplement).
REED, T. 1985. Estimates of British breeding wader populations. Wader Study Group Bull. 45: 11–12.
SALMON, D.G., PRYS-JONES, R.P. & KIRBY, J.S. 1987. Wildfowl and Wader Counts 1986–87. The results of the National Wildfowl Counts and Birds of Estuaries Enquiry in the United Kingdom. Slimbridge: Wildfowl Trust.
SHEPHERD, K.B., GREEN, M., KNIGHT, A.C. & STROUD, D.A., 1988. The breeding birds of Tiree and Coll in 1987/88 with special emphasis on breeding waders. NCC Chief Scientist Directorate commissioned research report No. 827. NCC, Peterborough.
SMITH, K.W. 1983. The status and distribution of waders breeding on wet lowland grasslands in England and Wales. Bird Study 30: 177–192.
THOMAS, J.F. 1942. Report on the redshank inquiry 1939–40. Brit. Birds 36: 5–14, 22–34.

Consultant: C.J. Cadbury

Greenshank
Tringa nebularia

The Greenshank is a species of special concern because of its dependence in Britain on the protection of the Flow Country of Caithness and Sutherland and other peatlands of north-west Scotland from afforestation. An estimated 960 pairs breed in northern and central Scotland. Afforestation of part of the peatland breeding grounds has already had a major effect on the population, and wide-ranging protection measures are urgently required.

LEGAL STATUS

Protected under Schedule 1 of WCA 1981; EC Birds Directive; Appendix III of the Berne Convention.

ECOLOGY

The Greenshank is a summer visitor to the open peatlands and forest bogs of northern Europe. It breeds on peatlands in Scotland where it is now largely restricted to the wet moorlands and Flow Country of the north. Nest: a thinly-lined scrape, more or less in the open, often close to a prominent feature such as a post or tree stump. Eggs: laid in May to mid-June. Clutch: 4 occasionally 3; one brood. The young fledge from the end of May.

Food consists chiefly of small invertebrates and small fish.

DISTRIBUTION AND POPULATION

Palearctic. The Greenshank breeds in a broad zone across northern Europe and Asia, mainly between 55°N and 70°N, from Scotland to the Kamchatka peninsula; it winters mainly in southern Europe, Africa, southern Asia and Australia. A few of the birds winter as far north as western Europe, including Britain and Ireland, where between 600 and 1,000 (occasionally more) regularly occur (Lack, 1986) — mainly, it is thought, involving birds from the Scottish breeding population.

In Europe outside the British Isles, breeding is confined to Norway (17,000 pairs), Sweden (50,000 pairs), Finland (40,000 pairs) and Russia where it is abundant in suitable habitat (Piersma, 1986).

Apart from one pair which occurs regularly at one site in Ireland, breeding in the British Isles is confined to northern and central Scotland where population estimates vary from 400–750 pairs during 1968–72 (Sharrock, 1976), between 805 and 905 pairs in 1977 (Nethersole-Thompson, 1979), and about 960 pairs in 1985 (Stroud *et al.*, 1987); however, although the latter figure may be more accurate, due to intensive surveys of the habitat, numbers are variable from year to year. Nevertheless, some decline has certainly taken place—notably in Caithness and Sutherland (see under 'Threats')—and a population in the Spey Valley of Scotland has almost gone.

THREATS TO SURVIVAL

Threats include a reduction in suitable habitat, disturbance, and egg-collection. Threats from afforestation are having marked effects on the population, even in remote areas of the Scottish breeding habitat (Stroud *et al.*, 1987). Figures produced by Stroud *et al.* show a loss of 130 pairs due to the afforestation of parts of the Caithness and Sutherland peatlands; this represents a 12% reduction in the national population. Evidence from Nethersole-Thompson's (1979) studies indicates that these territories have been lost, ie, it is not simply a question of birds having been displaced. Thus, it is possible that the maximum number of Greenshanks has been reached, or perhaps even passed, with the numbers now a reduction from the peak of the breeding population.

Recreational improvements, disturbance, and planting of the habitat in the Spey Valley destroyed the finest forest breeding habitat in Britain. Other habitats have been damaged or destroyed through the growth of heather and the drying-up of pools used for feeding. The loss of habitat surrounding lochs and rivers used by feeding birds will inevitably promote competition, increase predation, give a reduction in available food, and—ultimately—the production of less-viable eggs (as a result of birds laying later and lighter clutches) (Thompson *et al.*, 1986).

Egg-collecting continues to be a problem in some areas, but the notorious difficulty of locating Greenshanks' nests suggests that the effect is likely to be limited, although given the site-fidelity of the bird this could be a problem if the collectors became aware of a locality and returned to nests in successive years.

If, as seems to be the case, some of the Scottish breeding population winters in southern Britain and Ireland, estuary barrage schemes, marinas and other large-scale developments which would destroy coastal habitats are also likely to be a long-term threat.

CONSERVATION

Large tracts of the birds' breeding habitat in the Scottish uplands are being destroyed by afforestation. Elsewhere, recent surveys have shown quite large numbers of breeding pairs on Lewis—where land is already being ear-marked for future forestry planting (Stroud *et al.*, 1988). The available data show quite clearly that there have been significant historical and recent losses solely due to afforestation (Stroud *et al.*, 1987). It is vital to restrict the afforestation of deep peatlands; not only should adequate large areas of moorland be declared SSSIs, but other areas should also be maintained as open moorland free of conifer plantations.

REFERENCES

NETHERSOLE-THOMPSON, D. & M. 1979. Greenshanks. Calton: Poyser.
PIERSMA, T. (ed.). 1986. Breeding Waders in Europe: a review of population size

estimates and bibliography of information sources. Wader Study Group Bulletin 48, Supplement.

REED, T.M., LANGSLOW, D.R. & SYMONDS, F.L. 1983. The breeding waders of the Caithness Flows. Scot. Birds 12: 180–186.

STROUD, D.A., CONDIE, M., HOLLOWAY, S.J., ROTHWELL, A.J., SHEPHERD, K.D., SIMMONS, J.R. & TURNER, J. 1988. A survey of moorland birds on the Isle of Lewis in 1987. NCC: CSD Report 776: Peterborough.

THOMPSON, D.B.A., THOMPSON, P.S. & NETHERSOLE-THOMPSON, D. 1986. Timing of breeding and breeding performance in a population of Greenshanks (*Tringa nebularia*). J. Anim. Ecol. 55: 181–199.

Wood Sandpiper

Tringa glareola

The Wood Sandpiper is a rare breeding summer visitor to Britain. It has nested in small numbers (up to 10 pairs) in the Scottish Highlands since 1959, and is also a regular passage-migrant, especially in the autumn. Preservation of habitats from afforestation at the main breeding sites, and avoidance of disturbance of nesting birds, are the main conservation requirements.

LEGAL STATUS

Protected under Schedule 1 of WCA; Annex 1 of EC Birds Directive; Appendix II of the Berne Convention.

ECOLOGY

The Wood Sandpiper breeds in Scotland in northern marshes, swamps, boggy moorland and clearings in forests, or in scrub woodland — these nesting habitats being similar to those in Scandinavia. On passage, birds frequent freshwater habitats rather than tidal areas. Nest: on the ground; rarely in an old nest of a thrush or other tree-nesting species. The nest can be some distance from the marsh where the young are raised. Eggs: laid mid-May to mid-June. Clutch: 4, very rarely 3; one brood. The young are cared for by both parents in the first week, but often by a single adult in the remainder of the fledging period (to the end of July).

Food consists of insects, spiders, earthworms and small molluscs.

DISTRIBUTION AND POPULATION

Palearctic. The Wood Sandpiper breeds locally in Scotland, and from Fenno-Scandia, north Germany and east Czechoslovakia to eastern Siberia in the boreal and sub-arctic zones. It winters in Africa, southern Asia and Australasia.

Pairs bred in Northumberland in 1853, and possibly also in 1857. After nearly annual records of single birds summering in suitable habitats in the Scottish Highlands, breeding was recorded in Sutherland in 1959. A small population has built up since, with birds at nearly 20 sites in Caithness, Sutherland, Ross and Cromarty, Inverness, Badenoch and Strathspey, Lochaber, Perth and Argyll (Thom, 1986). Only six of these sites have been used regularly; the best sites (in Badenoch and Strathspey) have been used for 18 years, with breeding recorded during 13. The next most used site has been occupied for nine years, with breeding recorded in six. Overall, the best years have been 1968 (with ten pairs, three recorded breeding), 1978 (seven or eight pairs, four recorded breeding) and 1980 (eight to ten pairs, six recorded breeding). There are suggestions that loose colonies have formed, and that sometimes extra single birds are involved with pairs. This small population seems reasonably well established, although it is disappointing that no birds were recorded as having bred at the best site from 1986 to 1988.

Wood Sandpipers are common in northern Europe, with estimated breeding populations of 250,000 pairs in Sweden, 180,000 pairs in Finland and 27,000 pairs in Norway. There are also about 100 pairs in Denmark, and less than 50 pairs in West Germany; both countries have reported declines (Cramp *et al.*, 1983).

THREATS TO SURVIVAL

Threats include the loss of the best sites to afforestation—this appearing to be the only major threat to the small Scottish population. With recent increases in commercial forestry on peatlands and boggy moorlands, some sites have already been damaged. The loss of birch scrub and open flushes to plantations is also a threat.

In the past, drainage of marshes would have been a concern but this threat has been lifted to a certain extent due to changes in agricultural priorities.

Egg-collecting and human disturbance may cause local problems but it is likely that climatic changes will be the main factor influencing the future of this bird as a British breeding species.

CONSERVATION

Two of the best sites are nature reserves, and several have SSSI status or have been proposed as suitable SSSIs or SPAs; all the regular sites should be afforded such protection from land-use change. One nature reserve where Wood Sandpipers are occasionally recorded is being positively managed: a previously drained area of peat-mosses and marshland beside woodland has been reflooded, and the species is now regularly breeding there. It would appear that similar suitable sites could be enhanced for this (and other) species.

All breeding sites should be kept free from human disturbance. The species is monitored by the RBBP and details appear in the RSPB reports.

REFERENCE

THOM, V.M. 1986. Birds in Scotland. Calton: Poyser.

Consultant: R.H. Dennis

Turnstone
Arenaria interpres

The wintering population of the Turnstone in Britain is of international importance; breeding has never been recorded in this country, although it was suspected
in 1976. In winter birds are widely distributed on rocky shores and estuaries,
making census work very difficult. The size of the Icelandic and Norwegian
wintering population is unknown, but Britain probably holds at least 25% of the
western European wintering total. The main threat which affects only part of the
population, is estuarine land-claim.

LEGAL STATUS

Protected under WCA 1981; EC Birds Directive; Appendix II of the Berne
Convention.

ECOLOGY

Wintering birds are confined to coastal habitats where they are widely distributed on estuaries, sandy beaches and rocky shores. Turnstones generally forage in
small groups, congregating in larger flocks—and with other species—at high-tide
roosts Foraging generally takes place on rocky or stony substrata, especially on
mussel beds or along strand lines where fronds of seaweed or stones are turned over
or pushed aside. A variety of invertebrates are taken, but the birds feed mainly on
shrimps, winkles and barnacles (Harris, 1979; Cramp *et al.*, 1983). The Arctic
breeding season is short; most birds leave Europe during May and start to return
in July, the juveniles following mainly during September. There is a tendency for
birds to return to the same wintering site in subsequent years (Metcalfe & Furness,
1985).

DISTRIBUTION AND POPULATION

Holarctic. The Turnstone breeds within a thin coastal band encircling the
Arctic along the highest terrestrial latitudes, but with a southward extension along
the Scandinavian and Baltic coasts. The world range is divisible into five
populations, two of which regularly occur in Britain. The north-western population, which breeds in north-east Canada and Greenland, winters in western

Europe from the North Sea south to Iberia. The Fenno-Scandian and west Russian population migrates through Europe and the North Sea to winter in Morocco and west Africa.

The size of the west European wintering population is given as 67,400 by Smit and Piersma (1989), but this is undoubtedly an under-estimate because of the difficulty of counting along rocky shorelines. There are no estimates for the sizes of the populations wintering in Iceland or Norway, but this could number tens of thousands, possibly 100,000 (Prater, 1981).

Estimates of numbers wintering in Britain were formerly based on BOEE counts alone; this gave an annual figure of about 11,000 birds, contributing to an estimated total of 25,000 (Prater, 1981). A survey of non-estuarine coastline in the winter of 1984/85 located 35,000 birds in Britain (Moser & Summers, 1987) which, when combined with the estuary counts, gives a British total of the order of 45,000–50,000 birds. Using Smit and Piersma's figure of 67,400 for western Europe, and the upper limit of Prater's estimate of up to 100,000 for Norway and Iceland, the British population probably represents at least 25% of the western European population. There is one unproven instance of breeding in Britain: in Sutherland in 1976 (Sharrock, 1978).

THREATS TO SURVIVAL

Threats to birds associated with an estuarine habitat are discussed on pages 302–16. However, with less than 25% of British wintering Turnstones located within estuarine habitats, such threats are of less importance than they are to other estuarine waders, as this bird occurs mainly on rocky shores and will adapt to some artificial structures.

CONSERVATION

General conservation measures applicable to birds associated with an estuarine habitat are given on pages 317–27. In view of the widespread distribution of the wintering population no other conservation measures are necessary.

REFERENCES

HARRIS, P.R. 1979. The winter feeding of the Turnstone in North Wales. Bird Study 26: 259–266.

METCALFE, N.B. & FURNESS, R.W. 1985. Survival, winter population stability and site fidelity in the Turnstone *Arenaria interpres*. Bird Study 32: 207–214.

MOSER, M.E. & SUMMERS, R.W. 1987. Wader populations on the non-estuarine coasts of Britain and Northern Ireland: results of the 1984–85 Winter Shorebird Count. Bird Study 34: 71–81.

PRATER, A.J. 1981. Estuary birds of Britain and Ireland. Calton: Poyser.

SHARROCK, J.T.R. 1978. Rare breeding birds in 1976. Brit. Birds 71: 11–13.

SMIT, C.J. & PIERSMA, T. 1989. Numbers, mid-winter distribution, and migration of Wader populations using the East Atlantic flyway. *In* Boyd, H. & Pirot, J.-Y. (eds), Flyways and reserve networks for water birds. IWRB Special Publication No. 9. Slimbridge: IWRB.

Red-necked Phalarope
Phalaropus lobatus

The Red-necked Phalarope is a rare breeding summer visitor to Britain. It underwent a marked population decrease during the 20th century, probably due to drainage and to habitat loss due to successsion; about 20 'pairs' still breed, the majority on RSPB reserves in Shetland. The management of breeding sites, through the creation of small pools and the prevention of their drainage, is the most important conservation measure.

LEGAL STATUS

Protected under Schedule 1 of WCA 1981; Annex 1 of EC Birds Directive; Appendix II of the Berne Convention.

ECOLOGY

The Red-necked Phalarope breeds at sites with open water, emergent swamp, and wet and dry mire—often in old peat workings. Open water is necessary for courtship and copulation, and for some feeding. Emergent swamp, usually of bottle sedge (*Carex rostrata*), is important for much of the feeding by adults. Wet mire with water horse-tail (*Equisetum fluviatile*), common spike-rush (*Eleocharis palustris*), bogbean (*Menyanthes trifoliata*), marsh cinquefoil (*Potentilla palustris*), etc, is used as a feeding area by chicks and adults. Dry mire with common sedge (*Carex nigra*), creeping bent (*Agrostis stolonifera*), creeping buttercup (*Ranunculus repens*), red fescue (*Festuca rubra*), sweet vernal grass (*Anthoxanthum odoratum*) etc. is the main vegetation utilized for nesting. Maintenance of all these components is critical for the survival of the breeding colony.

The breeding cycle is short, adapted to the brief northern summer of the high Arctic, with its short-term abundant invertebrate food source. Birds arrive in May and mate during late May to early June. The mating system is monogamous or serially polyandrous, with pair-bonds lasting for a few days only (Hilden & Vuolanto, 1972). Nest: a scrape lined with grass and leaves, usually well hidden in a grass tussock or other vegetation. Eggs: laid early June, within about 4 days. Clutch: about 4 (3–7); one brood. The male alone incubates for 18 days. The chicks hatch in late June to late July; they are quickly able to fend for themselves, but are attended by the male—fledging in late July to mid-August. Adults moult in July–August, and all birds depart in late July–August, after residing for 8–12 weeks.

Food in the breeding season consists predominantly of small insects, especially dipteran flies and their larvae.

Red-necked Phalaropes feed in daylight at the breeding site, local swamps, mires and stony lochs, and sometimes at the sea edge; the preferred feeding is amongst emergent vegetation, especially tall and sparse *Carex rostrata*. No information on pelagic wintering birds is available.

DISTRIBUTION AND POPULATION

Circumpolar, within tundra and sub-arctic climatic zone. In the Palearctic breeding occurs in Iceland, the Faeroes, northern Fenno-Scandia, Estonia, northern USSR and, on the southern edge of its range, very locally in northern Scotland and Ireland. The Russian population winters at sea off Arabia and southeast Asia. The winter quarters of the western European population is unknown but is probably in the southern Atlantic off the west coast of equatorial Africa.

British breeding has long been concentrated on the Scottish Northern and Western Isles, with single 'pairs' having bred at two or three places on the Scottish mainland. There is also a rapidly declining, or possibly extinct, population in Ireland.

The present British population of about 20 'pairs' represents a relic of a formerly much more numerous one. After a serious decline in the 19th century, probably aggravated by the collection of eggs and adults, there was some local recovery in the early 20th century as a result of protection, but this proved only temporary, and numbers decreased again from the 1930s (Everett, 1971; Yates *et al.*, 1983). The population is now almost entirely confined to an RSPB reserve in Shetland. Trends in the population in Britain are given in the table below.

Red-necked Phalarope: trends in population in Britain

Counts of 'pairs' on Shetland

1950	1968	1970	1971	1976	1978	1980	1983	1988
27–34	35–45	28+	10–16	16–19	19–24	20–24	18–21	16

Counts of 'pairs' on the Outer Hebrides

1921–40	1951–60	1961–70	1971–81	1982–84	1988
27–35	21–30	2–12	2–8	3–6	3

On other Scottish islands there were 7–8 'pairs' in 1968 and about three in 1983 and 1988. The Scottish mainland population was 3–4 'pairs' in 1968, two in 1970, and one in 1983; there were none in 1988. Trends in the Irish population are given in the table below.

Red-necked Phalarope: trends in population in Ireland (County Mayo)

1905	1929	1968	1969	1970	1983	1988
50	40	7+	3+	c. 10	1	0

The total British and Irish population was 25–65 'pairs' at six sites in 1968–1970 (Everett, 1971), 29 at ten sites in 1983 (Yates *et al.*, 1983), and about 19 in 1988.

The Red-necked Phalarope is also a scarce passage-migrant, mainly in April–June and August–September, chiefly on the east coast.

In Northern Europe, breeding populations are estimated for Iceland at 50,000–

100,000 pairs, the Faeroes 40–50 pairs, Norway 9,500 pairs, Sweden 50,000 pairs, and Finland 15,000 pairs (Piersma, 1986).

THREATS TO SURVIVAL

Threats include the effects of drainage and the loss of a suitable mosaic of habitats in the remaining breeding sites; however, human disturbance, trampling by cattle, flooding, cold and wet weather, and predation—especially by Arctic Skuas (*Stercorarius parasiticus*)—are also potential problems.

Collecting is probably no longer a serious threat, but over-zealous birdwatchers and photographers are increasingly so. The close wardening of traditional sites during the breeding season reduces threats to a minimum.

The impact of increasingly intensive agricultural methods on breeding and feeding areas has accelerated the decline in Scotland, but the loss of open water originally created by peat-cutting, first to emergent swamp and then to wet and dry mire, is also very important. Most sites are now protected from total drainage by SSSI status, and active management is proceeding on some to provide suitable conditions for breeding and feeding.

CONSERVATION

Many traditional sites are now protected by SSSI or RSPB reserve status. Indeed, the most important site on Fetlar, Shetland, has been an RSPB reserve since 1973. Management agreements are also in operation at several other sites.

Elsewhere, bird-watchers and photographers should be encouraged to show more concern for the birds, and any unprotected sites should be kept secret.

Cattle should be excluded from breeding sites during the nesting period, but grazing at other times of the year is probably beneficial as it helps to maintain the important patchwork of open water, emergent vegetation and wet and dry mire.

Gaining control over water levels is the most important management measure. Thereafter, a mosaic of small non-acidic pools, emergent swamp vegetation and wet and dry mires needs to be created and maintained. At the RSPB reserve on Fetlar such conditions are controlled, and the population of Red-necked Phalaropes has been held at a reasonably stable level.

Farmers with Red-necked Phalaropes nesting on their land should be informed of the rarity of the species, encouraged not to drain the land, and to enter into a management agreement with a conservation organization.

REFERENCES

EVERETT, M.J. 1971. Breeding status of Red-necked Phalaropes in Britain and Ireland. Brit. Birds 64: 293–302.

HILDEN, O. & VUOLANTO, S. 1972. Breeding biology of the Red-necked Phalarope *Phalaropus lobatus* in Finland. Ornis Fenn. 49: 57–85.

PIERSMA, T. 1986. Breeding waders in Europe. Wader Study Group, Bull. 48, supplement.

YATES, B., HENDERSON, K. & DYMOND, N. 1983. Red-necked Phalaropes in Britain and Ireland 1983. RSPB unpublished report.

Consultant: N.D. Burgess

Great Skua
Catharacta skua

The Great Skua breeds in Britain in internationally important numbers. Increases in this species during the present century have resulted in 7,860 pairs in northern Scotland, which is about 57% of the world population. The Great Skua is threatened mainly by food shortages stemming from a reduction in sand-eels, and discarded whitefish from trawlers, the latter due to an increase in the mesh size of fishing nets. Close monitoring of the population and the diet of Great Skuas will be necessary.

LEGAL STATUS

Protected under WCA 1981; EC Birds Directive; Appendix III of the Berne Convention.

ECOLOGY

The Great Skua or Bonxie as it is commonly known, breeds in loose colonies on coastal grassy moors, showing preference for wetter areas. Nest: a scrape in the open on flat or gently sloping ground. Eggs: laid in May and June. Clutch: 2 (90%), 1 (10%); one brood. The young fledge from early July.

Food in summer consists mainly of fish, obtained chiefly from surface shoals of sand-eels, but also by scavenging waste (chiefly whiting and haddock) from fishing boats at sea, or by piratically chasing and harassing other seabirds and forcing them to drop or disgorge their prey. Bonxies also take the eggs, young and adults of other seabirds, and recently in Shetland they have begun to scavenge at rubbish-tips in small numbers (Furness & Hiscop, 1981).

DISTRIBUTION AND POPULATION

Northern hemisphere. The Great Skua has a very restricted breeding range which is confined to parts of the west Palearctic, although several closely related species/sub-species breed in the south Atlantic and Antarctic. Modern taxonomists are still not agreed on which merit full species status (see Furness (1987) for a discussion). The bird breeds in Iceland, the Faeroes and north Scotland, and it is also a recent colonist in Norway (about 4 pairs), Spitsbergen (30 pairs), and Bear Island (30 pairs) — and probably on Jan Mayen; it winters mainly coastally or offshore in the Atlantic, south at least to the equator, particularly off Iberia.

The Icelandic breeding population is now probably stable at 5,000 to 6,000 pairs after recent declines since the 1930s; the Facroes' population has been declining from about 530 pairs in 1961, to 400 in 1978 and to 250 pairs in 1984.

In Britain, the population has increased dramatically since the 1960s to about 7,150 pairs in 1985 and 7,860 pairs in 1988, about 57% of the world population of between 12,500 and 12,800 pairs. This is due particularly to less persecution and probably increased food supplies and seabird populations. Most of the birds breed in Shetland, where the population of 60 or fewer pairs in the 19th century has increased steadily to about 3,060 pairs in 1969–70 and 5,392 pairs in 1977. A fall to 4,700 pairs in 1982 was largely a result of the decrease from 3,000 pairs (in 1977) to 2,500 pairs (in 1982) at the species' main stronghold on Foula. In Orkney (first colonized in 1915) numbers increased gradually to 90 pairs in 1969–70, 525 pairs in 1977, and 1,532 pairs in 1982. About 50 pairs breed on the Outer Hebrides (first colonized in 1945), and about 35 pairs on St Kilda (first colonized in 1963). A further 30 pairs breed elsewhere, including the mainland of northern Scotland.

THREATS TO SURVIVAL

Threats include persecution by man, and a reduction in the availability of certain food items.

Great Skuas — in common with some species of auks and the Kittiwake — accumulate particularly high levels of organochlorine and heavy metal pollutants, but there is little evidence that these affect breeding performance or survival.

In the 19th century the population declined due to the shooting of adults for skins.

The collection of eggs for food by islanders was less harmful as these skuas lay up to three replacement clutches.

Persecution still occurs because of the alleged impact of these birds on sheep and lambs: many are illegally shot from fishing boats around Shetland, or by crofters. However the main breeding colonies are on reserves, and most of the breeding population seems reasonably secure from this persecution.

A further threat is the increases in fishing net mesh size used by trawlers; this will lead to a reduction in the availability of small discarded whitefish which may cause skuas to turn to other sources of food, such as predation of smaller seabirds. A decline in Great Skua numbers seems likely especially with the reduction in sand-eel numbers in parts of the North Sea — especially that surrounding the Northern Isles.

CONSERVATION

In view of the likely reductions in food supplies expected for Great Skuas, and their potential impacts on other wildlife, monitoring of their population and diets will be necessary.

REFERENCES

Furness, R.W. 1987. The Skuas. Calton: Poyser.
Furness, R.W. & Hiscop, J.R.G. 1981. Diets and feeding ecology of Great Skuas during the breeding season in Shetland. J. Zool., Lond. 195: 1–23.

Mediterranean Gull
Larus melanocephalus

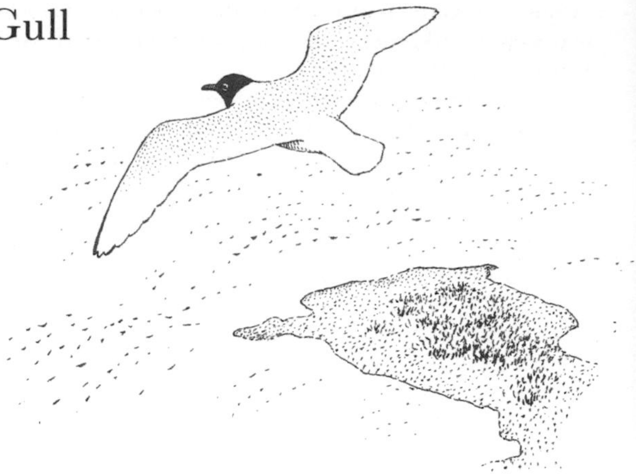

In Britain, the Mediterranean Gull is a rare breeding bird, a scarce winter visitor, and a passage-migrant. It was formerly a rare vagrant. Breeding in Britain was first recorded in 1968, and is now annual in small numbers (up to six pairs), but colonization is probably still dependent on immigration from Europe. The bird invariably nests within colonies of Black-headed Gulls where disturbance should be kept to a minimum.

LEGAL STATUS

Protected under Schedule 1 WCA 1981; Annex 1 of EC Birds Directive; Appendix II of the Berne Convention.

ECOLOGY

The Mediterranean Gull typically nests colonially, but in north-west Europe most breeding attempts have been made by odd pairs among Black-headed Gull or Sandwich Tern colonies. Nest: a cupped heap of vegetation on coastal marshes or islets in salt or brackish lagoons. Eggs: laid in continental nests, May–June. Clutch: 3 (1–3); one brood. The young fledge by late July.

Food consists of small marine fish, molluscs, water beetles, together with terrestrial and aquatic insects; also takes birds' eggs, and it has been known to scavenge at rubbish dumps and occasionally follows the plough where it feeds on worms.

DISTRIBUTION AND POPULATION

South-central Palearctic. The bird breeds in south Russia, Rumania and Greece, but scattered nesting occurs in small colonies—becoming more frequent across Europe through Hungary and Austria to Estonia, East Germany, the Netherlands, Belgium, France and England, south into Turkey and east towards the Caspian Sea.

In 1981 there were considered to be between 210,000 and 300,000 pairs nesting in the Soviet Union. Increases elsewhere are probably due to improved protection of the main colony in Tendra Bay (north-west Black Sea) where 272,530 nests were counted in 1981.

Away from the Soviet Union the only sizeable colonies are in north-east Greece, where at least four colonies together hold over 3,000 pairs (Glutz von Blotzheim & Bauer, 1982).

Breeding in Britain first occurred in Hampshire in 1968 (Taverner, 1970, 1972) but did not become regular until at least 1976. Since then the number of pairs attempting to nest has varied, with a maximum of six proven pairs in 1988 (with a further 10 pairs also in suitable habitat and possibly with nests in the same year) (Spencer, 1988).

Despite an increase in the number of birds visiting Britain in recent years there is not yet a regular, established breeding site.

THREATS TO SURVIVAL

Threats may include disturbance and predation.

Although the bird breeds in single-species colonies in south-east Europe, pairs on the limits of the present range tend to breed in Black-headed Gull or Sandwich Tern colonies, and may be overlooked.

As long as breeding attempts continue to be within established gulleries or terneries, many of which are in protected areas, the main threats will most likely come from disturbance and predation. Continued colonization will, however, probably depend for the foreseeable future on continued immigration from Europe, and on continued protection of the main breeding areas in the Soviet Union.

CONSERVATION

While only a small number of pairs breed in Britain, the protection of the bird in the remainder of its range is of vital importance. Pairs breeding in Britain should be given full protection to ensure that failure due to excessive human disturbance or predation does not occur. If a small colony starts to develop, then efforts should be made to ensure that the site is adequately safeguarded.

REFERENCES

GLUTZ VON BLOTZHEIM, U.N. & BAUER, K.M. 1982. Handbuch der Vogel Mitteleuropas. 81: 382–402.
SPENCER, R. 1988. Rare breeding birds in the United Kingdom in 1985. Brit. Birds 81: 99–125.
TAVERNER, J.H. 1970. Mediterranean Gulls nesting in Hampshire. Brit. Birds 63: 67–73.
TAVERNER, J.H. 1972. Mediterranean Gulls in Hampshire in 1970–71. Brit. Birds 65: 185–186.

Little Gull
Larus minutus

Single pairs of Little Gulls have nested in Britain on four occasions in recent years; all have failed at the egg stage, but with the increasing incidence of summering birds a successful attempt seems only a matter of time. The main conservation requirements will be to safeguard any nest from human disturbance, flooding or predation. The occasional, essentially opportunistic occurrence of these birds attempting to breed in Britain, although of little conservation significance, does represent a continuing range expansion of this species. Most existing European colonies are small, variable, and owe their existence to similar origins.

LEGAL STATUS

Protected under Schedule 1 of WCA 1981; EC Birds Directive; Appendix II of the Berne Convention.

ECOLOGY

The Little Gull breeds in lowland freshwater lakes and pools, in river valleys or along coasts; nest sites are normally immediately adjacent to areas of shallow water, either in open wetter parts of marshes, or on small islands or sand or shingle banks. Breeding has also been recorded on grazed saltmarshes and in reed beds. Nest: a shallow depression lined with grasses, reed-stems or leaves, but in wetter sites the nest may be a more substantial structure of such vegetation. The bird is colonial, but generally only small numbers of pairs occur together; the nests are scattered or in small groups. The birds are frequently attracted to nest amongst other colonial nesting species—particularly Black-headed Gulls, but they have also been recorded in association with Black Terns and Avocets. Eggs: laid in mid-May to early July (early June in the four British nesting attempts, which were all in Black-headed Gull colonies). Clutch: usually 2–3; one brood, but replacments are laid if the first clutch has been lost. The young normally fledge in July–August and become independent soon after leaving the nesting territory.

Food consists mainly of insects in the breeding season; at other times of year the diet includes fish and marine invertebrates.

This bird is mainly coastal in distribution outside the breeding season, some individuals clearly feeding way out at sea, with larger flocks seen along adjacent coasts in response to stormy weather. The bird may also occur briefly at inland or coastal freshwater sites. It prefers coastal sandy or muddy beaches, especially those around the mouths of rivers or streams, or even sewage outfalls.

DISTRIBUTION AND POPULATION

Other than a few pairs recently established in the Nearctic, the Little Gull is confined to the Palearctic in three distinct breeding populations—in east Siberia, western Siberia, and from north-west Russia to the Baltic area, including scattered colonies in Europe. The bird is a local breeder in Europe in small colonies which are highly variable in numbers, but it breeds regularly in the Netherlands (recently 7–61 pairs), Denmark (5–15 pairs), Sweden (90 pairs), Finland (a recent increase to 1,000 pairs), Poland (declined from 195 to 14 pairs at one site this century, another site 16–50 pairs recently) and in the USSR in Estonia (marked fluctuations) and Latvia (1,000–2,000 pairs). Occasional nesting attempts have also been recorded in West and East Germany, Austria, Rumania, and in the USSR and Armenia, Volhyria and the Sea of Azov.

In Britain, single pairs of Little Gulls laid eggs in Cambridgeshire/Norfolk in 1975 (Carson *et al.*, 1977), in Norfolk and north Yorkshire in 1978 (Madge, 1979), and in Nottinghamshire in 1987, but no young were hatched—all failures being at egg stage. Summering birds, adults and immatures, have been recorded in at least 12 counties, mainly in eastern England (from Kent to Yorkshire, with outlying records in Dorset, Cardigan and Cheshire) since the late 1950s, but with increasing frequency in the 1970s and 1980s. Breeding has occasionally been suspected in one or two of these cases, but has not been proven.

This pattern follows on from a very substantial increase in occurrences on spring and autumn passage, and also in winter in Britain and Ireland since the late 1940s; this is presumed to reflect either a large (but undocumented) increase in breeding populations further east in Europe and Russia, or a change in migration routes or wintering areas (Neath & Hutchinson, 1978). In view of the recent abundance of the Little Gull as a passage bird in Britain it is, perhaps, surprising that even more of these birds have not stayed or attempted to breed.

Wintering areas and migration are inadequately documented, but the two western-most populations probably migrate west to the Mediterranean or the north-west European seaboard, with the birds seen in Britain likely to originate from north-west Russia or the Baltic areas.

THREATS TO SURVIVAL

If the risks of flooding of the nest can be minimized, the only real threats are from human disturbance or predation by rats, mink, crows or other gulls. Predation seems to have been implicated in at least half the British breeding failures.

CONSERVATION

All four British nesting attempts have probably been largely opportunist where water-level conditions have temporarily produced attractive nest-sites and feeding habitat. Nonetheless, plenty of potentially suitable freshwater lakes, coastal lagoons, gravel pits and reservoirs exist in Britain—many associated with gull colonies. If the bird's requirements were better understood, experimental manipulation of water levels on wetland nature reserves might increase the likelihood of colonization.

When pairs settle, the main requirement will be to ensure protection from egg-robbery or accidental or other human disturbance which would leave the nest open to predation. The location of possible nests early in the season is recommended to ensure that protection can be given from the beginning of incubation. Although, so far, there have been no cases of attempts at nesting at any one site in successive seasons, a degree of secrecy seems prudent.

Consideration should be given to listing this species under Annex 1 of the EC Directive in view of the fact that limited numbers of pairs breed in the western Palearctic (and even more limited numbers within the EEC), and bearing in mind the dependence of these birds on threatened freshwater wetland habitats.

REFERENCES

CARSON, C.A., THOMAS, G.A. & CORNFORD, G.J. 1977. Little Gulls nesting on the Ouse Washes. Brit. Birds 70: 331–332.
MADGE, S.C. 1979. Attempted breeding of Little Gulls in Yorkshire. Naturalist 104: 143–146.
NEATH, C.D. & HUTCHINSON, B. 1978. Little Gulls in Britain and Ireland. Brit. Birds 71: 563–582.

Consultant: M. Davies

Sandwich Tern

Sterna sandvicensis

The Sandwich Tern breeds in Britain in internationally important numbers; the size of the British population—between 12,500 and 13,500 pairs in 1984—is steadily increasing, and there are no obvious reasons why this trend should not continue. A success story!

LEGAL STATUS

Protected under WCA 1981; Annex 1 of EC Birds Directive; Appendix II of the Berne Convention.

ECOLOGY

The Sandwich Tern is a colonial nester which associates with other *Sterna* species and gulls. Nest: a shallow excavated scrape, either unlined or with the addition of any available items; sand or shingle beaches are preferred, the bird is rarely found inland. Eggs: laid during late April–May. Clutch: 1–2 (1–3); one brood, but replacements are laid after egg-loss. The young fledge from late June to July. Breeding success in the major English colonies averages 0·73 chicks per nest.

Food consists of fish such as sand eels and herring.

First breeding takes place at 3–4 years of age; first-year juveniles normally remain in the winter quarters, while second-year immatures visit the colony from mid-June to display etc., but they do not lay.

DISTRIBUTION AND POPULATION

Holarctic; South Atlantic and Indian Ocean. The main population is within the west Palearctic, the Black Sea, Caspian Sea and north-west Europe—France, West Germany, East Germany, the Netherlands, Sweden, Denmark, Britain and Ireland. The bird also nests in the Mediterranean, Spain and occasionally Italy. In winter the Black Sea population moves to the Mediterranean, the Caspian Sea population moves to the Persian Gulf, and the northern European population moves to the west and south-west coasts of Africa.

In Britain the Sandwich Tern occurs in very localized populations in Orkney, the Firth of Forth, Northumberland, East Anglia, Hampshire, Anglesey and on the Clyde. Following a suspected decrease in the 19th century, the bird has shown a steady rise from less than 2,000 pairs in 1920 to more than 9,000 pairs at the time of 'Operation Seafarer' in 1969. Since 1969 the Scottish population has fluctuated at around 2,000 pairs, and the Welsh population has increased from a single pair in 1969 to 450 pairs in 1986. The English population of 7,142 pairs in 1969 had increased to 11,032 pairs by 1984, the maximum so far recorded. Overall, the British population reached its highest recorded level of 13,334 in 1982, with a slight fall to 12,725 in 1984. Since 1969, 59 sites have supported at least one breeding pair in at least one year, but the majority of the population is concentrated into six main colonies (the Farne Islands, Coquet Island, Blakeney Point, Scolt Head, Foulney and the Sands of Forvie), and these colonies have consistently held a total of over 10,000 pairs — over 80% of the British population (Cramp *et al.*, 1974; Lloyd *et al.*, 1975; Thomas, 1982; Thomas *et al.*, in press).

THREATS TO SURVIVAL

Threats relate to the species' susceptibility to the occurrence of disastrous events (eg, oil spillage) in the few large colonies which it forms.

This species is gradually but steadily increasing in numbers in Britain, and it appears to have had good breeding success. Its main British sites are reserves and therefore can be regarded as being relatively safe. Under these circumstances it is tempting to think that this species' future in Britain, at least in the short term, is relatively secure. However, the concentration of the species into a small number of large colonies means that it is susceptible to localized disastrous events — such as oil spillage or food shortage.

This species is trapped by man in its wintering quarters in West Africa — though the number taken is not known, and neither is it known what effect such trapping might have on the breeding population (Mead, 1971).

CONSERVATION

The intimate association of this species with Black-headed Gulls at many (but not all) of its main colonies is interesting since one of the management techniques used to protect this species is gull control. This arises from observations of gulls taking tern chicks or eggs. However, the only detailed study of this, in the Netherlands (Veen, 1977), shows that the advantages of nesting with the gulls outweighs the disadvantages. Studies are necessary to investigate the influence of gulls on the breeding success of Sandwich Terns in Britain. Only if gulls are proved to have a deleterious effect on the terns' nesting success should control measures be considered.

The RSPB and ICBP have funded an educational programme by the Ghanaian Government to try to reduce the incidence of winter trapping in Ghana. Further studies are necessary to measure the scale of the problem and to monitor any effects of the educational campaign.

REFERENCES

CRAMP, S., BOURNE, W.R.P. & SAUNDERS, D. 1974. The Seabirds of Britain and Ireland. London: Collins.
LLOYD, C.S., BIBBY, C.J. & EVERETT, M.J. 1975. Breeding terns in Britain and Ireland in 1969–74. Brit. Birds 68: 221–237.
MEAD, C.J. 1971. Seabird mortality as seen through ringing. Ibis 113: 418.

THOMAS, G.J. 1982. Breeding terns in Britain and Ireland, 1975–79. Seabird 6: 59–69.
THOMAS, G.J., UNDERWOOD, L. & PARTRIDGE, K. Breeding terns in Britain and Ireland 1980–84. Seabird (in press).
VEEN, J. 1977. Functional and causal aspects of nest distribution in colonies of the Sandwich Tern (*Sterna s. sandvicensis* L.). Leiden: E.J. Brill.

Consultants: M.I. Avery and F.L.R. Winder

Roseate Tern

Sterna dougallii

The Roseate Tern is rare and considered to be in danger of extinction as a British breeding species. After a marked population decline in the first half of the 19th century, the numbers of this bird increased in the 20th century to a maximum of perhaps 1,000 pairs by the late 1950s and early 1960s; however, numbers have since declined consistently to a current (1988) population of about 135 pairs in Britain. The causes of this decline are not known.

LEGAL STATUS

Protected under Schedule 1 of WCA 1981; Annex 1 of EC Birds Directive; Appendix II of the Berne Convention.

ECOLOGY

In Britain, the Roseate Tern nests with other species of tern, usually with Common but also with Arctic Terns. The colonies are almost always on offshore islands. The nest site is usually sheltered, often overhung by rock or vegetation, and sites such as the entrances to Puffin burrows are also used (in USA and France the bird readily uses artificial nest sites under boxes or planks). Nest: in piles of stones or in nest boxes—also amongst and below bushes of the Tree Mallow. The bird arrives in Britain later than other terns and begins laying soon after arrival; there is no prolonged period of courtship. Eggs: laid in May to late July. Clutch: 1–3 (average about 1·5); one brood, but one replacement clutch may be laid if the nest fails at the egg stage. The young fledge from late July to late August.

Food consists mainly of small fish, especially sand eels. Some food is stolen from other tern species.

The age of first breeding is 2–4 years (Nisbet, 1981).

DISTRIBUTION AND POPULATION

The bird is almost cosmopolitan, but the range is highly fragmented. In Europe it breeds only very locally in Britain, Ireland and Brittany. The stronghold of the European population is the Azores (Portugal), which hold more than half of the European population (Dunn, unpublished). The Roseate Tern has bred in small numbers in Spain, southern France, West Germany and perhaps Denmark. It was apparently formerly abundant in Tunisia, but it no longer breeds there.

The bird winters south to southern Africa, but British and Irish ringing recoveries suggest that West Africa, particularly Ghana, is the commonest wintering area (Nisbet, 1980; Gochfield, 1983).

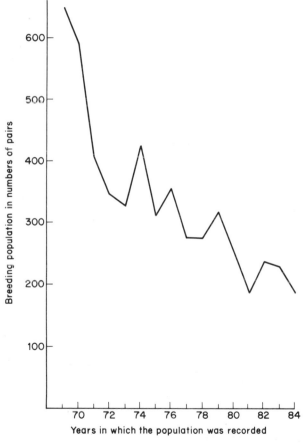

Breeding population of Roseate Terns (Sterna dougallii) in Britain during the years 1969–1984

After the population decreased in the 19th century (though it had always been local), there was a marked increase in the numbers of this bird in Britain and Ireland in the first half of the 20th century; however, numbers have again declined since the early 1960s, and in recent years the bird has been confined largely to one regular colony in Wales—which fared extremely badly in 1987 and 1988 (Cramp *et al.*, 1974; Everett *et al.*, 1987; Lloyd *et al.*, 1975; Thomas, 1982; Thomas *et al.*, in press).

An accurate assessment of breeding numbers is more difficult than for related species due to the difficulty of distinguishing the very similar eggs and chicks from those of other species, and the generally concealed nest sites. It is likely that a peak of perhaps 3,500 pairs in Britain and Ireland was reached in the late 1950s and early 1960s, though the British population probably did not exceed 1,000 pairs. The general picture since 1969 is given in the figure. In 1987 the British and Irish population numbered approximately 430 pairs, with approximately 250 of these at one Irish site, and only about 110 pairs at less than a dozen British sites. The main Welsh site dropped in numbers from 200 pairs in 1986 to only 40 pairs in 1987. In the year following (1988) there were signs of a reversal of the downward trend with a British population of about 135 pairs (of which there were 45 at the main site in Wales) but it remains to be seen whether this will be maintained.

The decline in British numbers has been accompanied by well-documented declines in Ireland and France, and there is evidence to suggest that the numbers now breeding on the Azores are lower than previously.

THREATS TO SURVIVAL

Threats include predation by mammals and by Peregrines.

The decline in numbers of the Roseate Tern since the early 1960s is as mysterious as the rise in numbers which preceded it. Without knowledge of the cause of these changes it is unlikely that much can be done to influence them. At the present rate of decline the species could cease to nest in Britain within the next decade.

This species is probably no more sensitive to human (or other) disturbance than are other *Sterna* species, but disturbance should certainly be avoided, particularly at the early stage of the breeding season. In some Irish and North American colonies birds have become accustomed to human presence and are extremely confiding (and successful).

The taking of adults by predators is a serious and rather intractable problem at the main Welsh colony, where, in 1987, 12 corpses of adult Roseates were found; these birds had been killed and stored away by a fox. At this same colony, predation by Peregrines has occurred every year since 1979, more than one pair of Peregrines being involved. In 1980, RSPB wardens estimated that 36 adult Roseates had been taken by Peregrines. Rats have caused problems at this colony in the past, but they now (appear to) have been effectively eliminated.

At present, loss of suitable breeding habitat is not a problem in Britain (though in Ireland one important site disappeared beneath the waves in 1976, and another is expected to disappear within the next few years). Many former sites still hold Common Terns, or other tern species, and would presumably be able to accommodate large numbers of Roseates if their numbers were to increase. At some sites the danger exists that the terns' nesting areas could become overrun by gulls if the latter are not controlled. The loss of habitat to Herring Gulls was a major factor in the decline of this species in the USA.

Trapping occurs in the winter quarters, but it has an unknown effect on the recruitment of young birds to the breeding population and the subsequent survival of breeding adults (Mead, 1971).

There is no evidence that a shortage of food in the breeding season is implicated in the decline, since the limited data available suggest that chick productivity is high.

CONSERVATION

The quality and quantity of information on breeding numbers and nesting success are at present inadequate. Standardized methods should be used at all colonies in the same year to provide a baseline from which to monitor further changes in numbers. Detailed information on breeding (clutch sizes, hatching success and fledging success) needs to be collected in order to provide comparisons with earlier British data and with current research in the USA, since, although there are no signs that breeding success (in the absence of predators) is low in Britain, this should be rigorously established.

A colour-ringing scheme, which will provide information on recruitment of young birds to the breeding population, and which identifies British and Irish born birds in the wintering grounds, has been established throughout Britain and Ireland. Sightings of colour-ringed birds should be sent to the RSPB at Sandy.

The small number of remaining colonies is a cause for concern. The creation of new sites should be considered. The (relative) strongholds of this species' British and Irish range are centred on the Irish Sea. It would be interesting to see whether a disused oil-rig moored or grounded off the Welsh (or Irish) coast would be colonized by this species.

Various attempts to solve the Peregrine problem in Wales have been ruled out or have failed. Artificial feeding has been attempted with little success; no suitable form of scaring has been suggested; the prevention of nesting by Peregrines, by modifying the local nest site, is impracticable since many suitable alternatives exist (and because not only the local birds are involved). Trapping (and removal) — or destruction — of the Peregrines have been ruled out as options.

Starting in 1988, artificial nest sites have been provided, and one has been used by Roseates on an experimental basis. These, it is hoped, may reduce the disturbance and predation of incubating adults.

The possibility of providing thicker vegetation at some sites is also being investigated.

Controlled public viewing of this species should be considered at a small number of colonies. This would allow people to see this attractive and endangered bird, and provide opportunities for the plight of the bird — and the measures being taken to help it — to be explained.

It is possible that the cause of the decline in this species' British population lies outside north-west Europe. Factors acting either in the Azores or in the wintering quarters in West Africa could be responsible for the decline. Little is known of the threats experienced by this species in the Azores, and research is needed to study it there. The RSPB and ICBP have funded an educational programme by the Government of Ghana to try to reduce the incidence of winter trapping in Ghana. Further studies are necessary to measure the magnitude of the problem and to monitor any effects of the educational campaign, though few people believe that trapping is the sole cause of the decline of this species.

REFERENCES

CRAMP, S., BOURNE, W.R.P. & SAUNDERS, D. 1974. The Seabirds of Britain and Ireland. London: Collins.

DUNN, E.K. 1984. Azores Tern Survey 1984. Preliminary ICBP Report (unpublished).

EVERETT, M.J., HEPBURN, I.R., NTIAMOU-BAIDU, Y. & THOMAS, G.J. 1987. Roseate Terns in Britain and West Africa. RSPB Conserv. Rev. 1: 56–58.

GOCHFIELD, M. 1983. The Roseate Tern: world distribution and status of a threatened species. Biol. Conserv. 25: 103–125.

LLOYD, C.S, BIBBY, C.J. & EVERETT, M.J. 1975. Breeding terns in Britain and Ireland in 1969–74. Brit. Birds 68: 221–237.

MEAD, C.J. 1971. Seabird mortality as seen through ringing. Ibis 113: 418.

NISBET, I.C.T. 1980. Status and Trends of the Roseate Tern *Sterna dougallii* in North America and the Caribbean. Report prepared for the US Fish and Wildlife Service.

NISBET, I.C.T. 1981. Biological characteristics of the Roseate Tern *Sterna dougallii*. Report prepared for the US Fish and Wildlife Service.

THOMAS, G.J. 1982. Breeding terns in Britain and Ireland, 1975–79. Seabird 6: 59–69.

THOMAS, G.J., UNDERWOOD, L. & PARTRIDGE, K. Breeding terns in Britain and Ireland 1980–84. Seabird. (In press.)

Consultants: M.I. Avery and F.L.R. Winder

Arctic Tern
Sterna paradisaea

The Arctic Tern breeds in Britain in internationally important numbers, in the early 1980s there were approximately 75,000 pairs in Britain representing about 33% of the breeding population in north-west Europe. In recent years there has been an almost total failure to produce fledged chicks in Shetland, apparently due to food shortage.

LEGAL STATUS

Protected under WCA 1981; Annex 1 of EC Birds Directive; Appendix II of the Berne Convention.

ECOLOGY

The Arctic Tern is a colonial nester; colonies number from a few pairs to over 10,000. The bird associates with other *Sterna* species where ranges overlap, particularly *S. hirundo*. Nest: a shallow scrape on open ground; a wide variety of substrates are used, generally along the coastline but also at inland lochs or on open, grazed areas. Eggs: laid mid-May to mid-June. Clutch: 2 (1–3); one brood, a replacement clutch being laid only if eggs are lost early in incubation. The young fledge in July.

Food consists mainly of small fish, but also crustaceans, worms and insects (Coulson & Horobin, 1976; Monaghan *et al.*, in press).

DISTRIBUTION AND POPULATION

Circumpolar. The bird breeds across northern Europe, the USSR, North America and Greenland. In Europe it breeds in Iceland, Norway, Denmark, Sweden, Finland, East and West Germany, the Netherlands, France, Britain and Ireland. Over much of the southern part of its range (France, Britain, Ireland, West Germany) the population has undergone a decline within recent years; which may have been the result of climatic amelioration. As with the other *Sterna* species, a decrease probably occurred in the 19th century followed by an increase during the beginning of the 20th century.

Annual migration covers a greater distance than for any other bird: from the Arctic to the Antarctic for some individuals. Most European birds move, via Britain, along the coasts of western Europe and West Africa, passage being completed in October–December. First-winter birds may remain in equatorial regions, or may travel to the antarctic with adults, but most overwinter off the coasts of South Africa and Chile. Some first-summer birds have undertaken partial northerly migration, but it is rarely until the second summer that they reach the breeding colonies (although they do not breed); breeding first occurs at 3–4 years.

The English population over the period 1969–1984 remained fairly constant at 3,000–4,000 pairs. The Welsh population has fluctuated between eight pairs (1973) and 982 pairs (1975), averaging 650 pairs in the last 14 years. The Scottish population is hard to estimate, with the bulk of it being scattered in 215 known Orkney colonies (33,069 pairs in 1980) and 396 known Shetland colonies (31,794 pairs in 1980). In 1980 the Scottish population was estimated at 70,970 pairs, considerably higher than any previous estimates (such as in 1969, when 30,182 pairs were estimated).

Taking the three countries together, the most recently available counts give a British total of over 75,000 pairs, about one-third of the population breeding in north-west Europe. Since 1969 however, the largest British colony, North Hill, Papa Westray, has declined from 17,500 pairs in 1969 to 1,500 in 1987. Counts over the last four years have shown a decline in Orkney, but the Shetland colonies have given cause for serious concern as the number of pairs at monitored colonies has steadily declined, and the number of chicks surviving to fledge has been virtually zero in recent years (Cramp *et al.*, 1974; Lloyd *et al.*, 1975; Thomas, 1982; Thomas *et al.*, in press). A complete census of breeding terns in Shetland in 1989 revealed that numbers there have declined by about 70% since 1980. On Fair Isle 283 pairs fledged only 36 chicks and less than 100 young were thought to have flown from all other colonies in Shetland (over 30,000 pairs in 1980) (Richardson, 1989).

THREATS TO SURVIVAL

Threats include a shortage of food at the Scottish breeding sites.

The major cause for concern is the very low, almost non-existent, breeding success in Shetland (and to a lesser extent, Orkney) in recent years. Current research by Glasgow University suggests that the cause of breeding failure is food shortage (as had been suspected by less detailed observations).

Arctic Tern populations in other areas of Britain have been less intensively studied, but data from Coquet Island, Northumberland suggest that breeding success there is high.

CONSERVATION

For such a dispersed and numerous species, comprehensive monitoring is not feasible, but the Orkney and Shetland populations have been surveyed in 1989 in order to assess any decrease in breeding numbers since 1980.

Food shortage is the most dramatic and obvious cause for concern. It is possible that food shortage may have been caused by overfishing by the commercial sand eel fishery established on Shetland, but it will be very difficult to establish whether the lack of sand eels is a natural event which has affected both the fishermen and the terns, or whether overfishing is the cause of the food shortage. If overfishing is proved to play an important role in the food shortage then it would be necessary to assess the effectiveness of curbs on fishing introduced in 1987 by the Shetland Fish Producers' Organization. These curbs ban the landing of sand eels if more than a quarter of the catch is made up of fish under three inches long, and are designed to protect the immature stages of the fish.

REFERENCES

COULSON, J.C. & HOROBIN, J. 1976. The influence of age on the breeding biology and survival of the Arctic Tern *Sterna paradisaea*. J. Zool. Lond. 178: 247–260.

CRAMP, S., BOURNE, W.R.P. & SAUNDERS, D. 1974. The seabirds of Britain and Ireland. London: Oxford University Press.

LLOYD, C.S., BIBBY, C.J. & EVERETT, M.J. 1975. Breeding terns in Britain and Ireland in 1969–74. Brit. Birds 68: 221–237.

MONAGHAN, P., UTTLEY, J.D., BURNS, M.D., THAINE, C. & BLACKWOOD, J. The relationship between food supply, reproductive effort and breeding success in Arctic Terns *Sterna paradisaea*. J. Anim. Ecol. (in press).

RICHARDSON, M. 1989. The 1989 Seabird Breeding Season. Shetland Bird Club Newsletter 79. November 1989.

THOMAS, G.J. 1982. Breeding terns in Britain and Ireland, 1975–79. Seabird 6: 59–69.

THOMAS, G.J., UNDERWOOD, L. & PARTRIDGE, K. Breeding terns in Britain and Ireland 1980–84. Seabird (in press).

Consultant: M.I. Avery

Little Tern
Sterna albifrons

The Little Tern breeds in Britain in internationally important numbers. After a decline in the 19th century, and a subsequent partial recovery, it began to decrease again in the mid-1930s; however, since 1969 it has increased to around 1,500–1,700 pairs, about 30% of the west European total.

LEGAL STATUS

Protected under Schedule 1 of WCA 1981; Annex 1 of EC Birds Directive; Appendix II of the Berne Convention.

ECOLOGY

The Little Tern is essentially a coastal breeding species on sand or shingle. Colonies are of much looser groupings than those of other *Sterna* species; the bird is normally found in small, single-species colonies, but at least seven British sites have held over 100 pairs in at least one year since 1969. The bird occasionally nests inland. Nest: a shallow scrape formed on sand or shingle in the absence of vegetation; it is sometimes only metres from the high-tide mark — flooding during high spring tides is a common cause of nest failure. Eggs: laid mid-May to end of June. Clutch: 2–3 (1–4), one brood, but up to two replacement clutches are laid if eggs are lost during incubation. The young fledge in July.

Food consists of small fish, crustaceans and invertebrates.

DISTRIBUTION AND POPULATION

The bird has a world-wide distribution. It breeds throughout Europe, parts of northern (Mediterranean) and West Africa, Asia, Australia and North America where, as in most of the USSR, it readily breeds inland. Within Europe, breeding occurs mainly in France, Spain, the Netherlands, West Germany, Poland, Denmark, Sweden, Italy, Greece, Britain and Ireland. Across most of this range there has been a contraction in population in the second half of the 20th century (except the colonization of Finland in 1960). This followed the decrease in the 19th century (common to all tern species) and subsequent increase at the beginning of the 20th century. The west European population migrates to winter along the coasts of West Africa. Breeding first occurs at three years; the first summer is spent in the wintering grounds, and the second summer at the wintering grounds or as a late visitor to the colony site. First-breeding does not necessarily occur at the natal colony, though older birds are generally site-faithful unless the habitat deteriorates or disturbance is high.

Within Britain the main colonies of the Little Tern are in south and south-east England, the north-east coast from Northumberland to Aberdeen, in the Hebrides, and on the north-west coast from the Clyde to Anglesey; at least 113 sites have held breeding Little Terns in at least one year.

'Operation Seafarer' in 1969 estimated the British population of Little Terns at 1,518 pairs; although fluctuations have occurred (a high of 1,912 in 1980, and a low of 1,283 in 1975) the 1984 figure of 1,584 is remarkably similar, and is surprising considering that this species has appeared to benefit from a growing number of protection schemes (Cramp *et al.*, 1974; Lloyd *et al.*, 1975; Thomas, 1982; Thomas *et al.*, in press).

THREATS TO SURVIVAL

Threats include predation, disturbance by man, and possibly egg collecting.

The Little Tern is less aggressive than the larger terns and is thus vulnerable to predators and to human disturbance. Human disturbance is the most obvious threat to the species' breeding success, and is perhaps the one threat for which a potential solution can be most easily seen.

Egg collecting is still perceived as a threat but there is little information to indicate the size of this problem.

At many sites protected from disturbance, breeding success has remained low due to predation of eggs and chicks by foxes and crows.

There is at present no evidence to suggest that food shortage is a problem for this species, though more data would confirm this.

CONSERVATION

Since it appears that protection schemes tend to concentrate the species into protected areas, it is important to know whether this leads to adequate breeding success. There is a danger that the birds could be concentrated into areas where their reproductive success is low.

Annual monitoring of sites needs to be carried out since pressure from predators can change from year to year, and single predators can have dramatic effects on breeding success in large colonies. The large number of potential colonies means that it is impracticable to collect detailed information from all sites or to protect all of them. Thus, a strategy of protecting the most productive sites is necessary. Where predation is reducing breeding success, chick shelters should be tried. These allow chicks to hide from predators such as foxes and crows.

In areas where flooding of nests by high tides is a problem, remedial steps have been taken for some years now with success. These involve either raising the nest site artificially, in order to protect it from the high water, or moving nests (very gradually) up the beach and past the danger area. Such techniques have become almost standard at some colonies (Everett, 1980; Knight & Hoddan, 1982, 1983).

REFERENCES

CRAMP, S., BOURNE, W.R.P. & SAUNDERS, D. 1974. The seabirds of Britain and Ireland. London: Collins.
EVERETT, M.J. (ed.) 1980. Little Terns: proceedings of a symposium on Little Terns (*Sterna albifrons*), Grafham Water, 4 November 1980.
KNIGHT, R.C. & HODDAN, P.C. 1982. Little Terns (*Sterna albifrons*) in England and Wales, 1977–79, with details of conservation work carried out at Rye Harbour Local Nature Reserve. Seabird 6: 70–85.
KNIGHT, R.C. & HODDAN, P.C. 1983. A guide to Little Tern conservation. RSPB, 114 pp.
LLOYD, C.S., BIBBY, C.J. & EVERETT, M.J. 1975. Breeding terns in Britain and Ireland in 1969–74. Brit. Birds 68: 221–237.
THOMAS, G.J. 1982. Breeding terns in Britain and Ireland, 1975–79. Seabird 6: 59—69.
THOMAS, G.J., UNDERWOOD, L. & PARTRIDGE, K. Breeding terns in Britain and Ireland 1980–84. Seabird (in press).

Consultant: M.I. Avery

Black Tern

Chlidonias niger

The Black Tern has bred in Britain on a few occasions since 1966, but not since 1978; otherwise it is a regular passage-migrant. The population of this bird has declined across much of its European breeding range due largely to drainage, but the bird may be encouraged to breed in Britain by the correct management of protected wetlands.

LEGAL STATUS

Protected under Schedule 1 of WCA 1981; Annex I of EC Birds Directive; Appendix II of the Berne Convention.

ECOLOGY

The Black Tern is a summer visitor which breeds in scattered localities across Europe. For nesting, the bird prefers fresh or brackish pools rich in low marginal, floating or emergent aquatic vegetation. Nest: a heap of aquatic plants either on floating mats of algae and pond weeds or anchored to sedges, reeds and other emergent vegetation in shallow water; alternatively, the nest may consist simply of a thinly lined scrape on firmer ground. The bird is loosely colonial. Eggs: laid (in continental nests) in mid-May to June. Clutch: 3 (2–4); one brood. The young fledge by late July.

Food consists mainly of insects and other invertebrates and small fish.

DISTRIBUTION AND POPULATION

Holarctic. The Black Tern breeds locally over much of continental Europe from Spain, France and the northern Balkans, north to Denmark, southern Sweden and the Baltic states, east across central and southern Russia; it winters in tropical Africa and South America, mainly along rivers and coasts. The European population has declined in recent years due largely to drainage of suitable habitat. Known populations are: France under 10,000 pairs (Yeatman, 1976), Belgium 20 pairs (Lippens & Wille, 1972), and the Netherlands 2,000–3,000 pairs (Teixeira, 1979).

The Black Tern formerly nested regularly in south-east and eastern England north to Yorkshire, particularly in East Anglia, but it became extinct before the mid-19th century as a result of extensive drainage. Since then, isolated breeding, usually in single pairs, has been recorded in 1853, 1858, 1966, 1969 (when up to seven pairs attempted to breed, at least one pair successfully rearing young) (Cottier & Lea, 1969), 1970 and 1975 in East Anglia, and in 1978 in Nottinghamshire. Otherwise the bird is a regular passage-migrant from April to June, and from July to October, chiefly in eastern and southern England. It also bred in Ireland in 1967 and 1975.

THREATS TO SURVIVAL

In Britain, nesting appears to have been attempted when food and weather conditions were right, at a time when significant numbers of migrants were passing through. However, few areas have the ideal combination of permanent extensive shallows and floating vegetation free from disturbance. The eggs of the pair that attempted to breed in Nottinghamshire in 1978 were taken by a collector.

CONSERVATION

Although the bird is now only an occasional breeder in Britain, recolonization must remain a possibility. The main aim must be the provision of the right habitat: sheltered shallow, open water with dense mats of floating vegetation such as *Glyceria* or filamentous green algae with open-water areas between. This management is likely to be possible only on reserves where other species, such as Black-necked Grebe, could also benefit.

Disturbance should be kept to a minimum, and the locality of any nest kept confidential. Should breeding become regular, site protection by way of SSSI notification should be considered.

REFERENCES

COTTIER, E.J. & LEA, D. 1969. Black-tailed godwits, ruff and black terns breeding on the Ouse Washes. Brit. Birds 62: 259—270.

LIPPENS, L. & WILLE, H. 1972. Atlas des Oiseaux de Belgique et d'Europe occidentale. Lanoo: Tielt.

TEIXEIRA, R.M. (ed.) 1979. Atlas van de Nederlandse Broedvogels. Vereniging tot Behod Van Natuurmonumenten in Nederlandte 's-Graveland.

YEATMAN, L.J. 1976. Atlas des Oiseaux Nicheurs de France. Paris: Ministere de la Qualite de la vie Environment.

Guillemot
Uria aalge

The Guillemot breeds in Britain in internationally important numbers; about 1,040,000 birds breed in Britain, about 65% of the European total outside Iceland

and Bear Island, and at least 25% of the Atlantic population. A high proportion of the west European population is to be found off British coasts in winter and during spring and autumn passage. Counts made in 1985–87 for the Seabird Group/NCC Seabird Colony Register suggest that breeding numbers have doubled since the last complete survey in 1969–70. This is confirmed by annual counts at a sample of sites throughout Britain.

LEGAL STATUS

Protected under WCA 1981; EC Birds Directive; Appendix III of the Berne Convention.

ECOLOGY

The Guillemot inhabits coastal and offshore waters; in summer it gathers at breeding colonies, which are often large and crowded, on coastal cliffs and rock stacks. There is no nest; a single conical egg is laid on bare ledges on sea cliffs or on level ground on top of stacks. Egg: laid in May to July. Clutch: 1; one brood. The young leave the colonies after about 20 days, unfledged, one-third grown, and in the care of the adult male, from the end of June to about mid-September.

Food consists mainly of small fish, especially sand eels in summer, crustaceans, molluscs and marine worms.

Adult birds undergo a period of flightlessness in July and August when the flight feathers are replaced.

DISTRIBUTION AND POPULATION

Holarctic. The Guillemot breeds on coastal cliffs of the north Pacific (about 5·5 million birds) and north Atlantic (3–5 million birds) oceans. Guillemots breed on the western seaboard of Europe and Scandinavia, at suitable localities, from Novaya Zemlaya to northern Spain and Portugal. Iceland holds 0·8–1·6 million pairs, Bear Island 0·4–1·0 million pairs, and the British colonies (excluding those in Ireland) about 1,040,000 birds — about 25–45% of the Atlantic population. Apart from these areas there are relatively small populations in (in declining order of numbers of pairs) the Faeroes (300,000), Norway (110,000), the USSR (Kola Peninsula and Novaya Zemlaya — 4,750), Denmark and Sweden (9,400), and Helgoland (2,000); Jan Mayen, Finland, France, Spain and Portugal all have colonies of less than 1,000 pairs (Nettleship & Birkhead, 1985). Within Britain the breeding distribution very closely resembles that of the Razorbill, with the largest colonies in the Shetlands (Noss, 37,700 birds; Foula, 37,500 birds; Fair Isle, 35,200 birds; and elsewhere at Sumburgh Head and Hermaness), the Orkneys (Noup Head, Westray, 33,200 birds, and populations at Marwick Head, Copinsay, Hoy and the Calf of Eday), and northern Scotland — particularly Caithness cliffs, Handa (98,700 birds) and Fowlsheugh (53,400 birds). In England the largest colonies are on the Farne Islands (14,900 birds) and at Flamborough Head–Bempton Cliffs (14,400 birds); other large colonies are at Skomer (6,200 birds), St Bees Head (4,900 birds), and Carreg y Llam (4,700 birds).

Comparison with counts of known colonies made during the 1969–70 'Operation Seafarer' census gives the following totals for Great Britain and the Channel Isles.

Guillemot: population figures for Great Britain and the Channel Isles*

	Seabird Colony Register 1985–87 (from Lloyd *et al.*, in press)	'Operation Seafarer' 1969–70 (from Cramp *et al.*, 1974)
Scotland	965,800 birds	461,410 pairs
England	42,400 birds	22,765 pairs
Wales	31,400 birds	14,010 pairs
Channel Isles	320 pairs	90 pairs

* Note the difference in units; 'Seafarer' data were probably equivalent to birds, not 'pairs'.

In 1981 it was estimated that the number of Guillemots in the North Sea in June would be about 1,700,000, rising to 2,073,000 in the autumn following the fledging of the summer's chicks from the colonies—most of which will have come from the colonies of eastern Scotland, Orkney and Shetland (Tasker *et al.*, 1987).

THREATS TO SURVIVAL

Threats include the effects of marine oil pollution and a shortage of food.

The former practice of taking Guillemots and their eggs for food, and shooting them for sport—prevalent in some areas until the 1930s—has now largely ceased.

Oil pollution close to major colonies, and at sea, remains a threat. While stronger legislation and wider awareness of the detrimental effects of oil pollution have reduced the number of incidents caused by deliberate cleaning-out of tanks or disposal of waste oil at sea, accidental spillages still occur regularly. The diving habits of auks render them especially prone to oiling: during 1968–70, between 21% and 100% of auks picked up dead on sections of coast all around Britain were oiled, with the highest incidence on the east coasts of Scotland and England (especially on the south coast of England).

Other forms of marine pollution, notably those arising from organochlorine pesticides used in agriculture—and polychlorinated biphenyls and heavy metals used in industry—are known to cause bird mortality and reduce breeding success, but as yet there is no firm proof that they have been the major cause of large-scale seabird mortality in Britain.

A shortage of food, possibly due to over-fishing, is the most serious problem; large-scale mortalities of starving birds have occurred in north-east Scotland in three recent winters, and once in the summer in west Scotland. The use of inshore drift fishing nets may be a problem in some localities.

CONSERVATION

Much further research is needed to improve our understanding of the complex ecology of the sea and its birds to enable proper assessment of present and future threats posed by overfishing, pollution and other factors.

The obvious main conservation need at present is for new research on the effects of industrial fishing of sand eels etc. Continued efforts are also needed to eliminate deliberate oil pollution at sea, and to find the most effective and environmentally safe methods of dealing promptly with oil spillages, especially when they occur in areas which hold important seabird populations.

Continued census-taking of auk colonies, and surveys of auks found dead on beaches, are important to give warning of any serious population reductions and to directly monitor the effects of oil and other pollutants.

REFERENCES

CRAMP, S., BOURNE, W.R.P. & SAUNDERS, D. 1974. The seabirds of Britain and Ireland. London: Collins.
LLOYD, C.S., TASKER, M.L. & PARTRIDGE, K.E. (in press). The status of seabirds in Britain and Ireland. London: Poyser.
NETTLESHIP, D.N. & BIRKHEAD, T.R. (eds) 1985. The Atlantic Alcidae. London: Academic Press.
TASKER, M.L., WEBB, A., HALL, A.J., PIENKOWSKI, M.W. & LANGSLOW, D.R. 1987. Seabirds in the North Sea. Peterborough: Nature Conservancy Council.

Consultants: M.L. Tasker and C.S. Lloyd

Razorbill
Alca torda

The Razorbill breeds in Britain in internationally important numbers; about 145,000 pairs breed in the United Kingdom—this being about 65% of the west European total, and about 20% of the world population. Similar proportions are to be found off British coasts in winter and during both spring and autumn passages.

LEGAL STATUS

Protected under WCA 1981; EC Birds Directive; Appendix III of the Berne Convention.

ECOLOGY

Razorbills inhabit coastal and oceanic waters, and in summer they gather at breeding colonies on coastal cliffs and stacks. The nest can be of pebbles, but single eggs are generally laid in crevices, ledges and holes in cliffs at sites which are less exposed than those favoured by Guillemots; eggs are also laid amongst boulders at the bases of cliffs, on cliff slopes and on top of rock stacks. Clutch: 1; one brood. In May to July the young leave the colonies unfledged, one-third grown, and still in parental care from the end of June.

Food consists mainly of fish, but the birds also feed on crustaceans and molluscs.

DISTRIBUTION AND POPULATION

North-eastern Nearctic and western Palearctic. The Razorbill breeds on coastal cliffs of the north Atlantic, wintering at sea mostly in northern waters south to the

Azores and the western Mediterranean. In Europe, the bird breeds from Brittany and the Channel Islands north to Iceland, northern Scandinavia, Bear Island and Russia (a distribution very similar to that of the Guillemot). Apart from relatively small colonies in Britanny, the Channel Islands and Helgoland, breeding in western Europe is confined to Britain and Ireland.

A complete census of known colonies in 1985–87 showed that there were 126,580 birds in Scotland, 9,578 birds in Wales and 8,370 birds in England; the British total of about 144,928 birds represented about 80% of the west European population (most of the remainder were in Ireland, where there were about 35,000 birds) (Lloyd *et al*., in press). In 1987 it was estimated that, following the breeding season, about 220,000 birds would be present in the North Sea (Tasker *et al*., 1987). When combined, the British and Irish totals represent about 20% of the world population of Razorbills.

Razorbills breed on most British coasts, except between Flamborough Head, Yorkshire, and the Isle of Wight—where there are few suitable cliffs. Most of the large colonies are in the north, particularly in Shetland and Orkney (Foula 6,200 birds, and Fair Isle 3,950 birds) and along the north and north-west coasts of Scotland (Handa 16,394 individuals, and Caithness cliffs 16,555 birds).

Limited historical information suggests that decreases have occurred at some sites—mainly in south-west England, where 1,000 pairs on the Isle of Wight in 1937 decreased to between 10 and 100 pairs in 1969–70, and eight individuals in 1985–87. Some 10,500 pairs on Lundy in 1939 decreased to 580 pairs in 1969–70 (Cramp *et al*., 1974), and 761 birds in 1985–87. Decreases have also been noted at some colonies in south Wales.

As for all the auks, decreases are mainly attributed to complex changes in the marine and fish ecology of inshore waters. The use of inshore drift fishing nets may be a problem in some localities.

Some mortality occurs from oil pollution at sea, but colonies in western and northern Scotland, where oil pollution incidents are generally less frequent than in the North Sea and English Channel, have fared best.

THREATS TO SURVIVAL

The Razorbill is one of the species most seriously affected by oil pollution—especially when birds are dispersing from breeding colonies into the North Sea in August. Other threats are as for Guillemot (see page 220).

CONSERVATION

As for Guillemot (page 220).

REFERENCES

Cramp, S., Bourne, W.R.P. & Saunders, D. 1974. The seabirds of Britain and Ireland. London: Collins.

Lloyd, C.S., Tasker, M.L. & Partridge, K.E. (in press). The status of seabirds in Britain and Ireland. London: Poyser.

Tasker, M.L., Webb, A., Hall, A.J., Pienkowski, M.W. & Langslow, D.R. 1987. Seabirds in the North Sea. Peterborough: Nature Conservancy Council.

Consultants: M.L. Tasker and C.S. Lloyd

Barn Owl

Tyto alba

The Barn Owl was relatively common in lowland agricultural habitats in the mid-19th century; it is thought to have declined since then but is still widespread. The decline has been attributed to a loss of food supply resulting from intensification of agricultural practices, severe winters, pesticides in the 1950s and early 1960s, and increased road traffic kills. The present population (about 5,000 pairs) is estimated to be less than one-half of that 50 years ago.

LEGAL STATUS

Protected under Schedule 1 of WCA 1981; EC Birds Directive; Appendix II of the Berne Convention.

ECOLOGY

The Barn Owl is largely nocturnal and crepuscular; it is active at dusk, roosts in trees as well as buildings, and is sedentary. Nest: no nesting material is used, the eggs being laid on a layer of old pellets in a dark, draught-free site in buildings, tree cavities or caves; hay barns, old elms and oaks are the most frequently-used sites. Eggs: laid in April. Clutch: variable (4–7), larger clutches being produced where prey is especially abundant (Baudvin, 1975); double-brooding is rare. Incubation is carried out for 29–34 days, and hatching occurs asynchronously. The young leave the nest site at about 60 days, and they disperse up to 20 km from the nest. Fledging success is particularly high in good vole years (Kaus, 1977), but there is a high rate of mortality among juveniles; the birds are able to breed when they are one year old. Adult birds remain paired throughout winter.

Food (based on pellet analysis) consists of voles, mice, rats and shrews (forming 90% of the diet), together with bats, moles, rabbits, weasels, birds, amphibians and invertebrates (making up the remaining 10%). The short-tailed field vole (*Microtus agrestis*) is the primary prey species, and the common shrew, wood mouse and brown rat are secondary prey species—of which the numbers eaten are inversely proportional to the numbers of *Microtus* taken.

DISTRIBUTION AND POPULATION

The Barn Owl is cosmopolitan, and it is said to be the most widespread land bird in the world; it has a mainly tropical and sub-tropical distribution between latitudes 40°N and 40°S. The British (nominate) race, *T. a. alba*, has a European distribution which includes countries adjoining the Mediterranean basin, and it also extends into North Africa—from Morocco to Cyrenaica—and south to northern Mauretania. The northernmost birds are in Scotland.

It is difficult to obtain an accurate census of the Barn Owl; the species is subject to marked annual fluctuations in population which are related to cycles in the abundance of voles. A national census in 1932 by RSPB (Blaker, 1934) was the first attempt to establish the numbers of Barn Owls in England and Wales by using questionnaires and ground searches. The breeding population was then estimated at 12,000 pairs, with an additional 1,000 non-breeding adults. The highest densities (41–50 pairs per 100 square miles) were recorded in Devon and Cornwall, Essex/south Suffolk, Hertfordshire, Anglesey, and Cumberland/Westmoreland; good densities (31–40 pairs per 100 square miles) were recorded in Dorset, Hertfordshire/Bedfordshire/central Northamptonshire and west Suffolk. Blaker estimated a fall of 33% from an estimated 18,000 pairs in 1922.

A BTO enquiry during 1953–1963 (Prestt, 1965), reported 'widespread long-term decline'; the 1968–1972 BTO Atlas of Breeding Birds (Sharrock, 1976) gave a conservative estimate of 2–4 pairs per 100 square kilometres and a total of 4,500–9,000 pairs. A survey by the Hawk Trust in 1982–1985 (Shawyer, 1987) recorded Barn Owls in 50% of 10-km squares, the population then being estimated at 3,750 pairs for England and Wales and 650+ pairs for Scotland. Highest densities (10–30 pairs per 100 square kilometres) were recorded for parts of the Isle of Wight, Anglesey, Cornwall, mid-Devon, Suffolk, Norfolk, Hampshire and Sussex. The current population is estimated at 5,000 pairs (Shawyer, 1987), but this does not necessarily represent the number that breed each year.

Short-term population changes are almost certainly linked to natural changes in the numbers of small mammals.

Shawyer (1987) states that the long-term decline of the Barn Owl in Britain is predominantly the result of the continuing deterioration of the winter climate. There is no evidence, however, of a long-term trend in winter severity to match the long-term decline in Barn Owl numbers. More research is needed to disentangle proximate from ultimate factors.

THREATS TO SURVIVAL

Threats include the loss of prey-rich foraging areas, the destruction of traditional breeding sites, urbanization, the increased use of toxic pesticides, and disturbance. Persecution by trapping and shooting is almost certainly less important now than in the past.

The main consensus is that the Barn Owl has declined primarily as a result of a drastic reduction in the amount of prey-rich foraging habitat, a process which is continuing. Habitat loss is attributed largely to changes in agricultural practice, although urbanization and road construction have caused local declines and have resulted in an estimated doubling in the numbers of road deaths since the mid-1950s (Shawyer, 1987).

Barn Owls are attracted to road-side verges because they represent prey-rich linear grasslands. The high incidence of road deaths has been interpreted as an important factor in limiting the population (Shawyer, 1987); however, there is evidence to suggest that birds killed on the roads are already in poor condition, and that they are likely to be the most susceptible to natural mortality agents (I. Taylor, *pers. comm.*).

A 41% loss of freehold rough grazing in lowland England between 1946 and 1981, and a 95% loss of hay meadows since the war—together with intensification of pasture management and the change from hay to silage production—have reduced the vole and shrew populations. Moreover, improved methods of storing food crops, and the loss of rick yards, have reduced the availability of mice and rats.

The dependence of Barn Owls on rough grassland in field margins and woodland edges has meant that the estimated loss of 225,000 km of hedgerows between 1946 and 1974, and the clearance of 35–50% of woodland since 1933, has probably had an adverse effect on the population. There is little scientific evidence to implicate the loss of nesting sites as a widespread cause of decline; locally, the lack of secure nesting sites may limit population density, but the provision of extra nesting sites does not necessarily result in an increase in breeding pairs.

Second generation rodenticides—including difenacoum and brodifacoum—are now widely used in and around farm buildings to control warfarin-resistant rodents; owls are potentially the most vulnerable avian predator to secondary poisoning, particularly where rodenticides are used illegally to control rodents away from farm buildings. The potential hazard of rodenticides depends on the extent and nature of their use, and on the intensity of owl predation on these rodents. This is an important area for future research and monitoring.

Taxidermy and disturbance represent minor threats; the existence or consequences of inter-specific competition with Tawny Owls (*Strix aluco*) also remains to be tested.

CONSERVATION

The provision of secure nesting sites, the restoration of foraging habitats, and the exercise of controls on the use of rodenticides may prove beneficial to Barn Owls. The success of many of these measures will depend on the degree to which individual farmers and landowners are willing to adopt slightly less intensive land-use practices which make provision for areas of unproductive rough grassland. Headlands of rough grassland could be provided adjacent to woodland, or along field margins, hedges and drainage ditches, and may favour Barn Owls, but these areas may need to be managed to prevent scrub encroachment. Recent reforms in agricultural policy designed to reduce cereal surpluses may provide financial incentives for implementing some of these proposed changes.

Safe nesting sites are required for successful breeding, but nestbox schemes have rarely produced a measurable increase in the number of breeding pairs; the haphazard provision of nesting boxes is unlikely to have any ecological benefit unless consideration is first given to the availability of suitable foraging habitat (Shawyer, 1987). However, in recently afforested areas, and in some coastal and fenland areas, the availability of nesting sites may limit population density, and the provision of nesting boxes may result in an increase in the number of breeding pairs; there is some evidence that productivity is enhanced if pairs are encouraged to use boxes where natural sites are vulnerable or have been removed (Kennedy, 1979; Colvin et al., 1984). Hay and straw stacks are important breeding sites in eastern England, but they can be inadvertently destroyed (Shawyer, 1987). Birds may be encouraged to select the least vulnerable part of the stack by providing tunnels into the bales. High priority should be given to the preservation of traditional nesting and roosting sites in old hollow trees in southern and south-east England.

Second-generation rodenticides fall into the category of highest pesticide toxicity, and their widespread misuse could have disastrous consequences for Barn

Owls. The limitation of use to professional operators, product-labelling which identifies the dangers to birds, and tighter controls on the indiscriminate use—or deliberate misuse—of rodenticides would provide some safeguards.

Barn Owls breed prolifically in captivity, and many birds are released back into the wild each year. There is little scientific evidence to assess the potential benefits of releasing birds bred in captivity as a means of supplementing the wild population. Given suitable nesting sites and abundant food, wild Barn Owls are perfectly capable of fledging large broods, and few parts of Britain are remote from existing wild pairs. Release schemes may damage the wild population if they encourage land owners to believe that re-introductions are a substitute for the provision of suitable habitat, and given the form usually practised they may be illegal under the Abandonment of Animals Act (1960).

REFERENCES

BAUDVIN, H. 1976. Biologie de reproduction de la chouette effraie (*Tyto alba*) en Cote d'Or: Premiers Resultats. Le Jean le Blanc 14: 1–51.

BLAKER, G.B. 1934. The barn owl in England and Wales. London: Royal Society for the Protection of Birds.

COLVIN, B.A., HEGDAL, P.L. & JACKSON, W.B. 1984. A comprehensive approach to research and management of Common Barn Owl populations. *In* Proceedings of a Workshop on Management of Non-Game Species and Ecological Communities. Lexington, Kentucky, June 1984.

KAUS, D. 1977. Zur Populationsdynamik, Okologie und Brutbiologie der Schleiereule *Tyto alba* in Franken. Anz. orn. Ges. Bayern 16: 18–44.

KENNEDY, R.J. 1979. A nest box study of Barn Owls (*Tyto alba*). Bird Ringing in SW Lancashire 9: 18–53.

PRESTT, I. 1965. An enquiry into the recent breeding status of some smaller birds of prey and crows in Britain. Bird Study 12: 196–221.

SHAWYER, C.R. 1987. The Barn Owl in the British Isles. Its past, present and future. London: The Hawk Trust.

Consultant: J.T. Cayford

Snowy Owl
Nyctea scandiaca

The Snowy Owl nested in Shetland in 1967–75, after which the single adult male disappeared; one or two females were still present into 1990, so that the arrival of other males could still result in recolonization.

LEGAL STATUS

Protected under Schedule 1 of WCA 1981; Annex 1 of EC Birds Directive; Appendix II of the Berne Convention.

ECOLOGY

Nest: an open scrape on the ground, often on a hummock, on moorland with rocky outcrops, barren fells, mountains and tundra. Pairs are solitary, but polygamy may occur. Eggs: laid in May–June. Clutch: 4–10 (3–15), depending on food supply; one brood. The young fledge in late July to August. Productivity is very high in some years, very low in others (Watson, 1957). Food consists typically of lemmings and voles, but arctic hares are taken in some areas, and rabbits are the preferred prey in Scotland. A wide variety of bird species is also taken, especially when mammal prey is scarce.

DISTRIBUTION AND POPULATION

North Holarctic. Arctic USSR, northern Alaska, northern Canada, north-east Greenland. The bird breeds in northern Fenno-scandia, but numbers are comparatively low there, even in good lemming years; it has also bred in Iceland. Some birds, particularly immatures, wander in winter, and irregular eruptive movements, dependent on food supplies (especially lemmings), take place south to central Europe, Asia, northern China and the United States. In Scotland the species was a regular vagrant in the 19th century, but it became much scarcer during the period 1900–60, presumably as a result of the climatic amelioration in the Arctic. During the 1960s the species again began to be recorded in the summer in the Shetlands; this followed a series of southward invasions in Scandinavia during 1960–63, as a result of which the bird was also increasingly seen on the Continent south to the Netherlands and Germany. Then, in 1967, a nest with seven eggs was found on Fetlar, Shetland (Tulloch, 1968). During the nine years 1967–75 a total of 23 young were reared; in 1973–75 the male also paired with a second female, but the resulting nests were always deserted (Robinson & Becker, 1986). Since the loss of the male in the winter of 1975/76 several females have remained in Shetland; in 1981, for example, up to four were reported on Fetlar, one of which laid an infertile clutch of eggs as did a lone female in the summer of 1987 also on Fetlar. Elsewhere, since the mid-1960s, single birds and, rarely, even pairs have occurred at various seasons, including the summer, in the central and north-eastern Highlands and in the Western Isles, though none are thought to have nested; two single females laid infertile eggs in 1982, and one did so in 1983. Otherwise, the bird is an occasional and irregular rare winter visitor, between September and April, mainly to Scotland and much less often south to England.

The introduction of a male onto the Shetlands to stimulate further breeding, with the females still present there, has been considered, but this idea has been rejected on the grounds that the natural course of events should ensue; that the area is too small to support a population in the long term and the threat which that might present to other rare naturally occurring species.

THREATS TO SURVIVAL

Threats to recolonization in Britain include disturbance and egg collection. At Scotland's comparatively low latitude, breeding is unlikely to be more than an exceptional event. Should any further attempt occur, disturbance by those wishing to see the birds is likely to be the main problem, unless the nest or nests are again on Fetlar or some other reserve where access can be readily controlled.

On the Scottish mainland there could be conflict with gamekeepers and shooting syndicates, who might perceive the owls as grouse predators; several species of grouse, especially Ptarmigan, are recorded as prey, but a wide variety of bird species is taken at times, and grouse species are not known to form a large part of the Snowy Owl's diet. Feeding mainly on small mammals, breeding was always more successful on Fetlar, when rabbits are abundant. Egg-collectors would also pose a considerable threat.

CONSERVATION

If a pair should be seen together in the breeding season the area should not be publicized unless it is a reserve, where public access can be controlled. Past experience on Fetlar has shown that the public can watch from a carefully-sited hide without causing any disturbance. Such a hide provides a guard as well as a visitor facility. There are certain reserves where such a treatment would be difficult and inappropriate, and here, increased wardening and monitoring of human movements during the critical stages would be the best strategy. Elsewhere, early liaison with landowners should be sought with a view to making some wardening arrangements.

REFERENCES

ROBINSON, M. & BECKER, C.D. 1986. Snowy Owls on Fetlar. Brit. Birds 79: 228–242.
TULLOCH, R.J. 1968. Snowy Owls breeding in Shetland in 1967. Brit. Birds 61: 119–132.
WATSON, A. 1957. The behaviour, breeding and food-ecology of the Snowy Owl *Nyctea scandiaca*. Ibis 99: 419–462.

Consultant: M.C. Robinson

Nightjar
Caprimulgus europaeus

The Nightjar is a summer visitor which is declining in numbers. The British breeding population is now about 2,000 pairs and is continuing to decrease in most areas—as it is elsewhere in western Europe. More than half the British population is now found in four southern counties: Dorset, Hampshire, West Sussex and Surrey. At least 20% (about 400 pairs, estimated) are found in Norfolk and Suffolk, where numbers have recently increased in two forested areas. A few heathland sites are protected as reserves, and many are SSSIs; the habitat is restricted, and it continues to be lost and fragmented. Currently the main threats are housing and other building developments, and encroachment by self-sown pine and birch.

LEGAL STATUS

Protected under WCA 1981; Annex 1 of EC Birds Directive; Appendix II of the Berne Convention.

ECOLOGY

Nest: a shallow, unlined scrape on bare or even burnt ground, often in a small clearing (less than 2 m in diameter) among bracken or heather, at the base of a sapling birch or pine (Berry, 1979). Eggs: laid in mid-May to mid-July. Clutch: 2 (1–3); second clutches (not repeats) are now infrequent and may be decreasing in view of cool springs delaying the start of the first clutches. A second brood may be possible only if the first clutch was started before the second week in June. The young begin flying by about 15 days, but they are probably dependent on their parents until 30 days (Berry & Bibby, 1981; Lack, 1930, 1932).

Food consists mainly of moths (50–60% of the items taken), beetles (particularly Scarabaeidae and Geotrupidae), and flies. Proportionately more microlepidoptera and flies are fed to small chicks; prey size increases as the young grow, with noctuid and hepialid moths becoming the main food.

Both sexes can breed in their second calendar year, but probably not all males do so. When breeding for the first time, only some birds return to their natal area, and after having bred they tend to return to the same areas (Alexander, 1984).

DISTRIBUTION AND POPULATION

Palearctic. The Nightjar breeds from Britain east to China and Mongolia. In the western Palearctic the breeding range extends north to southern Scandinavia and south to North Africa. Those birds which breed in Britain and Ireland belong to the nominate race. The western Palearctic population winters across the northern Afrotropics (away from the equatorial forest), in the eastern half of the continent and in South Africa and Namibia (Cramp et al., 1985).

National surveys undertaken by the BTO in 1952 (Norris, 1960), in 1957/58 (Stafford, 1962), in 1968–72 (as part of the BTO/IWC Breeding Bird Atlas project), and again in 1981 (Gribble, 1983), have demonstrated a marked contraction from the northern and western parts of the breeding range in Britain and Ireland.

An estimate of 3,000–6,000 pairs for 1968–72 is considered too optimistic. In 1981, only 1,784 churring males were recorded, and the total number is unlikely to have exceeded 2,000.

Acidic heathland areas on sandy or gravelly soils in southern England and East Anglia continue to be Nightjar strongholds in Britain. A little over half the churring males recorded in 1981 were in Hampshire (estimated 400), Dorset (273), Surrey (224) and East and West Sussex (158). A further 20% were recorded in Norfolk (273) and Suffolk (126), mostly in felled or re-stocked conifer plantation, areas in Breckland where numbers apparently increased from 165 in 1981 to about 200 in 1988. In similar habitat on the Suffolk Sandlings, near the coast, numbers have also increased, with over 90 churring males in 1986 and 1987 (only 34 recorded in 1981). Local concentrations in South Devon (on the Pebble Bed heaths), on Cannock Chase (Staffordshire), in the Dukeries (Nottinghamshire), in South Yorkshire, and on the North Yorkshire Moors (mostly in young conifer plantations, with many on poorly drained gley soils). Elsewhere, Nightjars are thinly distributed and scarce, especially in Wales (only three—apart from 33 in Gwent) and Scotland (only 25 recorded in 1981). None was recorded in the ten counties where Nightjars were found in 1957/58 (Gribble, 1983).

The total breeding population in north-west Europe (north of the Pyrenees, including West Germany and Finland) may at present be of the order of 22,000 pairs; France, West Germany and Sweden may each have about 5,000 pairs. Marked decreases have occurred in most European countries.

THREATS TO SURVIVAL

Threats include a loss of suitable habitat, a reduction in the availability of insect food, and (possibly) predation by adders. Over the last hundred years or so, the lowland heaths of southern and eastern England have continued to disappear as a result of agriculture, afforestation with conifers, housing and road developments, airfields and the creation of golf courses and gardens. There was a 40% overall loss of heathland in southern England between 1950 and 1984 (Nature Conservancy Council, 1984). In the Poole Basin, in Dorset, 39,960 ha of heathland in the mid-18th century had been reduced to 10,117 ha by 1960 (Moore, 1962); by 1983 only 5,670 ha (14%) remained (Bibby, 1978; Webb & Haskins, 1980). The rate of loss in Surrey has been even greater. The fragmented remnants have in many instances been degraded by frequent burning which has aided the spread of bracken in place of heather (particularly in Dorset), by overgrazing (in the New Forest), by the dumping of rubbish, and by activities such as motorcycle scrambling as well as the encroachment of dense thickets of self-sown birch and rhododendron (mostly in Surrey and North Hampshire) and Scots pine (Bibby, 1978).

Climatic changes influencing insect food have probably contributed to the withdrawal from the northern and western parts of the breeding range.

Predation by adders (*Vipera berus*) was considered a possible cause of some nest failures at some East Anglian nests (Berry & Bibby, 1981).

CONSERVATION

On the RSPB's Minsmere Reserve, in east Suffolk, the Nightjar population declined from up to 13 pairs in the mid-1970s to between five and seven pairs in the early 1980s, apparently largely as a result of encroachment of birch scrub on dry *Calluna*-dominated heathland. The following four types of management have been implemented to restore Nightjar habitats (Burgess *et al.*, 1989):

(a) On *Calluna* heath there has been selective felling of birch saplings, leaving scattered individuals around which small clearings have been made in tall heather. (There is some risk that such clearings will attract adders.)

(b) Dense birch scrub has been thinned out to leave small clumps of saplings as nest and roost sites.

(c) Clearings have been created in thickets of 20- to 30-year-old birch. Some

saplings have been left standing, but tree stumps have been treated with ammonium sulphamate to prevent regrowth.
(d) The wooded margins of the heath have been re-sculptured to increase the edge for nesting and feeding.

The Nightjar population on the reserve not only recovered to its former level but it actually increased to 20 pairs in 1986. At Arne Heath, in Dorset—another RSPB reserve—selective clearance of self-sown Scots pine has helped to maintain a population of 13–18 pairs during 1979–86 (Pickess, 1980–87).

To create nest sites in open woodland, where bracken is dominant as ground cover, the selective herbicide asulam can be used in July or August to create small litter-strewn glades among the bracken canopy. To keep these glades relatively free of growing fronds it should be necessary to treat the invading bracken only once every four or five years after the initial spraying (Cadbury, 1976).

A high proportion of the heaths in southern Britain which support more than one or two pairs of Nightjars are scheduled as SSSIs. Though such designation may prevent various developments destroying the heaths, unless the habitat is carefully managed, the disturbance controlled and the fire-risk minimized, it may become unsuitable for Nightjars. There is a need to know much more about the habitats used by Nightjars when feeding; it is probably as important to safeguard abundant sources of insect food as to provide nest sites.

REFERENCES

ALEXANDER, I.H. 1984. An examination of nightjar movements in south-east Dorset. Unpubl. Stour Ringing Group Ann. Rept. 1983: 28–37.
BERRY, R. 1979. Nightjar habitats and breeding in East Anglia. Brit. Birds 72: 207–218.
BERRY, R. & BIBBY, C.J. 1981. A breeding study of nightjars. Brit. Birds 74: 161–169.
BIBBY, C.J. 1978. Conservation of the Dartford warbler on English lowland heaths: a review. Biol. Conserv. 13: 229–307.
BURGESS, N.D., EVANS, C.E. & SORENSEN, J. 1989. Management of breeding Nightjars at Minsmere, Suffolk. Management Case Study. Sandy: RSPB.
CADBURY, C.J. 1976. Botanical implications of bracken control. 1976. Botanical J. Linn. Soc. 73: 285–294.
GRIBBLE, F.C. 1983. Nightjars in Britain and Ireland in 1981. Bird Study 30: 165–176.
LACK, D.L. 1930. Double-brooding of the nightjar. Brit. Birds 23: 242–244.
LACK, D.L. 1932. Some breeding habits of the European nightjar. Ibis 74: 266–238.
MOORE, N.W. 1962. The heaths of Dorset and their conservation. J. Ecol. 50: 369–391.
NATURE CONSERVANCY COUNCIL. 1984. Nature Conservation in Great Britain. Peterborough.
NORRIS, C.A. 1960. The breeding distribution of 30 bird species in 1952. Bird Study 7: 129–184.
PICKESS, B. 1980–87. Annual reports for Arne Reserve, Dorset, 1979–86. Sandy: Royal Society for the Protection of Birds. (Unpublished reports.)
STAFFORD, J. 1962. Nightjar Enquiry, 1957–58. Bird Study 9: 104–115.
WEBB, N.R. & HASKINS, L.E. 1980. An ecological survey of heathlands in the Poole Basin, Dorset, England in 1978. Biol. Conserv. 17: 281–296.

Consultants: C.G.R. Bowden and C.J. Cadbury

Hoopoe
Upupa epops

The Hoopoe is a sporadic breeder but an annual passage-migrant or casual summer visitor. As nesting in Britain is casual and unpredictable, the only conservation action is the safeguarding of nest sites from human disturbance, ideally by keeping them secret.

LEGAL STATUS

Protected under Schedule 1 of WCA 1981; EC Birds Directive; Appendix II of the Berne Convention.

ECOLOGY

The Hoopoe is a bird of open woodlands, parks, orchards, commons, sandy heaths or large gardens. Nest: an unlined structure in a cavity or a hole in a tree or old building, mainly in open country with scattered trees. The bird is solitary. Eggs: laid in early May to mid-June. Two broods are reared on the Continent. The young fledge in July or early August.

Food in summer consists mainly of large insects and especially larvae (eg, Orthoptera, Lepidoptera, Hymenoptera) together with spiders, centipedes, earthworms and small lizards.

DISTRIBUTION AND POPULATION

Palearctic, Oriental and Ethiopian. The Hoopoe breeds in most countries of continental Europe except Fenno-Scandia, but it is often scarce or irregular in the northern half (north-west France to Poland, Estonia and central Russia). The bird is fairly common throughout central and southern Europe, but there have been considerable fluctuations (and even a recent decline) in the north of the European range. Some of the birds winter in southern Iberia, but most do so in Africa and southern Asia.

In England the bird nests irregularly, with about 30 records up to 1950 (Glegg, 1942; Sharrock, 1974); in the 10 years 1968–77, however, there were seven or eight breeding records (four in 1977), but none during 1978–88—though there were several possible breeding attempts, including three in 1984 though none since and the bird is occurring less frequently in late spring and summer in the latter years. Counties in which definite breeding has been recorded since 1968 are Cornwall (twice at the same site), Avon, Somerset, Sussex and Surrey.

Otherwise, the bird is a regular migrant in spring and, to a lesser extent, in autumn. It has been recorded mostly in south-coast counties, and almost entirely in the southern half of England. Considering the frequency with which the species occurs on passage (currently about 150 a year, three-quarters of this total in the spring) (Sharrock, 1974), it is surprising that so few stay to breed. There appears to be plenty of suitable habitat available for a species which breeds at similar latitudes on the Continent.

THREATS TO SURVIVAL

Cold springs, wet summers, declines in the abundance of large insect prey, shooting on passage in the Mediterranean region, and the effects of pesticides have all been suggested as causes of decreases in Europe.

Isolated pairs breeding in Britain, usually in years with warm, dry springs or early summers, are open to some risk of human disturbance, though fortunately this conspicuous species can be surprisingly unobtrusive when nesting. Habitat and availability of holes seem unlikely to be limiting factors, but supplies of suitable insect food may well be.

CONSERVATION

Pairs should be safeguarded from human disturbance as far as possible. Indeed, as one site was occupied in Cornwall in successive years, it may be safer if the locality is not revealed even subsequently. Nevertheless, most instances of breeding in Britain are likely to be casual events, when conditions are right, and are not likely to be repeated.

REFERENCES

GLEGG, W.E. 1942. A comparative consideration of the status of the Hoopoe (*Upupa epops epops* Linn.) in Great Britain and Ireland over a period of a hundred years (1839–1938), with a review of breeding records. Ibis 84: 390–434.
SHARROCK, J.T.R. 1974. Scarce migrants in Britain and Ireland. Berkhamsted: Poyser.

Bee-eater
Merops apiaster

The Bee-eater has bred or attempted to breed in Britain twice, once in the early part of the 20th century and again in the mid-1950s. No subsequent attempts have been reported, but the bird has become much more numerous in Britain in late spring and summer in recent years; otherwise it is a scarce visitor from Spain, southern France or south-east Europe.

LEGAL STATUS

Protected under Schedule 1 of WCA 1981; EC Birds Directive; Appendix II of the Berne Convention.

ECOLOGY

The preferred habitat of this bird is open country, the edges or cultivated edges of wetland or irrigated areas, vineyards, ricefields or grasslands; it is occasionally seen on the edges of towns and villages where orchards with bee-hives are present (Cramp *et al.*, 1985). The bird breeds in the dryer and warmer areas of the Palearctic, including steppe and semi-arid desert zones. Nest: in a scrape in holes between 50 and 275 cm in length (average 118 cm), excavated by the bird in a sloping or vertical sand-bank in a quarry, gorge or river bank. Eggs: laid in mid-May to mid-June. Clutch: 6 (4–9); one brood. The young fledge by early August.

Food consists essentially of flying insects (the bird being an aerial feeder): predominantly bees and wasps, but a variety of other insects as well; the bird hunts from a high perch in a tree or from power lines, making flights of up to 100 m after prey (Fry, 1984).

DISTRIBUTION AND POPULATION

Palearctic (but also breeds in South Africa). The Bee-eater breeds in Spain, southern Portugal, north-west Africa (Morocco, Algeria, Tunisia and around Tripoli in Libya), east through southern France, Italy, Czechoslovakia and the Balkans to about 80°E in the USSR, south to northern Iraq and Iran, with isolated outposts in Israel, Jordan, Syria, Afghanistan and northern Pakistan. Some fluctuation occurs within the range, with recent increases in central Europe from the mid-1940s and in western Europe from the mid-1960s. The bird has bred in Scandinavia, in Sweden in 1976–78, and probably bred in Finland in 1954, and in Denmark in 1948, 1961–62, 1966 and 1973; also in the Netherlands in 1964, 1965 and 1983, in Belgium in 1956, and (unsuccessfully) in 1933, and in northern France—irregularly in Normandy and Finistere, but since 1968 regularly around Paris (Cramp *et al.*, 1985).

In Britain one pair attempted to breed near Edinburgh in 1920, and a group of three pairs nested in 1955, two successfully in Sussex. In the following year one pair bred on Alderney in the Channel Islands (Fry, 1984). In recent years (1981–1989) considerably higher numbers (often in small groups) have been recorded in Britain in the summer months than in the two previous decades; in 1981 there were 21 birds recorded, 26 in 1983 (including one group of at least 15), 17 in 1986, 37 in 1987 and 31 in 1988 (including groups of 6 in both years and another group of 4 in 1988). It is possible that odd pairs or groups may have bred undetected in Britain in the recent past, and with the present increase in summer records (matched by increases elsewhere in north-west Europe) it is certainly possible or anticipated that they will do so again.

Threats include climatic changes and disturbance.

There are plenty of potential nesting sites in sand-pits and quarries, many of which are now not in use.

Cold or wet springs and early summers pose a potential threat.

Food requirements are not fully understood, but many bees are kept in hives and they provide a substantial basis of the diet; whilst many birds at present often remain in the vicinity of bee-hives, others certainly do not—seeking instead adequate sustenance from a variety of flying insects.

Human and other predatory disturbance at potential nest sites should be kept to a minimum, and the location of any sites being prospected should not be widely disclosed.

CONSERVATION

Most of the factors affecting the species are beyond human control, but, should pairs begin to show an interest in a particular site, wardening, control of visitors, and the reduction of disturbance will help towards the success of the attempt.

REFERENCE

FRY, C.H. 1984. The Bee-Eaters. Calton: Poyser.

Wryneck
Jynx torquilla

The Wryneck is a rare breeding bird in Britain which, in recent years, has been virtually confined to Scotland. Otherwise it is a scarce passage-migrant, mainly on North Sea coasts. The Wryneck was formerly widespread as a breeding bird in England and Wales, but there has been a massive decline over the last 150 years, and the population is now reduced to occasional singing birds in southern and eastern England. Sporadic records of singing birds in the Scottish Highlands from

1951 culminated in the successful breeding of three pairs in 1969, since when a very small (1–4 pairs) fluctuating population has been present during most summers.

LEGAL STATUS

Protected under Schedule 1 of WCA 1981; EC Birds Directive; Appendix II of the Berne Convention.

ECOLOGY

In the breeding season the Wryneck occurs in open woodland, clearings, woodland edges and scattered trees (broadleaved in the south, coniferous and birch in the north), and also in orchards, parks and large gardens. Nest: in holes, usually in trees—both natural holes and those made by woodpeckers; the bird readily uses nest boxes. Eggs: laid in May to July. Clutch: 7–10 (5–14); occasionally two broods.

Food consists principally of ants and their pupae but also small quantities of other insects, beetles and spiders and occasionally berries (bilberry and elder).

DISTRIBUTION AND POPULATION

Palearctic. Europe (discontinuously from south-west Portugal to northern Spain) north to northern Sweden and Finland and east to northern China and Manchuria, Sakhalin Island and northern Japan; isolated breeding areas in Algeria, Turkey, southern USSR and central China. Winters in Africa north of the equator, India and throughout most of south-east Asia excluding peninsula Thailand and Malaysia. The Wryneck is now rare and very local in Britain, but it breeds over wide areas of continental Europe—except the far north and parts of the extreme south; it winters in small numbers in the Mediterranean region—wintering mainly in Africa and southern Asia. The bird was formerly common in central and south-east England, breeding—at least occasionally—north to Durham and Cumbria, and west to Devon and all counties in Wales.

Numbers began to decrease and the bird withdrew to the south-east in about 1830, and there was then a serious decline of the much reduced population from the 1950s onwards; the population fell from 150–400 pairs in 1954–58 to 20–30 pairs in 1966 (Monk, 1963; Peal, 1968) and only one pair in 1973. No pairs were known in 1974, but up to 3 pairs were recorded in 1975–77, since when there have been only sporadic individuals. The bird is a scarce passage-migrant to and from Scandinavia in the spring (mid-April to mid-June) and autumn (mainly mid-August to mid-September), principally during arrivals of migrants across the North Sea along the south-east and east coasts and the Northern Isles. Following these occurrences, singing birds were occasionally reported in the Scottish Highlands from 1951. Breeding was suspected in 1965, and three of five pairs nested in 1969 in Inverness-shire (Burton *et al.*, 1970). Singing birds occurred in subsequent years in Inverness-shire, Ross-shire, Perthshire and Aberdeenshire; nesting was proved in Ross-shire in 1974 and in Inverness-shire during 1975–77; by 1977 at least seven pairs had been confirmed. Proof of nesting is often difficult to obtain, but the situation was disappointing in the early 1980s when no confirmed breeding was reported. Breeding occurred again in Inverness-shire in 1985 (Thom, 1986) and has since continued with 1 pair (at least) reported (and others present in suitable habitat) every year. The numbers of singing birds/pairs have ranged during these years between 2 and 23.

There has been a decline, corresponding to that in England, in northern France, Belgium, the Netherlands, Denmark, North Germany, Austria, North Switzerland and Hungary, but the species is still fairly common in central and eastern Europe and Fenno-Scandia.

THREATS TO SURVIVAL

Threats appear to relate to climatic changes and the availability of the bird's insect food.

A tendency towards cooler, wetter summers in western Europe is thought to have reduced the population of ants, the species' staple food. Other factors suggested as reasons for the decline have included pesticides, loss of suitable habitat (in southern England), shortage of nest sites, and mortality on passage or in winter, none of which are entirely credible or supported by documented evidence.

Pesticides were probably involved to some extent in the rapid deterioration in numbers in the 1950s and 1960s, but the general decrease had begun much earlier.

There is still plenty of suitable habitat and no critical shortage of nest sites.

CONSERVATION

There is some evidence that the small population in Scotland prefers south-facing clearings in mixed open Scots pine and birch woodland, especially in the hotter inland valleys where ant populations are high. Protection and wise management of native Caledonian pine forest is important, and extensions to this resource would be valuable. Several of the main sites are now owned or managed as nature reserves or SSSIs, but this distinctive habitat is still under threat, and a proportion of the areas which have been lost to deforestation or commercial plantations should be restored.

Dead trees, especially those with woodpecker holes, should be left standing in woods suitable for this species.

The exact location of regular localities should not be publicized.

REFERENCES

BURTON, H., LLOYD-EVANS, T. & WEIR, D.N. 1970. Wrynecks breeding in Scotland. Scot. Birds, 6: 154–156.
MONK, J.F. 1963. The past and present status of the Wryneck in the British Isles. Bird Study, 10: 112–132.
PEAL, R.E.F. 1968. The distribution of the Wryneck in the British Isles, 1964–66. Bird Study, 15: 111–126.
THOM, V.M. 1986. Birds in Scotland. Calton: Poyser.

Woodlark
Lullula arborea

The Woodlark is a rare breeding bird in Britain. In 1983 the population was estimated at 210–230 pairs. The bird was widespread and numerous in the 19th century, and its numbers have fluctuated widely since; the range has contracted since the early 1970s, apparently because of habitat loss, but there have been local increases caused by expansion within the available habitat which may, however, be of a short duration.

LEGAL STATUS

Protected under Schedule 1 of WCA 1981; Annex 1 of EC Birds Directive; Appendix III of the Berne Convention.

ECOLOGY

The Woodlark breeds in open country with areas of bare ground and very short grass intermingled with areas of long grass, bracken or heather. Scattered trees or shrubs are used as song-posts. The main nesting habitats in Britain are lowland *Calluna* heaths, particularly during regeneration after burning, rabbit-grazed grass-heaths, derelict pasture, tree and shrub nurseries and clear-felled conifer plantations after restocking. Nest: on the ground, usually concealed in a tuft of long grass or bracken. Eggs: laid March to early August, with replacement nesting after failure at the egg or chick stage. Clutch: 3–4; second broods are frequent.

Food in summer consists mainly of beetles, caterpillars, spiders and other arthropods gleaned from grass or moss. Seeds are also taken outside the breeding season.

DISTRIBUTION AND POPULATION

West Palearctic. The Woodlark breeds from southern Britain and southern Fenno-Scandia to southern Europe and east to the Urals. It winters to the west and south of the range. In Britain, some birds winter near the breeding areas, especially in Hampshire and Surrey (Lack, 1986). However, the small total population in winter—compared with that in the breeding season—suggests that part of the population, particularly those birds from the Suffolk/Norfolk border (Breckland), may winter on the Continent (Sitters, 1986). The Woodlark had nested in most counties of England and Wales in the first half of the 19th century. A decline in numbers and a range contraction southwards began about 1850. There was some recovery between the 1920s and 1950s, but a further decline began in the 1950s. In 1965, soon after two consecutive severe winters, only 100 pairs were recorded (Parslow, 1967). By 1968–72 it was estimated that there might be 200–450 pairs (Sharrock, 1976), mainly in the south coast counties, Breckland, east Suffolk and south-central Wales. Numbers in Breckland increased in the 1970s as the area of felled and replanted conifer plantation increased. In the same area, numbers breeding on grass-heaths declined. On the Surrey/Hampshire border numbers increased after heathland fires created suitable habitat in the mid-1970s, but have declined again subsequently. Woodlarks no longer breed regularly in Wales. In 1983 the total population was estimated at between 200 and 231 pairs and by 1988 it was considered from reports submitted to the RBBP that there was a maximum of 226 pairs breeding.

THREATS TO SURVIVAL

Threats include severe winter and loss of habitat.

In Britain the Woodlark is on the northern edge of its range, and cold winters can decimate or even eradicate the population in areas where the birds winter locally. However, this is likely to result in local extinctions only where numbers have already been reduced by habitat loss or deterioration. Afforestation, the conversion of heaths to agriculture, and the growth of grass and scrub on remaining heaths following the decline of rabbits due to myxomatosis are probably the main causes of the recent decline.

A substantial part of the population nests in re-stocked conifer plantations, but Woodlarks are excluded from these for three to seven years after planting by the growth of long grass or bracken. The age structure of the forests where Woodlarks occur in this habitat indicates that there will be a shortage of plantations of suitable age in the 1990s and 2000s.

CONSERVATION

Effective management by livestock, rabbit-grazing of vegetation or grass, and the mowing, grazing or burning of *Calluna* heaths is required to recreate patches of suitably short vegetation and bare ground for Woodlarks. Most sites with semi-natural vegetation are protected from conversion to agriculture by SSSI or NNR status, or by military use, but in many cases current management does not favour habitat for Woodlarks.

The effects of the potential future bottleneck of suitably aged conifer plantations may be alleviated by modifications in felling patterns to smooth out local fluctuations in habitat availability. It may also be possible to reduce the rate at which the growth of ground vegetation renders plantations unsuitable for Wood-larks.

REFERENCES

LACK, P. 1986. The atlas of wintering birds in Britain and Ireland. Calton: Poyser.

Parslow, J.L.F. 1967. Changes in status among breeding birds in Britain and Ireland. Brit. Birds 60: 268–271.
Sitters, H.P. 1986. Woodlarks in Britain 1968–83. Brit. Birds 79: 105–116.

Consultants: C.G.R. Bowden and R.E. Green

Shore Lark

Eremophila alpestris

The Shore Lark is a rare breeding bird in Britain. It nested in Scotland in 1977, and almost certainly in 1973; singing males were present in suitable habitat during 1972 and 1976. The bird is a potential colonist if the Scandinavian population also continues to expand. It is a winter visitor in small numbers (less than 100) along the east coast of Britain.

LEGAL STATUS

Protected under Schedule 1 of WCA 1981; EC Birds Directive; Appendix II of the Berne Convention.

ECOLOGY

In the breeding season this bird is found in open tundra or barren montane uplands (becoming a shore bird only in winter). The bird is solitary or social (Shannon, 1974). Nest: a cup of grasses, plant down and hair on peaty, sandy or stony ground, usually sheltered by a tussock or a stone. Eggs: laid in mid-May to the end of July, in Scandinavia. Clutch: 4 (2–5); normally two broods.The young fledge by late August.

Food consists of seeds, buds, insects and larvae.

DISTRIBUTION AND POPULATION

Holarctic and locally Neotropical. The Shore Lark breeds in northern Fenno-Scandia and the USSR, and also in the Balkans and the Caucasus; part of the Scandinavian population (which has colonized the mountains of southern Norway in the last century) winters around the shores of the southern North Sea and the south-western Baltic. The bird is a regular autumn passage and winter visitor in small numbers, up to about 300, mainly during October to April, on the English east coast—especially from Lincolnshire to Kent, and more rarely elsewhere.

From about 1950 to 1975, the wintering population in Britain increased, but since 1975 numbers have been much reduced and there are now less than 100 birds seen annually along the North Sea coast of Britain. The species was unknown in the summer in Britain until a singing male was found on a mountain top in Scotland in July 1972. Then, in 1973, a male was seen singing about 1 km from that site in June, and at another site, a further kilometre away, a pair were seen carrying food in July–August. None was seen at that site in 1974 or 1975 (though there was a single bird elsewhere in June, 1975), but in 1976 a male was present in May and August, and in 1977 two or three were singing, and a nest with eggs was found and a juvenile seen later. Since then there have been no further records during 1978–88 (Watson, 1973; Thom, 1986).

THREATS TO SURVIVAL

Threats to colonization in Britain include disturbance by man and the limited number of these birds which arrive in this country. Suitable habitat seems plentiful in the Scottish Highlands.

Disturbance by birdwatchers and egg collectors could be a problem as long as the species is not firmly established.

The very small numbers of birds/pairs present is likely to be the main threat to this potential new colonist establishing a firm foothold in Britain. Further nesting attempts may be related to the strength of the population in the southern part of the Scandinavian range.

CONSERVATION

No measures are deemed feasible or possible beyond prevention of disturbance to further pairs, should they appear.

REFERENCES

THOM, V.M 1986, Birds in Scotland. Calton: Poyser.
WATSON, A. 1973. Shore Larks summering and possibly breeding in Scotland. Brit. Birds 66: 505–508.
SHANNON, G.R. 1974. Studies of less familiar birds. 174. Shore Lark and Temminck's Horned Lark. Brit. Birds 67: 502 511.

Consultant: R.H. Dennis

Black Redstart

Phoenicurus ochruros

The Black Redstart nested sporadically in southern England in the 1920s and 1930s, and regularly since then, in small numbers, mainly in industrial or urban areas, in south-east, east and central England; after a decline in the 1950s and early 1960s, the bird had increased to 60–75 pairs by the mid 1970s; by 1988 there were possibly as many as 112 pairs breeding. No special conservation or protection measures are considered necessary.

LEGAL STATUS

Protected under Schedule 1 of WCA 1981; EC Birds Directive; Appendix II of the Berne Convention.

ECOLOGY

Nest: a cup of grasses, moss, hair and feathers in a cavity or on a ledge in a building, ruin or rock-face, in towns, power stations and cliffs; the bird is solitary. Eggs: laid in late April to the end of June. Clutch: 4–6; usually two broods. The young fledge by mid-July.

Food in the breeding season consists of insects.

DISTRIBUTION AND POPULATION

Palearctic and Oriental. The Black Redstart breeds throughout Europe from England, south Sweden, the Baltic States and southern Russia to the Mediterranean and Black Seas; other races occur in Turkey and the Caucasus, in Central Asia, the Himalayas and China. The bird winters in west and southern Europe, North Africa and southern Asia.

After colonizing England in the 20th century, the Black Redstart is now a regular breeder in small numbers in south-east, east and central England; otherwise it is a regular but scarce passage-migrant, particularly on the east and south coasts, and it is an uncommon winter visitor.

The bird first nested in Sussex in 1923, and then for some years in Cornwall; from 1926 it nested in London. Breeding has been regular since 1939, at first mainly on bombed sites in London and Dover, then elsewhere in Kent, Sussex, the Home Counties and East Anglia, west and north to Wiltshire, the West Midlands and South Yorkshire—and sporadically in Cornwall, Shropshire and Lancashire (Fitter, 1965; Meadows, 1970); a female laid eggs in Orkney in 1973 (though no male was seen) (Fitter, 1976), and a pair was recorded in Grampian in 1976 (Morgan & Glue, 1981).

The population increased from 1939 to a peak of 53–56 singing males in 1950–52, a period which coincided with the main availability of bombed sites; the population then declined to only 17 by 1962, with rebuilding (Fitter, 1971). Since then, the development of modern power stations, and similar places such as gasworks and factories, has resulted in a consistent but fluctuating recovery leading to 100 males (61 proved breeding) in 1977, when a full survey was undertaken (Morgan & Glue, 1981). Up to 1976 it was included in the list of species monitored by the Rare Breeding Birds Panel (RBBP) but dropped thereafter. It was reinstated in 1985 and by the following year there were reports from 71 localities and a possible maximum of 87 breeding pairs. In 1988 there were reports to the RBBP of birds in 70 localities and the number of pairs breeding (or possibly breeding) had risen to 112, the highest ever. Most of these pairs were in south and east coast counties as far north as Cleveland and has now reached the Lancashire coast.

THREATS TO SURVIVAL

Threats include mainly demolition and construction work in the breeding season, a few nests being inevitably lost through building activities in urban and industrial areas. Many sites are quite safe from human disturbance, however, and plenty of presumably suitable urban, industrial and cliff habitats are not yet occupied.

CONSERVATION

The need for special measures is not foreseeable; however, this is still a rare species, and the number of approvals for photography and nest-examination should continue to be limited.

REFERENCES

FITTER, R.S.R. 1965. The breeding status of the Black Redstart in Britain. Brit. Birds 58: 481–492.
FITTER, R.S.R. 1971. Black Redstarts breeding in Britain in 1964–68. Brit. Birds 64: 117–124.
FITTER, R.S.R. 1976. Black Redstarts breeding in Britain in 1969–73. Brit. Birds 69: 9–15.
MEADOWS, B.S. 1970. Breeding distribution and feeding ecology of the Black Redstart in London. Lond. Bird Rep. 34: 72–79.
MORGAN, R.A. & GLUE, D.E. 1981. Breeding survey of Black Redstarts in Britain, 1977. Bird Study 28: 163–168.

Bluethroat
Luscinia svecica

The Bluethroat has bred in Britain on at least two occasions: in Scotland in 1968 and 1985. Otherwise, the bird is a scarce but regular passage-migrant in small numbers in eastern Britain. Two races, *L. s. svecica* (red-spotted) from northern Europe and *L. s. cyanecula* (white-spotted) from central Europe, are involved.

LEGAL STATUS

Protected under Schedule 1 of WCA 1981; Annex 1 of EC Birds Directive; Appendix II of the Berne Convention.

ECOLOGY

The north European race (*L. s. svecica*) has adapted to regions intermediate between forest and open plains or valleys with shrubby wetlands; the central European race (*L. s. cyanecula*) is much more strongly attached to bushy sites by water. Nest: a cup of grass stems and leaves, with roots and moss, lined with hair and finer vegetation, on the ground in dense vegetation, in a tussock or under a bush, or in a hollow in a low bank. Eggs: laid in April (in central Europe) but not until late May in Scandinavia. Clutch: 5–6; one brood in the north of the range, and two in the south.

Food in the breeding season consists mainly of insects, but earthworms and other small invertebrates have been recorded; in winter the bird also takes seeds and fruits.

DISTRIBUTION AND POPULATION

Palearctic and marginally Holarctic. Several races are involved. The nominate (*L. s. svecica*) from Scandinavia east through northern Siberia to western Alaska, south to 60°N in European USSR, and 57°N in western Siberia. *L. s. cyanecula*, of central Europe, from northern France, Belgium and the Netherlands, east to the Carpathian basin and also west to Spain. Other races occur in central Asia and the western Himalayas.

Population: France, 1,000–10,000 pairs, Belgium 900 pairs, the Netherlands 900–1,200 in 1976–77 (but numbers have decreased since), West Germany 600–1,050 pairs, Sweden 300,000 pairs and Finland 27,000 pairs (Cramp *et al.*, 1988).

In Britain the bird occurs chiefly as a scarce but regular passage-migrant on the south and east coasts, being more frequent in spring than autumn. Breeding has been recorded twice, both instances in Inverness-shire. In 1968 a female with nest and eggs was located (though a male was never seen); but this attempt subsequently failed (Greenwood, 1968). In 1985 a pair of the nominate *L. s. svecica* race fledged two young. The latter attempt came in a year in which there had been a heavy spring passage of Bluethroats in eastern Britain associated with a period of prolonged easterly winds during May (Murray, 1987).

THREATS TO SURVIVAL

There are probably no current threats to the status of this species in Britain. The northern race, *L. s. svecica*, appears not to be under threat in Europe, although the central European race, *L. s. cyanecula*, has declined in some areas due to habitat loss.

Future nesting attempts in Britain may be threatened by disturbance from birdwatchers, egg collectors and others.

CONSERVATION

There is little need for conservation action for this species in Britain. Should breeding occur again, care should be taken to avoid excessive disturbance and the attentions of collectors.

REFERENCES

GREENWOOD, J.J.D. 1968. Bluethroat nesting in Scotland. Brit. Birds 61: 524–525.
MURRAY, R.D. 1987. Bluethroats in Scotland during 1985. Scot. Birds 14: 168–174.

Fieldfare

Turdus pilaris

The Fieldfare is a rare breeding bird in Britain. It bred in Orkney in 1967, and now breeds annually in some parts of central Scotland and north-central England in very small numbers; the bird is on the edge of its continental range, and it is considered likely that it may slowly expand its range in Britain—possibly with small-scale contractions in some years, but at present there is still no sign of regular breeding—or a colony becoming established—in any particular area. A common winter visitor to the whole of Britain between late September and April.

LEGAL STATUS

Protected under Schedule 1 of WCA 1981; EC birds Directive; Appendix III of the Berne Convention.

ECOLOGY

A bird of deciduous or mixed woods, nesting in conifers, birch and alder but at other times of the year in more open habitat. Nest: a cup of grasses and twigs lined with mud, in a tree or bush, on a stump or on the ground, in open woodland, wood-edges, parks, orchards, gardens, even open moorland, often near marshes or water; the bird is social or loosely colonial. Eggs: laid early or in mid-May to July. Clutch: 4–6 (5–8); often two broods, at least on the Continent. The young fledge by August.

Food consists of slugs, snails, earthworms, insects, berries, seeds, grain and fallen fruit.

DISTRIBUTION AND POPULATION

North Palearctic and marginally Nearctic (south Greenland). The Fieldfare breeds in north Europe from Britain, Fenno-Scandia, Belgium, Germany and

northern Switzerland eastwards across Russia; the majority of northern populations move south in winter, reaching south Europe and south-west Asia, though
a few remain to winter in southern Scandinavia.

In Britain the bird was first recorded nesting in Orkney in 1967, when a pair
reared three young (Balfour, 1968), and a pair and three juveniles were subsequently seen in Tyne and Wear in the same year. In the following years, two or
three pairs bred for several years in Shetland, and in 1970 Inverness-shire
produced the first nest found on the Scottish mainland (Picozzi, 1973; Weir, 1970).
During 1971–77 singing or nesting Fieldfare were recorded in several Scottish
regions, including Grampian (Aberdeen, Banff, Kincardine), Tayside (Perth),
Lothian and Highland (Ross) (RBBP reports 1971–1977). Meanwhile in England,
there were scattered breeding records from the Peak District and nearby, with
breeding proved in eight years during 1969–80, but never more than two pairs in
any one year (Frost & Shooter, 1983). In 1976–79 summering individuals were
seen as far south as Bedfordshire and Essex, possibly linked with the westward
spread within north-west Europe which resulted in the colonization of Denmark in
1965 (Skov, 1970) and Belgium in 1967 (Arnhem, 1967), though the otherwise
generally northerly pattern of the British records indicates a Scandinavian origin.

Breeding has now been annual since 1967, but never more than a handful of
nests have been built in any year; the totals of breeding pairs recorded in 1973–77
were only 2–3, 3–7, 2–10, 3–12 and 4–6, respectively. Since then the expected
colonization has faltered, with 1–4, 1–6, 1–5 and 0–6 during 1978–81 (slightly
higher levels in 1981 and 1982, with 2–7 and 3–12), but reverting to 0–3 and 0–2 in
1984 and 1985, with two pairs breeding in 1986 and 1988 but only 1 proven case of
breeding in 1987, out of a maximum possible 6 pairs.

The Fieldfare is a common passage-migrant and winter visitor, mainly during
November to March, but some appear—mostly in Scotland—during September
to April; the bird occurs throughout Britain, with highest numbers in lowland
Scotland, northern and central England.

THREATS TO SURVIVAL

Threats to successful colonization in Britain include human disturbance.

Since there is much apparently suitable habitat for this wide-ranging and
spreading species, colonization is more likely to be dependent on late migrants
lingering in suitable habitat rather than any threat posed by man's activities.
Nevertheless, human disturbance should be avoided, wherever possible, while the
bird is becoming established.

CONSERVATION

Areas where the species is seen in summer should not be publicized, though the
naming of counties presents no risk in view of the plentiful habitat.

The development or creation of suitable nesting sites in areas where birds are
already present should be considered.

REFERENCES

ARNHEM, R. 1967. Premiere decouverte en Belgique d'une colonie de Grives Litornes
   (*Turdus pilaris*). Aves 4: 117–122.

BALFOUR, E. 1968. Fieldfares breeding in Orkney. Scot. Birds 5: 31–32.

FROST, R.A. & SHOOTER, P. 1983. Fieldfares breeding in the Peak District. Brit. Birds 76: 62–65.

PICOZZI, N. 1973. Fieldfares breeding on the Scottish mainland, 1972–1973. Scot. Birds 7: 406–408.

SKOV, H. 1970. Antallet af ynglende Sjaggere (*Turdus pilaris*) i Thy fordoblet. Dansk Orn. Foren. Tidsskr. 64: 271–272.

WEIR, D.N. 1970. Fieldfares breeding in East Inverness-shire. Scot. Birds 6: 212–213.

Redwing

Turdus iliacus

The Redwing is a rare breeding bird in Britain. It was found nesting in Scotland in 1925, and then sporadically to the early 1960s; nesting occurred in some numbers from 1967, but has apparently declined since 1973, and especially since 1976. The suggested population of 300 pairs in 1971–72 was based on annual totals of 40–50 singing males actually recorded during 'Atlas' fieldwork; however, in each year during 1977–81 only 7–12 singing males were reported, and only 2–3 pairs proved to be breeding. Since then, however, there has been a sizeable increase in the numbers possibly and proved breeding in the years 1982–88 with maximum totals (both possibly and proved breeding) of 79 (1984) and 50 (1987), although the number of pairs proved breeding remains low, since 1981 the highest has been 20 pairs (1986) and the lowest (9) in the year following. An abundant winter visitor, from late September to April, to the whole of the British Isles — principally the west, south-west and Ireland.

LEGAL STATUS

Protected under Schedule 1 of WCA 1981; EC Birds Directive; Appendix III of the Berne Convention.

ECOLOGY

Nest: a cup of grass, twigs, bracken, moss and wool, lined with mud and an inner layer of grass, in rhododendron, beech, birch, oak, conifer plantations or other shrub, hedge or tree, occasionally among tree-roots or on the ground, in shrubberies, or in mixed woodland with a good shrub layer, or scrub near water. The bird is solitary or loosely social. Eggs: laid mainly in May to mid-July, occasionally earlier. Clutch: 5–6 (2–7); two broods. The young usually fledge by early August, but have been known to fledge by the first week of May.

Food consists of insects, snails and slugs (Mollusca); many berries are eaten in autumn and winter.

DISTRIBUTION AND POPULATION

Palearctic. The Redwing breeds in Iceland, the Faeroes, Fenno-Scandia, the Baltic States, north and central Russia and locally in Scotland, north-east Germany and Poland; it winters in west, central and southern Europe and south-west Asia east to Turkestan—occasionally also north-west Africa.

The bird was first recorded nesting in Highland (Sutherland) in 1925, and then irregularly there or elsewhere in Scotland to the early 1960s. The period 1925–66 produced a total of under 30 breeding records in only 18 of those 42 years; breeding occurred mostly during 1953–66 (Ferguson-Lees, 1966; Sharrock, 1973), but seven pairs were found in 1967, and in 1968 as many as 20 pairs bred in Wester Ross alone (Williamson, 1973). In both 1971 and 1972 40–50 males were located on territory, and it was suggested, perhaps optimistically, that the total population was about 300 pairs. Since 1972 there appears to have been a marked decline, though this may have been at least partly the result of unfair comparison with the years of intensive fieldwork, eg, the 1968–72 'Atlas', during which there was confirmed, probable or possible breeding in 111 10-km squares, against a recorded total of 12–42 pairs in 1972 (Sharrock, 1976). In the years 1973–81 the totals, although varying from year to year, did not change significantly or suggest that the population was gaining ground from the rather tenuous foothold it appeared to have. To some extent this pattern is reflected in the population of Fieldfares breeding in Britain, although with smaller numbers involved. In 1982 however there was a sudden increase in the number of confirmed pairs breeding, 30 and 31 in 1984, at the same time as the possible maximum for proven and possible breeding pairs rose to 68 in 1983 and the peak (so far) of 79 in 1984. Since then there are signs that this sudden increase is on the wane as the maximum total (of possible and proven pairs) was 50 in 1987 and 39 in 1988. At the same time the numbers of proved breeding pairs have dropped to 9 and 10 pairs respectively. During 1967–88 breeding was proved in Shetland, Orkney, Highland (Caithness, Sutherland, Ross, Inverness, Nairn), Grampian (Moray and Aberdeen), Tayside (Perth) and Strathclyde (Argyll), and also in Northumberland, Lincolnshire and Kent.

The Redwing is a common passage-migrant and winter visitor, often in large numbers, from Iceland, Scandinavia, the Baltic states and Russia from late September to April (it is more numerous in October–March) and occasionally in early May. Although well distributed throughout Britain (though less commonly met with on upland moors and mountains), the highest numbers winter in the warmer west and south-west, the bird being severely affected by intense or prolonged cold weather—when large numbers depart south to Iberia and the coasts of the Mediterranean.

THREATS TO SURVIVAL

Threats may involve population and climatic factors.

Bird-watchers are not especially motivated to search in summer for a species that is a common winter visitor, and many of the recorded nests have been on private ground or in areas where human disturbance is unlikely to be significant; in any case, like other thrushes, this species readily breeds in large gardens, quickly replaces lost nests, and usually rears two broods.

The colonization of Scotland may have been connected with the eruptive nature of some movements of the Scandinavian population. Ringing has shown that Scandinavian Redwings may winter in widely separated areas in successive years, but it has also been suggested that the rapid growth in numbers in the late 1960s and early 1970s was more probably due to migrants returning from southern Europe being displaced by easterly winds (Williamson, 1975). Changes in migration and weather patterns may now be affecting the numbers, as cold or wet springs and early summers reduce the numbers of birds remaining to establish territories.

CONSERVATION

No particular protection or management activities seem feasible or necessary beyond the maintenance of suitable breeding habitat, for example, birch and willow scrub.

A thorough breeding survey would probably reveal a much higher proven total than exists at present.

REFERENCES

FERGUSON-LEES, I.J. 1966. Editorial comment on Redwings breeding in Scotland. Brit. Birds 59: 500–501.
SHARROCK, J.T.R. 1973. Habitat of Redwings in Scotland. Scot. Birds 7: 208–209.
WILLIAMSON, K. 1973. Habitat of Redwings in Wester Ross. Scot. Birds 7: 268–269.
WILLIAMSON, K. 1975. Birds and climatic change. Bird Study 22: 143–164.

Cetti's Warbler
Cettia celti

The Cetti's Warbler is a recent colonist to Britain which first bred in 1972, its population slowly grew in the following decade to a peak of over 300 pairs (possibly and confirmed) breeding in 1984. Since then the numbers have declined slightly and there seems to have been a shift in the centre of the population away from the area of south-east England colonized initially to south-west England. Its future status will be determined mostly by the intensity of ensuing winters. Effective policy and management advice concerning waterside vegetation on non-protected sites should play a small part.

LEGAL STATUS

Protected under Schedule 1 of WCA 1981; EC Birds Directive; Appendix II of the Berne Convention.

ECOLOGY

Cetti's Warblers favour scrubby margins of wet areas, including reed swamps, rivers and gravel pits or more extensive carr (Harvey, 1977; Bibby, 1982). Reed-beds might be more important habitats in winter (Bibby & Thomas, 1984). Invertebrates are taken throughout the year from low vegetation and frequently from bare ground beside water or beneath thick scrub. Males patrol large territories in which one or more females may breed (Bibby, 1982). Nest: well concealed in rank herbaceous vegetation, brambles or other low shrubs. Eggs: laid in late April to mid-July. Clutch: 3–5. The young fledge by mid-August to late August.

Food mainly consists of small insects, spiders, snails or even earthworms.

DISTRIBUTION AND POPULATION

This bird breeds almost continuously eastwards from Spain to Turkestan (Soviet Central Asia) and the borders with Mongolia; north to southern England and the Netherlands; and south (avoiding central and eastern Europe) to North Africa (Morocco to Tunisia), Israel, the Persian Gulf and northern Baluchistan. Cetti's Warblers are sedentary.

Following a northern spread in western Europe, the species first bred in Britain in Kent in 1972 and expanded rapidly in the next 10 years (Bonham & Robertson, 1975; Harvey, 1977) to a peak of 316 (confirmed and proven) pairs in 1984. Following the first breeding record, other areas of Kent were soon colonized and the bird became locally common in several areas within the county. The adjacent counties of Sussex and Hampshire and north to Essex, Suffolk and Norfolk increasingly recorded birds on territory, though Kent always remained the stronghold. Also at this time the bird had appeared—in some cases occasionally remaining to breed (eg, in Hertfordshire, Middlesex and Berkshire) whilst in other places only as a wandering individual—in most counties in southern Britain (north to Yorkshire). By the mid-1980s however, there had been a definite shift of emphasis with birds becoming scarce in south-east England (though still locally common or present at the initial places of breeding in Kent) and steadily becoming more numerous in Dorset, Devon, Cornwall and north to Glamorgan. By the late 1980s, there were about 200 (possible and confirmed) pairs (though only 24 of which were confirmed or proved breeding) in Britain south of a line from southern Norfolk/north Cambridgeshire to south Wales with the majority (76%) in the south-western counties.

Breeding Cetti's Warblers are notoriously difficult to count and have probably been under-recorded. For instance by 1983, numbers had reached some 250 pairs (RBBP), but allowing for these being mostly singing males, the number of true pairs of this habitually polygamous species would have probably been higher.

THREATS TO SURVIVAL

The spread of Cetti's Warblers was almost certainly related to winter severity, and the population will remain vulnerable to this factor; with a small population, this could lead to local or national extinction. At the moment, numbers are below what the available habitat could potentially support. Threats to sites are thus unlikely to limit populations in the near future.

CONSERVATION

Breeding sites are only modestly well protected by formal designation—unlike those of other more exclusively reed-dwelling species (Bibby & Lunn, 1982). Otherwise, no specific conservation measures have been taken.

Formal protection of sites is only likely to bring small benefit to this species. Unsympathetic management of waterside habitats outside the direct influence of nature conservation could be detrimental and should be resisted through policy and advisory channels.

REFERENCES

BIBBY, C.J. 1982. Polygyny and breeding ecology of the Cetti's Warbler *Cettia cetti*. Ibis 124: 288–301.
BIBBY, C.J. & LUNN, J. 1982. Conservation of reed-beds and their avifauna in England and Wales. Biol. Conserv. 23: 167–186.
BIBBY, C.J. & THOMAS, D.K. 1984. Sexual dimorphism in size, moult and movements of Cetti's Warbler *Cettia cetti*. Bird Study 31: 28–34.
BONHAM, P.F. & ROBERTSON, J.C.M. 1975. The spread of the Cetti's Warbler in north-west Europe. Brit. Birds 68: 393–408.
HARVEY, W.G. 1977. Cetti's Warblers in east Kent in 1975. Brit. Birds 70: 89–96.

Savi's Warbler
Locustella luscinioides

The Savi's Warbler is a rare breeding bird in Britain. A very small-scale recolonization took place during the 1960s after a 100-year absence. The bird has always been very scarce (up to 30 singing males, but fewer (less than half this figure) in more recent years (1988 and 1989)) and is confined to rather few large reed-bed sites. The numbers of this bird are probably regulated by factors beyond the control of man. Other than the continued safeguard of key sites, nothing beyond hope can be recommended.

LEGAL STATUS

Protected under Schedule 1 of WCA 1981; EC Birds Directive; Appendix II of the Berne Convention.

ECOLOGY

The bird breeds in large, wet reed-bed sites with adjoining fen vegetation. Singing birds have occurred, but have not been known to breed in dry or tidal reed-beds (Bibby & Lunn, 1982). Nest: built of grasses and placed low at the base of reeds, generally with sedges. Eggs: laid in mid-May to early July. Clutch: 4–5 (3–6); most probably one brood.

Food consists mainly of insects.

DISTRIBUTION AND POPULATION

West Palearctic. Savi's Warbler breeds locally from south-east England, the Low Countries, Germany, Poland and central Russia, south to the Mediterranean, the Black Sea and Caspian region; it winters in Africa. The bird formerly nested regularly in small numbers in Norfolk, Cambridgeshire, and probably Suffolk, but it became extinct by 1856, perhaps largely through drainage of the wetlands. After an absence of nearly 100 years, a singing male spent the summer of 1954 at Wicken Fen, Cambridgeshire. Then, in 1960, breeding was recorded in an extensive reed-bed in Kent where the species may already have been present for several years (Pitt, 1967). This population has continued ever since, usually with 2–6 singing males, though there were as many as 12 in 1965. Recently, records have also come regularly from Norfolk and Suffolk, with a scattering elsewhere in southern England and north to Humberside and Lancashire (Axell & Jobson, 1972).

Numbers overall reached a peak of 26–30 reported males at up to 15 sites between 1977–80. Since then, however, numbers have declined and there have been as few as 10 records from eight sites in only two counties (1981) with only a slight upward fluctuation in the intervening years to 20 records from 16 localities in 1987 and down to 13 records from 10 sites in 1988, both years in which for the first time consecutively there were no confirmed breeding records. The establishment of this tiny population has coincided with a range expansion into France, Denmark, Germany and Poland, though there seems to have been a decrease in Belgium and possibly also in the Netherlands through habitat destruction (Rappe, 1969; Yeatman, 1971).

THREATS TO SURVIVAL

Threats include drainage, or other loss of, or damage to, sites, and possibly disturbance of habitat by humans.

CONSERVATION

The major sites are well protected as reserves where human interference is controlled and steps are taken to maintain marshland vegetation communities (Bibby & Lunn, 1982). Savi's Warblers have not become as numerous as the available habitat in Britain would probably allow. It is very likely that future population levels in Britain will be regulated by factors beyond our control, for example, climatic influence, edge of range population fluctuation. No further measures can be suggested beyond continuing management of major sites.

REFERENCES

AXELL, H.E. & JOBSON, G.J. 1972. Savi's Warblers breeding in Suffolk. Brit. Birds 65: 229–232.
BIBBY, C.J. & LUNN, J. 1982. Conservation of reed beds and their avifauna in England and Wales. Biol. Conserv. 23: 167–186.
PITT, R.G. 1967. Savi's Warblers breeding in Kent. Brit. Birds 60: 349–355.
RAPPE, A. 1969. Notes sur la locustelle de Savi en Belgique. Aves, 6: 148–155.
YEATMAN, L.J. 1971. Histoire des Oiseaux d'Europe. Paris. Ministère de la qualité et vie Environment.

Marsh Warbler

Acrocephalus palustris

The Marsh Warbler is a rare breeding bird in Britain. It was never common, but it formerly bred regularly in several southern counties of Britain. The population in the middle to late 1970s was up to 200 pairs, but is now less than 20 pairs. Numbers in the main area of the west Midlands have recently declined rapidly, and local extinction appears imminent; however, a few scattered pairs breed elsewhere in southern England. The causes of decline are believed to be largely due to isolation, birds breeding in Britain are at the most north-western part of the Marsh Warbler's range, and no conservation action likely to reverse this trend can be proposed. Some local earlier declines may have been due to habitat loss.

LEGAL STATUS

Protected under Schedule 1 of WCA 1981; EC Birds Directive; Appendix II of the Berne Convention.

ECOLOGY

Favoured habitats are generally in damp areas with well developed herbaceous vegetation—such as sizeable clumps of nettles, meadowsweet or willowherb, and a scattered shrub or tree-cover (Price, 1969). Nest: cup-shape, made of grasses and hair, and characteristically built around the stems of herbaceous plants or shrubs. Eggs: laid in June to early July. Clutch: 3–5; one brood.

Food consists of invertebrates, especially insects and spiders.

DISTRIBUTION AND POPULATION

West Palearctic. The bird breeds from southern England and eastern France to central Russia, north to southern Sweden and the Baltic states, south to northern Italy, the Balkans and Caucasus, with otherwise only limited extensions into south-west Asia. Across the range the distribution is patchy, and numbers are locally erratic (Dowsett-Lemaire, 1981). Numbers have increased markedly in southern Sweden, Finland, and the Leningrad area of Russia, but there is otherwise no evidence of range or population change elsewhere in Europe (Kelsey, 1987; Kelsey *et al.*, 1989) where, in suitable habitat, the bird is often abundant. It winters in East Africa.

In Britain, historic records are difficult to assess as local populations appear to have waxed and waned. The most regular and numerous breeding in Britain has been in Worcestershire, Gloucestershire, Somerset, Sussex and Kent, but with more sporadic records in another 15 southern counties. In the years 1975–80, there might have been a total of 150–200 pairs: 100+ in Worcestershire, 50+ in Gloucestershire, perhaps about 20 in Somerset, and 10+ elsewhere (Kelsey, 1987). Numbers seem to have been declining since about the 1950s; in the main county, Worcestershire, numbers declined rapidly in the 1980s, so that by 1986 there were just eight singing males (Kelsey, 1987) and by 1988 only two breeding pairs. Elsewhere in 1988 there were up to 16 pairs possibly breeding (of which 4 were confirmed) at 10 sites.

THREATS TO SURVIVAL

The recent decline in numbers does not appear to be explicable in terms of habitat loss, though this, and climatic change, may have been factors in the 1950s and 1960s. The species probably suffered from habitat loss locally due to the policy of water authorities of tidying banks. By the time this policy was modified the population was at too low a level to buffer itself against random events and short term climatic variation. There are abandoned sites with apparently suitable vegetation surviving, and there is no evidence for changing trends in the climate to explain the timing of the decline. Breeding productivity does not appear to have declined, though it is lower here than elsewhere in Europe. Kelsey (1987) concluded that the small population in Britain is isolated, so that emigration losses are not made up from elsewhere. Numbers are thus probably vulnerable to random factors; the effects of these factors will probably become more severe as the population declines.

CONSERVATION

Some key sites have reserve status, and vegetation management has been undertaken. Steps were taken to oppose a major flood-control scheme in the main breeding area which would have reduced habitat availability; the scheme was shelved for economic reasons.

Existing site protection and management should be continued, and the control of birdwatchers may be needed as the tiny numbers breeding in Britain concentrate attention. It is however likely that the fate of the species in Britain will rely largely on chance beyond human control, and the Worcestershire population may (at the current rate of decline) become extinct in the very near future.

REFERENCES

Dowsett-Lemaire, F. 1981. Eco-ethological aspects of breeding in the Marsh Warbler *Acrocephalus palustris*. Rev. Ecol. (Terre et Vie) 35: 437–491.
Kelsey, M.G. 1987. The Ecology of Marsh Warblers. DPhil thesis, University of Oxford.
Kelsey, M.G., Green, G.H., Garnett, M.C. & Hayman, P.V. 1989. Marsh Warblers in Britain. Brit. Birds 82: 239–256.
Price, M.P. 1969. Nesting habitat of Reed and Marsh Warblers. Bird Study 16: 130–131.

Consultant: M.G. Kelsey

Dartford Warbler

Sylvia undata

The Dartford Warbler is a vulnerable species because its population is concentrated in a scarce and threatened habitat. The bird was formerly fairly common and more widespread in England but has suffered high mortality in the past from the effects of severe winters and is currently threatened by the loss, destruction or fragmentation of habitat. At present the population has increased again in recent years largely due to the series of mild winters in the mid to late 1980s and by 1988 it was estimated that there were in excess of 600 breeding pairs. Stronger site protection mechanisms are needed, as well as more extensive management of surviving heaths.

LEGAL STATUS

Protected under Schedule 1 of WCA 1981; Annex 1 EC Birds Directive; Appendix II of the Berne Convention.

ECOLOGY

The Dartford Warbler is mainly sedentary, but there is some partial migration from Britain in winter (Bibby, 1979a). The main habitat is dry lowland heath dominated by *Calluna vulgaris*. Nest: either in heather or gorse. Eggs: laid generally between mid-April and early July, occasionally later. Clutch: 3–5; one or two broods, depending on the starting date (Bibby, 1979c).

Gorse (*Ulex europaeus*) is a source of food disproportionately important in relation to its abundance because of higher invertebrate densities (Bibby, 1979b). (In winter, gorse also offers greater shelter.) Most territories contain some gorse, and densities of pairs are higher on heaths with a scatter of gorse.

Winter mortality is variable, and can be high, but population increase can be rapid, with numbers approximately doubling every two years in a recovery phase of good breeding seasons and mild winters.

South-west Palearctic, also Iberia, west and southern France, southern England, southern Italy, Sicily, Corsica and Sardinia. The winter range of this bird is similar, though some reach North Africa. The British breeding population is decidedly the northern outlier of this range.

In the 19th century the bird was more widespread in Britain than it is at present, breeding from Kent to Cornwall and north to Wiltshire, Oxford, Suffolk, and locally to Shropshire and perhaps Staffordshire. It is now mainly confined to Surrey, Hampshire and Dorset, with small numbers irregularly in Sussex, the Isle of Wight, Devon and Cornwall.

In 1961 the population was estimated to be in the region of 450 pairs, but numbers fell dramatically with 80–90% mortality in the severe winters of 1961/62 and 1962/63. By the summer of 1963 there were only about 12 breeding pairs (in two counties) in Britain, by 1966 this figure had risen to 22 pairs (Tubbs, 1963, 1967). Since then with an absence of severe or prolonged winter weather the population has increased and spread again to most of the heathlands formerly occupied in southern England (south of the Thames) and recent highs in the population have estimated 560 pairs in 1974 (Tubbs, 1975), 430 pairs in 1984 (Robins & Bibby, 1985) and by 1988 it was estimated from reports sent to the RBBP that there were up to 639 (proven and possible) breeding pairs in Britain, the highest numbers ever reported to the panel.

Threats include the destruction, deterioration and fragmentation of habitat (Moore, 1975; Bibby, 1978).

The history of the Dorset heaths is well documented. An area of 30,000 ha late last century had been reduced to 10,000 ha by 1960 and 5,832 ha in 1980. These losses have been due to agriculture, forestry and urbanization. Lowland heaths are also vulnerable to successional change, especially colonization by birch (*Betula* sp.) and pine (*Pinus* sp.). Large areas of former heathland have been overrun and converted to woodland.

Uncontrolled fire is a problem in that it periodically destroys suitable habitat for several years. More seriously, fire may promote the spread of birches or bracken (*Pteridium aquilinum*), which, once established, are hard to eradicate.

In the New Forest, heavy grazing by ponies can damage or eliminate gorse.

Local damage to heaths—destruction of vegetation—has been caused by the pressure of public usage or by military training.

Because the numbers of these birds fluctuate widely, fragmentation of habitat may be a problem. Outlying areas are recolonized after local extinctions have been caused by severe winters. This process is slower in the more isolated habitat fragments.

Both the extreme vulnerability of lowland heaths and their considerable value have been recognized in a very thorough spread of SSSIs and reserves, both NNR and other. However, SSSI designation is not sufficient to defend sites from development proposals, especially in places such as densely populated Dorset. SPA status would be a further protection not yet granted to key sites for this Annex 1 species. Specific attention could also be given to the large holdings of the Ministry of Defence.

Control of invasive vegetation by spraying (bracken) or hand removal (birch, pine and, locally, *Rhododendron ponticum*) is carried out on most reserves.

The spread of fire is generally curtailed by provision of fire-breaks, beaters, water supplies and fire-plans. Some positive management for Dartford Warblers has been practised by cutting or burning gorse in rotation to restrict the less attractive degenerate growth phase.

A substantial initiative to raise public interest in heaths would be beneficial, and the problem of vegetation encroachment, even on 'protected' sites, needs more effort. The consequences of heavy grazing and deliberate burning in the New Forest remain unresolved problems.

REFERENCES

Bibby, C.J. 1978. Conservation of the Dartford Warbler on English lowland heaths: a review. Biol. Conserv. 13: 299–307.
Bibby, C.J. 1979a. Breeding biology of the Dartford Warbler *Sylvia undata* in England. Ibis 121: 41–52.
Bibby, C.J. 1979b. Mortality and movements of Dartford Warblers in England. Brit. Birds 72: 10–22.
Bibby, C.J. 1979c. Foods of the Dartford Warbler *Sylvia undata* on southern English heathland (Aves: Sylviidae). J. Zool. 188: 557–576.
Bibby, C.J. & Tubbs, C.R. 1975. Status and conservation of the Dartford Warbler in England. Brit. Birds 68: 177–195.
Moore, N.W. 1975. Status and habitats of the Dartford Warbler, Whitethroat and Stonechat in Dorset in 1959–60. Brit. Birds 68: 196–202.
Robins, M. & Bibby, C.J. 1985. Dartford Warblers in 1984 Britain. Brit. Birds 78: 269–280.
Tubbs, C.R. 1963. The significance of the New Forest to the status of the Dartford Warbler in England. Brit. Birds 56: 41–48.
Tubbs, C.R. 1967. Numbers of Dartford Warblers in England during 1962–66. Brit. Birds 60: 87–89.

Firecrest

Regulus ignicapillus

The Firecrest is a localized breeding visitor with a fragmented and vulnerable population; it is also a regular passage-migrant and a scarce winter visitor, mainly near coasts. Breeding in Britain was first recorded in 1962, and subsequently single males or pairs were recorded in about 20 counties, with a peak count of 175 singing males at 75 localities in 1983. The recorded population fluctuates considerably from year to year and by 1988 the breeding population was estimated to be about half of the 1983 figure. Where Firecrests occur in forestry plantations clearfelling activities should leave some blocks of at least 3 ha intact.

LEGAL STATUS

Protected under Schedule 1 of WCA 1981; EC Birds Directive; Appendix II of the Berne Convention.

ECOLOGY

The Firecrest is found in conifer plantations and in mixed or even mainly broadleaved woodlands. Most early reports of breeding were in Norway Spruce (*Picea abies*) or Douglas Fir (*Pseudotsuga menziesii*) plantations at least 30 years old. Nest: usually on a side branch. Eggs: laid in mid-May to the second half of July. Clutch: 6–12; there is no evidence yet of more than one brood in Britain. The young fledge by early August.

Food consists of small invertebrates.

The Firecrest occasionally hybridizes with the Goldcrest (Cobb, 1976; Thorpe, 1983).

DISTRIBUTION AND POPULATION

The Firecrest is confined to the west Palearctic. It breeds in western and southern Europe north to southern England, Denmark and Poland, east to western Russia and the Black Sea, otherwise only to Asia Minor, north-west Africa, Madeira and the Canaries. The bird is partially migratory, wintering in the west and south of the range.

Colonization of Britain followed northward extensions of the range in France and Germany this century. The species is now increasing in Belgium; it spread to the Netherlands in 1928 and to Denmark in 1961, and it became more numerous on passage in southern England in the 1960s and 1970s. Three singing males were located in Hampshire in 1961, and breeding was recorded in 1962 (Adams, 1966); since then, singing males or pairs have been recorded in the summer in some 20 counties from Kent to Devon as well as Gwent and Powys north to Yorkshire and Merseyside. Otherwise the bird is a regular passage-migrant from mid-March to April and from mid-September to early November, mainly along south and East Anglian coasts; it also winters chiefly in south-west England and, to a lesser extent, along the south coast. The wintering distribution does not appear to differ from that recorded before colonization, although there are more records (Marchant, 1986).

This tiny species, nesting high in conifers, is not easy to watch and there were less than 20 confirmed records of breeding during 1961–78; doubtless many singing males are missed—indeed, the species may well have been overlooked in summer much earlier than 1961. Thus, only general conclusions on distribution and population are possible; Hampshire has remained one of the main areas (the highest number of males reported being 27 in 1969), but in 1971 a strong population was discovered in Buckinghamshire (a peak of 46 males in 1975) (Batten, 1971, 1973) and another was found in 1975 in Kent (a peak of 36 males in both 1975 and 1981). A maximum of 175 singing males from 75 locations was recorded in 1983, followed by a reduction to 82 in 47 locations and 46 in 25 locations in 1984 and 1985, respectively, by 1988 the trend was upwards with a possible maximum total of 80 pairs in 43 sites. Local and perhaps national populations fluctuate markedly from year to year.

THREATS TO SURVIVAL

Threats include loss of habitat and disturbance by man.

All Firecrest colonies based on even-aged forestry plantations are vulnerable to clear-felling.

Incidental human disturbance from recreational activities in the breeding grounds appears to have had no effect, but the species is very sensitive to investigation of the nest during building and laying.

CONSERVATION

The species is monitored by the RBBP; some areas, such as Hampshire, receive poor cover, however, and a more systematic approach is desirable.

Clear-felling of the plantations where Firecrest breed should be avoided from April to August and if, when clear-felling does take place, blocks of 3 ha or more are left, Firecrests may be able to maintain a presence. Clear-felling should, if possible, be carried out in such a way that there are always some stands of trees at least 30 years old remaining in the area.

REFERENCES

ADAMS, M.C. 1966. Firecrests breeding in Hampshire. Brit. Birds 59: 240–246.
BATTEN, L.A. 1971. Firecrests breeding in Buckinghamshire. Brit. Birds 64: 473–475.
BATTEN, L.A. 1973. The colonisation of England by the Firecrest. Brit. Birds 66: 159–166.
COBB, F.K. 1976. Apparent hybridization of Firecrest and Goldcrest. Brit. Birds 69: 447–451.
MARCHANT, J.H. 1986. Firecrest. In Lack, P.C. (ed.), The atlas of wintering birds in Britain and Ireland. Calton: Poyser.
THORPE, R.I. 1983. Apparent hybridization between Goldcrest and Firecrest. Brit. Birds 76: 233–234.

Bearded Tit

Panurus biarmicus

The vulnerability of the Bearded Tit is due to its concentration in rather few sites. The most recent survey of the population found that there were slightly under 600 pairs breeding in Britain. Active management to maintain the domination of reeds in wet sites should ensure the long-term future of Bearded Tits in Britain.

LEGAL STATUS

Protected under Schedule 1 of WCA 1981; EC Birds Directive; Appendix II of the Berne Convention.

ECOLOGY

The Bearded Tit is almost entirely confined to reed-beds (*Phragmites australis*) in the breeding season, and only slightly less so in the winter. The breeding season can last from March to August, occasionally longer. Nest: built low down in reed litter, sedges, or grass, usually near or in the drier parts of wet reed-beds. Clutch: 5–6; two, three or possibly four broods are produced in a season.

Food consists of invertebrates in the summer, especially chironomids and the larvae of reed-dwelling moths (Bibby, 1981). In winter the bird takes seeds, especially those of the reed—but also those of other plants such as sedges, nettle (*Urtica dioica*) or willowherb (*Epilobium hirsutum*).

DISTRIBUTION AND POPULATION

Palearctic, north to Sweden and in most southern European countries. The Bearded Tit is widely but thinly distributed across the eastern palearctic. Early in the 19th century it was fairly widespread in southern and eastern England from Lincolnshire to Hampshire. There was a marked reduction in its range in the first half of this century until it was virtually confined to Norfolk and Suffolk. There was a subsequent expansion to the present—mainly coastal—range from Yorkshire to Dorset, with an outlying population in Lancashire and sporadic breeding elsewhere.

In Britain the numbers of Bearded Tits were very low after the hard winters of 1916/17, 1939/40 and 1946/47 (below ten known pairs after the latter). From the mid-1950s an increase started and, surprisingly, it was barely slowed by the winters of 1961/62 and 1962/63 (Axell, 1966). At the last full review, in 1974, there were at least 590 pairs in 11 counties (O'Sullivan, 1976). Numbers have probably increased slightly since then. By 1979 the species was breeding regularly in 36 of the 109 reed-beds greater than 2 ha in extent in England and Wales (Bibby & Lunn, 1982).

Winter movements are irruptive (Axell, 1966), and are probably related to failure of the food supply based on a single plant species (Bibby, 1983). Very large irruptions into England from the Dutch polders—mainly in the 1960s to early 1970s—probably helped the spread of the British range. Bearded Tits are susceptible to high mortality in cold winters, but their breeding rate can rapidly make up numbers.

THREATS TO SURVIVAL

The sole threat is from habitat loss—which can occur by drainage, or by natural succession as reed-beds dry out and develop unsuitable vegetation and poorer food supplies.

Although numbers may be reduced by cold winters, high dispersive ability and high breeding rates do not make this species particularly vulnerable to habitat fragmentation; all but the remotest sites can be rapidly re-populated after a decline.

CONSERVATION

Most of the major reed-bed sites in Britain are scheduled as SSSIs, and a high proportion are managed as nature reserves. Active management includes water control, to keep the areas wet, and the control of invading scrub by cutting or burning.

Major dredging or other works might be needed at some sites to maintain suitable habitat in the face of accumulating silt and plant debris. Large new sites could readily be created. Many of the most important sites in Britain for this species are recent, and of artificial origin, and the population explosion of Bearded Tits on the Dutch polders indicates their potential to exploit new sites. Winter survival might be locally enhanced by artificial feeding in periods of severe weather.

REFERENCES

AXELL, H.E. 1966. Eruptions of Bearded Tits during 1959–65. Brit. Birds 59: 513–543.

BIBBY, C.J. 1981. Food supply and diet of the Bearded Tit. Bird Study 28: 201–210.

BIBBY, C.J. 1983. Studies of west Palearctic birds: Bearded Tit. Brit. Birds 76: 549–563.

BIBBY, C.J. & LUNN, J. 1982. Conservation of reed-beds and their avifauna in England and Wales. Biol. Conserv. 23: 167–186.

O'SULLIVAN, J.M. 1976. Bearded Tits in Britain and Ireland, 1966–1974. Brit. Birds 69: 473–489.

Crested Tit

Parus cristatus

The Crested Tit is a largely sedentary species restricted to the Moray Basin catchment area of the Highlands, with an estimated population of about 900 pairs. It has shown an increase in distribution over the last century coinciding with colonization of mature commercial plantation woodlands.

LEGAL STATUS

Protected under Schedule 1 of WCA 1981; EC Birds Directive; Appendix II of the Berne Convention.

ECOLOGY

The Crested Tit occurs typically in mature, open scots pine (*Pinus sylvestris*) woodland, but also in mature mixed scots pine and birch (*Betula*) woods, and mature commercial plantations of scots pine. Nest: a self excavated hole in a decaying scots pine stump, very occasionally a birch stump [less than 3 m from the ground in 90% of cases (Nethersole-Thompson & Watson, 1974)], lined with mosses, hair and feathers. Eggs: laid late April to early May. Clutch: 6 (3–9); second broods are produced only after predation of the first, and then only occasionally. The young fledge from late May to early June.

Food consists of a wide range of invertebrates and pine seeds. The bird stores food extensively during the early winter for use later in the winter.

DISTRIBUTION AND POPULATION

West Palearctic. Entirely European: the Highlands of Scotland, Scandinavia, eastern Prussia, Poland, the Baltic States, Russia (west of the Urals) and the Balkans, central Europe from Iberia to Rumania, except Italy (Campbell, 1974).

In Scotland the bird has shown an increase in range over the last 100 years— with birds utilizing mature or maturing commercially grown Scots Pine. Crested Tits now breed from Strathspey (Inverness-shire) north into Morayshire, Banff-shire, Nairn, Easter Ross and southern Sutherland, and west into the Strathglass (Inverness-shire) (Cook, 1982; Lack, 1986; Sharrock, 1976; Thom, 1986).

Densities of between 0·01 to 0·15 pairs per ha in plantations and in open, mature Scots Pine give the population an estimated 900 pairs. This comes from the potential areas occupied in the 35,000 ha of plantation, 4,000 ha of low-density natural Scots Pine wood, and 3,300 ha of pure natural Scots Pine wood (Cook, 1982).

From ringing it is clear that about one-third of the breeding population consists of birds at least two years old, and that pairs remain together throughout the winter. Outside the breeding season the bird forages in mixed flocks, mainly with Coal Tits and Goldcrests.

THREATS TO SURVIVAL

Threats include habitat loss and severe winter weather.

Only about one-fifth of the woodlands occupied by breeding Crested Tits is directly protected. In those areas which are not protected, removal of dead wood and clear-fellings pose a threat to about one-half of the population (over 400 pairs).

It has been suggested that very severe winter weather was responsible for the reduction of up to 60% in the breeding population over a single winter; however, the evidence is contradictory, and following some very severe winters the breeding population remains stable or even shows a slight increase (Thom, 1986). Despite large reductions in the breeding population, the Crested Tit shows a remarkable ability to recover its numbers: even in years of severe reductions, full recovery is made within three years (Thom, 1986).

CONSERVATION

Of the woodlands where the Crested Tit breeds, about one-third are owned by the Forestry Commission and the rest are privately owned. Of these woodlands only two-fifths are nature reserves or SSSIs. In some of these woods, and notably in Corsican Pine (*Pinus nigra*) plantations, Crested Tits have used the nest-boxes provided.

On the RSPB reserve at Loch Garten, Inverness-shire, young woods are thinned with a large proportion of dead-wood left standing in the form of short stumps. However, the influence of this management will become clear only after long-term study. Changes in commercial management, which allows dead-wood to be left standing, may be a major contribution to population expansion.

Research is currently being done on this species to establish its exact habitat requirements and with the hope of providing future guidelines for both reserve and commercial management.

REFERENCES

Campbell, B. 1974. Forestry Commission. Forest Records 98. Swindon: HMSO.
Cook, M.J.H. 1982. Breeding status of the Crested Tit. Scot. Birds 12: 97–106.
Nethersole-Thompson, D. & Watson, A. 1974. The Cairngorms. London: Collins.
Thom, V.M. 1986. Birds in Scotland. Calton: Poyser.

Consultant: H. Young

Golden Oriole
Oriolus oriolus

The Golden Oriole is a rare breeding bird in Britain; a few pairs have occasionally bred in scattered parts of southern England since about 1840, and some increase has taken place since 1949, with summering or breeding birds present in over 20 counties. From 1965 the bird has bred regularly in East Anglia; in the period 1974–1988, between 4 and 40 pairs were present in the breeding season. Golden Orioles in Britain clearly have a preference for poplar plantations, and it would benefit from increased planting of this species.

LEGAL STATUS

Protected under Schedule 1 of WCA 1981; EC Birds Directive; Appendix II of the Berne Convention.

ECOLOGY

The Golden Oriole breeds in broadleaved woodland, shelter belts and orchards. Poplar plantations are widely used in East Anglia, but oak and alder are also favoured trees elsewhere in Europe (Feige, 1986). It is not known why such a narrow range of tree types is chosen in England when other apparently suitable and widespread trees are not used. Nest: a hammock-like structure, formed from grass and other fibrous material woven around tree branches. Eggs: laid between late May and early June. Clutch: 3–5; one brood is normal, and replacement clutches are laid only after early failures.

Food in the breeding season consists of mainly insects gleaned from leaves within the tree canopy; Lepidopteran larvae are particularly important (Feige, 1986). In Europe immatures feed on fruit once they are independent, and before they migrate.

DISTRIBUTION AND POPULATION

West and central Palearctic, and Oriental. The Golden Oriole breeds throughout most of continental Europe north to southern Sweden, southern Finland and north-central European USSR. In central and western Europe it is widespread, and it breeds throughout in suitable woodland; however, it has declined in many areas in recent years—particularly in Denmark and parts of East Germany. In West Germany the population has fluctuated recently with an overall downward trend. It winters in sub-Saharan Africa and India.

The bird bred occasionally in southern and eastern England, especially in Kent, during the period 1840–1890, and thereafter even less frequently until 1949 when records of summering birds increased again, with occasional breeding north to Lancashire, Northumberland and Fife (Parslow, 1967). Regular breeding in Suffolk began in 1965 where one site has since held up to 14 pairs.

The total number of suspected breeding pairs in Britain increased to a peak of 30 in 1979, but declined to 18 in 1984 with the gradual felling of trees from the main Suffolk site which previously held several pairs. However, by 1987 and 1988 a new site had been discovered (where there was no threat from felling) which held a substantial part of the the total of 31 (1987) and 41 (1988) pairs that were possibly or proved breeding. At least 16 of the 41 pairs present in 1988 were confirmed as breeding.

THREATS TO SURVIVAL

Threats include adverse weather, loss of habitat, and disturbance by man.

This bird is near the northern edge of its breeding range, and there is evidence of poor breeding success in the recent tendency towards cool springs and wet summers.

Much of the population in East Anglia nests and forages in poplar plantations, many of which are privately owned and are being felled—or are likely to be felled in the near future—or could deteriorate through neglect. Replanting with poplar is not on a sufficient scale to replace the habitat being lost.

Disturbance by birdwatchers could be a potential problem, and losses of eggs to egg collectors have occurred recently.

CONSERVATION

The planting of poplars in those parts of East Anglia where Golden Orioles occur can be expected to increase their population there. Breeding pairs are relatively inconspicuous, and they need little protection from human disturbance except at well-known and accessible sites.

REFERENCES

FEIGE, K-D. 1986. Der Pirol. A Ziemsen Verlag, Wittenberg. Lutherstadt.
PARSLOW, J.L.F. 1967. Changes in status among breeding birds in Britain and Ireland. Brit. Birds 60: 268–271.

Consultant: R.E. Green

Red-backed Shrike
Lanius collurio

The Red-backed Shrike is now most probably a lost breeding species in Britain. It was formerly widespread in England and Wales but has suffered a marked decline since the mid-19th century. By the 1980s it was confined to East Anglia, where only one or two pairs bred in 1987 and 1988. A few pairs bred in Scotland during 1977–1979 but only one pair has bred since 1980, and hopes of colonization have proved to be unfounded. The reasons for this decline are still not fully understood, and it is unlikely that any action can be taken to reverse this trend. Extinction as a breeding species in Britain is considered imminent as for the first time no birds nested or were in pairs in the summer of 1989.

LEGAL STATUS

Protected under Schedule 1 of WCA 1981; Annex I of EC Birds Directive; Appendix II of the Berne Convention.

ECOLOGY

In Britain this bird formerly nested on commons and waste ground, in overgrown hedgerows, and in young plantations and other scrub, but in recent years it has been restricted to lowland heaths in southern England and East Anglia. Nest: a thrush-like cup-nest, placed at a height of up to 2·5 m well inside a thorny bush such as gorse, bramble, holly or hawthorn. Eggs: laid from late May through to late July. Clutch: 3–6; one brood. The young fledge by early August.

Food consists of a variety of prey—mainly large flying insects of the orders Orthoptera (grasshoppers), Lepidoptera (butterflies and moths), Hymenoptera (bees) and Coleoptera (beetles), but also small or young birds, small mammals and frogs, lizards and earthworms.

DISTRIBUTION AND POPULATION

Palearctic. The Red-backed Shrike breeds throughout most of Europe except in Iceland, Ireland, northern Fenno-Scandia, northern USSR, central and southern Iberia and many of the Mediterranean Islands. It winters mainly in tropical and southern Africa east to the Persian Gulf and north-west India.

The bird was formerly widespread over much of England and Wales, but it has been decreasing continuously since the mid-19th century. Although the decline initially began well over a century ago, the species was still widespread in 1920, and even in 1940 the bird nested in many parts of England and Wales south of a line from the River Dee to the Humber (Durango, 1950; Peakall, 1962; Ash, 1970). The decline apparently accelerated during this time, and the population of 300 pairs in 1952 had become a mere 80–90 pairs by 1971 (Bibby, 1973). By 1986 the population had fallen to four pairs, only two of which bred successfully (Hoblyn, 1983; Elliott, 1987), there were only one or two pairs in 1987 and 1988 and none at all in 1989. The presence of up to 6–8 pairs annually in five Scottish counties during three summers (1977–79) gave hopes of colonization from Scandinavia (which also appeared likely for several other species, eg, the Wryneck); several pairs did breed successfully, but there has been only one further nesting attempt in Scotland in 1987. The reason for this decline is not fully understood, although Bibby (1973) suggested that the major cause of the decline is almost certainly the effect of climatic change on food supply—but that the mechanism of the process is complex and elusive. The area of East Anglia which has been the species' stronghold in recent years is the driest part of Britain, and it is less under the influence of Britain's maritime climate.

In France the species has also declined in the more maritime climatic zone. The species appears to be doing well in those parts of Europe which are exposed to a drier or more continental climate.

THREATS TO SURVIVAL

Threats include climatic factors, changes in habitat, and (possibly) disturbance by man.

The major decline that has taken place in Britain has been linked with climatic trend, although other factors such as changes in land use, and agricultural practice (ie, spraying), may well have influenced the availability of a suitable supply of food. In recent years, since the decline set in, areas where habitat has remained unchanged have been deserted for no apparent reason. However, Bibby (1973) presented evidence to show that both habitat destruction and egg collecting can adversely affect scarce species, and suggested that these activities could have resulted in the elimination of local populations.

Birdwatchers are naturally keen to see this species, and if a small number of pairs continue to breed in Britain they may suffer from disturbance—even though the species is notoriously tolerant of people in its continental breeding range.

CONSERVATION

The species decline has been documented, and it seems that little can be done to affect the general trend. It is likely that the Red-backed Shrike will (if it has not already) become extinct in Britain as a regular breeding bird in the very near future. Until this happens it may prove necessary to ensure that breeding birds are free from undue disturbance; wardening of sites may prove necessary and, in the interests of the birds, breeding localities should continue not to be publicized.

REFERENCES

Ash, J.S. 1970. Observations on a decreasing population of Red-backed Shrikes. Brit. Birds 63: 185–205, 225–239.
Bibby, C.J. 1973. The Red-backed Shrike: a vanishing British species. Bird Study 20: 103–110.
Durango, S. 1950. Om klimatets inverkan po tornskatans (*Lanius collurio* L.) utbredning och levnadsmojligheter. Fauna och Flora 46: 49–78.
Elliott, G.D. 1987. Rare Breeding Birds. RSPB Conserv. Rev. 1: 84.
Hoblyn, R.A. 1983. The Status of the Red-backed Shrike in the Breck 1974–1983. Nar Valley Ornithological Society Annual Report 1983: 61–67.
Peakall, D.B. 1962. The past and present status of the Red-backed Shrike in Great Britain. Bird Study 9: 198–216.

Chough

Pyrrhocorax pyrrhocorax

The Chough is a vulnerable species, with a breeding population of less than 300 pairs in Britain. Before the middle of the 18th century the range extended to north and east Scotland, Yorkshire and Kent, but following a widespread decline since then it is now confined to Wales, the Isle of Man and western Scotland. About 130 pairs were recorded in 1963, but that number was probably underestimated; a national survey in 1982 counted 249–274 pairs and indicated that there had probably been an increase in Wales and Scotland.

LEGAL STATUS

Protected under Schedule 1 of WCA 1981; Annex 1 of EC Birds Directive; Appendix II of the Berne Convention.

ECOLOGY

Nest: an outer structure predominantly of coarse heather twigs, with a cup formed of finer twigs, rootlets and grasses; there is a lining of wool hair and some feathers. The nest is built in traditional sites: in a crevice or on a deeply sheltered ledge, mainly in sea-cliffs and sea-caves but also in quarries and old mine-shafts — especially in ruined buildings in Scotland, Wales and the Isle of Man; the bird is usually solitary when breeding, but is colonial in some areas. Eggs: laid during April to early June. Clutch: 3–5 (1–6); one brood. The young fledge by mid July.

Food consists mainly of larval and adult soil invertebrates, particularly beetles, crane flies, ants, spiders and flies, as well as invertebrates associated with animal dung—especially fly and beetle larvae and adults. Seasonal changes in diet have been recorded in many areas (see eg, Roberts, 1982); the birds also eat worms, grain, some crustaceans, molluscs, and moth larvae.

DISTRIBUTION AND POPULATION

Palearctic, north-east Ethiopian. The Chough breeds in Ireland, western Britain, north-west France and southern Europe from Spain and Portugal, north-west Africa (Morocco) and the Canary Isles (Palma) east to the Balkans, and the eastern Mediterranean, the Caucasus, Turkestan, Hindu Kush, Himalayas, Mongolia and China. Also in the mountains of Bale Province, Ethiopia. The bird is sedentary.

In the British Isles this bird was formerly much more widespread, extending to north, east, and inland Scotland and the coastal cliffs of Cumbria, Yorkshire and Cornwall to Kent and the Channel Isles; however, there was a marked decrease and a contraction of the range in the 18th and 19th centuries, and the bird is now confined to Wales, the Isle of Man and western Scotland, though it nested in Devon until about 1910, and Cornwall to 1952, and was more widespread in west Scotland before about 1940. The Chough rarely wanders outside its breeding range.

It should be added that there has also been a slow retraction of range in some other parts of Europe over the last two centuries (notably France, Portugal and Italy).

A census in 1963 (Rolfe, 1966) put the British population at about 130 breeding pairs, comprising 99–104 in Wales [seven counties, but mostly in Dyfed (Pembroke) and Gwynedd (Caernarvon)], 20 in the Isle of Man, and 11 in western Scotland [islands of south Strathclyde (Argyll)], as well as a number of non-breeders. The bird does not nest until it is three years old, and as much as 30% of the population may be in this category. The 'Atlas' showed much the same distribution, with confirmed or probable breeding in 64 10-km squares that included eight counties of Wales and two additional areas of west Scotland (one of these in the Outer Hebrides). The 1982 national survey found little change in distribution: 249–274 breeding pairs in Britain (about 1,000 pairs in Britain and Ireland), and a further 210–235 non-breeding immatures. While it was suggested that the 1963 figures may have been underestimated, there has probably been a real increase in Wales and Scotland: regional totals were: Wales 139–142 pairs, Scotland 61–72 pairs, and the Isle of Man 49–60 pairs. Two birds were seen at two sites in Cornwall in 1987 but both have subsequently disappeared. The origins of these are unknown, but it does indicate that re-establishment in Cornwall is physically possible if suitable habitat exists. In 1986 a survey in Scotland found 105 pairs, 95 of which were on Islay (but there were none found on the mainland) (Bignal *et al.*, 1988); in 1987 and 1988 a pair was present on Mull for the first time in over 50 years, and there were sightings on Iona and Tiree where the last breeding records were for 1890 and 1871, respectively.

THREATS TO SURVIVAL

Threats include changes to habitat, a reduction in the dung-associated fauna which the young birds use for food, and human disturbance.

Historically, habitat loss and land-use changes, coupled with persecution, have been important threats to this species. Disturbance and severe winters have been most significant, and competition from the successful Jackdaw has often been put forward as a cause of the decline—though neither the food nor the nesting requirements of these two species seriously overlap.

The 1982 survey showed the importance to this specialist feeder of rough, unimproved grassland grazed by cattle and sheep; machair and coastal turf were also important, but improved pasture and arable land are not as attractive, and it is suggested that changes to these habitats and landscape simplification may have been one of the main factors in the decline.

While numbers now seem to be stable, or increasing, clearly the main threat is the removal of livestock (allowing bracken and scrub development) or the introduction of intensive dairy or arable farming in areas at present attractive to Choughs.

The injection into livestock of certain anti-parasite drugs (eg, Ivermectin) ultimately results in their dung and urine containing an insecticide which consequently destroys those insects which feed on, or lay eggs in, cattle dung. Since dung is known to be an important source of invertebrates for Choughs throughout the entire range, any reduction in the dung-feeding/living fauna could significantly affect the bird—particularly recently fledged birds which may rely heavily on coprophilous insects for food.

Although frequently associated with humans (more in some parts of its range than in others) Choughs are vulnerable to disturbance, both at the nest and in feeding areas. At high disturbance levels on the coast—through tourism, rock-climbing, etc.—feeding areas can become unusable as a result of the disturbance and through developments (besides agricultural improvement) such as holiday areas.

In some parts of the range (especially Spain and Portugal), afforestation alters and drastically affects feeding habitats. This is often associated with changes in agricultural regimes (from pastoralism to cereal production), and these combined changes affect both breeding and non-breeding birds.

Other threats arise from egg-collecting (though on a very small scale), and some of these birds are still illegally shot.

Gapeworm infection has also been found in birds in this country, but to what extent this affects survival is not known (Bignal et al., 1987; Meyer & Simpson, 1988).

The species apparently suffers losses in severe weather, and the series of hard winters in the 19th century may well have contributed to the bird's decline; certainly, the winters of 1939/40 and 1962/63 badly affected the numbers in Western Scotland and Ireland.

CONSERVATION

Preservation of suitable feeding areas of poor-quality, rough grazing and semi-natural vegetation with relatively high stocking levels—particularly of cattle—in the main areas is the most important conservation need. Habitat management is feasible at local level together with the provision of artificial nesting sites developed experimentally by NCC research (Bignal & Bignal, 1987). Because Choughs are closely related to agricultural systems and land management over relatively large areas, site-based conservation policies need to be augmented with 'wider-countryside' policies that can maintain the conditions that they require. In this respect an Environmentally Sensitive Area (ESA)-type designation is urgently required for the Hebrides. The protection of certain key sites, particularly in the Inner Hebrides, is vital. Islay and Colonsay are of crucial importance as they support virtually the entire Scottish breeding population (97%), the principal flocking areas and the largest communal roost known in the British Isles. The re-establishment of more traditional forms of pastoralism in Wales (and Cornwall) could significantly assist the expansion of Choughs in these areas.

Management and maintenance of derelict and occupied buildings in remote areas to provide nesting sites has been successfully developed on Islay, and information (together with details of possible grant-aid) is available from the Nature Conservancy Council.

Monitoring and research of Chough populations by colour-ringing is still needed as there is relatively little known about the detailed movements of these birds. In 1988 an International Workshop on Chough Conservation produced a number of recommendations (Bignal & Curtis, 1989) and suggested the establishment of an International Forum on birds and pastoralism to investigate in more detail the needs of Choughs and other birds on Annex 1 of the EC Directive.

REFERENCES

Bignal, S. & Bignal, E. 1987. The provision of artificial nesting sites for choughs. NCC. CSD Report 765.

Bignal, E.M. & Curtis, D.J. (eds) 1989. The Chough and Land-use in Europe: Proceedings of an International Workshop of the Conservation of the Chough *Pyrrhocorax pyrrhocorax* in the EC. Scottish Chough Study group.

Bignal, E.M., Bignal, S. & Still, E. 1987. Gapeworm infection in Choughs. Ringing and Migration 8: 56–57.

Bignal, E., Bignal, S. & Easterbee, N. 1988. The recent status and distribution of chough in Scotland. NCC. CSD Report 843.

Bullock, I.D., Drewett, D.R. & Mickleburgh, S.P. 1983. The Chough in Britain and Ireland. Brit. Birds 76: 377–401.

Meyer, R.M. & Simpson, V.R. 1988. Gapeworm infection in Choughs *Pyrrhocorax pyrrhocorax*: further evidence. Bird Study 35: 223–226.

Roberts, P.J. 1982. Foods of the Chough on Bardsey Island, Wales. Bird Study 29: 155–161.

Rolfe, R. 1966. The status of the Chough in the British Isles. Bird Study 13: 221–236.

Consultant: E.M. Bignal

Brambling
Fringilla montifringilla

The Brambling is a winter visitor and passage-migrant that arrives in Britain in variable numbers; the bird has bred in Britain on a number of separate occasions in recent years; never more than 1–2 pairs have been proved to breed but there are increasing signs of birds holding territories in a number of areas. Wintering flocks are highly mobile, concentrating in areas of good beech-mast throughout Europe. Breeding is irregular in Britain, and special conservation measures are unlikely to change this.

LEGAL STATUS

Protected under Schedule 1 of WCA 1981; EC Birds Directive; Appendix III of the Berne Convention.

ECOLOGY

The Brambling breeds in coniferous and birch forest, mixed woodland or birch scrub across northern Europe and Asia. Nest: a deep cup of grasses, moss, hair and feathers, decorated with lichens and flakes of silver birch, situated in the fork of a tree at a height of 2–3 m. Eggs: laid in mid-May to July. Clutch: 5–7; one brood. The young fledge by early August.

Food in the breeding season consists mainly of the larvae of geometrid moths; in winter the birds feed on beech-mast, seeds, grain and berries.

DISTRIBUTION AND POPULATION

North Palearctic. The Brambling breeds throughout northern Europe and Asia in a broad band stretching from Norway to Kamchatka; it winters in west, central and southern Europe and in southern Asia. The bird occurs in Britain mainly as a winter visitor and a passage-migrant; it arrives in variable numbers, with the majority of birds coming from Norway, Sweden and Finland. Bramblings normally arrive in Britain in October or November, but the scale and timing of this arrival depends upon the availability of adequate food elsewhere in Scandinavia and Europe (Lack, 1986).

Breeding in Britain was confirmed for the first time in Sutherland in 1920, though the nest was later robbed (Baxter & Rintoul, 1953). More recently, singing males and pairs have been seen, in the summer, in various parts of the Scottish Highlands as well as in England. Between 1968 and 1972 four probable and two possible instances of breeding were recorded. A singing male was located in 1977, but breeding was not confirmed again until 1979 when a nest with three eggs, later deserted, was located in Grampian. The first successful breeding attempt occurred at Inverness-shire during 1981 when a pair was proved to have bred; birds were also present at a number of other sites. The following year two pairs were confirmed as breeding and there were at least 8 other pairs possibly breeding. Breeding occurred again in 1983 and 1984 when between one and seven pairs were located, all in Scotland but only one pair in each year was proved to have bred (Thom, 1986). Birds were then recorded during the summer in each successive year until 1987, when a single pair was confirmed as breeding and again in 1988. However, the number of sightings elsewhere during the summer months declined to only two.

There is no real evidence that this bird is spreading in Fenno-Scandia, and it may be that isolated nesting in Britain is probably the result of late migrants finding the right conditions in suitable habitat rather than indications of colonization.

THREATS TO SURVIVAL

Threats may include egg-collecting and disturbance by man.

With such a mobile wintering population, and a small occasional breeding population, there are probably no avoidable threats that could significantly change the current status of the Brambling in Britain. Individual nesting pairs would be at risk from the attentions of egg collectors, and perhaps over-zealous birdwatchers, should a breeding site become widely known.

CONSERVATION

Provided that no large-scale land-use changes occur within the breeding range of this species, there are probably few conservation actions that need to be—or could be—undertaken.

In Britain the wintering population would benefit from a widespread planting of broadleaved woodland with a high beech content, whilst the maintenance of birch woodland in Scotland would appear to be essential if breeding is to continue.

REFERENCES

Baxter, E.V. & Rintoul, L.J. 1953. The birds of Scotland. Edinburgh: Oliver & Boyd.
Lack, P. 1986. The atlas of wintering birds in Britain and Ireland. Calton: Poyser.
Thom, V. 1986. Birds in Scotland. Calton: Poyser.

Serin

Serinus serinus

The Serin is a rare breeding bird in Britain. After an upsurge in the number of records from about 1961, nesting was recorded in Dorset in 1967, in Sussex in 1969, and in Devon in 1978; between 1981 and 1985 up to two pairs bred in Devon, and there have been several other records of singing males elsewhere with a possible maximum of 9 pairs in 6 localities in 1988. The species has been spreading slowly north in Europe since the early 19th century, but it would appear that the barrier of the English Channel tends to inhibit a definite movement into Britain.

LEGAL STATUS

Protected under Schedule 1 of WCA 1981; EC Birds Directive; Appendix II of the Berne Convention.

ECOLOGY

Nest: a neat cup of stems, moss, rootlets and lichens, lined with plant down, hair and feathers, at a height of 1·5–6 m in a bush or tree, in parks, orchards, churchyards, avenues, suburban gardens, cultivated land near towns, copses and open woodland. The bird is solitary to social. Eggs: laid in the northern part of the Continent in late April to early July. Clutch: 4 (3–5); often two broods. The young fledge by late July.

Food consists of the seeds of wild and garden plants, and of alder (*Alnus*) and birch (*Betula*).

DISTRIBUTION AND POPULATION

South-west Palearctic. The Serin breeds in continental Europe north to the English Channel, Denmark, southern Sweden and southern Finland, and east to the Baltic States and Black Sea, but otherwise only in Asia Minor and north-west Africa; it winters chiefly in Iberia and countries round the Mediterranean.

Early in the 19th century a slow northward spread began from the original range in Mediterranean countries, and by 1875 central Europe had been colonized; this expansion accelerated in the east, and the south Baltic coast was reached by 1925, southern Sweden and the Baltic States by 1960, and southern Finland to Leningrad by 1970 (Olsson, 1969, 1971). Farther west, the spread was much slower, and, though the species was breeding widely in northern France by 1925, it had still barely reached the Channel coast by 1960; the bird first nested in the Netherlands in 1922, but was still scarce there by 1970 and remains rare in Denmark. Nevertheless, much of the Channel coast of France was colonized in the 1960s and early 1970s, and many more began to be recorded in Britain from about 1961 (only 76 during 1852–1957, but 268 during 1958–78) (Rogers, 1979). Unfortunately the rarity records committee stopped collecting records after 1982 so that no comparative figures have been compiled for the 1980s.

Breeding was established in Dorset in 1967 (Ferguson-Lees, 1968), and in Sussex in 1969, and was strongly suspected in four other areas in those counties, and in Hampshire, up to 1972; however, during 1973–77 no further nesting was recorded, though odd pairs and singing males were occasionally seen briefly in the summer north to Lincolnshire. In 1978 a pair reared two broods in Devon, and pairs or singing males were found at two other sites in that county, and one in Worcestershire. In 1980 a male sang and displayed for three weeks in Devon, and at three sites in the same county in 1981 one pair raised six young from two broods, and another pair raised at least three young; there were at least a further four singing males. In 1982, at the same site, one pair raised seven young in two broods, while in 1983 and 1984 two pairs were successful in raising at least eleven young to the flying stage. In 1985 only one pair bred, although there were four other possible pairs, but no females were reported with the three males that had been recorded in 1986. Since 1985 there have been no confirmed breeding records anywhere in Britain but the small number of singing males or birds possibly on territory continues to grow with a maximum of 9 birds in 6 localities in 1988. This slow progress, with periods of recession, has been characteristic of the range expansion, and more widespread colonization is still hoped for. It would appear however that the barrier of the English Channel tends to inhibit movement into Britain (Spencer, 1988).

THREATS TO SURVIVAL

There are probably no threats—other than human disturbance in the early stages of nesting and chick-rearing. Apparently suitable habitat and food are plentiful in southern England and, as this is a spreading species, nothing in Britain is likely to prevent its successful colonization when the time is right. Disturbance should be kept to a minimum at the first nests, but odd pairs of such a small species are easily overlooked, and a number may breed successfully whatever happens.

CONSERVATION

This species is monitored by the Rare Breeding Birds Panel. Localities where pairs or singing males are seen in summer should not be publicized. Some nests are likely to be safeguarded by being on private ground such as large suburban gardens.

REFERENCES

FERGUSON-LEES, I.J. 1968. Serins breeding in southern England. Brit. Birds 61: 87–88.
OLSSON, V. 1969. Die Expansion des Girlitzes (*Serinus serinus*) in Nordeuropa in den letzen Jahrzehnten. Vogelwarte 25: 147–156.
OLSSON, V. 1971. Studies of less familiar birds. 165. Serin. Brit. Birds 64: 213–223.
ROGERS, M.J. 1979. Report on rare birds in 1978. Brit. Birds 72: 503–549.
SPENCER, R. 1988. Rare Breeding Birds in the United Kingdom in 1986. Brit. Birds 81: 417–444.

Twite
Carduelis flavirostris

The Twite is one of very few passerine birds which breeds in Britain and whose population is of international importance. As a breeding bird in Europe it is virtually confined to Britain and western Norway; these populations are completely isolated from the main range of the species in south-west and central Asia. The main conservation action needed is to safeguard the bird's heather moorland breeding habitat in upland areas (and crofting land in coastal parts of north and west Scotland), the saltmarsh wintering areas on the east coast of England and in the Low Countries.

LEGAL STATUS

Protected under WCA 1981; EC Birds Directive; Appendix II of the Berne Convention.

ECOLOGY

The Twite breeds on open heather moorland, in upland areas, but also in coastal areas in the north and on Scottish islands. It often commutes from moorland to areas of pasture or other grassland nearby to feed (Orford, 1973). Birds are semi-colonial and build small groups of nests together. Nest: grass stems with moss and a few twigs, lined mainly with wool, some hair and feathers; nests are built on or near the ground, usually amongst tall heather or sometimes gorse — or, in the north, around crofts, in bushes, stone walls, etc. Eggs: laid from mid-May to mid-July. Clutch: 5–6 (4–7); two broods are not unusual. The young fledge in June–August and, with the adults, form autumn flocks.

Food consists mainly of small seeds and some insects in summer; in winter, on the east coast, the birds specialize on the seeds of saltmarsh plants — notably the marsh samphire (*Salicornia* spp.) and the sea aster (*Aster tripolium*).

DISTRIBUTION AND POPULATION

Palearctic. A strongly disjunct world range: a bird of the steppe and mountain areas of central and south-west Asia, from eastern Turkey and the Caucasus east to western China and Tibet, but with a completely isolated population along the north-west seaboard of Europe, mainly in northern Britain, western Ireland and western Norway.

In Britain the main breeding concentrations are on the north and west of mainland Scotland, Orkney, Shetland, the Hebrides and western Ireland, but with an isolated population in the English southern Pennines. In Norway the bird is found mainly along the western seaboard and on offshore islands; some of the birds occur on high fells north to Dovre, and north along the coast to the North Cape, but they are much scarcer here and are nowhere common inland.

No population figures are available, but density estimates of 25–75 pairs per 10 km^2 would suggest a population of between 19,625 and 58,875 pairs if applied to BTO Breeding Atlas data for occupied areas of 10 km^2 (1968–72) in Britain and Ireland (Davies, 1988). No estimates are available for the Norwegian birds, but the British population is clearly a significant proportion of the European total.

Scottish and Irish birds are probably largely sedentary in winter, though some move to milder coasts, vacating upland sites. Southern Pennine birds migrate to winter on saltmarshes, especially on the Wash and along the coast of Essex and in the Low Countries. Norwegian birds move south into Denmark, Germany, Poland and the Low Countries, but there is no evidence that any of them winter in Britain (Davies, 1988). Scandinavian and British birds are recognized as separate races — *C. f. flavirostris* and *C. f. pipilans*, respectively (Snow, 1971).

THREATS TO SURVIVAL

Threats include loss of habitat, a reduction in the food supply at wintering sites, and trapping.

The loss of heather moorland through afforestation or agricultural reclamation poses a major threat in upland breeding areas, even though some improved grassland areas are used for feeding. Agricultural intensification schemes on the Scottish west coast and islands — especially in crofting areas — could lead to deterioration in the coastal breeding habitat through loss of scrub and weed seeds.

Saltmarsh wintering areas are being threatened by estuarine reclamation projects, tidal barrages, etc., though the pioneer zone of saltmarshes provides preferred feeding areas.

Overgrazing of some saltmarshes probably greatly reduces the potential for seed production and thus threatens the bird's food source.

The Twite is reportedly trapped in large numbers in Belgium for the cage-bird trade; this is likely to involve both British and Norwegian breeding birds.

CONSERVATION

Improved information is needed on population numbers and distribution to identify key areas, both for breeding and wintering.

Protection of mature heather moorland in all upland breeding areas seems vital, as does the protection of winter saltmarsh feeding areas. In view of its international importance, wider recognition of this is required when considering upland and estuarine conservation issues.

Reported trapping of this species for the cage-bird trade in Belgium requires investigation, and the practice should be stopped.

REFERENCES

DAVIES, M. 1988. The importance of Britain's twite. RSPB Conservation Review No 2 (1988): 91–94.
ORFORD, N. 1973. Breeding distribution of the twite in central Britain. Bird Study 20: 51–62, 121–126.
SNOW, D.W. (ed.) 1971. The status of birds in Britain and Ireland. BOU. Oxford: Blackwell.

Consultant: M. Davies

Scottish Crossbill

Loxia scotica

The Scottish Crossbill is included in this book primarily as Britain's only endemic bird; it is now regarded as specifically distinct from other Crossbills. The bird is resident in the central and eastern Highlands (being confined mostly to the Caledonian pine forest). Little is known of the long-term population trends, but marked local fluctuations are known to be connected with food supply; the population was estimated at about 300 pairs in the early 1970s, though this figure is possibly too low.

LEGAL STATUS

Protected under Schedule 1 of WCA 1981; Annex 1 of EC Birds Directive; Appendix II of the Berne Convention.

ECOLOGY

The Scottish Crossbill is entirely restricted to the Caledonian pine forests of the Scottish Highlands. Nest: usually at a height of 8–20 m near the end of a side-branch or at the top of a Scots Pine (*Pinus sylvestris*) — or, less typically, other conifers — but sometimes close to the trunk, in natural pine forest; nests are also built locally in larches and in other predominantly coniferous woodland, but not in dense plantations. The bird is solitary to social. Eggs: laid mainly in March–May, sometimes from mid-February. Clutch: 3–4 (2–5); normally one brood. The young mostly fledge before the end of June.

Food consists very largely of seeds of the Scots Pine, extracted with the tongue after splitting the scales with its specially adapted bill; the seeds of spruce (*Picea* sp.), larch (*Larix* sp.) and rowan (*Sorbus aucloparia*), as well as buds, catkins and insects, are also eaten.

DISTRIBUTION AND POPULATION

West Palearctic. The bird is entirely confined to the central and eastern Scottish Highlands, where it is resident from parts of north Tayside, south Grampian through Badenoch and Strathspey, Highland (Inverness and Nairn) to mainly eastern Ross and Cromarty and south-eastern Sutherland; only sporadic movements have been recorded south to Fife and Dumfries and Galloway. Since it is fairly difficult to separate this bird in the field from the closely related Crossbill (*L. curvirostra*) [with which it was until very recently regarded as conspecific (Voous, 1978)], and because the bird is liable to annual fluctuations and distributional shifts or irruptions due to the availability of local food supplies (Newton, 1972; Nethersole-Thompson, 1975), precise population figures are difficult. Such behaviour may result in the species being common in one particular area one year and almost absent in another.

The population was estimated at 1,500 adults (not pairs) in the early 1970s, but interpretation of the 'Atlas' data of 1968–72 (when breeding of Crossbills was confirmed in over 60 squares in this species' range, and was considered possible or probable in over 40 others) suggests that this number is too low, and that 1,000–1,250 pairs may be nearer the mark.

THREATS TO SURVIVAL

Threats include habitat destruction and a corresponding reduction in the related food-supply.

Human disturbance causes few problems for this high-nesting species, but the distribution is essentially a relict one based on the now-fragmented Caledonian pine forests.

Since the bird does not adapt to dense conifer plantations, its long-term survival is likely to be dependent on the maintenance of sufficient areas of open mature semi-natural Scots Pine.

CONSERVATION

Effective protection of native Caledonian pine forest containing old or mature trees and open spaces, long-term management plans to increase the extent of native pine-forest-type habitat, and the use of buffer zones of commercial Scots Pine rather than exotic·conifers, are very important. Trees over 100 years old which remain in loose clusters after the surrounding forest has been felled may attract nesting pairs. As it is Britain's only endemic bird, further assessments of its numbers would be well worthwhile.

REFERENCES

NETHERSOLE-THOMPSON, D. 1975. Pine Crossbills. Berkhamsted: Poyser.
NEWTON, I. 1972. Finches. London: Collins.
VOOUS, K.H. 1978. The Scottish Crossbill: *Loxia scotica*. Brit. Birds 71: 3–10.

Parrot Crossbill

Loxia pytyopsittacus

The Parrot Crossbill has bred in Britain on at least two occasions: in 1984 and 1985; otherwise the bird occurs as a vagrant in this country. Occurrences in Britain are undoubtedly related to the failure of the pine-cone crop in Scandinavia and northern Europe, and are unlikely to lead to colonization. No special conservation measures are required.

LEGAL STATUS

Protected under Schedule 1 of WCA 1981; EC Birds Directive; Appendix II of the Berne Convention.

ECOLOGY

The Parrot Crossbill is restricted in range to the boreal forests of the north-west Palearctic. Nesting depends upon the size of the cone crop of the scots pine (*Pinus sylvestris*), and nesting populations fluctuate in relation to this (Olsson, 1964). Breeding normally takes place from March to June, with occasional second broods being reared. Breeding is timed to coincide with the opening of pine cones (Dementiev & Gladkov, 1970; Olsson, 1964). Nest: generally built high in a Pine amongst dense needles. Eggs: laid in February and March. Clutch: usually 3–4. The young fledge from late March to June.

Breeding in Britain in 1984 and 1985 followed an influx of birds the previous autumn, and was most probably related to the failure of the pine-crop in northern Scandinavia. In both years the nests were located in mature Corsican Pine (*Pinus nigra*); incubation began in February, and two broods were produced in each year (Davidson, 1985; Seago, 1986).

DISTRIBUTION AND POPULATION

North-west Palearctic. During the breeding season the Parrot-Crossbill is restricted to the boreal forest zone of Norway, Sweden, Finland and the north-west USSR. Outside this period it occurs further south, but only in years of poor pine cone production does it penetrate as far south as western and central Europe.

Population estimates for this bird are not readily available, but the bird is considered to be comparatively common in the north-western part of the Soviet Union (Dementiev & Gladkov, 1970). Occasional breeding takes place outside the normal range following 'irruptions' in response to the failure of the pine cone crop. Such breeding records are unlikely, without a good-sized nucleus population, to lead to the permanent colonization of areas away from the species' current range.

Breeding occurred in Britain in 1984 and 1985 following such an invasion: in Norfolk, a single pair raised two broods in each year. Elsewhere, nests were built but not used, and at another location in East Anglia newly fledged young were seen (Catley & Hursthouse, 1985; Davidson, 1985; Seago, 1986).

THREATS TO SURVIVAL

Threats to colonization in Britain include disturbance by man, and egg collecting.

Parrot Crossbills depend upon the Pine forests of northern Europe for their continued existence, and as long as these forests do not become over-exploited then there are probably no serious threats.

Isolated nesting attempts in Britain may, when discovered, attract the attention of birdwatchers, egg collectors and even aviculturists which may jeopardize the chances of successful breeding.

CONSERVATION

There are probably no conservation measures that could be taken or indeed that are needed to benefit this species in Britain, other than the protection of the occasional nest from excessive disturbance or egg robbery.

REFERENCES

CATLEY, G.P. & HURSTHOUSE, D. 1985. Parrot Crossbills in Britain. Brit. Birds 78: 482–505.

DAVIDSON, C. 1985. Parrot Crossbills: a new breeding species. Norfolk Bird and Mammal Report, 1984.

DEMENTIEV, G.P. & GLADKOV, N.A. 1970. Birds of the Soviet Union. Israel Programme for Scientific Translations, Jerusalem.

OLSSON, V. 1964. Studies of less familiar birds, Parrot Crossbill. Brit. Birds 57: 118–123.

SEAGO, M. (ed.) 1986. Nesting Parrot Crossbills at Wells, Norfolk. Bird and Mammal Report, 1985.

Scarlet Rosefinch
Carpodacus erythrinus

The Scarlet Rosefinch is a rare breeding bird in Britain; after considerable westward extension of its range to Scandinavia and northern Europe in recent years, one pair bred in Scotland in 1982. Subsequently only (single) singing males have occurred, usually in Scotland, though one in Devon in 1984 was seen briefly with a female on one occasion. Otherwise the bird is an annual but very scarce visitor, principally in autumn, to the east and south coasts of Britain.

LEGAL STATUS

Protected under Schedule 1 of WCA 1981; EC Birds Directive; Appendix II of the Berne Convention.

ECOLOGY

The Scarlet Rosefinch breeds in thickets, copses or scrub with tall trees, either in mountainous regions or in forests, lowland swamps, usually near water, sometimes dry oak woods, occasionally open country or (further east) in gardens. Nest: in low cover, often at the base of a tree or bush, and hidden by thick vegetation; it is loosely constructed of grass, roots, plant material and is lined with hair. Eggs: laid (in Scandinavia) at the end of May to late June. Clutch: 5 (4–6); one brood in the north of the range, but occasionally two in the south. The young fledge by late August.

Food consists of buds and the young leaves of birch (*Betula*), wild cherry (*Prunus*), wild apple (*Malus*), lilac (*Syringa*), rowan (*Sorbus*) or sallow (*Salix*), together with the seeds of grasses, dandelions, etc., berries and various insects.

DISTRIBUTION AND POPULATION

Palearctic. The Scarlet Rosefinch breeds locally in southern Scandinavia, continuously from southern Finland and East Germany eastwards across the northern USSR to northern Mongolia, northern China and Kamchatka; in the south, in the mountains of eastern Turkey eastwards through the Hindu Kush, the Himalayas and western China. The bird winters south of the breeding range around the Persian Gulf eastwards through India, northern Burma and Thailand to southern China and northern Vietnam. It arrives in late spring in Europe (late May) and usually departs early (late August) (Newton, 1972). Since about 1900 the bird has spread westwards in two stages, predominantly since 1930 (Newton, 1972); it now breeds in suitable habitat in scattered localities in Poland, East

Germany, West Germany (since 1985), Finland, Denmark (since 1981), southern Sweden, southern Norway (first bred in 1971), Czechoslovakia (1973), Austria (1977), Yugoslavia (1977), Switzerland (1983), Belgium and France, and is still consolidating its numbers and continuing to expand its range (Sharrock & Hilden, 1983).

Against this background it is perhaps not surprising that one pair bred in Scotland in 1982, and since then others have either attempted to breed (apparently unsuccessfully) or else single males have held territory (Mullins, 1984; RBBP reports). In 1983 a male held territory at the previous year's breeding site (and another at a second site); single males have held territory in Scotland every year from 1984 to 1988. In 1986 a second singing male was present in western Scotland and elsewhere there were two other singing males during the summer months in Scotland and one for a few days in June in England. In 1987 there were males singing briefly at two localities in Scotland in early June and in 1988 a lone male sang for two days before disappearing. In England, a male sang at a locality in Devon from early June to mid-July 1986 and was seen briefly with a female on one occasion, but there was no further proof of breeding.

The bird otherwise occurs annually (mostly immature in the autumn) in the British Isles, chiefly on the east coast of England (also on Fair Isle), and occasionally on the south and south-west coasts; it also occurs in spring, but much less frequently.

THREATS TO SURVIVAL

Threats include climatic changes and disturbance.

As with all incipient colonizing species, certain conditions have to be right to permit or stimulate colonization. The presence of preferred habitat and food may encourage passage birds to linger, but unless there is a return to warm or hot early summers, as there was in the early 1980s, it is unlikely that the present run of wet or damp summers in the highlands will induce males to sing or pairs to remain on potential territory.

Human and other predatory disturbance at potential nest sites should be kept to a minimum, and the location of any sites being prospected should not be widely disclosed.

CONSERVATION

The species is monitored by the RBBP. Most of the factors affecting the success of the anticipated colonization of Britain (or more particularly, Scotland) are beyond human control, but if pairs begin to show interest in a location, the control of visitors and the reduction of disturbance to a minimum will help towards the success of the attempt.

REFERENCES

MULLINS, J.R. 1984. Scarlet Rosefinch breeding in Scotland. Brit. Birds 77: 133–135.
NEWTON, I. 1972. Finches. New Naturalist Series. London: Collins.
SHARROCK, J.T.R. & HILDEN, O. 1983. Survey of Europe's Breeding Birds. Brit. Birds 76: 118–123.

Lapland Bunting
Calcarius lapponicus

The Lapland Bunting is a rare sporadic breeder in very small numbers. It was recorded summering in Scotland between 1974 and 1981 — with breeding recorded in four years, but none subsequently. In view of the remoteness of the locations, and the apparent abundance of habitat, the only conservation action needed is to safeguard any birds located from human disturbance, ideally by keeping them secret.

LEGAL STATUS

Protected under Schedule 1 of WCA 1981; EC Birds Directive; Appendix II of the Berne Convention.

ECOLOGY

The Lapland Bunting breeds in arctic and subarctic areas above the tree-line, inhabiting well-vegetated tundra, marshes, swampy areas, heath and even low scrub of dwarf birch and arctic willow — but avoiding barren areas. The bird is solitary or social. In Britain, it has been recorded in high montane areas, with one site described as 'hummocky frost bumps with short grass and heather between melting snowfields' (Cumming, 1979). Nest: a deep cup of grasses and moss, lined with feathers, on the ground or inside a hummock, often hidden by vegetation. Eggs: laid (in Scandinavian nests) between late May and July. Clutch: 5–6 (2–7); probably only one brood. The young fledge in July–August. Young often leave the nest with their wing feathers still in pin at around nine days old, whilst still flightless.

Food in the breeding season consists of insects, notably crane-flies (*Tipulidae*) and also some seeds.

DISTRIBUTION AND POPULATION

Northern Holarctic. The breeding range of this bird extends from the mountains of Norway, northern Sweden, Finland and northern Russia, east through Siberia to Kamchatka, the Bering Sea Islands, Alaska, northern Canada, east to Labrador and the western and southern parts of Greenland; it is absent from Spitsbergen and Iceland. No population estimates are available.

In the western Palearctic the bird winters around the shores of the southern North Sea (coasts of the low countries), and from eastern Hungary and southern Russia into central Asia.

It is a scarce or local winter visitor to Britain in highly variable numbers; in a good year the Lapland Bunting sometimes occurs in small flocks of 50–100 birds, occasionally more, mainly on the English east coast from Northumberland to Kent. The bird is a regular—if uncommon—passage-migrant in autumn (from late August to early November), largely in coastal areas of north-west, east and south Britain, but is a rare and irregular passage-migrant in spring (from mid-April to mid-May). The bird was unknown in summer in Britain until a male in breeding plumage was seen in Scotland in June 1974; subsequently there was a total of 16 instances of proved breeding during 1977–80 (11 pairs in 1979), with a further 21 instances of possible breeding at up to six Scottish sites annually. In 1981, only one bird was located, and since then none have been seen. It is tempting to suggest that this was another example of colonization in Scotland by Scandinavian populations, but the preponderance of autumn records came from the northern and north-western islands of Scotland, and from north-west Ireland, and it seems likely that these migrants originate largely from Greenland (Williamson & Davis, 1956). However, wintering birds on the Wash saltmarshes have wing-lengths significantly shorter than birds from the Greenland population, but show no significant difference from Norwegian birds, suggesting a Scandinavian origin (Davies, 1987). The Scandinavian breeding population is of the nominate race, *C. l. lapponicus*; they are not only shorter-winged than the Greenland birds but they have smaller, less robust bills, and in summer their plumage has broader buffish fringes to the feathers on the upper parts—giving the mantle a paler impression. The darker, larger Greenland birds have been recognized in the past as a separate race, *C. l. subcalcaratus*, but without biometrics it is doubtful whether the plumage differences could be confidently determined in the field for Scottish breeding birds (Williamson & Davies, 1956).

THREATS TO SURVIVAL

Threats to colonization in Britain include disturbance by man or egg collecting.
There seems likely to be plenty of suitble habitat and food in the Scottish Highlands and, if the species is indeed in the throes of establishing itself there, disturbance by birdwatchers and egg-collecting are probably the only dangers.

CONSERVATION

To avoid the risk of disturbance, areas where the species are seen in summer should not be publicized, even as counties.

REFERENCES

Cumming, I.G. 1979. Lapland Buntings breeding in Scotland. Brit. Birds 72: 53–59.
Davies, M. 1987. Twite and other wintering passerines on the Wash saltmarshes. NCC Focus on Nature Conservation Series: The Wash (Proceedings of the Wash Conference, Horncastle, Lincolnshire—April 1987): 123–132.
Williamson, K. & Davis, P. 1956. The autumn 1954 invasion of Lapland Buntings and its source. Brit. Birds 49: 6–25.

Consultant: M. Davies

Snow Bunting

Plectrophenax nivalis

The Snow Bunting is a rare breeding bird in the Scottish mountains; it has nested in very small numbers since the late 19th century. In recent decades numbers have risen to 10–30 pairs from a low of 1–6 pairs in the 1940s and 1950s. The bird is also a regular winter visitor to the British Isles; the current estimate of 10,000–15,000 birds is lower than in previous decades.

LEGAL STATUS

Protected under Schedule 1 of WCA 1981; EC Birds Directive; Appendix II of the Berne Convention.

ECOLOGY

The breeding areas of this bird are on the highest mountains of Scotland—those mainly above 900 m—and usually near late snow fields. Nest: a cup of grass and moss lined with feathers, well hidden in a hole or under rocks or scree boulders. Pairs can be solitary or in small groups. Eggs: laid between late May and the end of July. Clutch: 4–6 (2–6); often two broods. The young fledge in July–August.

Food in the breeding season consists largely of insects together with seeds and buds.

DISTRIBUTION AND POPULATION

North Holarctic. The Snow Bunting breeds in Iceland, Fenno-Scandia and arctic USSR, locally in Scotland and the Faeroes; it winters in southern to central Europe, Asia and the northern United States, but mainly on the coasts in western Europe—although flocks are often seen in the Scottish mountains in winter.

The bird was first recorded breeding in Scotland in 1886, and then more or less regularly to 1913; breeding was then sporadic to the 1940s and has probably been regular again since 1945—but always in very small and fluctuating numbers (Nethersole-Thompson, 1966). Otherwise the bird is a passage-migrant and a winter visitor between mid-September and mid-April (or even May) chiefly in the northern half of Britain.

The first breeding record was in Sutherland, but the main areas have been in the Cairngorms and the Ben Nevis range as well as in northern Inverness-shire, Ross-shire and Perthshire, with an isolated nesting record in 1901 on St Kilda.

Since the 1960s, numbers have in general been higher, with breeding proved in six counties and possibly in three to five others (Thom, 1986). Breeding is often difficult to confirm, and there are numbers of unmated males; numbers have ranged from 6–20 pairs and may have even reached 30 pairs in the best recent years.

THREATS TO SURVIVAL

Threats include climatic factors and disturbance by man.

Breeding numbers are probably most dependent on long-term climatic trends, with local adverse weather, small population size and human disturbance being other factors.

The years of regular breeding can be correlated with colder periods of climatic deterioration and with the years following severe winters in Iceland and Scandinavia.

With the increasing invasion of the Scottish mountains by hill-walkers and tourists there may be some risk of disturbance to nest sites and breeding success. Over zealous bird-watchers and egg-collectors are additional hazards.

CONSERVATION

The exact nesting localities should continue not to be publicized. The best nesting areas should be safeguarded from tourist developments and from proposals for new ski-lifts which encourage easy access.

REFERENCES

NETHERSOLE-THOMPSON, D. 1966. The Snow Bunting. Edinburgh and London: Oliver & Boyd.
THOM, V.M. 1986. Birds in Scotland. Calton: Poyser.

Cirl Bunting

Emberiza cirlus

The Cirl Bunting is a rare breeding bird in south-west Britain. It is a vulnerable and declining resident with a continuing retraction in the range it now occupies. It is confined to Devon and some isolated sites in Cornwall and Somerset, but there have been occasional breeding records from other southern counties in the recent past. Prior to 1957 it was more widespread and abundant, but has shown only a limited recovery following the severe winter of 1962/63. Away from the Devon stronghold there has been a marked reduction in range. In 1982 the British population was estimated at 167 pairs, by 1989 this figure had dropped to 118 pairs. Research begun by the RSPB in 1988 includes an investigation into the bird's habitat requirements.

LEGAL STATUS

Protected under Schedule 1 of the WCA 1981; EC Birds Directive; Appendix II of the Berne Convention.

ECOLOGY

Breeding territories are found within coastal scrub adjacent to arable land or on agricultural land with hedgerows. Territories are often on hillsides with scrub and bushes and on the sheltered aspects of hills and river valleys. A diversity of land use to include arable, pasture, horticulture and hedgerows appears to be important within a territory (Sitters, 1988). A typical nest would be well hidden in the lower part of a dense hedge, sitting atop an earth bank, but nests can also occur in isolated bushes. The nest is a deep cup built of grass and lined with fine grasses and occasionally moss. Eggs: end April–May to August. Clutch: 3–4 (2–5). Two to four young usually raised but often only two young raised. Second broods common while third broods are likely.

Food: cereal grains and seeds of weeds and grasses as well as insects, including Orthoptera. The young are fed almost exclusively on insects. In winter usually recorded singly or in discrete flocks often in proximity to larger mixed flocks of finches and buntings. The availability of cereal stubble, especially when containing arable weeds, is very important in winter. Flocks disperse in February and March.

DISTRIBUTION AND POPULATION

South-west Palearctic. Restricted to the Mediterranean and temperate climatic zones (Voous, 1960). North of the Mediterranean it is found throughout the Iberian peninsula and then eastwards to northern Turkey. Restricted in North Africa to northern Morocco and Tunisia, vagrant east to Egypt and south-west Iran. Birds in Britain are at the northern edge of the range.

Generally found below 100 m in Britain and not above 1,200 m in France. Principally a sedentary bird, its winter range is the same as the breeding range, but occasional records suggests some migration or dispersal.

In Britain currently restricted to south Devon, with several pairs in the adjacent counties. Formerly more widespread; prior to 1938 widely distributed in north Wales, the Malverns and throughout southern England south of a line from Gloucestershire to the Thames. Between 1968–70 county bird reports estimated at least 300 pairs. During the 1970s the population contracted leaving isolated pairs throughout its former range. In 1982 167 pairs were recorded with 136 in Devon. A further 14 pairs were located on Jersey. In 1989 a repeat survey found 118 pairs of which all but 4 were in south Devon.

Since 1982 the species has ceased to breed in Avon, Dorset and Buckingham-shire (Sitters, 1985). The Devon population is considered to have declined slowly between 1974–82 and since that data a continuing decline was established by the 1989 survey.

Within Europe declines in the population and range have been noted in

Belgium, France and Luxembourg. Limited expansion was considered to have occurred in Rumania and Switzerland, although in the latter the bird is known to be vulnerable to periodic extreme fluctuations in numbers (Appert, 1970; Talpaneanu and Paspaleva, 1979). Very few details on the European population are available apart from Luxembourg where there were 700 pairs in 1920–25 but none in 1942; the West German population in 1980 was estimated to be about 100–120 pairs and placed on the red list as 'threatened by extinction' (Federschmidt, 1988).

In France, although considered to be numerous in 1976 (Yeatman, 1976), a decline has been noted, especially in northern France.

THREATS TO SURVIVAL

Loss of habitat through scrub and hedge clearance and agricultural changes influencing the availability of seed and insect food could all be considered to have contributed to the decline. In winter the present research has found a strong correlation between the birds' distribution and weedy cereal stubble. The birds feed close to hedgerows on cereal grains, especially barley and other arable weed seeds. The retention of such stubbles throughout the winter is now an uncommon farming practice. Changes in the feeding of stock, including horses, may have reduced the amount of arable weed seed available in crops and this species may well be vulnerable to the use of agricultural chemicals as a seed dressing.

During the nesting season the availability of insect food for the young has been affected by changes in agriculture.

The threat posed by egg collectors is not seen as a major problem, however there may be an effect on small local populations.

No clear implications of the effect of climatic change on Cirl Buntings exist. Records from Dorset in the mid-1940s show that at that time the resident population appeared to survive severe winters and food was available in stock yards, barns and as feed for horses. However, the severe winter of 1962/63 had a dramatic effect on the population, reducing it to a very low level. Changes in farming in the late-1950s and early-1960s had removed many of the supplementary feeding sites formerly available in winter in the countryside (Ash, 1964).

With the population now at such low numbers local alternative feeding during winter may be playing an important role in protecting this species. The small number of sites providing weedy stubble increases this species' vulnerability.

Current developments and road building within the area of the core population continue to fragment and destroy suitable habitat. This is likely to cause further decreases in the population.

CONSERVATION

A few pairs enjoy protection within coastal SSSIs but the majority receive little habitat protection. The southern coastal area of Devon should be considered as an area suitable for ESA status.

Rotational annual fallow entered into 'Set Aside' has provided winter feeding sites.

Current research will identify what changes in land management are required to help Cirl Buntings. Supplementary winter feeding may, during harsh conditions, help individual birds survive and so support local populations. Liaison with farmers and landowners, currently operated by RSPB, aims to alert landowners to the presence of birds. This, together with local authorities recognizing the need to protect the species, should prevent the unnecessary destruction of nesting habitat.

A move towards revitalizing a mixed farming system, involving reinstatement of hedgerows, the reduction in the use of chemicals and the retention of stubble in close proximity to stock would benefit the species.

REFERENCES

APPERT, J. 1970. Breeding of the cirl bunting in the Canton of March, Switzerland. Orn. Beobab. 67 (2): 58–59.

ASH, J.S. 1964. Observations in Hampshire and Dorset during the 1963 cold spell. Brit. Birds 57: 229.

SITTERS, H.P. 1985. Cirl buntings in Britain in 1982. Bird Study 32: 1–10.

SITTERS, H.P. 1988. Tetrad Atlas of the Breeding Birds of Devon. Devon Bird Watching and Preservation Society.

TALPANEANU, M. & PASPALEVA, M. 1979. Recent expansion of some species of birds in Rumania. Trans. Mus. Nat. His. Grigore Antipa 20, 1 (0): 441–450.

VOOUS, K.H. 1960. Atlas of European birds. London and Amsterdam: Nelson.

YEATMAN, L. 1976. Atlas des oiseaux nicheurs de France. Paris: Ministère de la qualité et vie Environment.

Consultant: J. Waldon

Bird Habitats in Britain

Britain comprises a mosaic of habitat types, some of which provide the feeding and breeding requirements of our Red Data species. In this chapter the main habitats, the threats to them and their important birds are described pictorially and by way of expanded captions. For a more complete treatment of this subject see Fuller (1982).

The montane areas of Britain above 611 m cover 560,000 ha, whilst those above 915 m cover just 40,200 ha, over 90% being in Scotland (Ball *et al.*, 1983). Past and future predicted degradation—largely through overgrazing, built development and recreation—is localized. This is fortunate as they are important breeding areas for nine of the Red Data species: Golden Eagle, Peregrine, Merlin, Dotterel, Golden Plover, Purple Sandpiper, Shore Lark, Snow Bunting and Lapland Bunting.

Upland heaths and grasslands include the traditional heather-dominated grouse moors, usually above 300 m, and the maritime heaths of northern Scotland, Orkney and Shetland. Together they form the largest extent of semi-natural habitat still remaining in Britain with over 1,700,000 ha (Usher, 1988) and are prime habitat for Red Grouse, Golden Plover and wide-ranging species such as Hen Harrier and Merlin. This habitat faces threats of fragmentation with vast areas now being afforested with non-native conifers, widespread overgrazing by deer or sheep and agricultural improvements in previously untouched areas.

Upland mires are survivors of our prehistoric landscape and include blanket and valley bogs, raised mires, peatlands and the wet hummocks and pools of the 'Flow' Country. Red-throated Divers, Greenshank, Red-necked Phalaropes, Golden Plover and Wood Sandpipers breed. Present estimates suggest that about one and a half million hectares of Britain are covered by bogs and mires (Usher, 1988) but this is decreasing as large areas are planted with forest.

Broad-leaved and mixed woods provide a major habitat for the common species that make up the majority of Britain's bird life. In the upland and northern areas broad-leaved and mixed woodlands provide breeding sites for Red Kite, Goshawk and Black Grouse as well as Fieldfare, Redwing and Brambling. More generally, and in the lowlands, such woods are important for Honey Buzzard, Barn Owl and Firecrest. Older mature woods provide the most important nesting habitats for large birds of prey. Lowland broad-leaved woods are not under threat, though such woods in the uplands do suffer from overgrazing.

Native pine woods are vital for three Red Data species, all of which occur in Scotland—Capercaillie, Scottish Crossbill (Britain's only endemic bird) and Crested Tit. Past losses of this habitat—which now covers only 12,500 ha in 25 principal sites—have been severe (Bain, 1987), clearance of the forest—often followed by commercial replanting—being the main threat. This may now have been alleviated by changes to the Native Pine Wood Grant Scheme which strengthens its conservation impact. The main threat to existing native pine woods is overgrazing by deer.

Lowland heath supports three Red Data species—Dartford Warbler, Woodlark and Nightjar. It is one of Britain's most threatened habitats with 78% lost between 1830 and 1980 in the six main heathland areas in England (NCC, 1984). This was largely through agricultural improvement, built development, recreational pressure, abandonment of management, afforestation and fire. Approximately 60,000 ha remained in 1980, representing 18% of the European total (Farrell, 1989).

Swamp, fen and carr mainly comprises reed beds of which those over 2 ha in size aggregate to only 2,300 ha in Britain. Associated areas of open water, swampy ground, beds of marsh-loving vegetation and willow scrub are important aspects of this habitat mosaic. It suffers mostly from pollution of ground and surface waters, with other lesser threats being changes to the hydrological regime, natural plant succession and recreational pressure.

It is a very important habitat group for several Red Data species: Bittern, Pintail, Garganey, Pochard, Marsh Harrier, Wood Sandpiper, Spotted Crake, Cetti's and Savi's Warbler and Bearded Tit. It is also used by occasional breeders such as Little Bittern, Black Tern and Bluethroat. In winter, swamp, fen and carr provide part of the feeding and roosting area for several species of wildfowl—notably Bean Goose, Whooper Swans, Shoveler, Teal, Gadwall and Pochard—as well as an important hunting area for Hen Harriers.

Wet lowland grasslands are one of Britain's most threatened habitats, with less than 45,000 ha remaining. The major threats are agricultural improvement brought about through drainage, and changes to hydrological regimes which bring unpredictable flooding. In the breeding season wet lowland grasslands are important for a range of Red Data species: Pintail, Garganey, Pochard, Spotted Crake, Ruff, Black-tailed Godwit, Curlew, Barn Owl, Montagu's and Marsh Harrier. For the last three it is mainly a feeding area. In winter it is important for Bewick's and Whooper Swan, White-fronted, Bean and Brent Geese, Shoveler, Pintail, Teal, Wigeon, Gadwall, Pochard, Shelduck, Black-tailed Godwit, Golden Plover, Redshank and Hen Harrier.

It is easy to forget that the sea is an important habitat for birds, providing food for Britain's breeding sea birds. We have an international responsibility for many species such as Gannet, Manx Shearwater, Storm Petrel, Leach's Petrel, Guillemot, Razorbill, Roseate Tern, Arctic Tern, Little Tern, Sandwich Tern and Great Skua. Breeding Black-throated Divers and particularly Red-throated Divers also feed at sea, as do Osprey and White-tailed Eagles. The waters around our coasts are also important feeding grounds in winter for all three species of diver, Common and Velvet Scoter, Long-tailed Duck and Scaup and provide roosting sites for Brent Geese, Shelduck, Teal and Wigeon.

Sea cliffs, rocks and islets provide breeding grounds for several species of sea bird for which Britain has an international responsibility. The main species are Gannet, Manx Shearwater, Storm Petrel, Leach's Petrel, Guillemot, Razorbill, Great Skua, Arctic, Sandwich and Roseate Tern. They also provide nesting sites for Golden Eagle, Peregrine, Chough and reintroduced White-tailed Eagle. Threats to sea cliffs and rocks are minor and localized.

Intertidal flats. There are just under 236,000 ha of this habitat in Britain (NCC, 1989). The major threats come from land claim, coastal developments and recreational disturbance. Additional but local problems include bait digging, *Spartina* colonization and chemical pollution. Since 1945 less than 10% of the area of this habitat has been lost, but with the present scale of threats losses in the next 25 years could be worse. This habitat is important primarily for wintering and passage birds which use it for feeding and roosting. Particularly dependent are Brent Geese, Shelduck, Pintail, Oystercatcher, Ringed Plover, Grey Plover, Black-tailed Godwit, Curlew, Redshank, Knot, Dunlin and Sanderling, whilst Grey Geese and Whooper Swan may use the habitat for roosting.

There are approximately 38,000 ha of salt marsh in Britain (NCC, 1989). Salt marshes are threatened mainly by coastal development and land claims. More locally, agricultural improvements and recreational activities may cause problems for the birds using this habitat. Salt marshes are threatened in the future along with intertidal flats. They provide roosts for many of the species which feed on the intertidal flats. They also provide feeding areas, notably for Barnacle Geese and Twite.

Beaches, be they sand or shingle, are the main breeding habitat of the Little Tern and of the Kentish Plover—which is one of the very few regular breeding birds to have been lost from Britain. Other important birds include nesting Arctic Tern and roosting waders such as Oystercatcher. Sand and shingle areas are locally threatened by built development and by mineral winning, but the main hazard to the birds comes from recreational disturbance.

The fast-declining Corncrake is now mainly a bird of the cultivated machair of the Inner and Outer Hebrides in Scotland. This habitat is also notable for its concentrations of breeding waders, such as Dunlin, Lapwing and Ringed Plover. The richness of traditionally farmed machair is at risk from agricultural change involving either intensification or abandonment.

Brackish lagoons, which may be natural or man-made, are the major breeding habitat of the Avocet. A variety of terns, waders and wildfowl may occur in summer or winter, though barely in nationally important numbers since the habitat is rare in Britain. The total area of natural sites is about 3,300 ha but the largest, Poole Harbour, makes up 2,500 ha of this. Artificial sites total some 100 ha and include some very rich creations such as the famous Scrape at Minsmere. Threats to the larger sites come from development and recreation. The management of artificial sites demands constant attention to water levels, salinity and nutrient status.

Oligotrophic waters tend to be located in northern Britain. Although the densities of breeding birds are generally low, they support almost the entire populations of Black-throated Diver, Common Scoter, Osprey and Goldeneye. In the winter such lakes are important for Pink-footed Goose, Greylag Goose, Pochard, Whooper Swan, Teal and Wigeon—and particularly Greenland White-fronted Goose. The major threats to oligotrophic waters come from eutrophication due to agricultural run-off, acidification and changes to hydrological regimes.

Eutrophic waters are generally absent from the far north and west but widely distributed throughout the remainder of Britain. Although densities of breeding birds may be high, such lakes are important for only two Red Data species: Black-necked Grebe and Pochard. Threats include changes to hydrological regimes, chemical pollution, eutrophication and recreation.

Rivers and streams and their environs provide an important habitat for a range of breeding birds, but only for small numbers of five Red Data species: Temmink's Stint, Marsh Warbler, Goldeneye, Osprey and Cetti's Warbler. There are no significant populations of Red Data Book species represented in the riverine habitat during the winter. The major threat is still pollution but changes to hydrological regimes, recreation and acidification are also important.

Extraction pits and reservoirs account for an increasing proportion of standing water in Britain covering approximately 27,300 ha (Owen *et al.*, 1986). Breeding Red Data species include Red-necked Grebe, Mediterranean Gull, Black-necked Grebe, Pochard, Osprey and Sandwich Tern. Larger numbers of wintering wildfowl are supported by this artificial habitat, including eight Red Data species: Gadwall, Pochard, Teal, Greylag Goose, Wigeon, Pintail, Bewick's Swan and Shoveler. The main threat to this habitat is recreation.

Plantations are increasingly abundant. They account for over 2,112,000 ha in Britain, of which about 75% is conifer (Forestry Commission, 1988). The majority of conifer plantations are of non-native species and are located in Scotland, whilst the majority of the broad-leaved plantations are of native species and are found in England. Red Data species supported by plantations are Goshawk, Firecrest, Crested Tit and—when clear-felled, or in the early stages of growth—Nightjar, Woodlark and Hen Harrier. Black Grouse will nest in plantations as well as Goldeneye (where nest boxes are provided) and Osprey (when older trees are present). A recent development has been Merlin nesting in conifer plantations. In eastern England, Golden Orioles have colonized poplar plantations.

Arable land is the most abundant habitat in Britain, with nearly $4\frac{1}{2}$ million ha (MAFF, 1988). The main threats to birds are intensification, which can lead to hedgerow and woodland removal, drainage, changes in cropping regimes and pesticide usage. The proportionally small losses in this ecosystem which have occurred—and may occur in the future—do not pose as great a threat as changes in farming practices. These reduce the suitable habitat for breeding birds such as Grey Partridges, Stone Curlew, Cirl Bunting, Barn Owl, Montagu's Harrier and Marsh Harrier. Wintering Red Data birds include several geese as well as Golden Plover, Teal and Hen Harrier.

Downland. There were only 9,418 ha of this habitat left when a census was last taken (NCC, 1984). The main threat concerns changes in agricultural practice which result in reduced grazing or harvesting. Over 40% of this habitat has been lost since 1945, and the future outlook is not good with predicted losses of a further 40% in the next 25 years. The Red Data birds at risk are Stone Curlew in the summer and Hen Harrier in the winter.

Improved pastures and leys, with just over 1,750,000 ha, account for about 28% of the agricultural land in Britain (MAFF, 1988). Locally they may be threatened by afforestation, chemical pollution and urbanization, but these together are likely to lead to only relatively small losses in the future. The use of chemicals however may be more serious. Grasslands are important for breeding Grey Partridge, Corn-crake, Barn Owl and Cirl Bunting and are also used by Red Kite, Montagu's Harrier, Marsh Harrier, Whimbrel, Chough and Redwing for feeding. In the winter they provide feeding grounds for a host of species, including various geese, wild swans, Golden Plover and Hen Harrier.

Built-up areas are not threatened. The only Red Data species to have benefited from them is the Black Redstart.

REFERENCES

Bain, C. 1987. Native Pinewoods in Scotland. RSPB, unpublished.

Ball, D.F., Radford, G.J. & Williams, W.M. 1983. A Land Characteristic for Great Britain. Bangor ITE, occasional paper No. 13.

Farrell, L. 1989. The Different Types and Importance of British Heaths. Bot. J. Linn. Soc. 101: 291–299.

Forestry Commission. 1988. Report for 1987–1988.

Fuller, R.J. 1982. Bird Habitats in Britain. Calton: Poyser.

Maff. 1988. Agriculture in the United Kingdom 1988. London: HMSO.

Ncc. 1984. Nature Conservation in Great Britain. London: NCC.

Ncc. 1989. Extracts from Coastal Resources Database. London: NCC.

Owen, M., Atkinson-Willes, G. & Salmon, D. 1986. Wildfowl in Great Britain. Cambridge: Cambridge University Press.

Usher, M.B. 1988. Ecological Change in the Uplands. Oxford: Blackwell.

Threats to Bird Survival in Britain

This chapter considers the current threats to the British avifauna. Many factors combine to influence the status, distribution and population trends of a species, and, in this account, adverse factors are treated as threats and have been grouped under four main headings: land use changes (which cause most change or loss of habitat); pollution; the direct effects of other human activities; and 'natural' factors. It is clearly vital that threats are not only identified and understood, but are also graded in terms of their seriousness. Conservation efforts should be directed towards removing the major—or limiting—threat first. Unfortunately, it is not always possible to identify the limiting factor with certainty and indeed it may vary over a species range. In many cases, further research is essential before the nature of these threats can be fully understood and before effective conservation measures can be implemented.

Adverse factors, or threats, are often habitat-related. It is therefore important to realize that the extent and nature of habitats in 20th century Britain have been largely determined by the hand of man. It is instructive to reflect that if one were considering threats to birds in, say, the 17th century, there would probably be an outcry deploring the loss of breeding common cranes and spoonbills through the drainage of the Fens, or grave concern about the anticipated loss of great bustards from southern England due to the destruction of open grassy plains as well as persecution by man (Reid-Henry & Harrison, 1988).

It is also important to remember that, in some circumstances, changes to the vegetation and landscape of Britain may have positive as well as negative effects since a threat to one species might well be a benefit to another. For example, the draining of a marsh for conversion to arable land clearly threatens breeding Snipe and Redshank, but it is likely to provide more habitat for Skylarks. In this example, one's attitude to the event would be shaped by the knowledge that Redshank and Snipe are declining as freshwater wetlands disappear, while Skylarks are widespread and extremely common. More often, the changes are wholly detrimental because they involve the loss of scarce natural habitats and those semi-natural habitats developed by long-established interactions. They also tend to be rapid and widespread, unlike the more gradual changes of previous centuries. The usual result is the loss of scarce or specialized bird species.

This chapter is concerned primarily with threats to the Red Data birds identified in this book, but certain other species whose status must be kept under careful review are also mentioned. It is a depressing thought that, if present trends continue, all the 30 species listed in the Appendix (p. 345) might become eligible for a future Red Data inventory.

CATEGORIES OF THREAT

LAND-USE CHANGES

Agricultural intensification
Agricultural abandonment
Afforestation
Felling or destruction of woodland
Loss of habitats to buildings or roads
Changes in hydrological regimes
Land claim and coastal development
Lack or abandonment of traditional forms of land management

Fifty-one Red Data species are threatened by land-use changes.

POLLUTION

Oil pollution
Other chemical pollution
Acidification

Fifteen Red Data species are threatened by pollution.

KILLING OR DISTURBANCE BY MAN

Hunting
Legal (licensed) killing
Illegal persecution
Accidental killing
Recreational pressure and disturbance

Forty-seven Red Data species are threatened by killing or disturbance by man.

'NATURAL' THREATS

The term 'natural' is used rather loosely, as some of these threats may be a result of man's activities.

Climatic change
Inter-specific competition
Natural ecological change
Predation or disease

Thirty-six Red Data species are threatened by 'natural' threats.

SPECIES CATEGORY: NOT THREATENED OR RARE

Nineteen Red Data species were considered to be exposed to no identifiable threat. For a further 28 species the only 'threat' is their extreme rarity. Fourteen of these are only irregular breeders; little can be done to secure their future in Britain — chance or events elsewhere largely control their fate. Note that the totals above include some species twice because they occur in more than one category.

DEGREE OF THREAT

The various categories of threat described above were rated according to three degrees of severity, for each of the 117 species dealt with in this book. Severe, moderate and minimal threats were defined as follows, though of course a species facing two categories of threat may be severely threatened by one but only minimally threatened by the other.

SEVERE THREAT

Where extinction as a British breeding or wintering population, or a considerable reduction in range or a sustained reduction in numbers (more than 20% in 25 years) is likely to occur if the threat continues at the present level.

MODERATE THREAT

Where local contractions in range or small sustained reductions in total numbers (between 10% and 20% in 25 years) are likely to occur if the threat continues at the present level.

MINIMAL THREAT

Any factor less severe than a moderate threat but where an extension in range or an increase in numbers is likely to occur if the threat is removed.

Analysis of all the known and suspected threats revealed a great deal of uncertainty about the importance or extent of each, and of necessity this chapter can give only a broad overview. This compilation has drawn attention to the need for more research to clarify whether perceived threats are real or not. Until we understand the relative importance of specific threats to particular species, we are unlikely to be able to devise effective measures for their conservation. Even then we may be able to do very little in cases where we are at the extreme edge of a species range and the factor affecting or threatening the population lies outside Britain.

The figure opposite shows the the number of Red Data species under the various threats and the percentage of those species severely, moderately and minimally threatened.

THE THREATS IN DETAIL

Details of the threats to each species are given in the individual texts. Here we confine ourselves to broader aspects, but with examples where appropriate, including reference to future potential candidate species which are not covered by individual texts.

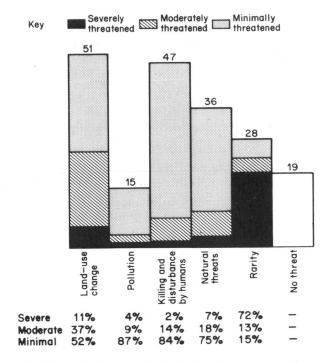

	Severe	Moderate	Minimal
Land-use change	11%	37%	52%
Pollution	4%	9%	87%
Killing and disturbance by humans	2%	14%	84%
Natural threats	7%	18%	75%
Rarity	72%	13%	15%
No threat	—	—	—

Numbers of Red Data Book species affected by the major categories of threat discussed in this chapter, and the percentage of those species severely, moderately and minimally threatened

LAND-USE CHANGE

• *Agricultural intensification*

There are changes in management which enhance agricultural production, leaving aside the use of chemicals (eg, pesticides or herbicides) which are considered separately. Agricultural intensification includes drainage and the conversion of natural or semi-natural habitats to arable or pasture, re-seeding, increase in grazing intensity, hedgerow and woodland removal or mis-management, and the destruction of other habitats, notably heathland and wetlands, to make more agricultural land.

The Red Data species for which these changes pose a severe threat (but not necessarily the only or limiting one) include Grey Partridge (hedgerow removal); Corncrake (changes in crofting practice); Stone Curlew (change from heath to unsuitable arable land); Barn Owl (agricultural intensification); Cirl Bunting (hedge removal and loss of stack yards). Species affected to a lesser extent are Merlin (loss of heather moorland); Red Grouse (loss of heather moorland); and Red-necked Phalarope (drainage). In addition, land-use changes pose a lesser threat to a further 11 species.

Looking to the future, Snipe, Lapwing and Yellow Wagtail might well be candidates for the Red Data listing if further drainage of marshland and wet pasture takes place. Linnet, Tree Sparrow and Corn Bunting may be included also because of the reduction of weed seeds, spilt grain and breeding sites. If agricultural set-aside policies are effective, the threats to such species may however be removed.

Wigeon and most species of geese have benefited from recent agricultural changes, particularly the increase in cereal growing which now provides a widespread and abundant winter food supply for them. In the 1970s, when there was widespread conversion of grazing marsh to arable land, the increasing population of Brent Geese extended their feeding habitat from salt marshes to coastal fields where they now graze the developing shoots of grass and cereals.

Agricultural abandonment

These are changes in agricultural practice which result in reduced grazing or harvesting leading to vegetational change. The effects of such changes are relatively local but represent threats to four species, namely Corncrake (abandonment of haymaking on crofting land), Stone Curlew, Bean Goose and Chough. The last three species are all affected by the reduction or abandonment of grazing.

Afforestation

This includes the wide-scale planting of mainly non-native conifers, such as sitka spruce, and their management as a commercial crop. This usually results in a blanket cover of even-aged trees, mostly in the uplands, and effectively removes feeding and breeding areas for a number of species which require extensive open spaces. Birds most threatened by afforestation are Greenshank and Golden Plover, but it also reduces the habitat for Red Grouse, Merlin, Dunlin, Curlew, Golden Eagle, Black Grouse, Hen Harrier and Twite. Initially, afforestation can have short-term benefits for Hen Harriers, Black Grouse and Short-eared Owls. These newly planted areas provide suitable nesting habitat and abundant food supplies (Avery & Leslie, 1990; Thompson, Stroud & Pienkowski, 1988), but these effects are short-lived.

As the forest ages the canopy closes, and a community of woodland birds replaces the ground-nesting species (Moss, Taylor & Easterbee, 1979). More species of conservation importance occur on moors than in forests, so these changes can represent a net loss of conservation value. The effects of afforestation may not be confined to the area of land actually under trees. It has been suggested that, close to the forest edge, rates of egg, chick and adult predation by foxes, etc., harboured by the forest, may be higher than in areas further away (Thompson *et al.*, 1988) though this has not actually been demonstrated (Avery, Winder & Egan, 1989). The drainage of water-logged peatlands associated with afforestation can profoundly influence their hydrology with adverse consequences for breeding waders (Lindsay *et al.*, 1988; Thompson *et al.*, 1988). Acidification of ground and surface water may follow afforestation (Stoner & Gee, 1985). Work carried out on habitat selection by breeding waterfowl in northern Scotland, indicated that Black-throated Diver, Wigeon and Common Scoter selected the waters of lowest acidity. Many of the lochs of greatest importance for these birds have been surrounded by forestry in the last few years. The impact of this land-use change on these and other species will need monitoring (Fox *et al.*, 1989).

Increase in woodland cover (whether of native or non-native species) in lowland areas no longer threatens any Red Data species. Many of the commoner species that now make up the bulk of our bird life have benefited. In the past, losses of the heath and breckland habitats of Dartford Warbler and Stone Curlew have, however, been due to afforestation. Nightjar and Woodlark have benefited from the clear-fells of pine cropping in the Brecklands (Gribble, 1983; Bowden, in press).

One species, the Golden Oriole, has thrived in one area of non-native poplar plantations in East Anglia, as it does overseas.

Felling or destruction of woodland

Woodland destruction currently threatens the three species which are confined to native pinewoods in Scotland: Capercaillie, Crested Tit and Scottish Crossbill. In addition, the Golden Oriole, having successfully colonized some commercial poplar plantations in eastern England, appears ironically to be threatened by the clear-felling of those same trees.

Loss of habitats to buildings or roads

Lowland heath, which supports three Red Data species (Dartford Warbler, Nightjar and Woodlark) is the semi-natural habitat most threatened by building developments. Recent destruction has been mainly through the creation of new towns and the rapid expansion of existing urban areas and their infra-structure which obliterates or fragments heathland, one of Europe's rarest and most threatened habitats.

Changes in hydrological regimes

In this category we include sudden or pronounced changes in water levels resulting from human activities. These may occur during river flooding, causing overspilling onto adjacent land, or controlled changes to levels of lochs and lakes which may be used for water supply or electricity. The drainage of wetlands for farmland, or other permanent water-table changes, is not included in this category but is dealt with under agricultural intensification.

Certain species can be affected by their nests being flooded or stranded. In the latter case, the nest may become vulnerable to predators or be too far from the water for the adults to reach.

Red-throated Divers and, even more so, Black-throated Divers are affected by fluctuating water levels in lochs, particularly those used as water supply reservoirs, as are Black-necked and Slavonian Grebes. Pintail, Garganey, Ruff and particularly Black-tailed Godwit are adversely affected by late spring flooding of washlands used to contain flood waters generated by improved drainage up-river, though it must be acknowledged that if washland areas did not exist there would be much less breeding habitat for these species. The scarcity of suitable undrained breeding habitat for these species means that any localized flooding of nesting areas can have a marked effect on breeding success for the whole British population (Green *et al.*, 1987).

Land-claim and coastal developments (the threats to estuaries)

Land-claim for barrages, bunding, infilling and other purposes is a major threat to estuarine birds which depend on sand, saltmarsh or mudflats as their feeding habitat. Significant loss of, or alteration to the estuarine habitat, means that the numbers and abundance of food species available to these birds would decrease (Evans & Dugan, 1984; Goss-Custard, 1985). The scale of the threat posed varies from scheme to scheme but there are many current proposals and each contributes to a decrease in the total amount of estuarine habitat. Large developments are increasing, but many smaller ones also take place and their total effect can be sizeable. Virtually every large estuary in Britain has some potential problem, either planned or underway.

A decrease in the feeding area or a reduction in the food availability in an estuary is likely to result in fewer waders being supported by that site. As the area decreases the birds could be forced to seek food in sub-optimal habitats, where there is less food, or in areas already fully occupied by others, thus increasing competition for resources. In these circumstances food may be depleted more quickly, resulting in increased competition and conflict for food between individuals, and a lower intake of food. Over-exploited food species may be reduced beyond their capacity to recover from predation pressure and disappear altogether. All these effects are most serious during severe winter weather when bird mortality is already higher (Evans & Pienkowski, 1984; Prater, 1981).

Sixteen Red Data species are considered to be threatened by insensitive estuarine developments. The most seriously affected are wintering and passage Black-tailed Godwit, Redshank, Dunlin, Knot and Bar-tailed Godwit. Species less seriously affected include Shelduck, Turnstone, Oystercatcher, Curlew, Ringed Plover, Grey Plover, Sanderling and Twite. Estuarine developments also pose a threat to one breeding Red Data species, the Little Tern.

Lack or abandonment of management

This category, which excludes agriculture, covers a range of situations from the abandonment of old methods of waste disposal (which favoured wintering Scaup) to the scrub encroachment on heathlands (causing a threat to Woodlark, Dartford Warbler and Nightjar). It also includes the abandonment of moorland management for game birds causing a degree of threat to Red Grouse, Black Grouse, Golden Plover and Dunlin. This will be especially significant if land is then transferred to afforestation

POLLUTION

Marine oil pollution

Of the nine species affected by marine oil pollution, the most vulnerable are Velvet Scoter and Long-tailed Duck because they winter inshore in rather sizeable concentrations. Other species affected but where the overall threat has been minimal include all three divers, Common Scoter, Scaup, Razorbill and Guillemot.

Although there have been several major oil spills which have killed long-lived birds with low annual productivity and small populations such as divers, there is no evidence that the population of any species has suffered a long-term decline through oil pollution. Indeed, two major victims, Razorbill and Guillemot, have been increasing in numbers in the last twenty years (Stowe, 1982). However, an oil pollution incident still has the potential to kill a significant proportion of the population of birds such as sea ducks and divers.

Chemical pollution

This category includes eutrophication, pesticides and industrial pollution. Leaching from refuse tips and the discharge of sewage occurs in many places around the coast. Eutrophication arises from leaching or discharge of nitrates and phosphates from fertilizers or sewage. In some enclosed estuaries, such as the Ythan or Langstone Harbour, eutrophic conditions have had major ecological effects but the impact on birds has not been clear (Raffaelli *et al.*, 1989; Tubbs, 1977). The result can be major changes or reductions in estuarine flora and fauna, with a substantial decrease in the diversity of the invertebrate species present. Waste and sewage outfalls have attracted certain sea ducks, such as Scaup and Pintail, which feed either on the grain in the effluent or on the invertebrates supported by it. Improvement of standards of sewage disposal has led to the loss of some concentrations of birds such as Goldeneye and Scaup (Campbell, 1984).

Acute or chronic poisoning can occur when pesticides, heavy metals or certain other discharges or accidents take place. Incidents such as those involving tetra-ethyl lead may result in immediate mortality. An example occurred in the Mersey estuary in the winter of 1979–80 when 3,000 waders and gulls were found dead with high residues of lead in their tissues (Prater, 1981; Bull *et al.*, 1983).

The worst of the era of the direct effects of persistent pesticides is perhaps past. During the period between the late 1950s and the late 1960s some bird of prey populations (eg, Peregrine, Sparrowhawk and Merlin) were severely affected by indirect poisoning resulting from the use of organo-chlorine seed dressings or insecticides. Highly toxic chemicals such as aldrin and dieldrin increased mortality, whilst DDT derivatives caused egg-shell thinning and lowered breeding success (Newton, 1979). Herbicides pose a threat to birds such as the Grey Partridge by removing the food plants of the insects which provide the main food of the newly-hatched chicks (Potts, 1986). Other affected species include the Merlin, where mercury contamination is a problem of uncertain significance at present (Newton & Haas, 1988). In coastal areas of north Scotland and its islands, PCBs originating from various sources may be inhibiting the recovery of Peregrine populations (Ratcliffe, 1980). Barn owls may be threatened by modern rodenti-cides, which cause either the loss of their food supply or direct poisoning through the birds eating affected animals (Shawyer, 1987). Incidents of mass mortality of Whooper Swans and geese after eating poorly sown dressed grain are recorded from time to time (Bailey *et al.*, 1972). Ingestion of spent lead gunshot at certain wintering sites leads to excessive mortality of waterfowl (Mudge, 1983; Pain, 1990).

Acidification

Whilst considerable concern has been expressed about the widespread effects of acidification, research has been unable to demonstrate any direct effects of acid emissions on Red Data species in Britain. Recent work in Wales on Dipper populations (a candidate Red Data species) has shown that acidification affects the species by reducing the invertebrate populations on which it feeds (Ormerod & Tyler, 1987).

KILLING AND DISTURBANCE BY MAN

Hunting

This covers legal hunting (trapping and killing) only, both in Britain and elsewhere in the birds' range, though the only Red Data species believed to be seriously affected by hunting abroad is the Roseate Tern on its wintering grounds in West Africa. The effects on certain species such as Osprey, Honey Buzzard and Montagu's Harrier which may be legally hunted in certain African countries are not known but are a potential threat. Hunting in Britain poses only a minimal threat to a very few species. Those currently considered to be most at risk are Capercaillie and Black Grouse, although voluntary bans on their hunting exist in some areas and other factors are probably more important in the case of the Black Grouse. In Denmark it has been totally protected since 1973 but is still declining. The winter range of certain wildfowl (eg, Pintail, Teal and Wigeon) may be restricted by hunting pressures, as demonstrated by the aggregations that develop following the creation of sanctuaries such as the Ouse Washes and the Ribble. The Greenland White-fronted Goose population has increased since the species was removed from the quarry list for Scotland in 1982 and since it has also been protected elsewhere (Stroud *et al.*, in prep.).

Illegal persecution

Under this heading are included illegal activities such as egg collecting, trapping, shooting and poisoning. Egg collecting is a constant threat, in which there may be a resurgence of interest, which affects the rarer species (Bibby & Robinson, 1990). Those considered at risk from it include Red Kite, Osprey, Black-throated Diver, Slavonian Grebe, White-tailed Eagle, and Honey Buzzard.

Persecution, including the poisoning of birds of prey, has its most serious effect on the Hen Harrier, Goshawk, Golden Eagle and Red Kite, probably limiting the numbers and distribution of all these species (Newton, 1979; Cadbury *et al.*, 1988). The range of one candidate for inclusion in the Red Data list, the Buzzard, may be partly limited by persecution (Moore, 1975; Elliott & Avery, in press).

The effect of shooting for taxidermy is not known but since large numbers have been found during RSPB enquiries into taxidermists' activities, it may have a local effect on another candidate for the Red Data list, the Short-eared Owl.

Whilst the illegal taking of birds of prey for falconry continues, the introduction of registration for captive birds and the encouragement of captive breeding programmes under the requirements of the Wildlife and Countryside Act 1981 should result in falconry becoming largely self-sustaining from birds bred in captivity.

A total of 14 Red Data Book species are considered to be adversely affected by illegal persecution in Britain. The effects of illegal persecution of migrant birds passing through European countries where they are protected are not known.

Accidental killing

This covers a wide range of circumstances, from road casualties to the destruction of nests and young during agricultural operations and the effects of monofilament nets used in fishing.

The accidental destruction of nests and young during agricultural operations can be a threat to Stone Curlews, Montagu's Harriers and Corncrakes, though effective measures are in progress with the help of farmers to reduce this unintentional killing of all these species.

Not a great deal is known about the effects of monofilament nets, and clearly more research is needed on this subject. They are a potential threat to diving seabirds because of their near-invisibility. British ringing recoveries show that 5% and 6% respectively of all Guillemots and Razorbills recovered up to 1970 were reported as found in fishing nets or netting. In the period from July 1987 to June 1989, those percentages had increased to 37% and 26% respectively, thus replacing oiling as the largest man-made threat to these species (Mead, 1989). The modern monofilament nets are so cheap as to be disposable and are frequently discarded at sea, becoming long-term hazards for diving sea birds since they do not rot. This matter clearly requires urgent international attention.

Recreational disturbance

This covers a wide range of activities in both summer and winter—for example, disturbance by birdwatchers who try to get close views of nesting birds or roosting waders; disturbance during legal hunting; and unintentional disturbance by the public when walking in the hills or around estuaries, and sailing or fishing on lochs and lakes. Whilst 27 Red Data species are affected by such recreational activities, only two are thought to be seriously affected: Black-necked Grebe, and to a lesser extent, Slavonian Grebe suffer from water sports, fishing and perhaps birdwatching disturbance.

The effects of recreational disturbance, particularly from aquatic sports such as sailboarding, water skiing and jet skiing, is most noticeable on the upper shore zones of estuaries where vital feeding areas exist and where roosts are formed at high tide. Disturbance denies access to, or the utilization of, feeding or roosting areas by birds. The deleterious affect of disturbance is potentially more telling during severe winter weather, since it is then that many waders need to feed throughout the tidal cycle and additional energy expenditure must be avoided. Public access to estuary shores seriously affects coastal breeding waders and little terns, particularly those on sandy or shingle beaches. Although not a Red Data species for its breeding population, the Ringed Plover had widely disappeared as a breeding bird from public beaches in Britain (Prater, 1974). The extinction of Kentish Plover as a regular British breeder may also have been due to recreational pressure. Aquatic sports, especially sailboarding which can extend into the shallow waters of estuaries and lakes, and landings on islands or other isolated areas, can have an impact on roosting waders or wildfowl feeding at or near to the edge of the tide. Similar types of disturbance can also affect breeding terns and waders which may, for example, be disturbed by people landing on islands from boats and by holidaymakers on beaches. It is clear that disturbance can affect the distribution of birds and reduce their breeding success. However, as it is difficult to demonstrate precisely the damaging impact of recreational disturbance on populations, we may be underestimating the scale of the problem.

Boating, water skiing and angling can reduce the use birds make of reservoirs, but these effects can sometimes be alleviated by appropriate zoning of the activities in time and space.

Further threats, as yet not fully understood, are the harvesting of bivalve molluscs (mainly cockles, *Cerastoderma*) through the increasing use of mechanical methods, such as suction dredging and the semi-commercial digging of lugworms (*Arenicola marina*) (Heiligenberg, 1987) and ragworms (*Nereis diversicolor* and *N. virens*) for baiting fishing hooks. Both have indirect effects by reducing food stocks for estuarine birds and by restricting feeding bird distribution through disturbance. In some areas, such as Lindisfarne National Nature Reserve, bait digging became so intensive that bye-laws had to be introduced to control it. This case also demonstrates the problem of interacting threats since the bait-digging prevented birds from using the shooting sanctuary area, potentially disrupting the management of this activity.

It should be remembered that since 1967 it has been illegal intentionally to disturb rare breeding birds (those on Schedule 1 of the Wildlife and Countryside Act 1981). This has undoubtedly had a beneficial effect both in drawing attention to and in lessening disturbance that would otherwise be caused by an ever-increasing number of birdwatchers and photographers, though the precise effects of such disturbance cannot be adequately quantified without further research.

'NATURAL' THREATS

Climatic change

Minor effects of weather are always apparent and may pose a low to medium threat for various species: cold winters can reduce the populations of Dartford Warblers, Cetti's Warblers, Bearded Tits and Bitterns. Cold springs tend to reduce the numbers of 'southern' species such as Garganey breeding (or even arriving) in Britain. Wet summers can affect the breeding success of birds such as the Honey Buzzard, which feeds largely on wasp larvae.

Climatic change is long term and its impact on birds is not fully understood. It may be affecting species such as the Capercaillie, Barn Owl, Nightjar, Cirl Bunting, Woodlark, Red-backed Shrike, Wryneck and Marsh Warbler, possibly through changes in habitat or the abundance of invertebrates or by affecting breeding success or survival rates. In the case of migrants these changes could be either on the breeding or wintering grounds, or both. The reduction in numbers of some candidate species such as Sand Martin and Whitethroat has been attributed to drought in the Sahel (Winstanley, Spencer & Williamson, 1974).

There is however a major threat now manifesting itself to many more species in the form of global warming due to the so-called 'greenhouse effect'. According to some predictions, the most obvious effect will be the flooding of coastlands and the loss of estuarine habitat. This might be a threat or an opportunity depending on how the resulting changes are managed. Major changes to vegetation and the availability of food, particularly in the marine environment could also affect birds. This potential threat is not further considered in this book, but could cause 'southern' populations to move north, and northern ones to retreat.

Interspecific competition

Some species compete with others for nesting and feeding areas. The most notable are Roseate and Sandwich Terns which suffer from competition for nesting space with large gulls which have increased greatly due to man's activities. This threat, however, is considered to be low as long as present management efforts continue on reserves where most of these populations now nest.

Natural ecological change

This concerns a small group of species. In some cases, changes in their populations or distribution cannot be fully explained by known threats and are believed to be due to unidentified ecological changes. The Roseate Tern's decline in numbers since the early 1960s is as unexplained as the rise in numbers that preceded it. Whatever the factors responsible, they pose a severe threat.

Natural ecological changes include vegetational succession which affects any unmanaged habitat below the tree-line such as seral change from open water created by peat cuttings, through a swamp and eventually dry mire. This results in a loss of suitable breeding habitat, for example for the Red-necked Phalarope, and is thus a threat to that species.

The decline of the Bittern population may in part have been caused by the deterioration of its habitat due to scrub growth and the colonization of ditches by invading plant species. Similarly, the drying out of reed beds and subsequent development of unsuitable vegetation can be a threat to Bearded Tits. This excessive invasion of dry heathland by scrub is a threat to Nightjars though their preferred habitat does include a small scrub component (Berry, 1979). Dartford Warblers may be adversely affected by the invasion of bracken on heathlands (Bibby, 1978).

Loss of or changes in fish populations, notably those of the sandeel, have caused a considerable decrease in breeding success in the Shetland and, to a lesser extent, Orkney Arctic Tern populations (Monaghan *et al.*, 1989). Commercial fishing may have contributed to these changes (Avery & Green, 1989). Such changes, however, have occurred in the past, before the sandeel fishery had developed (Bourne, 1989). The Red-throated Diver is another species vulnerable to possible changes in the fish populations in the waters around Shetland and Orkney.

The spread of the introduced *Spartina anglica* over upper shore mudflats is a threat to wintering Dunlin since it can destroy crucial winter feeding grounds for that species (Goss-Custard & Moser, 1988).

Predation or disease

These factors sometimes have significant impact locally (eg, parasite infection in grouse) and in some situations predation may be unnaturally severe due to man's activities: for example the introduction of rats and cats to seabird islands. These could particularly affect burrow-nesting species such as Storm and Leach's Petrels and Manx Shearwater. Predation is considered to be a moderate threat to three Red Data species, Roseate Tern, Grey Partridge and Red Grouse, and a minimal threat to a further 18. However, it should be remembered that predation becomes a threat only when prey populations are at considerably lower densities than normal or when the habitat has deteriorated for the prey species or improved for the predator.

Land-use changes in the uplands, resulting in increased afforestation and thus more breeding habitat for predators such as foxes and crows, may have led to increased predation of Black Grouse, Red Grouse and Golden Plover. Dotterel may be vulnerable to predation by gulls and crows attracted to scraps left by hill walkers and skiers (Watson, 1988; Galbraith *et al.*, in prep.) — a threat that used not to exist before the increased ease of human access.

The very large increase in the fox population, and hence predation pressure from this species, is a problem for many ground-nesting species in addition to those already mentioned, especially Stone Curlew, Capercaillie and Black-throated Diver. Feral and domestic cats are important predators of Corncrake, whilst pike take a toll of Black-necked and Slavonian Grebes, particularly young birds. Some populations of species with restricted ranges are likely to be more vulnerable to predation.

REFERENCES

Avery, M. & Green, R. 1989. Not enough fish in the sea. New Scientist 123: 28–29.

Avery, M. & Leslie, R. 1990. Birds and Forestry. London: Poyser.

Avery, M.I., Winder, F.L.R. & Egan, V. (in press). An investigation of predation rates on artificial nests adjacent to forestry plantations in northern Scotland. Oikos.

Bailey, S., Bunyan, P.J., Hamilton, G.A., Jennings, D.M. & Stanley P.I. 1972. Accidental poisoning of wild geese in Perthshire, November 1971. Wildfowl 23: 88–91.

Berry, R. 1979. Nightjar habitat and breeding in East Anglia. Brit. Birds 72: 207–218.

Bibby, C.J. 1978. Conservation of the Dartford Warbler on English lowland heaths: a review. Biol. Cons.13: 299–307.

Bibby, C.J., Robinson, P.J. & Bland, E. 1990. The Impact of Egg Collecting on Scarce Breeding Birds. RSPB Conserv. Rev. 4: 22–25.

Bourne, W.R.P. 1989. Shetland's sand eels. New Scientist 123: 71.

Bowden, C.G.R. (in press). Selection of foraging habitats by woodlarks *Lullula arborea* nesting in pine plantations. J. Appl. Ecol.

Bull, K.R., Every, W.J., Freestone, P., Hall, J.R. & Osborn, D. 1983. Alkyl lead pollution and bird mortalities on the Mersey estuary, UK, 1979–1981. Environmental Pollution, Series A 31: 239–259.

Cadbury, C.J., Elliott, G.D. & Harbard, C.J. 1988. Birds of prey conservation in the UK. RSPB Conserv. Rev. 2: 9–16.

Campbell, L.H. 1984. The impact of changes in sewage treatment on seaducks wintering on the Firth of Forth, Scotland. Biol. Cons. 28: 173–180.

Elliott, G.D. & Avery, M.I. (in press). A review of Buzzard persecution 1975–1987. Bird Study.

Evans, P.R. & Pienkowski, M.W. 1984. Population dynamics of shorebirds. *In* Evans, P.R., Goss-Custard, J.D. & Hale, W.G. (eds), Coastal waders and wildfowl in winter: 83–123. Cambridge: Cambridge University Press.

Evans, P.R. & Dugan, P.J. 1984. Coastal birds: numbers in relation to food resources. *In* Evans, P.R., Goss-Custard, J.D. & Hale, W.G. (eds), Coastal waders and wildfowl in winter: 8–28. Cambridge: Cambridge University Press.

Fox, A.D., Jarrett, N., Gitay, H. & Paynter, D. 1989. Late summer habitat selection by breeding waterfowl in northern Scotland. Wildfowl 40: 106–114.

Galbraith, H., Murray, S. & Thompson, D. (in prep.) Status and distribution of breeding Dotterel in Britain.

GOSS-CUSTARD, J.D. & MOSER, M.E. 1988. Rates of change in the numbers of Dunlin, *Calidris alpina*, wintering on British estuaries in relation to the spread of *Spartina anglica*. J. Appl. Ecol. 25: 95–109.

GOSS-CUSTARD, J.D. 1985. Foraging behaviour of wading birds and the carrying capacity of estuaries. *In* Sibly, R.M. & Smith, R.M. (eds), Behavioural Ecology: Ecological consequences of adaptive behaviour: 169–188. Oxford: Oxford University Press.

GREEN, R.E., CADBURY, C.J. & WILLIAMS, G. 1987. Floods threaten Black-tailed Godwits breeding at the Ouse Washes. RSPB Conserv. Rev. 1: 14–16.

GRIBBLE, F.C. 1983. Nightjars in Britain and Ireland in 1981. Bird Study 30: 165–176.

HEILIGENBERG, T. VAN DEN 1987. Effects of mechanical and manual harvesting of lugworms *Arenicola marina* L. on the benthic fauna of tidal flats in the Dutch Wadden Sea. Biol.Conserv. 39: 165–177.

LINDSAY, R.A., CHARMAN, D.J., EVERINGHAM, F., O'REILLY, R.M., PALMER, M.A., ROWELL, T.A. & STROUD, D.A. 1988. The Flow Country. The Peatlands of Caithness and Sutherland. Peterborough: Nature Conservancy Council.

MEAD, C.J. 1989. BTO News July–August 1989, No. 163: 8.

MITCHELL, J.R., MOSER, M.E. & KIRBY, J.S. 1988. Declines in midwinter counts of waders roosting on the Dee estuary. Bird Study 35: 191–198.

MONAGHAN, P., UTTLEY, J.D., BURNS, M.D., THAINE, C. & BUCKLAND, J. 1989. The relationship between food supply, reproductive effort and breeding success in Arctic Terns *Sterna paradisaea*. J. Animal Ecol. 58: 261–274.

MOORE, N.W. 1957. The past and present status of the Buzzard in the British Isles. Brit. Birds 64: 412–420.

MOSS, D., TAYLOR, P.N. & EASTERBEE, N. 1979. The effects on song-bird populations of upland afforestation with spruce. Forestry 52: 124–147.

MUDGE, G.P. 1983. The incidence and significance of ingested lead pellet poisoning in British wildfowl. Biol. Conserv. 27: 333–372.

NEWTON, I. 1979. Population ecology of Raptors. Berkhamsted: Poyser.

NEWTON, I. & HAAS, M.B. 1988. Pollutants in merlin eggs and their effects on breeding. Brit. Birds 81: 258–269.

ORMEROD, S.J. & TYLER, S.J. 1987. Dippers *Cinclus cinclus* and Grey Wagtails *Motacilla cinerea* as indicators of stream acidity in Upland Wales. *In* Diamond, A.W. & Fillion, E. (eds), The Value of Birds: 191–208. ICBP.

PAIN, D.J. 1990. Lead poisoning of waterfowl: a review. *In* Matthews, G.V.T. (ed.), Proceedings of the IWRB Symposium on the Management of Waterfowl Population, Astrakhan, USSR, 1989 (in press).

POTTS, G.R. 1986. The Partridge: Pesticides, Predation and Conservation. London: Collins.

PRATER, A.J. 1974. Breeding populations of the Ringed Plover in Britain. Bird Study 21: 155–161.

PRATER, A.J. 1981. Estuary Birds of Britain and Ireland. Calton: Poyser.

RAFFAELLI, D., HULL, S. & MILNE, H. 1989. Long-term changes in nutrients, weed mats and shorebirds in an estuarine system. Cah. Biol. Mar. 30: 259–270.

RATCLIFFE, D.A. 1980. The Peregrine Falcon. Calton: Poyser.

REID-HENRY, D. & HARRISON, C.J.O. 1988. The History of the Birds of Britain. London: Collins.

SHAWYER, C.R. 1987. The Barn Owl in the British Isles: its Past, Present and Future. London: The Hawk Trust.

SMIT, C.J., LAMBECK, R.H.D. & WOLFF, W.J. 1987. Threats to coastal wintering and staging areas of waders. Wader Study Group Bull. 49, Suppl./IWRB special Publ. 7: 105–113.

STOWE, T.J. 1982. Recent population trends in cliff-breeding seabirds in Britain and Ireland. Ibis 124: 502–510.

STROUD, D.A., FOX, A.D., WILSON, J.W. & NORRIS, D. (in prep.) The population of Greenland White-fronted Geese in Ireland and Britain: 1982/83–1986/87.

THOMPSON, D.B.A., STROUD, D.A. & PIENKOWSKI, M.W. 1988. Afforestation and upland birds: consequences for population ecology. *In* Usher, M.B. & Thompson, D.B.A. (eds), Ecological change in the uplands: 237–259. Oxford: Blackwell.

TUBBS, C.R. 1977. Wildfowl and waders in Langstone Harbour. Brit. Birds 70: 177–199.

WATSON, A. 1988. Dotterel *Charadrius morinellus* numbers in relation to human input in Scotland. Biol. Conserv. 43: 245–256.

WINSTANLEY, D., SPENCER, R. & WILLIAMSON, K. 1974. Where have all the white-throats gone? Bird Study 21: 1–14.

Bird Conservation in Britain

Stuart Housden

INTRODUCTION

The advent of legislation to protect wild birds owes a considerable debt to those pioneering individuals who pamphletted and lobbied tirelessly at the turn of the century, many of whom were motivated by welfare considerations rather than the conservation of species *per se*. Their contribution should not be underestimated for it gave the legal protection of birds a flying start over that enjoyed by flora and other fauna which is still apparent today. This early attention concentrated on the *exploitation* of birds, their plumes, skins and eggs and not on the conservation of their habitat, an understandable bias in an age where changes in farming and forestry practice were slow and the spread of industry and the conurbations less marked than now.

AN HISTORICAL PERSPECTIVE

It is chauvinistic to assume that Britain led, or indeed now leads, in the field of bird protection. The first attempt to encourage bird protection on an international scale originated at the 26th General Assembly of German agriculturalists and foresters held in Vienna in 1868, when a resolution was passed and despatched to the Austro-Hungarian Government requesting efforts to procure international agreements for the protection of animals useful to agriculture and forestry (ICBP, 1952). Over the next 20 years this idea was pursued by other European countries but no formal agreements were reached. In 1895 a conference on the protection of birds was held in Paris, and a draft convention comprising 10 Clauses was tabled by the French Government. This draft was to form the basis of the International Convention for the Protection of Birds which was signed in Paris in 1902 by the representatives of 12 European states (not including Britain). The Paris Convention accorded protection to 'useful' bird species and their nests and eggs and prohibited their sale during the close season; 'harmful' species were exempted from protection. The Paris Convention attracted numerous signatories and was reviewed on a regular basis throughout the first half of the 20th century. A major review of the Paris Convention in 1950 saw the adoption of new measures including controls on the use of poisoned or stupefying baits, repeating or

317

automatic shot guns, motor vehicles or mechanically propelled boats and so on, all of which can now be found in British legislation. Despite this, the British Government never ratified the Paris Convention. In 1966 the Home Office informed the British Section of the International Council for Bird Preservation: 'The main problem in our view is that the convention contains too much detail; the United Kingdom fully supports the principles embodied therein but is prevented from ratifying it because of inability to accept all the detailed requirements' (Barclay-Smith, 1967).

BIRD PROTECTION IN BRITAIN

Within Britain the RSPB had, from its earliest days, been actively pressing the Government to pass comprehensive legislation to protect wild birds (Samstag, 1988). The Wild Birds Protection Act 1880 offered only limited protection for certain birds during the 'close' (breeding) season. Amended many times (for example the Wild Birds Protection Act 1904 added a prohibition on the use of pole traps), this legislation was piecemeal, poorly understood and difficult to enforce. The RSPB however had influential supporters who used their connections to good effect, and in 1913 the Government finally responded to their demands by establishing a committee to review the protection of wild birds. The Departmental Committee's work was finished before the outbreak of the Great War but it did not report until 1919 (HMSO, 1919). Its report made many pertinent recommendations, a number of which still featured in debates on the Wildlife and Countryside Bill during its Parliamentary scrutiny 60 years later. For example, on taxidermists they reported: 'In many cases it is through a taxidermist that a collector obtains specimens of rare birds or eggs which may or may not have been legally taken'. The Committee recommended that all taxidermists should be required to keep a register of all birds and eggs which pass through their hands, which should be open to inspection at reasonable times by an authorized person. The Wildlife and Countryside Act 1981 at last implemented this recommendation for birds (but not their eggs).

In 1921 the Home Office appointed a Wild Birds Advisory Committee. Numerous attempts to improve the legislation followed, but no comprehensive legislation was to reach the Statute Book until 1954.

THE PLUMAGE TRADE

The importation of exotic plumes for the millinery trade was a spur to bird protectionists on both sides of the Atlantic. Campaigners stressed the cruelty involved in the mass killings and the fact that young birds were left to die a lingering death by starvation once the adults had been killed. The scale of the slaughter is hard to imagine today, but from the 1870s onwards thousands of pounds of weight of plumes were imported, with dealers selling millions of bird skins each year. Against such vested interests it took until 1921 to see the Importation of Plumage (Prohibition) Act onto the Statute Book. London's pre-eminence as a centre of the world trade in bird plumes and skins ceased.

BIRD TRAPPING

Alongside the plumage trade the other 'evil' which concerned the early bird protectionists was the trapping of song birds for the cage bird market. In a strongly worded RSPB pamphlet published in 1904, W.H. Hudson wrote: 'It (the linnet) is captured in tens or hundreds of thousands all over the country . . .'. This trade, which largely ignored the limited protection afforded to birds by the 1880 Act and its county schedules, was eventually controlled by The Protection of Birds Act 1933. This made it an offence to take wild birds, or offer for sale such birds unless they had been close ringed and bred in captivity.

HABITAT PROTECTION

As mentioned earlier, most bird protectionists campaigned for legislation to control or prohibit the exploitation of wild birds. It was the naturalist the Hon. Charles Rothschild who set the pace with regard to habitat protection measures; he financed his own review of wildlife habitats, and in 1915 he published a list of 251 sites worthy of protection. 'The Rothschild list' was in effect to become a shopping list for the Society for the Promotion of Nature Reserves (SPNR) in which Rothschild was a driving force. The SPNR, RSPB and National Trust all established reserved areas for wildlife in the years leading up to the second war. However, unlike the United States, there were no statutory national parks or nature reserves where the habitat of wild birds was specifically maintained and protected.

The RSPB and SPNR (now the Royal Society for Nature Conservation) agreed to promote an initiative to rectify this and a conference was held in 1941 to consider 'Nature Preservation' in post-war reconstruction. The conference, organized by SPNR, made several important recommendations and concluded that the Government should itself establish an official body to consider the whole issue. The conference proceedings attracted much interest including a favourable leader in the Times. The relevant Government Minister of the day, however, preferred that as an interim measure the conference should appoint a Nature Reserves Investigations Committee. This was done in June 1942 and evidence was collected from the RSPB, British Ecological Society and other sources. Three reports duly followed dealing with Nature Conservation, National Geological Reserves and National Nature Reserves (Sheail, 1976). Meanwhile the National Park Movement, led by John Dower, renewed its efforts to persuade the Government to establish parks. In 1942 Dower was appointed by the Minister of Works and Planning to review the whole question of National Parks, and in his report, Dower (1945) clearly recognized the importance of wildlife in determining national park management.

In 1945, following opposition from the Minister of Agriculture and the Treasury, a special Government Committee under the chairmanship of Sir Julian Huxley was established (Huxley, 1947) with the remit of examining the proposals made for National Parks and considering such other matters relating to Wildlife Conservation as may be referred by the Minister of Town and Country Planning. In order to keep the National Park initiative alive, the Minister, W.S. Morrison, appointed a committee under Sir Arthur Hobhouse, and directed that they use the Dower report as the basis for their work. Similar committees were appointed to review national park and wildlife conservation in Scotland (Hobhouse, 1947; Douglas Ramsay, 1947). Thus the development of the Government's thinking on National Parks and on nature conservation during the war years was achieved in parallel, but sprang from different sources, a dual approach still very evident in Britain today.

The Wildlife Conservation Special Committee reported to Parliament in July 1947 (Command 7122). This report was nothing if not comprehensive, and it is fair to say that the post-war development of wildlife conservation in Britain owes the committee a clear debt. The Committee during its investigations reviewed the 1915 Rothschild list and commented as follows: 'It is a depressing exercise to examine the Rothschild list—some have been destroyed, others are on the way to destruction, and some have so declined they can no longer be rated as of outstanding national importance'. They went on to state that it is 'unfair to infer that these sites had mainly been swamped by the advancing tide of bricks and mortar. They have been lost to hurried and sometimes ill-considered plans for agricultural expansion; to pressing demands for timber; to increasing drainage of surface waters, coupled but not co-ordinated with a steady increasing drain on underground water supplies . . .'. To remedy this state of affairs the Committee suggested the establishment of national nature reserves, conservation areas, geological monuments, local nature reserves and the formation of a biological service who would be charged with the scientific survey of land and the preparation of schedules of sites of special scientific importance. They also endorsed the need for national parks.

Anyone reading Command 7122 cannot be fired with enthusiasm and recognize the wisdom that, to be effective, conservation action must be integrated into all aspects of planning and resource use affecting the countryside and that powers are required to protect sites from damaging developments.

These various official reports paved the way for the National Parks and Access to the Countryside Act 1949. This Act became the cornerstone for the development of post-war conservation in Britain. It is humbling to think that after a long and exhausting war the nation could find the time and energy to set in hand such a comprehensive review of the needs of landscape and wildlife conservation.

THE POST-WAR ERA

The 1949 Act established the Nature Conservancy (Biological Service) and the framework for establishing national parks and sites of special scientific interest (SSSIs). The areas identified as conservation zones in Commands 6628/7122 became known as Areas of Outstanding Natural Beauty (AONBs).

Significantly, Parliament rejected recommendations that in certain circumstances farming and forestry activities within these protected areas should be subject to control measures. The 1949 Act instead relied upon voluntary means to achieve conservation. National Park Authorities were able to offer management agreements to secure access to land or the management of countryside for conservation. Similarly, the Nature Conservancy (NC) had powers to enter into agreements or to acquire land for the purposes of establishing National Nature Reserves (NNRs). This decision was to lead to a widespred loss of important wildlife habitats and landscape features to farming and forestry operations. The NC was given compulsory purchase powers but in practice these were used only where land ownership could not be determined.

SPECIES PROTECTION

The passage of the Protection of Birds Act 1954 introduced for the first time comprehensive legislation to protect all wild birds. This was an historic achievement which owed much to the RSPB's powers of campaigning and persuasion. The Act followed the principle of 'reverse listing', ie, all birds were protected except those listed on quarry or pest schedules. Certain rare species were offered a higher degree of protection, and they, too, were listed in a special schedule to the Act. Many unselective methods of bird pest control, such as poisonous baits, were outlawed.

The 1954 Act was amended in 1967. Two new matters were particularly noteworthy. First, the rarest species (those listed on Schedule I of the 1954 Act) were protected from wilful disturbance at the nest. Second, the sale or exchange of dead wild geese was prohibited.

THE MODERN INFRASTRUCTURE AND LEGISLATIVE SAFEGUARDS

The principal statutes currently protecting wild birds and their habitats are the Wildlife and Countryside Acts 1981–5. These statutes are the means by which the British Government implements relevant international obligations (as described below) and they build on the systems established under the National Parks and Access to the Countryside Act 1949 and the Protection of Birds Act 1954–67. The 1981 Act was introduced specifically to meet the Government's duties to bird conservation as laid out in the European Community Council Directive on the Conservation of Wild Birds (although the Act's provisions go much wider than this). At the time of writing, this is the only Directive requiring EC member states specifically to protect a specific part of the community's fauna.

EC COUNCIL DIRECTIVE ON THE CONSERVATION OF WILD BIRDS (79/409/EEC)

This Directive was adopted by the Council in April 1979, and came into force two years later. The European Commission can investigate complaints of breach of the Directive and this sanction can be deployed to ensure observance since alleged breaches can ultimately result in member states being challenged in the European Court. All EC member states are required to take measures to protect wild birds and to preserve sufficient diversity of habitats for all species naturally occurring within their territories, so as to maintain their populations at an ecologically and scientifically sound level. Species whose status is a cause of some concern are specially identified (in Annex 1) for special conservation measures. Member states are required to classify the most suitable areas for these species as Special Protection Areas (SPAs). The same measures apply for migratory species. Significant pollution of or deterioration of habitats must be avoided. To date, 216 important sites have been identified in Britain, 40 of which the Government has listed with the European Commission as SPAs.

There is no doubt that the EC Directive has provided a great stimulus to bird conservation, particularly through the conservation of habitats which has also benefited all our flora and fauna. Its requirements contributed in large measure to the protection afforded to all SSSIs in the Wildlife and Countryside Act (see below).

THE RAMSAR CONVENTION ON WETLANDS OF INTERNATIONAL IMPORTANCE, ESPECIALLY AS WATERFOWL HABITAT

In 1976 the United Kingdom ratified the 'Ramsar Convention' (HMSO, 1976), so-called after the meeting venue of Ramsar in Iran. Contracting parties are required to promote the conservation of 'listed' wetlands. More generally contracting parties are exhorted to plan the 'wise use' of wetlands in all areas of policy planning and formulation. Where listed sites are involved, damaging development can proceed only in the 'urgent national interest'. Alternative sites are required to be listed in place of any so developed. The criteria used to identify 'Ramsar' sites depend on factors such as the numbers of waterfowl which they support and complementary criteria for 'non-bird' sites are currently under discussion. Within Great Britain, 150 sites qualify for listing—of which 43 have been so listed to date. The majority of qualifying sites under the Convention are also potential SPAs (see above).

THE BERNE CONVENTION ON THE CONSERVATION OF EUROPEAN WILDLIFE AND NATURAL HABITATS

The UK ratified this Convention in 1983. The Convention carries an obligation to protect and conserve a wide range of flora and fauna (including their habitats), especially those listed as endangered or vulnerable. The mechanisms for habitat protection measures are not closely defined, and in Britain the Government seeks to meet its obligations via the SSSI provisions in the Wildlife and Countryside Acts 1981–5. Contracting parties are encouraged to declare 'Biogenetic Reserves' (like the Convention, a Council of Europe measure) as a contribution to the convention's aims; thus far no such sites have been declared in Britain.

OTHER INTERNATIONAL OBLIGATIONS

The UK is also a party to the Bonn Convention (The Convention on the Conservation of Migratory Species of Wild Animals) and the Convention concerning the Protection of the World Cultural and Natural Heritage, ('World Heritage Convention', which encourages the declaration of 'natural' world heritage sites). The UK is a party to the Convention on International Trade in Endangered species (CITES), which places strict controls on the import and export of rare or vulnerable flora and fauna.

THE WILDLIFE AND COUNTRYSIDE ACTS 1981–5

These statutes are the reference point for modern bird protection and conservation. *Part 1* of the 1981 Act deals with the protection of species, including birds, and protects all wild birds, their nests and eggs and places controls upon their sale and possession. As with the 1954 Act, the reverse listing procedure is followed. The number and range of species afforded 'special protection' is similar to the 1954 Act, but a few extremely rare breeding species have been added. Falconry and taxidermy are now controlled by licensing procedures. The Agriculture Departments are provided with powers to issue licences (under Section 16) to permit the control of protected species in order to prevent *serious* damage to crops or other forms of property. Following the passage of the Act, problems with the administration of this Section were encountered, particularly in Scotland where for example licenses to 'control' Barnacle Geese on the island of Islay for agricultural reasons permitted sport shooting to continue (illegal under the EC Directive on the Conservation of Wild Birds). Although the sport shooting problem has been resolved there remains confusion and concern over the interpretation of what constitutes 'serious damage' under the Act, and the granting of licenses by Government to allow the control of otherwise protected species.

Part II of the 1981 Act gave greatly enhanced protection for SSSIs (see 1949 Act). Sites of Special Scientific Interest have existed in Britain for 40 years, but have provided few safeguards against changes in land use. The Nature Conservancy was split in 1973 to form the Institute of Terrestrial Ecology (ITE) and the Nature Conservation Council (NCC) (Nature Conservancy Council Act 1973). The NCC continued the task of identifying SSSIs as set out in the 1949 Act. Since the early 1970s consultation with NCC was required by local planning authorities before deciding a planning application affecting an SSSI. This helped to protect some sites, but many were destroyed. Where changes in farming or forestry practice were concerned, however, few safeguards existed prior to the passage of the 1981 Act. As a consequence the NCC estimated in 1980 that 13% of all SSSIs (over 4,000 sites existed by 1980) were damaged in one year alone (NCC, 1982), the majority by farming operations.

After the passage of the 1981 Act the NCC was required to renotify all SSSIs using new procedures. Once notified, owners and occupiers were obliged to give the NCC advance notice of their intention to carry out a potentially damaging operation (PDO). Once notice of a PDO had been received the NCC could endeavour to prevent damage by offering the owner a management agreement, or seeking to persuade him to withdraw or modify his plans. If this voluntary approach failed the NCC could seek a Nature Conservation Order from the Secretary of State which would delay any damaging work from being carried out on the site and pave the way for compulsory purchase as a last resort. Such Orders are subject to appeal, but most owners whose land is subject to an Order come to an agreement with the NCC reasonably quickly thereafter. As the management agreements which the NCC are obliged to offer rely upon a negotiated settlement, the NCC is not always able to secure the optimum afteruse or management. Nevertheless, the system has worked quite well and the number of SSSIs damaged or destroyed each year has fallen: in 1988/9 some 160 sites were affected (most damaged). The total number of SSSIs has, as NCC survey work has progressed, grown to some 5,000 (NCC, 1988).

Since SSSIs form less than 10% of the country's land area and are widely recognized as the prime areas for conservation it remains unacceptable that so many sites should suffer damage in this way. Although not all damaged sites will suffer permanent loss of interest this erosion of the best semi-natural habitats found in Britain is of serious concern.

BIRDS IN THE WIDER COUNTRYSIDE

Most attention in respect of statutory or treaty commitments concerning conservation has tended to focus on site-related matters. However, many measures also make reference to the need for conservation outwith discrete areas. This is important as most wildlife populations occur outside designated 'sites'. Site-protection measures are essential components of an overall conservation strategy, but cannot be the only component, because SSSIs and nature reserves can protect only certain features, species and populations. Wide-ranging birds, such as many of the vulnerable raptors, require broader conservation measures. A strategy based on discrete sites alone is therefore bound to fail.

The need for work on wider countryside issues is emphasized in the Department of the Environment Circular 27/87 on Nature Conservation (issued to planning authorities), particularly in paragraphs 6–7: 'our natural wildlife heritage is not confined to the various statutorily designated sites. . . . . The survival of the nation's wildlife cannot be achieved solely by site-protection. It depends on the wise management of the nation's land resources as a whole. . . . Nature conservation must be taken into account in all activities which affect rural land use and in the planning process. . . . In the development of this comprehensive framework for the protection of natural resources, a central role has been played by the Nature Conservancy Council in advising Government and others on the development and implementation of policies for or affecting nature conservation in Great Britain. . . . It supports these functions by a substantial programme of research. . . the Secretaries of State attach considerable importance to the NCCs advisory role and wish to encourage close and effective liaison with it'.

The Government's ratification of the 'Ramsar' Convention accepts an obligation to promote the wise use of all wetlands, not just those on listed sites. EEC Directive 79/409 on the Conservation of Wild Birds similarly has a range of requirements including special protection measures for a list of vulnerable species, migratory birds and their habitats which goes beyond the designation of Special Protection Areas (see above). In particular, Member States are to develop general protection measures. Since species conservation by site-designation alone is not adequate, the UK Government has indicated to the European Commission that the NCC is conducting research on how to conserve birds in the wider countryside, for example, by adapting forestry or farming practice.

Despite this, it remains difficult to persuade land-using industries to give proper regard to the requirements of nature conservation in the wider countryside. The Forestry Commission, for example, will consult the NCC only where afforestation proposals directly affect SSSIs. Nature conservation arguments put forward by local authorities or non-Governmental Organizations regarding forestry schemes not affecting designated sites are usually ruled out of court. Where wetlands are concerned, land drainage interests usually accord conservation a lower priority than the needs of agriculture. This is the case even on SSSIs where drainage regimes may be implemented which reduce the conservation value of land. Particular difficulties have been experienced in this regard on the Somerset Levels and Moors, an area qualifying for protection under the EC Birds Directive.

Gradually, however, there are signs that a more integrated approach to land use is developing. For example, a number of regional councils in Scotland are developing forest planting strategies in order to give locational guidance to the Forestry Commission and private forest companies. These strategies consider the balance between forestry and other land uses, such as agriculture, tourism and nature conservation. The NCC, RSPB and others are providing advice to regional councils who are proving receptive to modifications of their strategies in favour of conservation, provided that hard evidence is available to support the nature conservation interest. In Strathclyde the evidence presented on natural interest caused the regional council to upgrade the conservation rating of 13% of the total area between published consultation draft and submission to the Secretary of State.

The British Government, with encouragement from conservation bodies, promoted the idea of 'Environmentally Sensitive Areas' (ESAs). Such areas are declared by Agriculture Ministers under Section 18 of the Agriculture Act 1986. Within these areas farmers are encouraged to continue traditional farming practices, to benefit landscapes, wildlife and the archaeological heritage. Payments are offered to the farmers to reimburse them for the costs of continuing these practices and foregoing the chance of improving their land for agriculture. There are now 19 such areas in the UK, covering 500,000 ha. A number are very important for birds—eg, the Machairs of the Uists, the Brecklands of East Anglia and the Somerset Levels and Moors. It is hoped that ESA schemes will provide a blueprint for future agricultural support in the countryside.

THE NON-GOVERNMENTAL SECTOR

Britain has a strong voluntary sector active in a wide range of conservation activities from reserves purchase, scientific survey and enforcement of the law to land-use policy work. Of particular note are the baseline surveys and monitoring undertaken by skilled volunteers (usually) organized by the British Trust for Ornithology (BTO). The willingness of thousands of amateurs to give freely of their time to participate in surveys has contributed considerably to our knowledge of bird numbers and population trends. Membership of the main orgnizations concerned with wild birds (RSPB, BTO, WWT, RSNC) is well over one million and is a potent force with increasing influence on Government land-use policy. The land-owning bodies (WWT, RSNC, RSPB and National Trust) also own or manage substantial areas of land as nature reserves, much of which is SSSI quality.

PROTECTED AREAS

The main categories of protected areas in Britain are as follows:

NATIONAL NATURE RESERVES

There are 234 NNRs in Great Britain, usually managed by the NCC for the conservation of flora and fauna, geological or physiographical features. There is a marine nature reserve equivalent for marine sites, although only two of these have so far been established.

SITES OF SPECIAL SCIENTIFIC INTEREST

SSSIs are the backbone of statutory sites protection in Britain. They are mostly in private ownership and are selected and notified by the NCC on scientific grounds relating to floristic and faunistic, geological or physiographical interest. Special consultation arrangements apply to land-use operations on these sites, but adequate protection depends on voluntary co-operation by owners and occupiers and the availability of NCC funds to back management agreements or compulsory purchase where necessary.

SPECIAL PROTECTION AREAS AND WETLANDS OF INTERNATIONAL
IMPORTANCE (RAMSAR CONVENTION)

SPAs and 'Ramsar' sites are designated by central Government under the terms
of EC Directive 789/409 on the Conservation of Wild Birds, and the 'Ramsar'
Convention, respectively. Their protection is by means of notification as a SSSI
and no extra statutory protection is provided over and above this. A significant
number of additional sites still await designation.

LOCAL NATURE RESERVES

LNRs are established by local planning authorities. They are often, but not
always, owned by the authorities, and are regulated by bye-laws for control of
access, protection of wildlife and so on; 133 exist to date.

NATIONAL PARKS

Generally, in upland areas, these were declared in the 1950s largely for
landscape and amenity purposes. There are currently 10 in England and Wales
only. They are inhabited and entail no special state ownership. There are some
special planning constraints and consultative arrangements, administered by a
National Park Authority for each park. General promotion of the parks is
undertaken by the Countryside Commission for England and Wales. In addition
to the 10 designated parks the Norfolk and Suffolk Broads are accorded a similar
status.

AREAS OF OUTSTANDING NATURAL BEAUTY

Forty AONBs are established for the conservation of natural beauty, by the
Countryside Commission in England and Wales. Special planning presumptions
apply but do not extend to most farming and forestry operations. They therefore
provide only limited guarantees for wildlife.

NATIONAL SCENIC AREAS

Forty of these replaced the five former National Park Direction Areas in
Scotland and are designated on landscape grounds. Special consultation arrangements between planning authorities and the Countryside Commission for Scotland apply. Again, the majority of farming and forestry operations are unaffected.

OTHER IMPORTANT DESIGNATIONS WHICH CAN BENEFIT WILD BIRDS

These include green belts; heritage coasts; environmentally sensitive areas;
areas of special protection; (bird sanctuaries not to be confused with special
protection areas—see above); areas of great landscape value; tree preservation
orders; country parks; forest nature reserves and a variety of local nature
conservation designations made by Local Planning Authorities. These are bios-
phere reserves (*re* UNESCO/MAB) and one 'natural' world heritage site (World
Heritage Convention); but no biogenetic reserves (*re* the Berne Convention) as yet.

CONSERVATION: THE UNCERTAIN FUTURE

Proposals announced by Government without prior consultation to break up the GB Nature Conservancy Council (HMSO, 1989), and replace it with three successor bodies for England, Scotland and Wales have attracted considerable opposition from non-Governmental organizations (Prestt, 1989). They fear that the national approach to nature conservation will be weakened as a result. At the tme of writing, the Bill to enact these changes is still being considered by Parliament. Assuming the changes go through, there is a real possibility that divergent conservation policies will be developed by each of the new agencies, resulting in changes in statutory conservation practice. The impact of any such new policies is difficult to predict, and in Scotland the powers of the new countryside agency have still not been decided. It will be vitally important to ensure that action to promote the conservation of Red Data species is pursued in a co-ordinated manner in future.

REFERENCES

BARCLAY-SMITH, P. 1967. Position of the International Convention for the Protection of Birds. Paris 1950 X Bulletin of the International Council for Bird Protection. London: ICBP.

DOUGLAS RAMSAY, J. 1947. National Parks, Cmd 7235. London: HMSO.

DOWER, J. 1945. National Parks in England and Wales, Cmd 6628. London: HMSO.

HMSO. 1919. Report of the Departmental Committee on the Protection of wild birds 1919. Command 295. London: HMSO.

HMSO. 1976. Convention on Wetlands of International Importance especially as Waterfowl Habitat 1976, Cmd 6465. London: HMSO.

HOBHOUSE, A. 1947. National Parks Committee, Cmd 7121. London: HMSO.

HOUSE OF COMMONS DEBATES 11 July 1989, col 482/436W. London: HMSO.

HUXLEY, J.S. 1947. Conservation of Nature in England and Wales, Cmd 7122. London: HMSO.

ICBP. 1952. International Convention for the Protection of Birds Government Conference, Paris 17–18 October 1950. VI Bulletin of the International Committee for Bird Preservation, 53–56. London: ICBP.

NATURE CONSERVANCY COUNCIL. 1982. 7th Report 1 April 1980–31 March 1981. Peterborough: NCC.

NATURE CONSERVANCY COUNCIL. 1988. 14th Report 1 April 1987–31 March 1988. Peterborough: NCC.

PRESTT, I. 1989. Birds 13(1): 3. Sandy: RSPB.

SAMSTAG, T. 1988. For Love of Birds, the Story of the RSPB. Sandy: RSPB.

SHEAIL, J. 1976. Nature in Trust, the History of Nature Conservation in Britain.

Future Action for Birds

The texts for individual species (pages 9–288) show that many of the threats and solutions to them are mentioned repeatedly. It follows that general problems could be tackled with benefit to a wide range of species. The following ten points summarize major areas in which the conservation of Britain's Red Data birds needs to be advanced. The reader is referred to the individual species texts for further detail.

1. A detailed conservation plan for Great Britain should be prepared for each species discussed in this book, to help conservation agencies to implement measures to maintain and enhance their populations. These species plans should be linked to land-use strategies covering groups of bird species and other conservation interests.

2. Conservation agencies should develop and implement a programme to monitor the status of all Red Data and candidate Red Data species, identify likely future threats to them and their habitats and initiate research programmes to further our knowledge of these species where necessary.

3. Distribution surveys of Red Data species should be completed to enable appropriate areas to be identified and given statutory protection, to advise decision makers of areas where detrimental land-use changes should be avoided, and to initiate positive land-use practices.

4. The UK Government should designate all sites identified as meriting Special Protection Area status (under the EC Birds Directive) and as 'Ramsar' Sites with the appropriate authorities as soon as possible. The Government should ensure that such sites (and candidate sites) are not damaged or destroyed by inappropriate developments or pollution. Powers to create SPAs over marine feeding areas for sea birds should be introduced.

5. Other policies should be developed by Government to provide (with SPAs) a suite of effective conservation measures especially for widely dispersed species, for example, those which occur in the uplands, whose conservation needs cannot be met fully by site safeguard measures alone. Such measures could include the wise use of ESAs and agricultural set-aside.

6. All major waterfowl sites, both inland and coastal, should incorporate an adequate refuge zone free from human disturbance to maintain their value to birds for feeding, breeding and roosting.

7. The Land Drainage Act 1976 should be amended to remove the legal imperative to drain wetlands. Instead, schemes to promote wetland conservation and the re-creation of wetlands should be adopted and enshrined in statute.

8. On land surplus to agricultural requirements, schemes to maintain and enhance the management of semi-natural habitats for birds by traditional low-intensity pastoral farming practices should be introduced. Imaginative recreation/restoration schemes should be encouraged into the structural reorganization of the Common Agricultural Policy. This should not be on land where traditional farming practices are important for birds.

9. Better government support for the enforcement of the legislation protecting wildlife is needed, particularly in relation to the illegal killing of birds of prey.

10. Nature conservation, especially habitat conservation, should feature more prominently in the duties of government departments/agencies who use and manage land. Specifically, such departments/agencies should be required to promote conservation as part of their duties.

Population Estimates of British Breeding and Wintering Birds

	Breeding (pairs)	Source[a]	Wintering (birds)	Source[a]
Red-throated Diver	1,200–1,500	Text	10–15,000 Br. & Ire.	Text/WA
Gavia stellata	(1988)		(1987)	
Black-throated Diver	150	Text	1,300 Br.	Text
G. arctica	(1985)		(1986)	
Great Northern Diver			3,500–4,500 Br. & Ire.	Text
G. immer			(1986)	
Little Grebe	9–18,000	BA	25–50,000 Br.	WA
Tachybaptus ruficollis				
Great Crested Grebe	c6,000	WA	7–10,000 Br.	WA
Podiceps cristatus				
Red-necked Grebe	0–2	Text	120–170 Br.	WA
P. grisegena	(1988)			
Slavonian Grebe	60–75	Text	c400 Br.	WA
P. auritus	(1986)			
Black-necked Grebe	25–37	Text	120 Br.	WA
P. nigricollis	(1988)			
Fulmar	528,100	SAST	1·6–1·8 million	WA
Fulmarus glacialis	(1988)		Br. & Ire.	
Manx Shearwater	c235,000	Text		
Puffinus puffinus	(1988)			
Storm Petrel	20–80,000	Text		
Hydrobates pelagicus	(1988)			
Leach's Petrel	c10,000	Text/BWP		
Oceanodroma leucorhoa	(1988)			
Gannet	159,000	Text		
Sula bassana	(1984/5)			
Cormorant	c8,000 Br. & Ire.	BA	20–25,000 Br.	WA
Phalacrocorax carbo				
Shag	36,100	SAST	100–150,000 Br.	WA
P. aristotelis	(1988)			
Bittern	20–25	Text	50–150 Br.	WA
Botaurus stellaris	(1990)			
Little Bittern	0–1	Text		
Ixobrychus minutus	(1984)			
Grey Heron	8,600	BTO[1]	30,000 Br.	WA
Ardea cinerea	(1986)			
Mute Swan	19,000 birds	WA	c20,000 Br.	WA
Cygnus olor				
Bewick's Swan			c6,000 Br.	Text
C. columbianus			(1987/8)	
Whooper Swan	0–2	Text	5,100 + Br.	Text
C. cygnus	(1988)		(1987)	
Bean Goose			4–500 Br.	Text
Anser fabalis			(1987/8)	
Pink-footed Goose			176,000 Br.	Text
A. brachyrhynchus			(1988)	
White-fronted Goose			5–7,000 Br.	WA
A. albifrons				

Population Estimates of British Breeding and Wintering Birds—*continued*

	Breeding (pairs)	Source[a]	Wintering (birds)	Source[a]
White-fronted Goose			13,000 Br.	Text
A. a. flavirostris			(1987/8)	
Greylag Goose	c2,300	Text	110,000 Br.	Text
A. anser	(1986)		(1985)	
Canada Goose	10–15,000	WA	35–50,000 Br. & Ire.	WWC
Branta canadensis			(1987/8)	
Barnacle Goose			c33,000 Br.	Text
B. leucopsis			(1988)	
Brent Goose			235,000 Br.	Text
B. bernicla			(1988/9)	
Egyptian Goose	150–200	WA	500 Br.	WA
Alopochen aegyptiacus				
Shelduck	10–12,000	Text	40–70,000 Br.	Text
Tadorna tadorna	(1987)		(1987)	
Mandarin Duck	850–1,000	WA	2,000 Br.	WA
Aix galericulata				
Wigeon	3–500	BA/Text	200,000 Br.	Text
Anas penelope	(mid-1970s)		(1987)	
Gadwall	5–600	Text	5,000 Br.	Text
A. strepera	(1986)		(1987)	
Teal	3,500–6,000	Text	100,000 Br.	Text
A. crecca	(1988)		(1986)	
Mallard	150,000	BA	500,000 Br.	WA
A. platyrhynchos				
Pintail	32	Text	25,000 Br.	Text
A. acuta	(1982/3)		(1986)	
Garganey	>50	Text		
A. querquedula	(1986)			
Shoveler	1–1,500 Br. & Ire.	Text	5–7,000 Br.	Text
A. clypeata	(1988)		(1986)	
Pochard	3–400	Text	35–50,000 Br.	WA
Aythya ferina	(1988)			
Tufted Duck	7,000+	WA	60,000 + Br.	WA
A. fuligula				
Scaup	0–3	Text	6–7,500 Br.	Text
A. marila	(1988)			
Eider	c25,000	BA	c72,000 Br.	WA
Somateria mollissima				
Long-tailed Duck			c20,000 Br. & Ire.	Text
Clangula hyemalis			(1988)	
Common Scoter	c100	Text	25–30,000 Br. & Ire.	WA
Melanitta nigra	(1988)			
Velvet Scoter			2,500–5,000 Br. & Ire.	WA
M. fusca				
Goldeneye	85–90	Text	10–15,000 Br. & Ire.	WA
Bucephala clangula	(1989)			
Smew			150–350 Br.	WA
Mergus albellus				
Red-breasted Merganser	1,500–2,200	WfGB	9,500 Br.	WA
M. serrator	(1976)			
Goosander	c1,245	WfGB	5,000 Br.	WA
M. merganser	(1975)			
Ruddy Duck	c3,000 birds	WWT	2,300	WWC
Oxyura jamaicensis			(1987/8)	
Honey Buzzard	max. 30	Text		
Pernis apivorus	(1980s)			
Red Kite	52	Text	130–140 Br.	WA
Milvus milvus	(1989)			
White-tailed Eagle	0–6	Text	max. 80 Br.	Text
Haliaeetus albicilla	(1988)		(1985)	
Marsh Harrier	<75	Text	c10 Br.	WA
Circus aeruginosus	(1988)			
Hen Harrier	500	Text	1,200 Br.	WA
C. cyaneus	(1989)			
Montagu's Harrier	7–10	Text		
C. pygargus	(1988)			

Population Estimates of British Breeding and Wintering Birds—*continued*

	Breeding (pairs)	Source[a]	Wintering (birds)	Source[a]
Goshawk	100–200	Text	c300 Br.	WA
Accipiter gentilis	(1988)			
Sparrowhawk	c25,000	WA	150–170,000 Br.	WA
A. nisus				
Buzzard	24,500–33,500 birds	BTO[2]	24–35,000 Br. & Ire.	BTO
Buteo buteo				
Rough-legged Buzzard			20–250 Br.	WA
B. lagopus				
Golden Eagle	424	Text	1–2,000 Br.	WA
Aquila chrysaetos	(1982)			
Osprey	c53	Text		
Pandion haliaetus	(1988)			
Kestrel	30–80,000	WA	100,000 Br. & Ire.	WA
Falco tinnunculus				
Merlin	550–650	Text	2–3,000 Br. & Ire.	WA
F. columbarius	(1983/4)			
Hobby	290–300	RBBP		
F. subbuteo	(1986)			
Peregrine	c900	Text	4,000 Br. & Ire.	WA
F. peregrinus	(1985)			
Red Grouse	>500,000	Text	1½ million Br.	WA
Lagopus lagopus	(1988)			
Ptarmigan	10,000	WA	10–15,000 Br.	WA
L. mutus				
Black Grouse	10–50,000	Text	10–100,000 Br.	Text
Tetrao tetrix	(1986)		(1986)	
Capercaillie	<2,000 birds	Text	1–2,000 Br.	Text
T. urogallus	(1988)		(1988)	
Red-legged Partridge	100–200,000	BA	500,000 + Br.	BA
Alectoris rufa				
Grey Partridge	500,000	BA	<1 million Br. & Ire.	WA
Perdix perdix				
Quail	100–200	Text		
Coturnix coturnix	(1987)			
Pheasant	100–500,000	BA	8–12 million Br.	WA
Phasianus colchicus				
Golden Pheasant	500–1,000	WA	1–2,000 Br.	WA
Chrysolophus pictus				
Lady Amherst's Pheasant	100–200	WA	200–500 Br.	WA
C. amherstiae				
Water Rail	2–4,000	BA	c12,000 + Br.	WA
Rallus aquaticus				
Spotted Crake	<18	Text		
Porzana porzana	(1987)			
Corncrake	550–600	Text		
Crex crex	(1988)			
Moorhen	300,000	BA	1 million + Br.	WA
Gallinula chloropus				
Coot	10–100,000	WA	200,000 Br.	WA
Fulica atra				
Crane	0–2	Text	8 Br.	Text
Grus grus	(1988)		(1990)	
Oystercatcher	33–43,000	Text	280,000 Br.	Text
Haematopus ostralegus	(1988)		(1988)	
Black-winged Stilt	0–1	Text		
Himantopus himantopus	(1987)			
Avocet	<400	Text	890 Br.	Text
Recurvirostra avosetta	(1988)			
Stone Curlew	135–155	Text		
Burhinus oedicnemus	(mid-1980s)			
Little Ringed Plover	610	BTO[3]		
Charadrius dubius	(1984)			
Ringed Plover	8,400–8,800	Text	23,000 Br.	Text
C. hiaticula	(1980)		(1988)	
Kentish Plover	0–1	Text		
C. alexandrinus	(1979)			

Population Estimates of British Breeding and Wintering Birds—*continued*

	Breeding (pairs)	Source[a]	Wintering (birds)	Source[a]
Dotterel	c550	Text		
C. morinellus	(1988)			
Golden Plover	22,600	Text	200–300,000 Br. & Ire.	WA
Pluvialis apricaria	(1987)			
Grey Plover			40,000 Br.	Text
P. squatarola			(1988)	
Lapwing	200,000 Br. & Ire.	BA	2,050,000 Br.	WA
Vanellus vanellus				
Knot			220,000 Br.	Text
Calidris canutus			(1988)	
Sanderling			14,000 Br.	Text
C. alba			(1988)	
Little Stint			30 Br. & Ire.	WA
C. minuta				
Temminck's Stint	<8	Text		
C. temminckii	(to 1988)			
Purple Sandpiper	3	Text	16,000 Br.	Text
C. maritima	(1987)		(1987)	
Dunlin	c9,150	Text	430,000 Br.	Text
C. alpina	(1988)		(1986)	
Ruff	<32	Text	1,400 Br.	WA
Philomachus pugnax	(to 1986)			
Jack Snipe			10–50,000 Br.	WA
Lymnocryptes minimus				
Snipe	10–80,000	BA	300,000 + Br.	WA
Gallinago gallinago				
Woodcock	10–50,000	BA	200,000 + Br.	WA
Scolopax rusticola				
Black-tailed Godwit	c50	Text	4–5,000 Br.	WA
Limosa limosa	(1987)			
Bar-tailed Godwit			c61,000 Br.	Text
L. lapponica			(1985)	
Whimbrel	470	Text	c30 Br.	WA
Numenius phaeopus	(1985)			
Curlew	33–38,000	Text	91,000 Br. & Ire.	WA
N. arquata	(1988)			
Spotted Redshank			80–200 Br.	WA
Tringa erythropus				
Redshank	30,000	Text	75,000 Br.	Text
T. totanus	(1900)			
Greenshank	960	Text	600–1,000	WA
T. nebularia	(1985)			
Green Sandpiper			500–1,500 Br.	WA
T. ochropus				
Wood Sandpiper	<10	Text		
T. glareola	(1986)			
Common Sandpiper	c50,000	BA	100 Br.	WA
Actitis hypoleucos				
Turnstone			45–50,000 Br.	Text
Arenaria interpres				
Red-necked Phalarope	c20	Text		
Phalaropus lobatus	(1988)			
Arctic Skua	3,350	SAST		
Stercorarius parasiticus	(1988)			
Great Skua	7,860	Text		
S. skua	(1988)			
Mediterranean Gull	<6	Text	100–150 Br. & Ire.	WA
Larus melanocephalus	(1985)			
Little Gull	0–1	Text	c700 Br.	WA
L. minutus	(1981)			
Black-headed Gull	122,800	SAST	3 million Br. & Ire.	WA
L. ridibundus	(1988)			
Ring-billed Gull			c40 Br. & Ire.	WA
L. delawarensis				
Common Gull	60,000	SAST	635,000 Br.	WA
L. canus	(1988)			

Population Estimates of British Breeding and Wintering Birds—*continued*

	Breeding (pairs)	Source[a]	Wintering (birds)	Source[a]
Lesser Black-backed Gull	83,400	SAST	58,200 Br.	WA
L. fuscus	(1988)			
Herring Gull	150,300	SAST	275,600 + Br.	WA
L. argentatus	(1987)			
Iceland Gull			70–300 Br.	WA
L. glaucoides				
Glaucous Gull			500–600 Br. & Ire.	WA
L. hyperboreus				
Great Black-backed Gull	17,860	SAST		
L. marinus	(1988)			
Kittiwake	486,900	SAST		
Rissa tridactyla	(1988)			
Sandwich Tern	<13,500	Text		
Sterna sandvicensis	(1984)			
Roseate Tern	135	Text		
S. dougallii	(1988)			
Common Tern	10,900	SAST		
S. hirundo	(1988)			
Arctic Tern	c75,000	Text		
S. paradisaea	(1988)			
Little Tern	1,500–1,700	Text		
S. albifrons	(1984)			
Black Tern	0–1	Text		
Chlidonias niger	(1978)			
Guillemot	1,040,400 birds	SAST		
Uria aalge	(1988)			
Razorbill	145,000	SAST		
Alca torda	(1988)			
Black Guillemot	40,000 birds	SAST	58–80,000 Br. & Ire.	WA
Cepphus grylle	(1989)			
Puffin	563,500	SAST		
Fratercula arctica	(1988)			
Rock/Feral Dove	100,000	BA	200,000 + Br.	BA
Columba livia				
Stock Dove	100,000+	BA	200,000 + Br.	WA
C. oenas				
Woodpigeon	5·8 million birds	WA	10 million	WA
C. palumbus				
Collared Dove	50,000+	WA	150,000 Br.	WA
Streptopelia decaocto				
Turtle Dove	100–125,000	BA		
S. turtur				
Ring-necked Parakeet	500–1,000 birds	WA	500–1,000 Br.	WA
Psittacula krameri				
Cuckoo	17,500–35,000	BA		
Cuculus canorus				
Barn Owl	c5,000	Text	12,500–25,000 Br. & Ire.	WA
Tyto alba	(1987)			
Snowy Owl	0–1	Text	2–3	Text
Nyctea scandiaca	(1975)			
Little Owl	7–14,000	BA	19–38,000 Br.	WA
Athene noctua				
Tawny Owl	50–100,000	WA	50–350,000 Br.	WA
Strix aluco				
Long-eared Owl	3–10,000 Br. & Ire.	BA	10–35,000 Br. & Ire.	WA
Asio otus				
Short-eared Owl	1–10,000	BA	5–50,000 Br. & Ire.	WA
A. flammeus				
Nightjar	2,000	Text		
Caprimulgus europaeus	(1988)			
Swift	c100,000	BA		
Apus apus				
Kingfisher	5–9,000 Br. & Ire.	BA	9–15,000 Br. & Ire.	WA
Alcedo atthis				
Hoopoe	0–4	Text		
Upupa epops	(to 1986)			

Population Estimates of British Breeding and Wintering Birds—*continued*

	Breeding (pairs)	Source[a]	Wintering (birds)	Source[a]
Wryneck	1–5	Text		
Jynx torquilla	(1987)			
Green Woodpecker	15–30,000	BA	40–70,000 Br.	WA
Picus viridus				
Great Spotted Woodpecker	30–40,000	BA	150–200,000 Br.	WA
Dendrocopos major				
Lesser Spotted Woodpecker	5,000+	BA	20–40,000 Br.	WA
D. minor				
Woodlark	c230	Text	150–200 Br.	WA
Lullula arborea	(1983)			
Skylark	2–4 million	BA	25 million Br. & Ire.	WA
Alauda arvensis				
Shore Lark	0–3	Text	>100	Text
Eremophila alpestris	(to 1986)			
Sand Martin	250,000+	BA		
Riparia riparia				
Swallow	500–600,000	BA		
Hirundo rustica				
House Martin	300–600,000	BA		
Delichon urbica				
Tree Pipit	50–100,000	BA		
Anthus trivialis				
Meadow Pipit	3 million Br. & Ire.	BA	1–2½ million Br. & Ire.	WA
A. pratensis				
Rock Pipit	50,000 + Br. & Ire.	BA	100–150,000 Br. & Ire.	WA
A. petrosus				
Water Pipit			c100	WA
A. spinoletta				
Yellow Wagtail	175,000	BTO[4]		
Motacilla flava	(1984)			
Grey Wagtail	25–50,000 Br. & Ire.	BA	40,000 Br. & Ire.	WA
M. cinerea				
Pied Wagtail	500,000 Br. & Ire.	BA	2 million Br. & Ire.	WA
M. alba				
Waxwing			up to 11,000 Br.	WA
Bombycilla garrulus				
Dipper	c30,000 Br. & Ire.	BA	15–60,000 Br. & Ire.	WA
Cinclus cinclus				
Wren	3–3½ million	BA	12–20 million Br. & Ire.	WA
Troglodytes troglodytes				
Dunnock	5 million Br. & Ire.	BA	20 million Br. & Ire.	WA
Prunella modularis				
Robin	3½ million	WA	10 million Br. & Ire.	WA
Erithacus rubecula				
Nightingale	c4,800 Br.	BTO[4]		
Luscinia megarhynchos				
Bluethroat	0–1	Text		
L. svecica	(1985)			
Black Redstart	<112	Text	c500 Br. & Ire.	WA
Phoenicurus ochruros	(1988)			
Redstart	90–140,000	BTO[4]/BA		
P. phoenicurus				
Whinchat	20–40,000 Br. & Ire.	BA		
Saxicola rubetra				
Stonechat	30,000 + Br. & Ire.	BA	30–60,000 Br. & Ire.	WA
S. torquata				
Wheatear	80,000 Br. & Ire.	BA		
Oenanthe oenanthe				
Ring Ouzel	8–16,000 Br. & Ire.	BA		
Turdus torquatus				
Blackbird	4½–5 million	BTO[4]	14–20 million Br. & Ire.	WA
T. merula				
Fieldfare	0–10	Text	c1 million Br. & Ire.	WA
T. pilaris	(1988)			
Song Thrush	1½–3½ million	BA	6–10 million Br. & Ire.	WA
T. philomelos				

Population Estimates of British Breeding and Wintering Birds — *continued*

	Breeding (pairs)	Source[a]	Wintering (birds)	Source[a]
Redwing *T. iliacus*	80 (to 1988)	Text	c1 million Br. & Ire.	WA
Mistle Thrush *T. viscivorus*	300,000+	BA	400–800,000 Br. & Ire.	WA
Cetti's Warbler *Cettia cetti*	<200 (1988)	Text	1,000	WA
Grasshopper Warbler *Locustella naevia*	12,500–25,000 (1984)	BTO[4]/BA		
Savi'sWarbler *L. luscinioides*	<15 (1989)	Text		
Sedge Warbler *Acrocephalus schoenobaenus*	300,000 Br. & Ire.	BA		
Marsh Warbler *A. palustris*	>20 (1988)	Text		
Reed Warbler *A. scirpaceus*	40–80,000	BA		
Dartford Warbler *Sylvia undata*	<640 (1989)	Text	800–1,500 Br.	WA
Lesser Whitethroat *S. curruca*	50–80,000 (1984)	BTO[4]/BA		
Whitethroat *S. communis*	400–500,000 Br. & Ire.	BTO[4]		
Garden Warbler *S. borin*	200,000 Br. & Ire. (1984)	BTO[4]		
Blackcap *S. atricapilla*	400–800,000 Br. & Ire. (1984)	BTO[4]/BA	3,000 Br. & Ire.	WA
Wood Warbler *Phylloscopus sibilatrix*	10–20,000 (1984)	BTO[4]		
Chiffchaff *P. collybita*	400–500,000 (1984)	BTO[4]	500–1,000 Br.	WA
Willow Warbler *P. trochilus*	2½ million (1984)	BTO[4]		
Goldcrest *Regulus regulus*	500–600,000 (1984)	BTO[4]	2–4 million Br. & Ire.	WA
Firecrest *R. ignicapillus*	c80 (to 1988)	Text	200–400 Br. & Ire.	WA
Spotted Flycatcher *Muscicapa striata*	300,000 (1984)	BTO[4]		
Pied Flycatcher *Ficedula hypoleuca*	20–60,000 (1984)	BTO[4]/BA		
Bearded Tit *Panurus biarmicus*	590 (1976)	Text	3–5,000 Br.	WA
Long-tailed Tit *Aegithalos caudatus*	50–150,000 Br. & Ire.	BA	c96,000 Br. & Ire.	WA
Marsh tit *Parus palustris*	140–150,000 (1984)	BTO[4]	200–400,000 Br.	WA
Willow Tit *P. montanus*	50–100,000	BA	175–350,000 Br.	WA
Crested Tit *P. cristatus*	c900 (1988)	Text	3,600 Br.	WA
Coal Tit *P. ater*	1 million Br. & Ire.	BA	4 million Br. & Ire.	WA
Blue Tit *P. caeruleus*	3½ million (1984)	BTO[4]	15 million Br. & Ire.	WA
Great Tit *P. major*	2 million (1984)	BTO[4]	10 million Br. & Ire.	WA
Nuthatch *Sitta europaea*	20,000	BA	60–80,000	WA
Tree Creeper *Certhia familiaris*	200–300,000 Br. & Ire.	BA	1 million Br. & Ire.	WA
Golden Oriole *Oriolus oriolus*	<40 (to 1988)	Text		
Red-backed Shrike *Lanius collurio*	0–1 (last bred 1988)	Text		
Great Grey Shrike *L. excubitor*			150 + Br.	WA

Population Estimates of British Breeding and Wintering Birds—*continued*

	Breeding (pairs)	Source[a]	Wintering (birds)	Source[a]
Jay *Garrulus glandarius*	100,000 Br. & Ire.	BA	350–400,000 Br. & Ire.	WA
Magpie *Pica pica*	250–500,000 Br. & Ire.	BA	1 million + Br. & Ire.	WA
Chough *Pyrrhocorax pyrrhocorax*	280 (1982)	Text	3–5,000 Br. & Ire.	WA
Jackdaw *Corvus monedula*	500,000 + Br. & Ire.	BA	3 million + Br. & Ire.	WA
Rook *C. frugilegus*	1–1¼ million Br. & Ire.	WA	4 million + Br. & Ire.	WA
Carrion Crow *C. corone*	1 million Br. & Ire.	BA	3½ million Br. & Ire.	WA
Raven *C. corax*	5,000 Br. & Ire.	BA	20–30,000 Br. & Ire.	WA
Starling *Sturnus vulgaris*	4–7 million Br. & Ire.	BA	c37 million Br. & Ire.	WA
House Sparrow *Passer domesticus*	3½–7 million Br. & Ire.	BA	10–15 million Br. & Ire.	WA
Tree Sparrow *P. montanus*	250,000 Br. & Ire.	BA	800,000 Br. & Ire.	WA
Chaffinch *Fringilla coelebs*	5 million	WA	c30 million Br. & Ire.	WA
Brambling *F. montifringilla*	0–10 (1986)	Text	50,000–2 million Br.	WA
Serin *Serinus serinus*	0–9 (to 1988)	Text		
Greenfinch *Carduelis chloris*	1–2 million Br. & Ire.	BA	5–6 million Br. & Ire.	WA
Goldfinch *C. carduelis*	300,000 Br. & Ire.	BA	c100,000 Br. & Ire.	WA
Siskin *C. spinus*	20,000 + Br. & Ire.	BA	c150,000 Br. & Ire.	WA
Linnet *C. cannabina*	80,000–1·6 million Br. & Ire.	BA	c3 million Br. & Ire.	WA
Twite *C. flavirostris*	20–60,000 Br. & Ire. (1988)	Text	100–150,000 Br. & Ire.	WA
Redpoll *C. flammea*	300–320,000 Br. & Ire.	WA	350–850,000 Br. & Ire.	WA
Crossbill *Loxia curvirostra*	3,500	BA	1–15,000 Br. & Ire.	WA
Parrot Crossbill *L. pytyopsittacus*	0–2 (1985)	Text		
Scottish Crossbill *L. scotica*	300–1,000 (1988)	Text	c1,500 Br.	WA
Scarlet Rosefinch *Carpodacus erythrinus*	1 (1982)	Text		
Bullfinch *Pyrrhula pyrrhula*	5–600,000 Br. & Ire.	BA	1–1½ million Br. & Ire.	WA
Hawfinch *Coccothraustes coccothraustes*	10,000	BA	20,000 Br.	WA
Lapland Bunting *Calcarius lapponicus*	0–4 (none since)	Text	200–1,000 Br. & Ire.	WA
Snow Bunting *Plectrophenax nivalis*	10–30 (1986)	Text	10–15,000 Br.	WA
Yellowhammer *Emberiza citrinella*	1 million Br. & Ire.	BA	3½ million Br. & Ire.	WA
Cirl Bunting *E. cirlus*	167 (1982)	Text	c500 Br.	WA
Reed Bunting *E. schoeniclus*	600,000 + Br. & Ire.	BA	1,200,000 + Br. & Ire.	WA
Corn Bunting *Miliaria calandra*	30,000	BA	100–150,000 Br.	WA

For notes see overleaf

Notes to Population Estimate

^a *Source References*

Text   – Indicates that the figure given and further information is from the species text in the book.

BA   – Breeding Atlas, figures as given in 'The Atlas of Breeding Birds in Britain and Ireland' by J.T.R. Sharrock. 1976.

BTO¹   – British Trust for Ornithology. BTO News March–April 1986.

BTO²   – Bird Study 35: 109–118.

BTO³   – BTO News November–December 1987.

BTO⁴   – BTO report to NCC 'Population Estimates for British Breeding Birds' January 1984.

BWP   – Birds of the Western Palearctic, figures as given in the species accounts of Vols. 1–5 of 'Birds of Europe and the Middle East and North Africa (The Birds of the Western Palearctic'), by S. Cramp *et al.* (eds).

RBBP   – Rare Breeding Birds Panel, annual summaries of all rare breeding birds in Britain (to 1986) published in the journal 'British Birds'.

SAST   – Sea Birds at Sea Team, figures supplied annually by the NCC funded sea-birds research team surveying and monitoring the numbers and distribution of sea-birds around British coasts.

WA   – Winter Atlas, figures as given in 'The Atlas of Wintering Birds in Britain and Ireland' by P. Lack (ed.). 1986.

WfGB   – 'Wildfowl in Great Britain', by M. Owen, G.L. Atkinson-Willes and D.G. Salmon. 1986.

WWT   – Information provided by the Wildfowl and Wetlands Trust.

WWC   – Wildfowl and Wader Counts, annual summary of the numbers of wildfowl and waders wintering in Britain, published jointly by the BTO and the Wildfowl and Wetlands Trust.

Red Data Birds

117 species of conservation importance according to the criteria set out in this book

	1		2	3	4		5
	a BI	b WI	BR	BD	a BL	b WL	SC
Red-throated Diver *Gavia stellata*	*	*					
Black-throated Diver *Gavia arctica*		*	*				
Great Northern Diver *Gavia immer*		*	*				
Red-necked Grebe *Podiceps grisegena*			*				
Slavonian Grebe *Podiceps auritus*			*		*		
Black-necked Grebe *Podiceps nigricollis*			*		*		
Manx Shearwater *Puffinus puffinus*	*				*		
Storm Petrel *Hydrobates pelagicus*	*				*		
Leach's Petrel *Oceanodroma leucorhoa*	*				*		
Gannet *Sula bassana*	*				*		
Bittern *Botaurus stellaris*			*	*	*		
Little Bittern *Ixobrychus minutus*			*				
Bewick's Swan *Cygnus columbianus*		*				*	
Whooper Swan *Cygnus cygnus*		*	*				
Bean Goose *Anser fabalis*						*	

Red Data Birds — *continued*

	1		2	3	4		5
	a BI	b WI	BR	BD	a BL	b WL	SC
Pink-footed Goose *Anser brachyrhynchus*		*					
White-fronted Goose ssp. *Anser albifrons*		*				*	
Greylag Goose *Anser anser*		*					
Barnacle Goose *Branta leucopsis*		*				*	
Brent Goose (races) *Branta bernicla*		*				*	
Shelduck *Tadorna tadorna*		*				*	
Wigeon *Anas penelope*		*				*	
Gadwall *Anas strepera*		*				*	
Teal *Anas crecca*		*					
Pintail *Anas acuta*		*	*			*	
Garganey *Anas querquedula*			*				
Shoveler *Anas clypeata*						*	
Pochard *Aythya ferina*		*	*				
Scaup *Aythya marila*			*			*	
Long-tailed Duck *Clangula hyemalis*						*	
Common Scoter *Melanitta nigra*			*			*	
Velvet Scoter *Melanitta fusca*						*	
Goldeneye *Bucephala clangula*			*				
Honey Buzzard *Pernis apivorus*			*				
Red Kite *Milvus milvus*			*				
White-tailed Eagle *Haliaeetus albicilla*			*				
Marsh Harrier *Circus aeruginosus*			*				
Hen Harrier *Circus cyaneus*							*

	1		2	3	4		5
	a BI	b WI	BR	BD	a BL	b WL	SC
Montagu's Harrier *Circus pygargus*			*				
Goshawk *Accipiter gentilis*			*				
Golden Eagle *Aquila chrysaetos*	*						
Osprey *Pandion haliaetus*			*				
Merlin *Falco columbarius*							*
Peregrine *Falco peregrinus*	*						
Red Grouse *Lagopus lagopus*	*						
Black Grouse *Lyrurus tetrix*							*
Capercaillie *Tetrao urogallus*					*		
Partridge *Perdix perdix*				*			
Quail *Coturnix coturnix*			*				
Spotted Crake *Porzana porzana*			*				
Corncrake *Crex crex*				*			
Crane *Grus grus*			*				
Oystercatcher *Haematopus ostralegus*		*				*	
Black-winged Stilt *Himantopus himantopus*			*				
Avocet *Recurvirostra avosetta*			*		*	*	
Stone Curlew *Burhinus oedicnemus*			*	*	*		
Ringed Plover *Charadrius hiaticula*		*				*	
Kentish Plover *Charadrius alexandrinus*			*				
Dotterel *Charadrius morinellus*							*
Golden Plover *Pluvialis apricaria*		*					*
Grey Plover *Pluvialis squatarola*		*				*	

Red Data Birds—*continued*

	1		2	3	4		5
	a BI	b WI	BR	BD	a BL	b WL	SC
Knot *Calidris canuta*		*				*	
Sanderling *Calidris alba*		*				*	
Temminck's Stint *Calidris temminckii*			*		*		
Purple Sandpiper *Calidris maritima*			*		*		
Dunlin *Calidris alpina*		*				*	
Ruff *Philomachus pugnax*			*		*		
Black-tailed Godwit *Limosa limosa*			*		*	*	
Bar-tailed Godwit *Limosa lapponica*		*				*	
Whimbrel *Numenius phaeopus*							*
Curlew *Numenius arquata*	*	*					
Redshank *Tringa totanus*		*				*	
Greenshank *Tringa nebularia*							*
Wood Sandpiper *Tringa glareola*			*		*		
Turnstone *Arenaria interpres*			*				
Red-necked Phalarope *Phalaropus lobatus*			*		*		
Great Skua *Stercorarius skua*	*				*		
Mediterranean Gull *Larus melanocephalus*			*		*		
Little Gull *Larus minutus*			*				
Sandwich Tern *Sterna sandvicensis*	*				*		
Roseate Tern *Sterna dougallii*	*		*	*	*		
Arctic Tern *Sterna paradisaea*	*						
Little Tern *Sterna albifrons*	*				*		
Black Tern *Chilidonias niger*			*				

Red Data Birds—*continued*

| | 1 | | 2 | 3 | 4 | | 5 |
| | a | b | | | a | b | |
	BI	WI	BR	BD	BL	WL	SC
Guillemot	*						
Uria aalge							
Razorbill	*						
Alca torda							
Barn Owl							*
Tyto alba							
Snowy Owl			*				
Nyctea scandiaca							
Nightjar							*
Caprimulgus europaeus							
Hoopoe			*				
Upupa epops							
Bee-eater			*				
Merops apiaster							
Wryneck			*				
Jynx torquilla							
Woodlark			*				
Lullula arborea							
Shore Lark			*				
Eremophila alpestris							
Black Redstart			*				
Phoenicurus ochruros							
Bluethroat			*				
Luscinia svecica							
Fieldfare			*				
Turdus pilaris							
Redwing			*				
Turdus iliacus							
Cetti's Warbler			*				
Cettia cetti							
Savi's Warbler			*		*		
Locustella luscinioides							
Marsh Warbler			*	*			
Acrocephalus palustris							
Dartford Warbler			*		*		
Sylvia undata							
Firecrest			*				
Regulus ingnicapillus							
Bearded Tit					*		
Panurus biarmicus							
Crested Tit					*		
Parus cristatus							
Golden Oriole			*		*		
Oriolus oriolus							
Red-backed Shrike			*	*			
Lanius collurio							

Red Data Birds — *continued*

	1		2	3	4		5
	a	b			a	b	
	BI	WI	BR	BD	BL	WL	SC
Chough *Pyrrhocorax pyrrhocorax*			*		*		
Brambling *Fringilla montifringilla*			*				
Serin *Serinus serinus*			*				
Twite *Acanthis flavirostris*	*	*					
Scottish Crossbill *Loxia scotica*	*				*		
Parrot Crossbill *Loxia pytyopsittacus*			*				
Scarlet Rosefinch *Carpodacus erythrinus*			*				
Lapland Bunting *Calcarius lapponicus*			*				
Snow Bunting *Plectrophenax nivalis*			*				
Cirl Bunting *Emberiza cirlus*			*	*	*	*	

1a BI Breeding in internationally significant numbers (>20% of the north-west Europe population)

1b WI Non-breeding in internationally significant numbers (>20% of the north-west Europe population)

2 BR Rare breeder (<300 pairs)

3 BD Declining breeder (>50% sustained decline since 1960)

4a BL Localized breeder (>50% of the population in the ten most populated areas). Rare breeders are not included here unless they are additionally vulnerable because of confinement to vulnerable habitats

4b WL Localized non-breeder (>50% of the population in the ten most populated areas)

5 SC Special category—show cause for concern or declining numbers but inadequate data to quantify the extent of the problem

Red Data Bird Candidate Species

Buzzard *Buteo buteo*
Red-legged Partridge *Alectoris rufa*
Lapwing *Vanellus vanellus*
Snipe *Gallinago gallinago*
Redshank *Tringa totanus*
Herring Gull *Larus argentatus*
Arctic Skua *Stercorarius parasiticus*
Kittiwake *Rissa tridactyla*
Puffin *Fratercula arctica*
Rock Dove *Columba livia*
Turtle Dove *Streptopelia turtur*
Short-eared Owl *Asio flammeus*
Kingfisher *Alcedo atthis*
Sand Martin *Riparia riparia*
Swallow *Hirundo rustica*
Yellow Wagtail *Motacilla flava*
Dipper *Cinclus cinclus*
Nightingale *Luscinia megarhynchos*
Redstart *Phoenicurus phoenicurus*
Whinchat *Saxicola rubetra*
Stonechat *Saxicola torquata*
Wheatear *Oenanthe oenanthe*
Ring Ousel *Turdus torquata*
Sedge Warbler *Acrocephalus scheonobaenus*
Whitethroat *Sylvia communis*
Spotted Flycatcher *Muscicapa striata*
Raven *Corvus corax*
Tree Sparrow *Passer montanus*
Linnet *Acanthis cannabina*
Corn Bunting *Miliaria calandra*

Index